ISSUES IN HEALTH CARE ETHICS

ISSUES
IN
HEALTH CARE ETHICS

EILEEN P. FLYNN

St. Peter's College

Prentice Hall   Upper Saddle River, NJ 07458

Library of Congress Cataloging-in-Publication Data

Flynn, Eileen P. (Eileen Patricia)
    Issues in health care ethics / Eileen P. Flynn.
        p.   cm.
    Includes bibliographical references and index.
    ISBN 0-13-012230-0
    1. Medical ethics.   I. Title.
    R724 .F588 2000
    174'.2—dc21   99-33270
                                                     CIP

Acquisitions Editor: Karita A. France
Editorial Assistant: Jennifer Ackerman
Production Editor: B. Christenberry
Manufacturing Buyer: Tricia Kenny

An earlier version of this book
was published under the title
Issues in Medical Ethics
in 1997 by Sheed & Ward.

This book was set in 10/12 Palatino by A & A Publishing Services,
Inc., and was printed and bound by Courier Companies, Inc
The cover was printed by Phoenix Color Corp.

© 2000 by Prentice-Hall, Inc.
    Upper Saddle River, NJ 07458

Printed in the United States of America

10 9 8 7 6 5 4 3 2

ISBN 0-13-012230-0

PRENTICE-HALL INTERNATIONAL (UK) LIMITED, *London*
PRENTICE-HALL OF AUSTRALIA PTY. LIMITED, *Sydney*
PRENTICE-HALL CANADA INC., *Toronto*
PRENTICE-HALL HISPANOAMERICANA, S.A., *Mexico*
PRENTICE-HALL OF INDIA PRIVATE LIMITED, *New Delhi*
PRENTICE-HALL OF JAPAN, INC., *Tokyo*
PEARSON EDUCATION ASIA PTE. LTD., *Singapore*
EDITORA PRENTICE-HALL DO BRASIL, LTDA., *Rio de Janeiro*

To my very dear friend,
Doris Hershkowitz
and in loving memory
of Stanford Hershkowitz

Contents

PART FOUR ETHICAL RESPONSES TO SICKNESS

PART FIVE ETHICAL ISSUES AT THE END OF LIFE

PART SIX ETHICAL ISSUES FOR HEALTH CARE PROFESSIONALS

PART SEVEN MEDICINE AND THE COMMON GOOD

Preface

I have written this book so that readers might better understand what is at stake in health care ethics and so that they will become well enough informed to respond to issues in an appropriate manner.

Issues of health care ethics can be approached from two points of view. The first approach is that of the interested, but uninvolved, observer who considers an issue in a curious but detached fashion. The second approach is that of a person who is directly involved in an issue and for whom the matter is urgent and preoccupying. Over the past two decades I have worked inside and outside the classroom with both kinds of people, and I have come to realize how important it is for them to be able to understand ethical theory and medical information, as well as how to process this knowledge. Whether a person comes to health care ethics because of interest in the field or because her life has been turned upside-down by a clinical crisis, I hope she will find in this book a concise and systematic exposition which helps her come to grips with what is at stake.

Issues in Health Care Ethics is written in language which is meant to be accessible to students in colleges or professional schools as well as educated people in general. I hope that in the course of reading this book you find an incentive to nurture a life-long interest in its subject.

I owe thanks to many people, particularly my students at Saint Peter's College, my colleagues in the Theology Department, and members of the administration who supported my project. Special thanks are due to Mrs. Peggy Greenwood, College Secretary, for the superb job she did with producing my manuscript. Finally, I want to thank my friends on whom I depend for affirmation and assistance and my family: my husband John and our children, John, Tom, Annemarie and Peter, whose love makes my life truly blessed.

ISSUES IN HEALTH CARE ETHICS

PART ONE

FORMULATING A MORAL METHODOLOGY

CHAPTER 1

Ethical Decision Making in the Health Care Context

INTRODUCTION

How do we know that conduct is correctly situated in the "moral" or "ethical" sphere? This is not an easy question because there are a lot of subtle issues involved, but there are some clues which generally indicate that morality or ethics is an aspect of a situation.

Moral questions are intuitively understood as having a special kind of importance. It doesn't make much difference what flavor yogurt you have for lunch, but it does make a difference whether or not you tell the truth. The bonds of trust and community are strengthened if people are sincere and truthful; these bonds can be weakened or broken if they are untruthful. Truth, trust and the well-being of the community are ethically significant.

Moral discourse involves using terms such as *good and bad, right and wrong, should and should not, ought and ought not*. In moral discourse, people are also apt to disclose what their values are, what beliefs they hold, and what principles influence their decisions. Their values have been interiorized as part of the process of searching for truth. Those who have clarified their values and who seek to live by them tend to be clear in their thinking as well as capable of making their own choices. They make up their minds to swim *with* the current or *against* it according to deeply cherished values or principles.

Ethical people can be counted on to argue in favor of doing what they consider to be the right thing and against what they consider to be the wrong thing. This is because of the special kind of importance that moral matters possess for them. People recognize this importance and have a hard time letting go of moral issues they believe require attention. For example, I have personally found it impossible to keep silent about the injustice done to people I know who have been fired without cause from their jobs. And I admire nurses and physicians who do not hesitate to care for patients with contagious diseases even though they may be placing themselves at some risk.

There can be disagreements about how to go about deciding if an action or policy is right or wrong. In other words, in pluralistic United States society, as in most of the Western world, we lack consensus as to which moral **methodology*** is soundest and most coherent. In addition to the fact that the methodological issue is unresolved, the actual process of engaging in moral reasoning within any particular system is complex. While the existence of disagreement may be disconcerting, it is important not to become pessimistic about morality because people are **essentially good** and most people want to act in a morally upright manner.

There are frequently disagreements about moral judgments:

> X is a morally right action   versus   X is a morally wrong act

In this regard, what Dr. Jack Kevorkian does comes immediately to mind as an apt example. Thus one could conceivably judge:

> When Kevorkian releases a terminally ill suffering person from enormous pain and indignity (or helps the patient release herself) a morally right action takes place.

or

> When Kevorkian euthanizes sick people or assists them in suicide, morally wrong acts occur.

Sometimes moral questions are so difficult that people cannot even decide into which category to put them. While most people would classify rape as an evil deed, a moral wrong, and a crime because analyzing rape is fairly straightforward, other questions are much more perplexing. For example, people tend to be confused about evaluating government sponsorship of condom giveaways. Would such sponsorship constitute approval of irresponsible conduct, realistic public health policy which is tolerant of the **lesser evil**, or a simplistic and ill-fated attempt to deal with the worldwide **pandemic** of HIV/AIDS by suggesting a **problematic solution**?

In addition to disagreements about which moral judgments are correct, there are disagreements about who is competent to make these judgments. Some say individuals should decide for themselves; others contend that authorities such as judges, legislators, religious leaders, or philosophers are the ones who are equipped to say what is right or wrong. I maintain that the

---

*Throughout this book unfamiliar terms are printed in boldface. Explanations of these words appear in glossaries at the ends of the chapters.

decisive element in deciding what is right or wrong is the rationale on which the argument is based, not the status or title of the person who articulates the argument.

In order to engage in moral reasoning, one needs to analyze arguments and motives as well as conclusions. A critical assessment of contemporary culture will also be required. This task will be difficult because it is hard to achieve the necessary distance from one's culture in order to determine how it influences values, behaviors, and goals.

SOME METHODS OF MORAL REASONING

There are many ways to reason morally and these are summarized under the following headings:

Intuitionism and Subjectivism are not so much systems for doing ethical reflection as unsystematized ways by which people make moral decisions. Moral judgments are reached without recourse to supporting rationale or argumentation. Accordingly, with Intuitionism people follow their *hunches* and say things like "Do not provide my relative with any life-saving medical treatments because my instincts tell me she shouldn't receive them." Thus, an extremely important life-and-death decision is decided on the flimsiest of grounds, i.e., what the decision maker's instincts dictate. Ironically, people who reach ethical judgments based on Intuitionism do not seem to grasp the superficiality and arbitrariness inherent in their approach.

Subjectivism is also a superficial and arbitrary approach to ethical decision making. With Subjectivism the criterion for deciding what is morally right or what is morally objectionable is one's *feelings*. We are as likely to hear a terminally ill subjectivist proclaim, "I feel that I should not be resuscitated," as to say, "If I stop breathing, I have a feeling I should be resuscitated." What is missing from these two decisions is an answer to the question "Why?" which would provide evidence of wrestling with the sadness, complexities, medical realities, and **risk-benefit calculus.** All these need to be explored before a sound decision can be reached.

Hedonism is a system of ethical decision making which dates to the **ancient Greeks.** Hedonism holds that the ethically good act is the one which brings the actor pleasure and the unethical act is that which causes pain and suffering. Whether pleasure or pain are to be felt as bodily, intellectual, or spiritual experiences differs according to various schools of Hedonism. A person who follows a hedonistic approach to ethics could argue for or against donating bone marrow, depending on which type of pleasure he seeks. If it is physical sense pleasure, he would see bone marrow donation as immoral because the process is uncomfortable. But if it is intellectual or spiritual pleasure, bone marrow donation might be assessed differently because of the pleasant satisfaction gleaned from altruistic conduct. In presenting this example one of the principal drawbacks of Hedonism becomes apparent: Since there are different ways of being hedonistic (sense, intellectual, spiritual), and since different people experience pleasure in different ways, Hedonism cannot provide us with dependable, nonarbitrary answers for ethical questions.

In fact, a fault common to Intuitionism, Subjectivism, and Hedonism is that no one of these ways of doing ethics is capable of providing an objective basis for resolution of ethical problems. Since factors internal to the decision maker (hunches, feelings, or the experience of pleasure) determine the moral rightness or wrongness of actions, there is bound to be disagreement as to what constitutes right or wrong conduct. In the face of such disagreement, the way to preserve social harmony is to condemn as few ways of acting as possible, while tolerating the greatest possible diversity. In fact, it is in precisely this direction that contemporary Western society is moving. Such actions as rape, murder, fraud, arson, terrorism and abuse of children are condemned, but on most other ethical matters there is tolerance for a wide range of possible opinions. Consequently, some people oppose physician-assisted suicide, others favor it, and still others withhold judging the practice in the abstract, preferring instead to evaluate concrete instances. Moral relativism is thus encountered with great regularity as is the pervasive inclination to believe that one opinion is as good as another.

In regard to the next three ethical approaches to be considered, Authoritarianism, Utilitarianism, and **Natural Law**, factors external to the persons who make moral decisions determine whether actions are ethically right or wrong. In other words, one does not decide whether an action is moral or immoral based on variable **subjective factors** but, rather, by employing **objective criteria**.

With Authoritarianism it is the will, the analysis or the declaration of a person in authority, which makes an action ethical or unethical. People who follow any authority as their dependable guide to moral action can be counted on to justify their conduct by saying that it conforms to the orders of the person in charge. Certainly this was true of officials in **Nazi concentration camps.** Conceivably it could be true in respect to unethical conduct in a health care facility if such conduct is ordered by a high-ranking physician and is carried out by a health care worker of lesser rank. An example might be a live birth during an abortion, followed by a physician's orders to a nurse not to resuscitate a struggling newborn and the nurse's compliance. Ordinarily a nurse does well to follow a physician's orders, but would you be inclined to say that, in this case, the doctor's orders should be followed? If not, you understand the major flaw in Authoritarianism: Every decision which comes from an authority figure is not necessarily an ethical one so that those in subordinate positions need criteria by which to evaluate the soundness of decisions handed down from above.

Utilitarianism is an approach to ethics which seeks to avoid the arbitrariness of subjective approaches as well as the nonnegotiability of either Authoritarianism or Natural Law. Accordingly, Utilitarianism seeks to establish a method for arriving at ethical conclusions through means of mathematical calculation. The action or policy which is deemed ethically correct is that which will accomplish the greatest good for the greatest number. The action or policy which is considered morally wrong might benefit a small percentage but would not be beneficial for the majority. Ethical theoreticians associated with Utilitarianism are Jeremy Bentham (1748–1832) and John Stuart Mill (1806–1873). Bentham maintained that actions produce units of pleasure and that the task of ethics is to help people discern which actions will produce the greatest amount of pleasure for both the individual and the community. Mill differed with Bentham in that he challenged the idea of always being able to measure pleasure and he placed more emphasis on the social character of happiness.

The current practices of not allowing individuals to go into the marketplace seeking organs for themselves or loved ones and of not allowing payment to organ donors can serve as an example of utilitarian methodology. The rationale is that while it is understandable that a person who desperately needs an organ for herself or a loved one could conceivably benefit by cutting a deal with a potential donor or the donor's surrogate, to do so would disrupt the orderliness of the entire procurement-allocation process and might lead to grave abuses. The solution to the scarceness of organs for donation is seen not in setting in motion a wave of individuals paying high prices for organs or entrepreneurs bartering organs. Instead, a better policy is thought to be educating the public about the possibilities of organ donation, facilitating the process of designating oneself a donor, and separating the donation networks from financial incentives. By so doing, according to Utilitarianism, the greatest good for the greatest number is achieved.

As a methodology for resolving ethical issues, Utilitarianism has both strengths and weaknesses. Among its strengths is the attractiveness of equating ethically good acts or policies with those which bring pleasure or happiness to people because, on the surface, it seems a commendable goal. In addition, striving to achieve pleasure or happiness for the greatest number seems reasonable to citizens in democracies wherein it is customary to follow the will of the majority. Utilitarianism also manages to bypass intractable disagreements over conflicting principles by foregoing debate altogether and simply acting to bring about the greatest good for the greatest number. In spite of these strengths, however, Utilitarianism is a flawed methodology for three reasons.

First, actions or policies which bring pleasure to people may not serve their best interests and, therefore, may not be ethically sound. For example, making the medical school curriculum less demanding would probably increase the pleasure and decrease the stress experienced by students but would, in the long run, be a disservice to both future physicians and their patients.

Second, rules, actions or policies justified by Utilitarianism, because designed to bring about the greatest good for the greatest number, might violate the interests of a minority or undermine important principles. For example, cost-cutting measures such as employing medical assistants who receive only a few months of training to do work heretofore assigned to registered nurses could be justified because of the lowered cost of health care for everyone. However, this cost-lowering may be accomplished at the expense of sick patients who receive less than optimal care. In addition, the time-honored principle "Do no harm" may be compromised by having nursing care provided by nonprofessionals. Problems such as these undermine the rational adequacy of the methodology of Utilitarianism.

Third, if there is a basic principle at the core of ethics, it is the requirement to act justly, that is, to give to each person his due. In view of the fact that Utilitarianism avoids engagement with the demands of justice, it distinguishes itself as an inadequate ethical methodology.

Natural Law is a system for doing ethics which dates to the ancient Greeks. The philosopher Aristotle was its chief proponent. According to Natural Law, sane, mature individuals discover a reasoning process within themselves which is an accurate tool for determining the actions or courses of action that are morally appropriate or inappropriate. A key to understanding Natural Law is understanding the concept of substantial form. By substantial form is meant that each specific category of being has a particular nature and can be counted on to act according to its nature. Thus, we expect dogs to bark, horses to gallop, and apples to grow on apple trees. This is because dogs, horses, and apple trees act in accordance with their natures or, in other words, conform to their substantial forms.

The substantial form of the human person differs radically from those of plants and animals. Plants follow the natures inscribed in them and animals generally act in accordance with their instincts. Humans are different. According to Natural Law, in their essence humans possess reason, which will allow them to act in conformity with their nature or go against their nature. Thus, humans can respond to hunger by eating or by continuing a hunger strike. They can satisfy a desire to acquire possessions by going on a shopping spree, or they can deprive themselves of this satisfaction and give their money to a charitable cause. Human experience confirms that humans, by their substantial form, differ in fundamental ways from other beings. A primary focus of Natural Law ethics is to describe how human intellect and volition fit into a system of ethics.

The theory of Natural Law contends that the person has a goal: To become happy, or complete, or good. With this goal in mind the person acts in such ways as to bring about the desired result. It is morally good deeds which will bring contentment or satisfaction or the "happiness" which the person hopes for. In like manner, by good deeds, consistently performed, people complete and perfect themselves, becoming the morally good persons that they are meant to be. In the task of perfecting their nature, people perform morally good actions on a consistent, predictable basis. Their ease in performing these actions becomes second nature, and the name by which we call this predictability and ease is virtue. Such virtues as truthfulness, kindness, generosity, dependability, patience, prudence, and a host of others characterize morally good people.

The Natural Law approach to ethics is theoretically capable of yielding objective standards because of the assumption that people will agree that what promotes human dignity and the well-being of society is morally good and what retards dignity or the social order is morally objectionable. It is further held that by processes of both individual and group reflection fair-minded people will affirm the inherent soundness of this fact. Natural Law assumes that the consciences of the individual and the society will validate the premise that certain actions facilitate human development and are morally good and other actions retard development and are morally evil. Principles function within Natural Law as the fundamental truths or motivating forces from which norms, or rules of conduct, are derived.

In respect to health care ethics, the principle that confidentiality should characterize the physician-patient relationship dictates the norm that only under the most extraordinary and exceptional conditions may a physician disclose privileged information. An extraordinary, exceptional case would be that involving a psychiatrist who becomes aware that her patient is plotting to murder someone. In such a case confidentiality may be breached as the psychiatrist's duty to protect an innocent person from harm supersedes her duty to respect her patient's confidence. Law enforcement personnel must be informed in order to prevent a murder.

How useful is Natural Law to people in general and to those who do health care ethics in particular? Proponents of Natural Law tend to attribute greatness to the system. After all, it has been in existence for 2500 years, it holds out the lofty ideals of authentic human development, the practice of virtue and objective standards based in reason on which a consensus can be formed. Natural Law, however, is not without problems. It can deteriorate into **biologism** so that the physical, biological structure of acts, particularly human procreative acts, becomes prescriptive of right moral conduct. (Those who argue against employing artificial contraception, direct sterilization, and reproductive technologies such as artificial insemination and in vitro fertilization tend to conflate Natural Law with biologism.) Another reservation about the utility of Natural Law as a system for doing ethics comes from those who see it as too black and white an approach that fails to comprehend the full ambiguity and complexity of real life, or as a system which pays far too little attention to how human emotions impact on ethical choices.

In the process of moral deliberation, Natural Law relies heavily on act analysis. Humans perform two kinds of actions, acts of humans and human acts. Acts of humans, such as breathing, blinking, and digesting, are routine things that humans do. They have no particular ethical significance. Human acts, on the other hand, are those thoughtful deeds that disclose the individual's beliefs and values and are of ethical import. Infertile couples need to grapple with moral concerns as they try to decide whether or not to attempt to become parents through techniques of artificial reproduction. Decisions about starting, continuing, or stopping respirators, feeding tubes, and dialysis machines are also difficult and incorporate many ethical components.

In analyzing human acts, Natural Law proponents suggest that the four aspects of the act be examined and that the act be considered morally acceptable only if it is defensible in each of these aspects. The aspects are:

Object: That which is done. This is simply a description of what transpires without any elaboration in terms of values or appropriateness. For example, passerby administered **CPR** to pedestrian who fell to the sidewalk and who had no discernible cardio-respiratory functioning.

Intention: Describes why the object of the act happened. For example, in the situation just described, the pedestrian probably fell to the sidewalk without wanting or choosing to do so (the act of a human) while the passerby who administered CPR probably wanted to assist a neighbor in distress, a highly ethical motive, a "human act." (Of course, one cannot know for certain what motivates another person without the person's own testimony. Although it is hard to imagine, the fallen pedestrian's intentions could have been evil: To make a demand on the kindness of an unsuspecting passerby who would be vulnerable to the attack of a hiding accomplice while bent over in the act of providing CPR. Admittedly, this is far-fetched, but since it is a possibility, it provides a caution in regard to making assumptions about unknown intentions.)

Circumstances: These are the unique features of time and place under which the act takes place. If the pedestrian collapses in front of a hospital, and those in immediate proximity include medically trained personnel as well as lay people who have only the most superficial acquaintance with CPR, it would make sense for trained physicians and nurses to try to revive the stricken individual rather than those who are less qualified.

Effects or consequences: These are the foreseeable results of actions or omissions. With regard to the fallen pedestrian, without CPR it is very probable that she will die. With CPR there are three possibilities: It will work and she will recover in fairly good condition; it will work and she will recover in very poor condition, to suffer another cardiac arrest soon or to linger in a diminished state; or it will not work and the patient will die. Since life is a great good, and since, as members of the human race we are required to assist one another, there is general agreement in this country that, in the case of a person who suffers a cardiac arrest in emergency circumstances, CPR should be administered in the hope of restoring the person to well-being. If this desired result is not attained, the human task is to accept that sad fact with resignation, even while hoping that the result had been otherwise.

It sometimes happens that in carrying out human acts there are two effects, one good and the other evil. Consider the case of a pregnant woman who is diagnosed with advanced cancer of the uterus. In order to deal decisively with the cancer, a hysterectomy has to be performed but, as a result of the hysterectomy, the nonviable fetus will perish. What should the physician do? What should the woman allow? According to the Natural Law principle of double effect, as long as the intention for the hysterectomy is only to save the woman's life and not to cause the fetus harm, and under the circumstances there are no other possible medical techniques to deal with the kind of cancer from which she is suffering, the hysterectomy may be carried out. Thus, an action which includes a bad effect can be tolerated based on the fact that less than ideal situations often force morally good people to accept less than ideal solutions. There are two cautions to keep in mind in applying the principle of double effect.

1. The good and bad effects must occur simultaneously and the good effect cannot come about as the result of the bad effect.
2. There must be a truly proportionate reason for allowing the bad effect to happen. A trivial or frivolous reason would not provide sufficient justification to tolerate a bad effect.

The Natural Law approach to moral decision making has several strengths. This system is analytical so that in the process of justifying one's judgments the theoretical substructure from which one reasons inevitably is disclosed. Thus, one's objective standards are brought into the open and are laid out, allowing for subsequent questioning and defense. From the Natural Law system lofty ideals and concepts have emerged. Justice, fairness, truthfulness, fidelity, respect, and a host of other ideals have consistently been advocated as ethically mandatory. So have human rights and their correlative, obligations. An analysis of the foundations of English common law, upon which legal practice in the United States is based, would show clear lines of connection between Natural Law morality and our consensus on legal and illegal deeds, as well as the rationale for why we assign one or the other designation to a particular action.

Just as there are strengths to Natural Law morality, so there are weaknesses. A distressing weakness lies in the claim by Natural Law proponents that its principles and judgments are universally applicable even while there is widespread acknowledgment that these claims are not universally accepted. Is the reason for the lack of acceptance a failure of communication or of understanding, or are there real problems with the system which need to be addressed? This is a complex question and one which I raise so that the reader can be aware of it, not because there is a simple answer for it. Another difficulty with Natural Law theory is its historical association with the Roman Catholic Church. Many people are inclined to think of Natural Law as the "Catholic" approach to morality. While it is true that the great thirteenth century theologian, St. Thomas Aquinas, adopted Aristotle's method of ethical analysis, and the Catholic hierarchy after Thomas Aquinas accepted and utilized this approach, this fact does not alter Natural Law's capacity to serve as an objective, rational approach to ethical decision making.

In the approach known as proportionalism, an attempt is made to integrate subjective preferences into decision making. Patients do not make health care decisions in the abstract; each and every decision involves a specific individual with a clinical concern, as well as a unique history and set of values. According to Natural Law tradition, the patient who undertakes to make a decision has to do so in view of two distinct realities: First, binding moral principles which need to be acknowledged; and, second, his own health-related circumstances and personal values. Such principles as the following need to be honored:

- life is a good, although not an absolute good;
- autonomy is as much a responsibility as a right;
- reasonable treatments should be accepted.

The patient needs to integrate principles into his value system and to arrive at a decision which honors both relevant principles and his own values. This will not be easy because the outcomes of medical procedures cannot be known in advance. Often there are degrees of medical ambiguity, so that decisions frequently follow a trial-and-error approach. Accordingly, a patient decides to see how a treatment goes, prepared to make yet another decision based on its outcomes.

As it happens, personal values and preferences differ from person to person and give rise to different choices. This is because the overall human good for one person can differ from the overall good for another. In respect to the principles just listed, since life is not an absolute good and since people are autonomous, some people likely would refuse such medical treatments as chemotherapy, hemodialysis and respirator-assisted breathing in order to accommodate a desire for a quicker death. Others who want to live for as long as possible in order to be present for a specific event or because of the value they place on each moment of life would likely choose all available medical technologies. What constitutes a "reasonable treatment" for one patient would constitute a burdensome treatment for the other. This is because the two patients are different people with different values, and their value perspectives influence their choices.

The rationale which justifies either decision is known as *proportionate reason*. Proportionate reason determines *why* a person chooses one course of action over another. It reveals what motivates a person and suggests what the person intends his action or choice to accomplish. In a sense, the person who employs proportionate reason chooses one good over another, and what makes the good a good or value for him is his personal system of preferences and dislikes. Proportionate reason may be followed if

1. There are no clear absolute prohibitions forbidding a given course of action;
2. the person understands what his subjective values are and feels their exigence on him in such a way that he considers it important to honor them; *and*
3. it appears that he will experience more benefits than burdens as a result of his choice.

The burden-benefit calculus has a well-established place in health care ethics and, in a sense, the use of proportionate reason requires that a patient or surrogate employ this strategy of measurement. This strategy recognizes that medical procedures may be withheld when the burden or risk incurred exceeds the expected or actual benefit. This judgment cannot be dictated in advance but, rather, is made in light of specific clinical circumstances along with individual preferences. Factors to be considered when assessing benefits and burdens include the effects of a treatment on the quality and/or length of life and the effects on the patient's physical, mental, emotional, and spiritual well-being.

THE ROLE OF HOSPITAL ETHICS COMMITTEES

The way in which ethical questions are raised and resolved in today's medical practice entails their being the subject of discussion by ethics committees. These committees vary in size from a handful of individuals to close to two dozen. What happens when a complex question is addressed by a group of people from the fields of medicine, nursing, law, philosophy or religion, pastoral care, social services, and the community? Nothing too neat, I can assure you. For one thing, some ethics committee members are clear about the reasons for the judgments they make, and others are confused. For another thing, people from various fields tend to focus on a problem from different perspectives: Physicians are interested in how medicine can address a cluster of symptoms, attorneys tend to be preoccupied with trying to ascertain which legal precedents apply, and ethicists, depending on their methodology, may be searching for truth, or trying to decide what the patient would want, or trying to understand in what the best use of the hospital's resources might consist. Members of the clergy might be considering how the leaders of their denomination might respond to the kind of case under discussion, and members of the community might be thinking that one opinion is as good as another, so this case will never be settled.

In view of such a scenario, two things become apparent. First, it is good to be knowledgeable about the various methodological approaches to ethical decision making as well as the different perspectives from which issues can be approached. This allows for members of an ethics committee to step back from the discussion and describe what it is that is going on and, in a sense, to bring order out of chaos. This type of informed clarification is helpful to everyone on an ethics committee. The second thing which becomes apparent is the need to get things moving, to honor as many points of view, values and principles as possible, and to reach a conclusion. This is where pragmatism comes in. Pragmatism can be loosely described as solving problems by employing solutions which have worked in the past or which will likely work in this case. What works in other hospitals? What are the courts satisfied with? What can the community we serve live with? What can we all agree to? These are the kinds of questions which tend to surface and the answers they generate tend to dictate the course to follow. This is American Pragmatism at work in the health care setting. It is an established ideology which is here to stay.

There is a movement in contemporary health care ethics in the direction of giving renewed respectability to a medieval method for doing ethics called **casuistry**.[1] With Casuistry, paradigm cases are studied and discussed to decide what kinds of rules could be established to deal with these cases. These rules or maxims would hold true in the typical circumstances in effect when the rule was formulated, and they would provide practical guidance in the clinical setting. During the 1980s in hospitals and nursing homes in the United States a paradigm case arose with surprising frequency. The case involved once competent adult patients who sustained irreversible brain damage and who were maintained by feeding tubes in **persistent vegetative states**. The question raised time and again in hospitals, nursing homes, and courts was whether or not tube feeding could be discontinued and the patients allowed to die. Many cases were decided allowing for discontinuance of tube feeding and, as a result, both legal precedents and practical maxims were established. The relevant casuistic insight or maxim is: If a once competent adult patient in a persistent vegetative state has a valid advance directive, or a **surrogate** who can establish through anecdotal evidence or **substitute judgment** that the patient would not want his life continued by means of artificial nutrition and hydration, then it is ethically appropriate to discontinue treatment. In regard to casuistry, note that the maxim would apply only to situations which are similar in pertinent aspects.

TACKLING A PROBLEM IN HEALTH CARE ETHICS

In order to analyze any dilemma in a systematic fashion, one needs to have a system for problem solving. As we saw above, there are several ethical methodologies from which one can choose. It is important to be aware of the essential elements that should be taken into consideration in solving a health care issue. These elements include clarifying the medical facts pertinent to the case, including uncertain matters and points of disagreement; determining what is known of patient preferences, whether or not a health care proxy has been appointed to act for an incompetent patient, or if a surrogate is speaking for the patient without the benefit of the legal status conferred on a proxy and whether or not there is a dispute between the attending physician and decision maker, or disagreement within an incompetent patient's kinship circle; and knowing the ethical issues contained in the case and the various ways of resolving these issues. In light of relevant facts, an appropriate decision maker must decide on the best moral solution and provide rationale in justification of this decision.

CONSCIENCE

The human capacity most utilized in the process of moral decision making and the actual carrying out of moral conduct is conscience. Children of 4 or 5 or 6 usually discover that they have a conscience when they find themselves aware that they should *not* do something wrong like tell a lie or take something that doesn't belong to them. They don't make their conscience; they discover it.

Conscience is a power of the mind and will. The mind or intellect enables a person to reason as to what is the right action to perform and the will provides the capacity to carry out the decision. If a person acts against his conscience integrity is diminished and goodness lessened. Conversely, by following his conscience, his integrity and goodness grow.

Conscience is a specifically human capacity so that we do not think of nonhumans as exercising conscience. Just as humans are complex and have many levels of competence, so the way they exercise conscience is reflective of these realities. In order to act on their consciences, persons need to be sane, mature, and capable of self-discipline. It follows, therefore, that people who are mentally impaired or incapable of self-control cannot be expected to form or act on conscience.

In response to some horrible acts against others a question can be raised as to whether or not there can be people who have no consciences. This is a hard question to answer, but some elucidation is possible.

People can have *blind spots* which means that they can do ethically questionable things without ever realizing that they should not be doing these things. An example might be parents who give a nurse a considerable bribe to spend lots of time with their child. Nurses on pediatric floors often have large patient case loads and do not have much time to spare to socialize with their patients. Parents may be so anxious about their child's situation that they may not even be aware of the total picture and the unfair request they are making of the nurse along with the pressure they are applying through handing him a bribe. It is not difficult to recognize their blind spot. On the other hand, in regard to the nurse who takes the bribe, we would probably be much quicker to judge his action harshly because he has received sufficient training and has had enough experience to be able to recognize how unprofessional is his action.

Some people never grow up ethically. They never get to the point where they realize that they are responsible for what they do and, instead, operate from an inclination to blind obedience. With blind obedience one does the morally right thing if one's superior commands the right thing. But one would do the wrong thing if the command were unethical. Thus, in a hospital setting, it would be wrong to follow a doctor's order to do a "slow code." A "code" is to do CPR on a patient who suffers cardiac arrest. Conversely, "no code" means to refrain from doing CPR on a patient who suffers cardiac arrest, in accordance with the patient's instructions or those of the next of kin. Sometimes it happens that health care practitioners think that a patient who has a code status should be no code, and they decide to take matters into their own hands by doing a "slow code." This means that nurses and physicians take their time getting to the patient's side, and, once there, take their time getting started, and are not fully committed to their efforts at resuscitation. It is generally agreed that participating in slow codes is unprofessional as well as unethical.

Sometimes people do wrong things from misguided motivation. They have a conscience and they try to do the right thing, but they experience some impediment in carrying out their convictions. Consider the case of a proxy who is instructed by her father that he does not want to be kept alive by artificial means once the quality of his life is such that he has no capacity for pleasure or interaction. The gentleman suffers a serious stroke and his physician tells the daughter that there is a chance he might recover if he is artificially fed for a time, provided the experimental medication works. Only time will tell. The daughter agonizes over the decision and instructs the doctor to start the patient on medication. Several months pass with no improvement; there is steady deterioration and doctors eventually hold out no hope. According to her father's instructions, the daughter should ask for termination of tube feeding based on his quality of life so that her father's dying not be further prolonged. But she just cannot let him die because she thinks that that would be a cruel thing to do. She is motivated by misguided compassion, which is prompting her to instruct continuance of futile treatment in contradiction to her father's wishes. She also fails to justify her father's trust in her to carry out his wishes.

There are some other factors which keep people from being able to follow their consciences. Peer pressure and other environmental factors can cause physicians to close ranks rather than report a colleague who is a potential threat to patients. Impaired freedom as a result of psychological causes can undermine one's ability to follow one's conscience. For example, a health care provider who is clinically depressed can fail to properly question and listen to a patient's symptoms and needs so as to guide the patient toward recovery.

Even in view of the factors which can keep people from acting in accord with their consciences, it still happens that most people, under most circumstances, are capable of following conscience, making the living of the moral life a realistic possibility.

How do we go about reaching a decision of conscience in complex circumstances? Begin by elucidating the facts and alternatives particular to the situation, as well as the values and principles by which you want to live. Next, try to see the situation you are struggling with in the context of the total picture: What came before, what else is going on, and what can be expected to happen down the line? Then try out different solutions and ask yourself which hypothetical ones make sense and which ones do not, and why. At this point it would be appropriate to confer with respected advisors, share with them what you have been thinking, and ask their advice. It is also good to confer with someone who found herself in similar circumstances and ask for whatever wisdom she can offer. You may want to do some research in terms of health care, obtaining ethical, legal or religious leaders' thinking in regard to your dilemma so as to have consulted as many authorities as possible. Finally, you may want to seek solitude and time for your understanding to evolve to the point where you can make your decision, secure in the knowledge that it is the best that can be done.

CONCLUSION

In this chapter we have considered various ways of approaching ethics and have explored the reasons why it is important to work out ethical issues within a coherent, consistent, rationally adequate system.

The decisions we make about ethical issues determine whether or not we become people of integrity. In addition, the ethical standards which our society encourages influence our communal identity, for good or for ill. Therefore, it goes without saying that the importance we place on understanding and implementing ethical theory will have profound and far-reaching results. It is time consuming and intellectually demanding to clarify theoretical presuppositions but, in the long run, both the time and effort expended will come to be seen as worthwhile.

ENDNOTES

[1] An excellent history and explanation of casuistry is contained in A. R. Jonsen and S. E. Toulmin, *The Abuse of Casuistry* (Berkeley: University of California Press, 1988).

DISCUSSION QUESTIONS

1. In terms of the various ethical methodologies described in this chapter, discuss how subjective or objective factors lead to ethical judgments.
2. Does it make sense to base ethical judgments on subjective or objective considerations? Or both? Why?
3. Explain the basis for reaching an ethical judgment using each of the following methodologies: Intuitionism, Subjectivism, Hedonism, Authoritarianism, Utilitarianism, and Natural Law.
4. What is substantial form? How does human substantial form function within a system of Natural Law ethics?
5. Name three assets of Natural Law methodology and three weaknesses of this system.
6. Given the fact that hospital ethics committees are made up of people with a variety of ethical methodologies representing several different interest groups, how can ethical dilemmas presented to these committees get resolved?

7. What is conscience? How should a person reach a decision of conscience about a health care issue?

GLOSSARY

Methodology is one's organized, predictable system or method for approaching a question or issue which requires some degree of deliberation in order to be resolved.

By holding that people are **essentially good** one rejects an overly pessimistic or cynical view of human nature. One gives the benefit of the doubt to the probability that an individual's intentions are good. Of course, this will not always be the case, but, for the most part, it will hold true.

By tolerating a **lesser evil** one recognizes the imperfection inherent in individuals and society and seeks to bring about a compromise which takes reality into account. Thus, a hospital's policy might absolutely prohibit hospital employees from smoking in the building while making allowance for patients to smoke in designated areas only.

A **pandemic** is an epidemic which is worldwide in scope. A communicable disease is considered to be an epidemic when its incidence reaches numbers in excess of normal expectancy.

The use of condoms is a **problematic solution** to the genital spread of HIV because condoms do not provide absolutely dependable protection. Defective condoms, condoms which rip, or condoms which are put on improperly provide little or no protection. Hence, trying to halt the spread of HIV through advocacy of condoms is an inherently **problematic solution**. However, there is no question that regular use of condoms will save some persons from the dreadful effects of infection with HIV.

A **risk-benefit calculus** is an estimation of the minuses and pluses to be expected from a specific medical procedure. The benefit anticipated by a person with a broken leg who agrees to have the bone set and the leg encased in a cast will clearly outweigh the risks involved. The decision of a person with terminal cancer about exploratory surgery to ascertain the cause of an intestinal blockage will tend to be much more ambiguous because the risks of surgery in that situation may not offset the possible benefits.

Ancient Greek society of approximately 2500 years ago contributed significantly to subsequent Western societies, especially in respect to philosophy. Philosophers such as Aristotle, Plato, Socrates, and Plotinus exerted profound influence on both their educated contemporaries and educated people throughout the ages. Aristotle's exposition of **Natural Law** is instructive for people engaged in health care ethics today.

Subjective factors are such things as likes, dislikes, feelings, beliefs, and values which people experience within themselves. We tend to think of the subjective realm as personal, private, individual, and unique. Subjective factors come into being as a result of a person's heredity, temperament, upbringing, culture and life experiences; subjective factors differ from person to person. Accordingly, one person may be inclined to trust doctors and another person may be fearful. The reason behind the trust or fear would amount to a subjective factor such as a good relationship with a kindly pediatrician or the remembrance of a botched clinical procedure which resulted in disfigurement.

Objective criteria are standards about which there exist a consensus. These standards range from general to specific and have in common the fact that there is cross-cultural agreement about their validity. For example, consider the following objective criteria:

Morally right actions conform to reason because these actions *promote the good of the human person or the human community.*

Arranging for the provision of health care for the indigent is morally appropriate because the indigent are human persons and *health care is both a basic right and need of human persons.*

Note that objective criteria are derived from rational principles which are perceived as self-evident and, therefore, do not require justification by argumentation.

At the Nuremberg trials conducted in Germany after World War II high ranking officers who presided over the atrocities of the **Nazi concentration camps** offered as justification for war crimes the lame excuse that they were "just following orders." Society's refusal to accept that excuse was accompanied by the general consensus that all people are bound by a basic law of decency which cannot be denied and which prohibits carrying out cruel, barbarous acts against any person.

Biologism is a fundamental distortion of Natural Law which would conflate biological structures with proper human conduct.

CPR is the acronym for cardio-pulmonary resuscitation, which is the process of trying to revive a person who has stopped breathing.

Casuistry dates from the Middle Ages and is distinguished by its practicality. The term "casuistry" comes from the Latin verb *cadere*—to happen—and the method of casuistry involves similar situations which happen again and again and which are resolved by guidelines which become ritualized as policies.

Persistent vegetative state or **PVS** is a neurological diagnosis about an irreversible brain condition. In this condition a person has a functioning brain stem but has suffered irreversible destruction of the brain's cerebral-cortical functioning. Accordingly, the person is incapable of both any degree of sensate feeling and any possibility whatsoever of human interaction. The diagnosis of persistent vegetative state can be made after a brain-injured patient has been in a coma for six months.

A **surrogate** is a person who makes decisions for a child or for an adult who lacks the decisional capacity to make decisions for himself. A surrogate can be designated by a competent person before the onset of incompetence, or a surrogate can be appointed by a court. Oftentimes relatives function in the role of surrogates (parents for children; spouses for each other, etc.) without any official process of delegation. Another term for a surrogate is a proxy.

Substitute judgment is the judgment made by a surrogate about what an incompetent patient would want based on the surrogate's knowledge of the likes, dislikes, and idiosyncrasies of the incompetent patient. In an incident of substitute judgment one is likely to hear a surrogate say, "If John could speak for himself, this is what he would want. I know because John is my brother and I know better than anyone how he would think."

PART TWO

ETHICAL ISSUES AT LIFE'S BEGINNING

CHAPTER 2

Abortion

INTRODUCTION

In 1973, with its decision in *Roe v. Wade,* the United States Supreme Court made abortion legally available in the nation. The decision to have an abortion was to be a private one, reached between a woman and her physician. Not until the third trimester of pregnancy when a fetus could conceivably survive outside the uterus could the government intervene to act to protect the life of the fetus. In the United States close to 1.5 million women a year have abortions. Abortion is one of the most controversial and divisive issues in contemporary health care ethics as well as in the broader society. Members of hospital ethics committees are not likely to be asked to comment on the ethical aspects of abortion because whether or not a hospital provides abortion was probably decided more than 20 years ago. Still, abortion is a major ethical issue, a dilemma about which health care providers and women with unwanted pregnancies must decide. It is also a critical issue for so-called "pro-life" and "pro-choice" advocates who are committed to promoting their points of view. Abortion is an emotionally packed issue, one which can bring people beyond intellectual disagreement to seething hostility and even deadly violence.

WHY ABORTION WAS LEGALIZED IN THE UNITED STATES

In order to approach the issue of abortion in a dispassionate manner one needs to understand the factors which gave rise to acceptance of the practice.

Frequently in health care ethics it is from complex, emotionally packed, media-covered cases that discussion arises, consciousness changes, and new practices or policies evolve. As a result of the case of Sherri Finkbine[1] this phenomenon occurred in respect to tolerance for abortion. In 1962 Mrs. Finkbine, a California resident, told her story to a health writer for a local newspaper. An article appeared in which Mrs. Finkbine's predicament was described and readers were cautioned lest they place themselves in similar circumstances. When she was in her first trimester of pregnancy, Sherri Finkbine made two extremely distressing discoveries simultaneously: If taken by pregnant women, **thalidomide** was capable of causing very severe fetal abnormalities, *and* the medication which she was taking contained thalidomide. In the article cautioning pregnant women against taking thalidomide the author mentioned that Finkbine was scheduled for a thera-peutic abortion the following week, and she stated the name of the hospital where the procedure was going to be performed. Sherri Finkbine never dreamed of the floodtide the article would set in motion.

Pro-life advocates were outraged that a hospital would allow an abortion and a physician would be willing to perform it even though there was no legal sanction for the procedure. At the time, in the State of California, the only legally tolerated abortions were those which were performed to save the life of the mother. Sherri Finkbine's life was not in danger and so any physician or administrator who performed or facilitated the performance of a therapeutic abortion would be violating the law.

Opponents of Sherri Finkbine's scheduled abortion won the day. Her doc-tor decided not to go ahead with the procedure and she was left with choos-ing between continuing the pregnancy or leaving the United States to have an abortion. Sherri Finkbine flew to Sweden where her pregnancy was ter-minated. Consciousness of people in the United States in regard to the ille-gal status of abortion and the predicaments endured by women like Mrs. Finkbine was raised. This raised consciousness set the stage for the emer-gence of the pro-choice movement.

The United States in the 1960s and 1970s was a more liberal society than it had been in the previous decades of the twentieth century. The so-called "sexual revolution" had followed quickly on the heels of approval by the U.S. Food and Drug Administration of the birth-control pill in 1960, and peo-ple seemed to want far fewer restrictions in regard to sexual intimacy. The **double standard** was attacked, as men and women argued that women should not be bound by different sexual rules than men. Recreational sex was advocated and there were many attempts to sever the traditional con-nection between sex and marriage as well as sex and pregnancy. One possi-ble negative complication of heterosexual intercourse is that, even with the use of contraceptives, it can result in unwanted pregnancies. Neither unwanted pregnancies nor unwanted children was considered desirable by proponents of the sexual revolution, and so it is not surprising that they tended to favor the legalization of abortions performed by physicians.

Another factor which led to societal acceptance of abortion was a shift in ethical thinking towards relativism and subjectivism in morality. Accordingly, there was a discernible shift away from acknowledgment of principles such as the sanctity of human life which are binding on all to a pervasive belief that personal opinions, as variable and different as they are, ought to be honored, if at all possible. The move to moral relativism occurred simultaneously with the decline of community and the ascendancy of individualism as the salient feature of social organization in the United States. The ascendancy of individualism meant that people tended not to see themselves as members of families, tribes, or groups, bound to one another by customs and traditions and required to carry out responsibilities to each other. Instead, there was a much greater sense that each person stands alone, thinks for himself, works for herself, is encumbered by no one, and is required to act on no one's traditions or interests but his own.[2] Both moral relativism and individualism played a part in shaping an American society in which the majority was willing to accept *Roe v. Wade*.

The media plays an important part in shaping our attitudes. There is no question that many people became sympathetic toward the legalization of abortion as they read accounts of the plight of Sherri Finkbine or as they watched television accounts of other exceptional types of cases. These cases include pregnancies resulting from rape and incest as well as cases involving severely deformed fetuses and pregnant women in extreme distress because of mental or physical problems associated with their pregnancies. Cases of women suffering injury or even death as a result of botched attempts at abortions they performed themselves or obtained in so-called "back alleys" also influenced public opinion.

ABORTION AND SOCIAL DISSOLUTION

During the week between Christmas 1994 and New Year's 1995 John Salvi entered two Massachusetts abortion clinics and shot and killed two employees. These killings were not the first at abortion clinics in the United States, but Salvi's deeds represented the worst possible horror connected to abortion protests. The facts that Salvi's fanaticism was documented by the media, that neither woman who was killed actually performed or physically assisted in abortions, that the timing was absolutely dreadful, during one of the most festive seasons of the year, and that the killings represented the most distressing example of escalation led to a national questioning as to whether the time was right to reach some kind of compromise or at least tolerance for the range of viewpoints on abortion which does, in fact, exist.

In the wake of the killings, one centrist pro-life organization after another issued absolute condemnations of violence against abortion providers. Religious leaders joined the protest, too, pointing out that violence begets violence and is totally counterproductive. Given the near unanimity of disapproval for what John Salvi did, a national consensus that extremist factions need to be restricted is emerging. The question as to whether or not it might be possible for pro-choice and pro-life factions to reach some kind of compromise so as to establish a civil atmosphere, a situation which has not existed since *Roe v. Wade,* is also being addressed.

One often hears that there are too many abortions and that the two sides should join forces to lessen the number. How should this be done? Some suggest more sex education earlier, easier access to artificial contraception, ready availability of the so-called **"morning after" pill**, and more education of men as to their responsibilities as sex partners. People who oppose feminism, sex before marriage, and/or artificial contraception are not likely to accept the aforementioned suggestions. Neither are those who are absolutely opposed to abortion under any circumstances because, to them, a lesser incidence of abortion does not represent an acceptable compromise.

There is also a school of thought which would allow for abortion before a certain stage of fetal development such as during the first trimester, i.e., before quickening, when the pregnant woman has not yet felt movement. Others would move the time to the first week to ten days after pregnancy, before the embryo attaches itself to the uterine wall and an early stage pregnancy becomes established. There are others who attach significance to a beating heart, or brain function or some other biological criterion, and they contend that abortion is tolerable before that organic development but intolerable afterwards. Unfortunately, proponents of limiting abortions based on physiological characteristics of a fetus have not succeeded in generating significant support, and it does not seem likely that a future consensus will emerge along such lines.

A large segment of the United States population wants to allow for legal abortion when the pregnancy results from rape or incest, when the fetus is deformed, or when the fetus presents a threat to the life of the pregnant woman.[3] In view of the influence exerted by pro-choice thinking, however, it seems unlikely that limitations will become public policy.

PARTIES WITH INTEREST IN ABORTION

Roe v. Wade said that the issue of abortion concerned a woman and her doctor until the point in fetal development when the State might declare an interest in view of the fact that the fetus had grown into a viable being with potential for living outside the uterus. Over the years, however, it has become apparent that there are several other parties with an interest in abortion, and this is one reason why the issue of abortion will not go away. These parties include

the fetus who, if left undisturbed, would probably grow into an infant;

the fetus' other parent, its father, who, under current circumstances, cannot reverse an abortion decision;

the grandparents of a developing fetus who have no authority to cancel the choice of an abortion;

health care administrators and other health care professionals whose moral principles might be compromised by their complicity in the practice of abortion;

insurers who must decide whether or not abortion is a medical service which should be provided to clients;

the President of the United States, members of the U.S. Supreme Court, state courts, the U.S. Congress and state legislatures who need to reassess the rational adequacy and constitutional validity of current laws and practice, and who also need to deal with limit setting and novel questions which arise in connection with abortion;

taxpayers who need to search their consciences: Do they want their tax money used to pay for all medicaid abortions, some, or none, and to what extent are they willing to go to make their views known and insure that these views become law;

the media, which knows that abortion is a highly charged issue and needs to examine itself in order to understand how it might convey news about abortion in an even-handed manner;

educators in classrooms from primary schools through law schools and medical schools—at each level educators need to determine the morally right way to deal with abortion and related issues, such as prevention of unwanted pregnancies and need to decide how to communicate this information;

activists, both pro-choice and pro-life, striving to influence attitudes toward abortion. Because their goal is sensitive and the implications of their work are far-reaching, members of these groups need to bend over backwards to maintain their integrity and be above reproach in their tactics;

finally, under ordinary circumstances, leaders of religious institutions must call people to lofty ideals and commendable deeds. In the context of abortion, this has not always been true. Are there ways for religious leaders to encourage respect, cooperation, and tolerance between pro-life and pro-choice advocates without abandoning their principles and beliefs? If they were to do so perhaps the debate about abortion would move forward with less acrimony and hostility.

Will the issue of abortion be resolved? Will those who oppose it give up their opposition? Will *Roe v. Wade* be overturned? Will a constitutional amendment be adopted giving states the right to regulate the availability of abortion within their borders? Will abortion become so repugnant in medical schools that physicians will not receive training in how to perform the procedures? Will civil discourse bring about a civil atmosphere, so that the procedure's availability will no longer cause terroristic acts like those of John Salvi? The answer to each of these questions is probably "No," and so we are left with a seemingly unsolvable issue with incalculable ramifications. In view of this reality, the most constructive approach to take in regard to abortion may be to understand facts about abortion as well as the arguments offered against and for access to it so that we can appreciate its enormous complexity.

ABORTION FACTS

The following facts about abortion were published by the Alan Guttmacher Institute in 1994. These facts convey information about the ages, religious backgrounds, and rationale of the women who terminate their pregnancies by abortion.

More than 50 percent of the pregnancies among American women are unintended. Half are terminated by abortion.

Of the women seeking abortions, 43 percent have had at least one previous abortion, and 49 percent have had a previous birth.

The United States has one of the highest abortion rates among developed countries.

Fifty-six percent of women obtaining abortions are under age 25; 23 percent of that number are teenagers. Twenty-two percent are 30 and older.

Eighteen to nineteen-year-old women have the highest abortion rate: 59 per 1,000 women 18–19 years of age.

Catholic women are about as likely to obtain an abortion as are all women nationally, while Protestants and Jews are less likely. Catholic women are 30 percent more likely than Protestants to have abortions.

One in six abortion patients in 1987 described herself as a born-again or evangelical Christian; evangelical Christians are half as likely as other women to obtain abortions.

Three-quarters of women getting an abortion say having a baby would interfere with work, school, or other responsibilities. About two-thirds say they cannot afford to have a child, and one-half say they do not want to be a single parent or are having problems in their relationships with their husband or partner.

Of women having an abortion, 1 percent have been advised that the fetus has a defect, and 12 percent fear that the fetus may have been harmed by medications or other conditions.

Eighty-nine percent of abortions take place in the first trimester of pregnancy; of that figure, about half occur at eight weeks or less from the last menstrual period, and about one-quarter at nine to ten weeks.[4]

TYPICAL ARGUMENTS ABOUT THE MORALITY OF ABORTION

AGAINST ABORTION	*FOR ABORTION RIGHTS*
1. The embryo or fetus is a human life and abortion is morally wrong because it takes a human life.	1. The embryo or fetus is not a human life.
2. To be valid, law must be derived from sound principles such as respect for human life.	2. The function of law should be to protect women from inept practitioners and physicians from liability.
3. Taking an unborn life is an immoral act because the unborn is innocent and no combination of tragic circumstances or foreseeable post-birth situations can negate this fact.	3. The fetus can be an extremely difficult burden in the life of a pregnant woman; life for an unwanted or severely handicapped child may be tragic.
4. A fetus is not a part of its mother; instead, it is a separate entity with rights of its own.	4. The fetus is part of its mother and not a separate entity at that early stage of development.
5. The right of the unborn to life takes precedence over the right of a woman to control her body.	5. The rights of women are greater than those of fetuses, and it is moralistic to suggest women should have exercised their right not to become pregnant *before* they did so.
6. Abortion is *morally* wrong and the law should follow morality.	6. Religions seek to impose their creeds in regard to abortion; but in the pluralistic United States there is no justification for imposing beliefs.
7. The carrying out of abortion diminishes all parties in their humanity, the woman, the physician, and other accomplices.	7. Forcing unwanted pregnancies is a travesty with grave psychological consequences for both mother and child.

Let us consider the seven "typical arguments" which, taken as a whole, usually provide the rationale for opposing abortion or accepting it.

1. Against. The embryo or fetus is a human life and abortion is morally wrong because it takes a human life. At the moment of conception, when ovum and sperm combine, a unique human life is created. This life, if supported and nurtured, will develop over a period of nine month's gestation within the uterus and will be born as a live infant. Should its mother miscarry or should the fetus die in utero, it will not go on to develop into a living individual; either of these occurrences would constitute a reason for deep sadness. Human life is sacred at every stage of its development, and abortion constitutes a grave and inexcusable offense against a person-in-becoming. The young one's heart beats at 18-25 days gestation. Brain waves can be recorded as early as 40 days. By 11 or 12 weeks the young one can squint, swallow, and make a fist. She has fingerprints and can kick. She is sensitive to heat, touch, light, and noise, and sucks her thumb. She weighs about one ounce and is 2⅓ to three inches long and so could fit comfortably in the palm of one's hand.

1. For. The embryo or fetus is not a human life. Because it is just a cluster of cells, a pregnancy mass, it should not be of moral concern to us. By scraping it from the uterus or removing it with the aid of a suction device (first trimester techniques) we remove pregnancy tissue; we do not do harm to a being with rights. The same holds true with second trimester saline abortions which entail a woman's going into labor and delivering a **nonviable fetus.** By its nonviability, the fetus confirms that it is not a human life. Human life does not begin until a live human person, an infant which is capable of independent existence, is born.

2. Against. To be valid, law must be derived from sound principles. Law has an integrity of its own and is only valid if legal precepts conform to objective standards of justice and right conduct. To suggest that citizens and legislators can make laws be anything they want them to be is to distort the very nature of law, which requires that government leaders acknowledge the existence of objective standards of right and wrong and formulate regulations conforming to those standards. What would society be like if lawmakers decided to lower the age of consent for sexual intercourse to 12 years or if they decided that parents whose newborn infant was not of the desired gender could dispose of the baby in whatever manner they wanted? Both these possibilities are morally repugnant because there is widespread agreement that children have a right not to be exploited and a right not to be killed. Instinctively we shudder at the horrors to which we just alluded. In the same vein it is apparent that the most fundamental right of any human is the right to life. Since human life begins at conception, it is a responsibility of lawmakers, citizens, pregnant women, and members of the health care professions to respect the right to life. Therefore, the legal precedent estab-

lished by *Roe v. Wade* is inherently flawed because it allows for an action which visits a grave injustice on a human being.

Law is related to morality in that law should reflect sound morality. The most fundamental dictum of morality, the most basic nonnegotiable rule of thumb is "Do good and avoid evil." Because taking the life of a viable human fetus is so self-evidently evil, this action is unquestionably immoral. The most fundamental rule to which physicians are bound dates from the **Hippocratic Oath** and is contained in the instruction "Do no harm." Physicians who violate this stipulation erode the integrity of the medical profession and abandon more than 2,000 years of ethical tradition. The connection between law, morality, and health care ethics is indisputable, and it requires overturning the irrational decision reached in *Roe v. Wade*.

2. For. The function of law should be to protect women from inept practitioners and physicians from liability. Law is constructed by legislators and it reflects both the wishes of the populace and the mores of the society. The purpose of law is to keep order in society so that individuals can function without being afraid of wrongdoers or unnecessarily restricted by regulations which impede individual freedom. Law can and does prevent harm. Traffic laws prevent accidents, securities law prevents fraudulent financial misconduct, and laws legalizing abortion prevent injury and even death to women because women are not forced to procure "back alley" abortions. In addition, legalized abortion enables physicians who provide this service to do their work without fear of criminal penalty. Doctors who feel no ethical reservation about legal termination of pregnancies are thus able to meet with women who feel abortion is right for them in order to carry out the procedure. Law is at its sanest and best when it protects the privacy and consciences of people who exercise their right to provide or obtain procedures resulting in termination of pregnancy.

3. Against. Taking an unborn life is an immoral act because the unborn is innocent and no combination of tragic circumstances or foreseeable post-birth situations can negate this fact. The crucial idea in this argument against abortion is the fact that the embryo-fetus is innocent and there is a consistent tradition in ethics and law not to kill the innocent. The occasions on which society tolerates killing humans are limited to three and in each it is the non-innocent nature of the one killed which leads to tolerance of the act of taking that person's life. *First*, criminals who are guilty of horrible crimes may be condemned to death and their killings can be carried out in order to meet the demands of justice and serve as a deterrent to other would-be evil-doers. *Second*, in war, enemy soldiers may be targeted and killed, but enemy non-combatants, because they are innocent civilians, may never be directly targeted. And, *third*, an unjust aggressor may be attacked, with deadly force if necessary, in order to protect an innocent person in danger. Killing another person, depriving that person of life, is a matter of the utmost importance.

This is why, in Western ethical and legal traditions, the exceptional instances in which it has been allowed to take life by killing have been severely restricted. Even if the unborn is a dreadful burden to its mother, it does not follow that she has the right to abort it. One of the most consistent and compelling characteristics of civilized societies has been their commitment to protect innocent human life. A climate of ethical relativism and sexual permissiveness cannot revoke this compelling moral obligation.

3. For. The fetus can be an unfair burden in the life of a pregnant woman. She may have conceived as a result of rape or incest, and it would be a travesty to require that she carry the fetus. Or she may have other reasons for not wanting to be pregnant. Should a 12-year-old be forced to become a mother? What about women in menopause? Should we require women in troubled relationships to continue pregnancies? What about women who want to finish their studies, or women who already have enough children, or poor women who just cannot afford to have a child? Should a woman be forced to carry to term a deformed or retarded offspring if she feels she lacks resources to cope with that child after birth? People who answer "No" to these questions focus on the circumstances surrounding the pregnancy, such as whether or not the woman consented to participate in intercourse, her age, her finances, her ability to care for a child, or her readiness to become a mother, and they argue that in some circumstances the harm of carrying a pregnancy and giving birth would be so grave to a woman, or the situation after birth would be so disadvantageous for a child, that abortion is justified.

4. Against. A fetus is not a part of its mother; instead, it is a separate entity with rights of its own. At conception a new being (or in the case of multiple embryos, beings) is formed. Twenty-three chromosomes from each parent join to form a unique, never to be replicated individual. From the moment of conception until emergence from the womb approximately nine months later, an awesome process of biological development occurs. Even though it relies on its mother for provision of nourishment and the warm, secure environment in which it can grow, the embryo develops all its own systems, digestive, cardio-pulmonary, etc.

A troublesome tooth, appendix, or gall bladder is part of a woman over which she can rightly exercise jurisdiction. A developing fetus is a separate entity. Human decency requires of pregnant women and of the broader society that these unborn children be protected and not subject to harm. Should a woman make the decision to have an abortion, she will live with grief for the rest of her life because a pregnant woman knows that what grows in her uterus is an unborn child. The burden of this knowledge may be with the woman for years, or even for her whole life, causing her anguish, sadness, and guilt.

4. For. The fetus is part of its mother and not a separate entity at that early stage of development. It is merely pregnancy tissue which can cause a woman untold psychological trauma.

This argument seeks to put to rest any protestations that the embryo-fetus is close to being a separate, individual, personal human life. It assigns to the fetus much less status than it would to a person after birth, claiming that the biological clump of characteristics is nobody's business but the pregnant woman's. Since it exists within the woman's body and since it is an individual's right to decide what will or will not happen to her body, no one should interfere in a woman's decision about the disposition of pregnancy tissue. Furthermore, once women end unwanted pregnancies they experience enormous relief.

5. Against. The right of the unborn to life takes precedence over the right of a woman to control her body. The time to exercise control is *before* pregnancy. This argument presupposes that the conflict contained in an unwanted pregnancy is a conflict between an interest of the pregnant woman and the existence of the fetus. The interest of the pregnant woman could be that the fetus is a burden because she is unmarried, or poor, or at the beginning of her career, or in school, or that she has enough children already, or some other difficulty. Should she choose abortion she would remove the difficulty but she would do it at a terrible price to the fetus: Its life would be terminated. Those who hold this position contend that it would be disproportionate and unreasonable to deprive the fetus of life in order to deliver the woman from distressing circumstances. They point out that she can receive help with the expenses of pregnancy and beyond from government and private sources and that she can surrender the newborn for adoption if she cannot care for it. They point out further that becoming pregnant is a serious business which requires maturity and years of parental responsibility. The height of immaturity is for a woman to discover that she has become pregnant and try to figure out where to go from there. Precautions, planning, self-restraint, and prudence could prevent tragic situations from causing tragic consequences.

5. For. The rights of women are greater than those of fetuses and it is moralistic to suggest that women should have exercised their right not to become pregnant *before* they did so. The twentieth century has witnessed many liberating movements such as the labor movement, the movement for racial equality, and the women's movement. One aspect of the women's movement was that it ushered in a new awareness of the full dignity and equality of women. Prior to the women's movement, women were considered inferior to men and incapable of achieving the same level of competence as men in the business world or the professions. While no one would claim that women have achieved full equality in the workplace and the pro-

fessions, legal and moral commitments to correct injustices are now in place, and there is no argument as to the appropriateness of the goals of the women's movement. A natural carryover from the ideology of the women's movement in which women are understood to be equal to men is to think of women as greater than embryos or fetuses. Therefore, if the rights or potentialities of one or the other are to suffer, it is without question that the woman is entitled to more consideration than the fetus. She is a full, complete, developed, independent person and, as such, need not have her wishes countermanded by a being of far less development than herself. In this argument it is the woman's autonomy and full personhood which are stressed. In another variation of it, her usefulness to her family is of paramount consideration so that abortion is justified if it is necessary so that a woman will be able to continue to care for the husband, children or other relatives she already cares for based on the fact that another pregnancy or baby would impede her from so doing.

The second part of this argument that "it is moralistic to suggest that women should have exercised their right not to become pregnant *before* they did so" is not so much an endorsement of birth control as realistic about the facts that both poor decisions are made and that accidents happen. Whether conception occurs as a result of reckless passion, failed birth control, a drunken episode, or exploitation of a woman by a man does not alter the fact that the pregnancy occurs in a woman's body. In regard to her body and her relationship to an embryo or fetus, this argument goes, a woman is superior and may make whatever decision she chooses.

6. Against. Abortion is *morally* wrong and the law should follow morality. To think of opposition to abortion as a religious doctrine is to fundamentally misconstrue what is asserted by religious leaders and many nonreligious people as well. Religious leaders have an obligation to speak out on behalf of the vulnerable and defenseless and, in fact, many nonreligious people consider the same obligation to be theirs. Since embryos and fetuses are voiceless and among the most fragile members of the human community, people who are convinced of their humanity feel compelled to speak out on behalf of their right to life.

By calling for tolerance of all viewpoints and favoring the accommodation of legal abortion for those who want to choose it, a fundamental flaw in our nation's moral consciousness becomes apparent. This flaw is an outgrowth of the movement to moral relativism with its attendant absence of objective moral standards. A connection is proposed between moral relativism (one opinion on the morality of abortion is as good as another) and the permissive climate of tolerance which has become a leading characteristic of our culture. In the names of pluralism and tolerance, access to legal abortion is promoted because ironing out the fundamental differences which divide pro-life and pro-choice groups appears to be an impossible task. Those who cannot tolerate abortion on moral grounds, whether they argue from religious and moral grounds, or just moral grounds, feel compelled to hold on to a truth which they find ethically self-evident: Abortion takes the life of a person-in-becoming and is a direct and inexcusable violation of the humanity of the fetus. No more could they consider toleration of abortion than could they contemplate the reinstitution of the dehumanizing practice of buying, selling, and owning slaves.

6. For. Religions seek to impose their creeds in regard to abortion; in the pluralistic United States there is no justification for imposing beliefs. So called "conservative religions," such as conservative Judaism, the Roman Catholic Church, the Muslim religion, and some fundamentalist Christian churches consider abortion a grave sin or offense against God and are unequivocal in condemning the practice. Those who favor legal access to abortion are inclined to protest the fact that various religions seek to influence public policy on abortion by advocating that the law conform to their credal positions. They argue that women and physicians who want to follow religious teachings against abortion are free to do so, and they request that they not be constrained in their actions on the grounds of religious beliefs to which they do not adhere. The United States is a pluralistic society which seeks to tolerate the greatest possible range of cultural, philosophical and ideological diversity, and it does so by respecting all religions while steering clear of being unduly influenced by any specific creed. The United States Constitution and the American way of life dictate that we continue to follow our tradition of respect for separation of church and state by preventing religions from imposing their beliefs in regard to abortion.

7. Against. The carrying out of abortion diminishes all parties in their humanity, the woman, the physician, and other accomplices. To be a human person is to have for a goal to achieve the fullness of human development. The ideal of a fully developed woman includes responsibility, generosity, compassion, and conscientiousness. Such a person would be mature enough to accept and nurture a fetus growing within her and make the best possible arrangements for the baby after birth. She would follow her conscience and respect life and, if she did not, she would have to live with the negatives of a guilty conscience and a pervasive sadness she would likely find difficult to dispel.

Physicians who perform abortions and other health care providers who assist with the procedure likewise diminish themselves, primarily by contributing to a climate which is disrespectful of human life and violating the ethics of the Hippocratic Oath. The Oath stipulates: "Nor will I give a woman a pessary to procure abortion," thus situating mainstream medical practice in opposition to abortion. The taking of fetal life does nothing to enhance the dignity of those who perform abortions and toleration of abortion erodes the decency of the overall human community.

7. For. Forcing unwanted pregnancies is a travesty with grave psychological consequences. There is a time sequence in a typical pregnancy, nine months, followed by several additional months of post-partum stress. Pregnancy can be a difficult time for women who want to become mothers because of the physiological and psychological burdens which accompany it. If a woman conceives accidentally, or conceives against her will, or learns that she is carrying a defective fetus, or decides that she just does not want to be pregnant, she should not be forced by religion, law, or social custom to go through with the pregnancy. To force her to do this would deny her freedom and humanity, would diminish her status, and could compromise the quality of her parenting. This would be contrary to our nation's heritage and would contravene the notions of autonomy, self-determination, and privacy which are at the heart of health care decision making.

As we have just seen, there are many arguments for and against abortion and these arguments can be made singly or in combination. For example, an abortion foe can say that because abortion takes a human life it is morally wrong and the discussion is closed. On the other hand, a person who favors legal access to abortion may do so solely on the basis of the argument that a woman owns her body, and it is up to her to decide whether or not to continue a pregnancy. Further complicating matters is the fact that many people agree with some arguments *for* abortion rights and some arguments *against* abortion, causing them to experience feelings of ambivalence in regard to the matter.

RU 486, THE SO-CALLED "MAGIC PILL"

Given the fact that the United States has been riven apart by controversy surrounding legal abortion, the discovery of RU 486, a pill capable of terminating a pregnancy, may appear to be a fortuitous event which holds the promise of putting to rest much of the divisiveness associated with abortion. If women can self-administer RU 486 in the privacy of their own homes, then perhaps we will no longer need abortion clinics. In addition, it would become very difficult to determine which physicians prescribe this pharmacological agent, thus lessening dangers doctors now face from some antiabortion forces.

While RU 486 is a fairly effective means for causing abortion, it is not a "magic pill," i.e., one capable of resolving the social and moral issues attendant to abortion. RU 486 was developed in France by Dr. Etienne Baulier for the Roussel Uclaf Pharmaceutical Company. It consists of mifepristone, a progesterone-receptor blocker, and must be combined with a second drug, prostaglandin, in order to cause an abortion. Mifepristone and prostaglandin cannot be taken simultaneously but, rather, need to be taken separately, a few days apart. The combination of RU 486 and prostaglandin only works in women whose pregnancies are of less than two month's duration. These drugs cause abortion 85 percent of the time by breaking the fertilized ovum's bond with the uterine wall. For those who do not abort as a result of taking these drugs, surgical abortions are prescribed. Clinical trials of RU 486 are currently underway in the United States. The Population Council, a family-planning research group based in New York City, which is sponsoring trials of RU 486, received conditional approval to market the drug combination from the Food and Drug Administration on September 18, 1996.[5] However, the Population Council has had trouble finding a manufacturer, which has kept the Council from submitting enough information on the manufacturing process to win unqualified approval by the FDA to market the drug. It is still an open question as to whether and when RU 486 will be readily available in the United States.[6]

Would the availability of RU 486 improve the abortion situation in the United States? That depends on whether you take a pro-choice or a pro-life position. Although the number of abortion clinics would decline, there would still be need of clinics for women more than two months' pregnant, as well as for women for whom the drugs do not work. When the combination of RU 486 and prostaglandin is effective, women pass a small sac containing an aborted fetus; the individual woman must deal with the emotions surrounding the passing and disposal of this sac, a potentially wrenching experience. Mifepristone and prostaglandin are powerful drugs and need to be taken under a physician's supervision; handled safely, two or three visits to the doctor's office are needed. Should RU 486 become available, like all powerful drugs, there is the danger that some women may get it on the black market and take it without a physician's supervision. Uninformed girls and women who are more than two months' pregnant or who take larger doses than appropriate would place themselves at significant risk of harm. On the other hand, abortions resulting from RU 486 would be cheaper and would be done by women themselves. Thus some of the problems with violence at clinics would be reduced, and women would have greater privacy with their individual decisions. However, the key ethical objections of pro-life adherents, concerning the fetus' right to life and the woman's responsibilities to protect it, would not disappear.

CONCLUSION

Abortion is a medical procedure of which women avail themselves with surprising frequency. By listening to how we ourselves reason about abortion, as well as by analyzing the rationale presented by others, we can become aware of the controverted points. To be sure, there are plenty of relativists who reason that abortion is the right choice for some people while it would be a disaster for others. There are lots of subjectivists, too, for whom "It just feels right," or "It just does not feel right." Then there are authoritarians who reason that abortion is morally acceptable because of the United States Supreme Court's decision or that it is unacceptable based on what a particular religious leader has to say. People who argue most strenuously against abortion generally acknowledge the binding force of such objective standards as principles, norms, and rules of conduct to which all persons are bound and from which no judicial or legislative decision is empowered to excuse. Therefore, while abortion is a perennial issue of health care ethics, it is also a subject about which division of opinion appears to be irreconcilable. The only way in which this difference could possibly be resolved would be for one side to convince the other that it is in error but, in view of the prevalence of opposing opinions on abortion, this possibility seems to be highly unlikely.

In addition to being a complex moral issue, abortion also presents a personal dilemma for the physicians who have to decide whether or not to perform the procedure, as well as the women who have to decide how to deal with problem pregnancies. For them abortion is much more than a complicated ethical matter; it becomes a pressing question which requires that they identify their own beliefs, values, and principles, along with the courage to follow their consciences.

It is said that the more people consider the issue of abortion from a detached, dispassionate, studied perspective, the more they are likely to move toward the center of the spectrum. In other words, people who hear the other side and listen to the points which are being made are likely to yield some of the absoluteness with which they initially approach abortion to allow for some exceptions or some restrictions. Perhaps the solution to the polarization which has come to characterize the pro-life and pro-choice camps in this country could be respectful listening to the other side, with a mutual goal of lessening the overall incidence of abortion. Given the depth of the difference of opinion, perhaps, for now, working toward a climate of civility would be the best strategy to implement.

ENDNOTES

[1] For an account of how the case of Sherri Finkbine generated momentum in favor of legalized abortion, cf., Kristin Luker, *Abortion and the Politics of Motherhood* (Berkeley: University of California Press, 1984), pp. 62–65 and 78–89.

[2] These brief remarks about salient aspects of American society echo the opinions of Robert N. Bellah, et al., *Habits of the Heart* (San Francisco:

Harper & Row, 1985). The reader is referred to Bellah's excellent volume for a thorough analysis of contemporary culture in the United States. For a comprehensive scholarly analysis of how to retrieve a sense of commitment to the common good, cf., James Donahue and M. Theresa Moser, RSCJ, editors, *Religion, Ethics & the Common Good* (Mystic, CT: Twenty-Third Publications, 1996).

[3] From 1975 until 1992, in 13 separate Gallup Polls, the percentage of people polled who thought that abortion should always be legal ranged from a low of 21% to a high of 33%; those polled who thought that abortion should be legal in certain circumstances ranged from a low of 49% to a high of 58%. Adding together those in favor of access to abortion regardless of the circumstances of the pregnancy and those who favor access to abortion in certain circumstances, an average of over 80% of the population does not favor making abortion illegal in all circumstances. Cf., *Information Plus* (Wylie, TX, 1994), p. 125. Comparable statistics, established over a 17-year period from surveys conducted by the National Opinion Research Center, were reported by Anne Cronin, "Abortion: The Rate Vs. the Debate," *The New York Times*, February 25, 1996, p. 4E. A *New York Times*/CBS News Poll conducted from January 10–12, 1998 showed that U.S. public support for abortion was declining, with large majorities favoring limits. In answer to the question, "Should a woman be permitted or forbidden to have an abortion during the first three months of pregnancy?" 61% answered "permitted," and 28% answered "forbidden." Second trimester abortions were approved by only 15%; third trimester abortions by only 7%. Nearly 80% of respondents supported both parental consent and waiting periods. Cf., Carey Goldberg and Janet Elder, "Public Still Backs Abortion But Wants Limits, Poll Says: A Notable Shift from General Acceptance," *The New York Times*, January 16, 1998, pp. 1, A16.

[4] The Alan Guttmacher Institute, 1994, *The Record*, January 22, 1995, p. L 1.

[5] Gina Kolata, "Pill For Abortion Clears Big Hurdle To Its Sale In U.S.," *The New York Times*, September 19, 1996, p. 1.

[6] Tamar Lewin, "A New Technique Makes Abortions Possible Earlier," *The New York Times*, December 21, 1997, pp. 1, 30.

DISCUSSION QUESTIONS

1. What is your ethical assessment of abortion? Why do you hold this position?
2. Reread the arguments against abortion and the arguments for abortion

rights. Which of these arguments seem most convincing to you? Why? Which seem least convincing? Why?

3. In reading this chapter and participating in a discussion of abortion, have you become more or less convinced of the position you originally held? If you have shifted in your thinking, describe this shift and discuss the reasons for it.

4. Do you think there are too many abortions? What steps could be taken to lessen the number?

5. Assess the positive and negative consequences of the sexual revolution. How can the media, government, and religious institutions create a better climate with regard to sexual behavior?

6. If *Roe v. Wade* were overturned, how would women deal with unwanted pregnancies? What strategies could be put in place to assist them?

7. One of the reasons a common ground has not been reached in regard to the practice of abortion in the United States is because of the hostility and disrespect pro-life and pro-choice factions often manifest toward each other. Suggest at least four measures which might lessen this hostility and disrespect.

CASE STUDY

Marla Sitler, a 14-year-old retarded girl, was raped by her 16-year-old cousin. Since Marla's mother caught him in the act, there is no question that the assault occurred.

Mrs. Virginia Sitler believed that pregnancy could not follow rape because, she thought, the trauma associated with rape was so unsettling that conditions necessary to establish a pregnancy would be missing. As a result, Mrs. Sitler did not seek medical care for her daughter in the aftermath of the rape. Instead, she invested her energies in comforting and reassuring Marla.

When several weeks elapsed during which Marla did not menstruate Mrs. Sitler became concerned and made an appointment for Marla with her pediatrician. After an examination and urinalysis the doctor said that Marla was approximately six weeks' pregnant. Although he was not asked for advice, the doctor said that, in his opinion, Marla should have an abortion right away; his principal reason was that Marla should not have to experience the discomforts of pregnancy, labor, and delivery. Mrs. Sitler thanked the doctor and said that she would need to discuss the situation with Marla's father, from whom she was divorced.

Marla's mother is strongly pro-life and, therefore, she is opposed to an abortion. Mr. Sitler is pro-life, too, but not in cases of rape and, therefore, he wants the pregnancy terminated. Marla is too retarded to grasp the situation or participate in the decision. Because the parents are unable to resolve the conflict, they decide to schedule an appointment with a clergyperson, a pastor they both respect. The pastor agrees to meet with them to offer advice and, perhaps, to serve as a mediator.

Evaluation:

1. Identify ethical issues contained in this case.
2. Propose possible solutions for these issues.
3. Make a decision relevant to action to be taken or not taken and provide rationale supportive of this decision.
4. Are you satisfied with your decision? Why or why not?

GLOSSARY

Thalidomide is a prescription drug which was used in Europe in the late 1950s and early 1960s as a sedative or hypnotic agent. If taken early in pregnancy thalidomide may cause the birth of infants with phocomelia and other defects.

Double standard refers to an expectation that at the time of their weddings women would be virgins while men would be sexually experienced. According to the so-called **"double standard,"** women who have sex before marriage are not desirable mates, while men who have been sexually active are not thought less of on that account. With the coming of the sexual revolution, we witnessed the end of the **double standard** as a social expectation, except in groups where strong cultural traditions are retained.

The **"morning after" pill** usually consists in large doses of diethylstilbesterol (DES) in order to cause menstruation. DES is synthetic estrogen in the form of white crystalline powder. If an ovum is fertilized prior to a woman's taking DES, it will be discharged with the menstrual flow. In similar fashion, an unfertilized ovum would also be discarded, thus preventing the possibility of its being fertilized by sperm remaining in her body from prior sexual intercourse.

A **nonviable fetus** is at such an early stage of development that it probably cannot live outside the uterus. A **viable fetus**, on the other hand, is sufficiently mature to be able to continue its growth outside the uterus. The earliest premature infant for whom growth outside the uterus is possible is one of 24 weeks' gestation. (See Chapter 3, "Compromised Newborns," for coverage of low birth weight newborns.)

The Hippocratic Oath is a more than 2500-year-old pledge to which Western physicians traditionally considered themselves bound. The text of the Oath can be found in Elizabeth J. Taylor, Ed., *Dorland's Illustrated Dictionary*, 27th Edition, (Phila.: W. B. Saunders Co. 1988), p. 768.

CHAPTER 3

Assisted Reproduction and Cloning

INTRODUCTION

Some questions of reproductive ethics have been with us for hundreds of years. Among these issues are what to do with "unwanted" newborns (girls, in some societies, as well as retarded infants), the use of artificial contraceptives, and abortion. However, when the subjects of this chapter, assisted reproduction and cloning, are raised, people think of recent technological developments such as so-called "test tube" babies and surrogate motherhood. As we shall see, the fields of assisted reproduction and cloning comprise a vast territory which gives rise to some of the most difficult and complex questions in the entire field of health care ethics. Evaluating these technological possibilities will require articulating the essence of one's ethical theory, as well as utilizing the full range of analytical distinctions which come into play in reaching ethical decisions. Moreover, one will inescapably become aware of a slippery slope down which it is very easy to slide if one does not clearly stipulate limits in regard to what is ethically acceptable.

PRELIMINARY CONSIDERATIONS

The first step to take in approaching issues of assisted reproduction is to clarify several interrelated preliminary matters. In so doing, one must unavoidably confront an underlying dilemma. The dilemma is whether these issues yield an objective normativeness, which just about everyone can endorse, or whether they can be approached from so many different perspectives that it is impossible to speak definitively to them. An example of a reproductive issue which Western society unequivocally condemns is the killing of new-born baby girls. The rationale supportive of the ban on killing infant girls emanates from the values and ethics inherent in Western culture and is read-ily accepted by just about everyone in Western societies. Another reproduc-tive issue, the availability and use of artificial contraception, however, is a subject of disagreement. Proponents of population control, individual auton-omy, responsible parenthood, and many others argue for the availability and use of artificial contraception. Leaders and members of some religions, espe-cially Roman Catholicism, as well as those who interpret natural law from the perspective of **biologism**, object to artificial birth control for several rea-sons, based on rational argumentation and/or religious grounds. The way one views the following topics will play a part in determining how one comes to evaluate the various issues of assisted reproduction. Let us con-sider each in turn.

TECHNOLOGY

Technology involves knowing how things work, as well as developing skills to accomplish results. In regard to human reproduction, during the nineteenth century scientists learned that the human embryo results from the fusion of female and male gametes, ovum and sperm. Prior to this breakthrough, it was thought that the human was contained completely within the sperm. The woman's role was to provide in the womb a hos-pitable environment within which the deposited sperm could grow. Fol-lowing realization of how ovum and sperm function in reproduction, as well as creation and alteration in the laboratory of different species of ani-mals, it became possible to think about and subsequently implement the range of technological options currently available within the field of assisted human reproduction.

One prerequisite for considering any specific procedure of assisted repro-duction is determining whether or not technology ought to be part of the pic-ture at all and, if so, to what extent. There are several different ways to resolve this issue. At one end of the spectrum we find extreme negativity toward technology along with the conviction that nature's way of making a baby should be the only way. At the other end of the spectrum is an unfet-tered enthusiasm for technology so that whatever is technologically possible should also be ethically acceptable. Between these two rather extreme posi-tions there are many other possible assessments of technology. A middle ground suggests that technology is morally advantageous when it con-tributes to the well-being of individuals, families, and the human commu-nity. To the extent that technological assistance in human reproduction serves these goals it may be acceptable.

What is your opinion about the role technology should play in human reproduction and why do you hold this opinion? Answering this question is a necessary first step in clarifying matters. And, even as we engage in this exercise, it is important to remember the underlying ethical issue in the big picture, that is, whether or not there are objective standards binding on everyone and, if so, what these standards are.

AUTONOMY VERSUS BEING BOUND BY PREEXISTING STANDARDS

By autonomy is meant that individuals take responsibility for governing themselves according to their own wits. The liberal philosophy which asserts the right of autonomous individuals to determine for themselves the choices they will make stands in contrast to an approach to morality which holds that individuals are bound by preexisting standards in the form of rules or conventions and that they need to conform to these. People who admit a requirement to conform to objective standards also exercise autonomy; however, the standards which they observe limit the choices they feel they are entitled to make.

It is obvious that where one stands on the autonomy question will have a significant bearing on the manner in which one makes choices about using reproductive technology. An unmarried woman can now become a parent without engaging in sexual intercourse. Should she, and should society allow, tolerate, or endorse such choices? Answering questions such as this one requires clarifying one's position on autonomy.

SEXUAL INTERCOURSE VERSUS ASSISTED REPRODUCTION

Sexual intercourse is the "traditional" way to achieve human reproduction. There is no dispute about this. However, there is a conflict as to whether or not sexual intercourse plays an *essential* role in the generation of human life. If intercourse is judged to play an essential role, then assisted means of reproduction are not acceptable, even when it is not possible to procreate without help from technology.

Some people hold that sexual intercourse between married spouses should be the *only* way to generate life. This reasoning contends that it is the nature of the act of intercourse to be personal and intimate; only in such a close personal manner should human offspring come into being. Most who argue in this way reinforce their argument by citing a divine plan behind the way procreation should occur, and they say that this is the way God intends it to be.[1]

Those who would allow for assisted reproduction do not assert a necessary connection between sexual intercourse and procreation. They argue that people use technology to assist with many kinds of biological processes. False teeth, hearing aids, kidney dialysis, tube feeding, and pacemakers are just a few examples. There is nothing so sacrosanct about human reproduction that it needs to be kept in its pristine state, apart from technology. The love, warmth, and kinship which await children, this argument goes, are of more ethical significance than the manner in which the child is conceived.

Numbered among those who would argue for technological reproduction are both those who would restrict parenthood to married spouses and those who would allow it regardless of the status, relationships, or sexual preferences of those who use methods of assisted reproduction.

POPULATION

The earth's population has increased from an estimated 1.3 billion in 1850 to an estimated 2.49 billion in 1950 and an estimated 4.3 billion in 1980.[2] According to the United Nations Fund for Population Activities, the world's population is now estimated as in excess of 5.3 billion and it will likely reach 6.25 billion by the year 2000.[3] Assisted reproduction will add to the overall population. One's views about the earth's ability to sustain ever larger numbers of humans as well as each individual's responsibility in terms of population will impact on her assessment of the ethics of assisted reproduction. As with each of the other preliminary considerations, more than one assessment is possible.

Some people think that married couples have a right to procreate and that how many children they decide to have is best left to them. Others think that there are too many people already and that people who have difficulty procreating should adopt children rather than add to the population. Still others think that including considerations of population when ethically evaluating assisted reproduction is unwarranted because the numbers of humans so generated is not large enough to make a significant impact on the overall picture. Interestingly, by the very fact of introducing the issue of population, the nature of the issue comes into play. Is technological reproduction a question for individual moral consideration to be decided by those who are directly involved, or is it a matter of concern for society, justifying issuing restrictions based on concern for the common good, i.e., the well-being of the entire society?

PARENTHOOD AND CHILDREN

What is the nature of parenthood? Who has the right to parent a child? What does it mean to be a child? Does a potential child have any rights, either in respect to the way in which she is conceived or in the relationship to a parent or parents with whom he will grow up? As with the other topics we have considered, a variety of opinions can be expressed in answer to these questions.

One opinion in respect to parenthood is held by the **magisterium** of the Roman Catholic Church, which contends that married persons have a right to the act of intercourse but do not have a right to become parents. Should pregnancy follow intercourse, this manner of thinking goes, the child would be a gift of God given to the parents for them to nurture to maturity. The child would be their flesh and blood, but not their possession. This way of thinking underscores the beautiful reality of the relationship between parents and children while attempting to reject the notion that a child is an object owned by a person or persons. There is certainly merit in pointing out this fact because, given consumerist and materialistic aspects of our culture, we might be tempted to begin to think of children as among those things which we want to possess.

Another way of approaching this issue is to think that children and parents are a part of society and that there are no hard and fast rules about how children ought to come into existence or who is meant to be a parent. Accordingly, rights language which asserts that married people have a right to posit an act but do not have a right to a child seems abstract and far-fetched. More practical issues tend to hold sway: Are those involved psychologically, socially, and morally mature enough to reproduce? Will the child be wanted, loved, cared for? Are there obvious harms which we need to guard against? If not, assisted reproduction in its various forms and possible combinations ought to be identified as a **gray area** and those people who want to avail themselves of it should be left in peace and freedom to make their own responsible choices.

In summary, one's ideas about technology, autonomy, the connection between sexual intercourse and reproduction, limiting the number of people being born, and what it means to be parent or child will influence the way one considers the ethics of assisted reproduction. It goes without saying that the ethical methodology (or lack of same) espoused will also have a profound effect on the way issues of assisted reproduction are resolved.

POSSIBLE PROCEDURES

Prior to the birth of Louise Joy Brown on July 25, 1978, which resulted from in vitro fertilization, technology available to aid in procreation was limited to artificial insemination, dating from the 1930s. On the other side of the coin, technology used to prevent conception had its beginnings in the Middle Ages with primitively designed condoms. Since availability of the anovulant, or birth control pill, in 1960, research efforts aimed at developing new types of contraceptives have been undertaken on an ongoing basis. The

most technologically advanced contraceptive breakthrough in recent years is
Norplant, a synthetic which is surgically emplaced under the skin and which
renders a woman infertile for as long as five years. Norplant was approved
by the Food and Drug Administration in 1990.

In regard to technologies available to assist people in becoming parents,
several options have been developed over the past two decades. Within the
conventional category are drug therapy and surgery. Fertility drugs like Clo-
mid and Pergonal are frequently prescribed for women who have difficulty
getting pregnant and, in some cases, these help. Surgery to correct or reduce
endometriosis in women or to repair a **varicocele** in men is routinely done
in order to increase chances for conception.

In the United States there are approximately 5 million infertile couples,
who fail to conceive after one year of trying. One-half of these couples are
helped by conventional treatments, and the other half have to rely on
recently developed high-tech procedures or leave matters to fate. Over the
past 30 years, the percentage of infertile couples has remained constant but
the aging of the baby-boom generation has caused the total number of infertile couples to swell to 2.3 million.[4] Thus, issues of assisted reproduction are
of concern to a large segment of the population.

Assisted reproduction technologies, which actually separate reproduction
from intercourse can be accomplished in several ways.

Artificial Insemination. Sperm, either the husband's or a donor's, are shuttled
with a catheter into the uterus, where fertilization may occur. In 1993 an estimated 600,000 intrauterine inseminations were performed.[5] (When sperm
from the husband is used, the procedure is called *AIH, Homologous Artificial
Insemination. AID* is the acronym for artificial insemination by donor.)

In Vitro Fertilization (IVF). Ova or eggs are surgically removed from a
woman's body and fertilized by sperm in a petri dish. Some of the resulting
embryos are transferred by catheter to the uterus; extra embryos are frozen.
There are approximately 32,000 IVF procedures annually, at an average cost
of $7,800 each.[6]

Gamete Intrafallopian Transfer (GIFT). Ova are collected with a needle and put
into a catheter with sperm. The mixture of ova and sperm is then injected
into the fallopian tube for fertilizing. There were 4,992 reported procedures
in 1993.[7] (Since GIFT does not entail fertilization outside a woman's body in
a laboratory, this procedure is acceptable to the Roman Catholic hierarchy
provided sperm are not obtained by means of masturbation.)

Zygote Intrafallopian Transfer (ZIFT). Eggs are fertilized by sperm in a laboratory dish and resulting embryos are transferred to a fallopian tube. Reported
procedures in 1995 totaled 1,792.[8]

Micromanipulation. A variety of techniques can be performed by an embry-
ologist in a laboratory to manipulate egg and/or sperm in order to improve
chances of pregnancy. There were approximately 1,400 procedures in 1993.[9]

Intracytoplasmic Sperm Injection (ICSI). A single sperm is inserted into a single ovum in order to overcome problems inherent in poor-quality sperm. A resultant embryo would be transferred to the uterus.

Cryopreserved Embryo Transfer (CPE). Frozen embryos are thawed and then transferred to the uterus. In 1993 there were an estimated 6,672 procedures of this type.[10]

Egg Donation. Eggs are removed from a donor's ovary and fertilized in vitro before being transferred to the uterus of a contracting party. The donor is paid a fee from $1,500 to $3,000 or more and must submit to hormone therapy aimed at **superovulation** as well as **laparoscopic surgery** to remove ova. Egg donations carried out in 1993 totaled 2,766.[11]

TECHNOLOGICAL REPRODUCTION RESULTS IN NOVEL PATHS TO PARENTHOOD

Technological reproduction can result in novel paths to parenthood. Accompanying the innovations of the laboratory are changing social mores in regard to who should bear children and what constitutes the "family" in which children should be raised. Ironically, these changes are occurring simultaneously with an epidemic of out-of-wedlock births as well as a staggering number of abortions.[12]

It goes without saying that both individuals and society have a lot of sorting out to do in regard to establishing criteria for acceptable uses of assisted reproduction. What are some of the possibilities opened up by technological reproduction? This is a difficult question because, just as soon as we think we've thought of everything, another combination is reported. With this caveat in mind, let us consider the more obvious possibilities.

The Simple Case. The so-called "simple case" entails the use of assisted reproduction by a married couple. The husband's sperm, the wife's ovum or ova, and her uterus are featured in this instance, with resulting offspring being their child or children.

Surrogate Mothers. A surrogate mother is a woman who allows an embryo to grow to term in her womb and then turns the newborn infant over to the party or parties who contracted for her services. A surrogate mother is usually paid a fee, but this is not always the case.

A surrogate may carry the embryo of a contracting couple, made from the sperm and egg of that couple. In such an instance, the surrogate provides a womb, but is not genetically related to the resultant offspring.

A surrogate may also carry an "adopted" embryo unrelated to either herself or a contracting couple or party(ies). As in the previous case, the resultant child or children would be unrelated to the surrogate.

A surrogate's own ovum (ova) might be used in a contractual arrangement. Accordingly, the surrogate could be artificially inseminated or the in vitro process could be employed. Where could the sperm come from? It could be from the husband of a heterosexual couple, married or not married; it could be a donor's sperm which was being utilized by a heterosexual couple; or it could be a donor or gay man's sperm, to be used to create a child for him or for a gay couple.

A surrogate is usually unrelated to the party or parties for whom she carries a child. This, however, is not always the case. A sister may be a surrogate, or a sister-in-law, or cousin. In addition, there is no necessity that the surrogate be from the same generation as the contracting would-be parent or parents. A daughter could carry a child for a mother, or a mother for a daughter. There have not been reports of grandmothers or granddaughters becoming involved in such arrangements, but it is conceivable and may happen.

A Lesbian woman or a heterosexual single woman can make use of assisted reproduction techniques to conceive a genetically related child by either artificial insemination using donor sperm or by laboratory fertilization, again with donor sperm. The woman may or may not know the donor. Furthermore, Lesbian and other single women could become pregnant using donor ova as well, these ova emanating from partners, friends or unidentified donors.

Cryopreservation of Gametes and Embryos. Cryopreservation, i.e., the freezing of sperm, makes it possible for women to conceive children by men even after these men have died. The freezing of embryos makes possible future pregnancies for women without repeat processes of hormone therapy and in vitro fertilization.

SPECIFIC ETHICAL ISSUES RAISED BY REPRODUCTIVE TECHNOLOGIES

As with other advances in medical science, such as artificial feeding, assisted reproduction technologies have come so far so fast that there are numerous complex moral questions about which there is little or no ethical consensus as to what should be done. Part of the reason for this state of affairs is the prevalence of ethical **pluralism** and **relativism** in society, resulting in reluctance to formulate and enforce hard-and-fast rules. Another reason is the extremely complex and sensitive nature of this subject. People want to have children; they long for them and dream of loving and nurturing them; they seem willing to go to almost any lengths to have children. The relationship between a parent and a child is profound and infused with meaning. In a sense this very relationship contributes enormously in ways known and unknown to both the child and the parent, as well as to the human community. It is apparent that it is the quality of this relationship, especially on the part of the parent(s), that is of greatest consequence for the well-being of children and society, more than the manner in which offspring are conceived. Nevertheless, society has already witnessed enough examples of reproductive technology run amuck to realize the need for ethical caution and/or reservation about some uses of assisted reproduction.

In this regard four widely publicized cases come to mind.

In 1986, Mary Beth Whitehead, a married woman, contracted with William and Elizabeth Stern to be inseminated with William Stern's sperm, carry an ensuing child to term, and give the baby to the couple. As it happened, however, Mrs. Whitehead bonded to Baby M and wanted to keep the infant and raise her. In a widely followed case, in 1987 Judge Harvey Sorkow of the Family Court in Hackensack, New Jersey awarded custody to the Sterns and the judge declared that Mrs. Stern was the adoptive mother. In 1988 the decision was overturned on appeal to the New Jersey Supreme Court, with Mary Beth Whitehead reinstated as the child's mother and ample arrangements established for her to visit her daughter. As society considered this highly emotional case it could not help but come to acknowledge the fact that surrogacy can be very problematic and that both legal and ethical guidelines need to be established in regard to the practice.[13]

In 1983, a New York couple, Alexander Malahoff and his wife Nadja contracted with a Michigan woman, Mrs. Judy Stiver, to bear Mr. Malahoff's child. The contract which Mrs. Stiver signed stipulated that she was not to have sexual intercourse with her husband for 30 days before the artificial insemination.

Mrs. Stiver became pregnant, apparently fulfilling her part of the contract. As the pregnancy evolved, however, Mr. and Mrs. Malahoff experienced marital problems and agreed to separate. In spite of his marital difficulties, Mr. Malahoff did not attempt to withdraw from his arrangement with Mrs. Stiver and he was on hand for the baby's birth. As it turned out, the baby was born with the same hereditary anomaly as some of Mr. and Mrs. Stiver's other children, prompting Mr. Malahoff to demand blood tests to determine paternity before agreeing to accept the child. The blood tests proved that Malahoff was not the father and so he was free to walk away from the child.[14]

In 1981, Elsa and Mario Rios attempted to become parents through in vitro fertilization. Mrs. Rios had an embryo transfer and had two other embryos frozen. The initial transfer resulted in a miscarriage and the couple intended to try again using the embryos which were stored in a freezer at a laboratory in Australia. In 1983, before having a second transfer, Elsa and Mario Rios died in a plane crash and the story of the orphan embryos became headline news in Australia. Some people thought the embryos should be thawed and allowed to disintegrate in the laboratory. Others thought that they should be put up for adoption by a woman or a couple who wanted to get pregnant with a nonrelated embryo. Mario Rios' son from a previous marriage opposed bringing a potential sibling into existence because he did not want to share the estate he was due to inherit. But his concern turned out to be unfounded when it was revealed that the sperm used in conception was donor sperm, not Mario Rios' sperm, so that it could not have happened that the son would have a sibling. Needless to say, in both the developing story and debate about the fate of the embryos the complexities of possible situations resulting from technological reproduction surfaced.[15]

In recent years a number of cases, such as the Stowe-Davis embryos case, involving divorced couples whose embryos were created and frozen before they divorced have come to light. The pattern these cases typically take is that the woman wants to use the embryos to become pregnant and the former husband attempts to prevent this because he does not want to be related to a child of which his ex-wife is mother, or because he does not want paternal or financial responsibility, or for a combination of reasons.[16] The difficulty of resolving such scenarios is obvious.

In order to prevent injury to innocent parties and exploitation of naive individuals, society has been grappling with the need to put safeguards in place. There are also concerns about protecting the institution of the family and the well-being of human embryos which only in the relatively recent past have existed outside the human body. Complicating matters is disagreement about how to resolve each and every derivative issue, arising from different ethical methodologies and a wide range of differing presuppositions. While it is not possible at this time to resolve all that is disputed, it is possible to identify the derivative issues and discuss possible responses to them.

EXTRACORPOREAL CONCEPTION

If reproduction apart from sexual intercourse or outside the maternal milieu is evaluated as morally wrong and, therefore, an inappropriate mode of human reproduction, then almost all the issues raised in conjunction with assisted reproduction would disappear because of the manner in which the threshhold question is resolved. As we have seen, this is the way it works out for people who follow the teaching of the Roman Catholic Church[17] which finds **extracorporeal conception** morally unacceptable. Although there are no statistical data, it is probably reasonable to think that most people do not adhere to this teaching and, hence, think that reproductive technologies are morally appropriate, at least in some cases.

TOLERANCE OF ASSISTED REPRODUCTION ONLY IN THE "SIMPLE CASE"

Some people argue that it is ethically acceptable for married spouses to "trick" nature if nature does not allow them to become parents. After all, it would be their gametes, her womb, their baby, born within a loving, personal union. It would be possible to move forward from the conception and birth of the child to a predictably "normal life" without danger of troubling complications. Those who argue in this way understand reproductive technologies as potentially beneficial; those who reject this usage see technology employed to result in conception as essentially deficient.

THIRD PARTY INVOLVEMENT IN CONCEPTION

AID. Third party involvement in conception dates from the first usage of artificial insemination by donor. AID was originally implemented in cases in which the husband was infertile and AID was the only **asexual** way for the couple to have children. In some cases the child who resulted from AID was treated by the woman and her husband as "their" child. In other cases, the child was told that his genetic father was an anonymous donor.

Some people object to AID as a technological act replacing a physically intimate act as the locus for procreation. Additional reservations about AID focus on the dynamics of the relationship between spouses that could suffer as a result of the procedure. There has been speculation that the woman's love and commitment to her husband could be undermined if she fantasized about her novel relationship with an anonymous donor. In respect to the woman's husband, he might become jealous of the donor or feel inadequate because he could not accomplish what a stranger did. With respect to the child, he would be in different relationships to his parents; he would truly be his mother's son but he would only be in a pretend relationship with his "father." Distance, aloofness, and alienation would thus be possible outcomes for the "father" and the "son," as well as the husband and wife. Similar reservations are voiced in respect to use of donor sperm or ova in the laboratory because, in these cases, a third party would be involved and comparable issues could surface.

Surrogacy. Some people argue that there should be no surrogacy arrangements on the grounds that the potential problems which could occur make these arrangements unwise. Others say that with proper counseling and screening surrogates and contracting prospective parents can work out mutually acceptable terms. There are several other issues relevant to surrogacy. Is the ideal surrogate a relative or a stranger? How much compensation should a woman get for her work as a surrogate? If she is not going to be a surrogate, but rather, an egg donor, what would constitute reasonable compensation for submitting to hormone therapy and surgery so that technicians can obtain her ova? Will monetary incentives lead to exploitation of women who lack money and education and who turn to surrogacy in order to make money?

These are significant questions and they expose the fact that surrogacy involves a very different and profound kind of involvement, that of a woman with a baby which is destined to be handed to someone else, an involvement with which we have little experience, historically. However, the biggest issues concerning surrogacy require deciding what to do when the surrogate mother wants to keep the baby or, highly unlikely, but still possible, what to do when the contracting parties change their minds and do not want to accept the child.

FROZEN EMBRYOS OR GAMETES

At the present time it is technologically possible to freeze sperm and embryos; the freezing of ova has recently begun. By having sperm and embryos in freezers the processes of technological reproduction become simpler. Accompanying the simplicity, however, are ethical issues of theoretical as well as practical consequence.

In respect to sperm, donors are paid modest amounts for their sperm material. Several offspring can result from a single donor and the possibility exists that siblings with different mothers but the same genetic father could marry. Careful monitoring of inseminations should decrease chances of this remote possibility.

Another question about frozen sperm is whether it should be available to a man's widow to create his children after he has died. There have been a few cases of this kind in recent years with ethical opinion pretty much split.[18] Those in favor argue that a child is the last and most beautiful gift a husband could give his wife. Others reason that a child should have a father and a mother, and that to create a child knowing that she will never have a relationship with her father is unwise and irresponsible.

In respect to frozen embryos, there are several questions. If people do not want their spare embryos, should they be destroyed, given away, or simply left on the shelf? If one party wants to retrieve an embryo but the other refuses, what should happen? Should future generations have access to embryos which are frozen today? If so, a woman could give birth to her sister—and could establish a mother-daughter relationship with her. Should she?

In the summer of 1996 an ethical furor erupted in England over the announcement that more than 3,000 frozen embryos stored in 33 clinics would be destroyed. The reason for the proposed destruction was that a law passed in 1991 stipulated that embryos not be kept in storage more than five years if their donors failed to respond to inquiries about what they wanted done with them. Since 3,000 four-cell embryos fell into the category of unclaimed or unwanted, authorities decided to thaw them, administer a few drops of alcohol to destroy them, and, finally, incinerate the remains. This procedure was carried out in spite of protests from individuals and groups which argued that it would be more humane to allow infertile couples to adopt the embryos.[19]

If it becomes known that sperm or an embryo could carry a disease or significant genetic defect, what should be done with the sperm or embryo? In asking this question a significant insight becomes apparent: The sperm is less than an embryo because, by itself, it cannot become a person. The embryo, however, has the potential to develop into a human person. Each and every person who is alive or ever lived began as an embryo. Since the embryo is the most vulnerable form of human life, what safeguards should be established to protect it from harm?

REGULATION OF LABORATORIES

At the satisfactory conclusion of an episode of assisted reproduction a person takes a healthy baby home. However, it is apparent that many pitfalls can impede this storybook outcome. One of these pitfalls can be sloppy management of a laboratory so that women receive the wrong sperm or embryo. When this occurs consequences can be devastating, as in the case of a Caucasian woman in Holland who received the sperm of a man of African heritage in addition to her Caucasian husband and who gave birth to two sons, one Caucasian and one black.[20] When things go wrong in life people try to make the best of it. But, in respect to giving birth to the wrong baby because of a technician's error, it would seem that facile platitudes will not be much help to those who have to adjust to the error.

There is no disagreement that it is ethically imperative that reproductive laboratories be supervised and regulated so that sperm and embryos are properly stored and so that safeguards are in place to prevent tragic mistakes.

SAFEGUARDING VULNERABLE PATIENTS

People can exhaust their savings as well as their emotional equilibrium in trying to make a baby. At the same time, providers of assisted reproduction can earn handsome incomes. The traditional rule of the marketplace is "Let the buyer beware." In respect to assisted reproduction a question naturally arises as to whether this maxim is sufficient advice to give to prospective parents or whether measures should be enacted to prevent their being exploited. This is not a simple issue; it is one that reveals the obvious need for truth-telling on the part of providers and unvarnished realism on the part of would-be parents.

DECISION MAKING BY INTERESTED PARTIES

Several parties are directly impacted by assisted reproduction. Medical professionals who are involved in this field or who consider the possibility of entering it need to clarify what they find acceptable and unacceptable and need to understand the rationale undergirding their positions. Matters such as virtue and integrity come into play here, so that a person needs to justify what she is doing so as to be able to consider herself an upright person.

Individuals and couples need to think through the actions by which they might make a baby. Are these actions/arrangements acceptable or tolerable to them; do they consider them morally appropriate or inappropriate; or do they feel a repugnance which they cannot overcome? It is essential to soul-search in advance and to be prepared to live with the outcome.

The child-to-be is an important party to consider. Will he be accepted by parents, extended family and the broader society? Will he be able to accept himself? If there are realistic possibilities of foreseeable harm, it would be ethically preferable to refrain from creating the child who would be the recipient of this harm.

Society needs to get interested and actively involved in questions of assisted reproduction. How medical resources are used, whether individuals are exploited, and how the well-being of children is affected are ethical issues of concern to society. Raising the level of awareness, discussing pros and cons, and formulating guidelines are societal responsibilities which need to be shouldered.

"HIGHER ORDER" PREGNANCIES

"Higher order" pregnancies entail conceiving three, four, five, or more fetuses. According to U.S. government statistics, 6,000 babies were born in sets of three, four, or more in 1996, a one-year leap of 19 percent. The number of twins has also increased, but not as dramatically as for triplets and beyond.[21]

The instances of "higher order" pregnancies occurring in the ordinary course of things is very rare. The large number of such pregnancies in recent years is attributed to increased use of fertility drugs as well as employment of in vitro fertilization. While approximately half of all natural conceptions are unplanned and may be unwanted, conceptions following technological assistance are eagerly desired by would-be parents who are heavily invested, both emotionally and financially, in the quest for biological offspring. It seldom happens that the end of the wait for a baby of their own turns out to be triplets, quadruplets, or more, but when this does happen, people find themselves grappling with a complex and distressing situation.

There is no question that it is the parents' prerogative to make decisions. Since our legal and medical systems consider conception a personal, private matter, resolving issues connected to "higher order" pregnancies is up to the parents. Bobbi and Kenny McCaughey, parents of septuplets born in Carlisle, Iowa, on November 19, 1997, decided to see the pregnancy through to its conclusion. They learned early on through ultrasound imaging that

Mrs. McCaughey was carrying seven fetuses and, based on their religious beliefs, they rejected pregnancy reduction. "Just how can you decide that you're going to have this one and you're not going to have that one? How do you choose which one? You know, they're all babies and I'm gonna have them all."[22]

The McCaugheys are admirable for their faith and courage and the fact that all seven of their children seem to be faring well is reason for gratitude. The McCaughey situation notwithstanding, however, the reality faced by couples in "higher order" pregnancies is far from sanguine. This reality consists in the possibility or probability of miscarriage so that none of the fetuses survive or premature birth with its attendant risks. These risks include lung problems that can lead to chronic lung disease; retinal damage that can lead to blindness; strokes that can bring on mental retardation and cerebral palsy; bowel infections that can require surgery and lead to damaged intestines; and long-term learning disorders.[23] Little ones may also be so frail and sick as to be incapable of surviving for more than a short time.

Faced with multiple fetuses the decisions parents make are to continue the pregnancy as is or to reduce the number of fetuses, generally to one or two. The reasoning behind pregnancy reduction can be either the best interests of prospective children, or of parents, or of both. Thus, parents may decide that it would be better to have one or two probably healthy babies than to have several who are at risk or none because of miscarriage. Or, they could shift the focus from their offspring to themselves and rationalize that they would not be able to deal with the stresses of more than one or two children. Parents could also decide that it would be better for all concerned, their offspring and themselves, to reduce a pregnancy and improve the chances of their child or children being full-term and healthy.

Regardless of what decision parents make, those who experience "higher order" pregnancies must work through an emotional and ethical minefield. Their emotional struggles involve coming to grips with a situation that they probably never thought they would have to face, circumstances replete with sadness and confusion. Ethically they cannot escape confronting the principle that human life is sacred. The McCaugheys' belief in the sacredness of human life meant they could not act to terminate any of their fetuses. Other couples adopt a different approach, terminating one, two, three, or more for the sake of the one or two whom they believe will fare well because of the intervention.

There is an emerging consensus that the medical community should do what it can to lessen the incidence of "higher order" pregnancies. One tactic would be to limit the number of embryos transferred at in vitro fertilization to three at most. Another would be to monitor women taking fertility medication and to switch from corporeal to extra-corporeal conception if it is determined that treatment has resulted in a large number of ova which are ready to erupt. In this way, even if all the ova are fertilized in the laboratory and develop into a large number of embryos, only a few embryos will be transferred and the rest can be stored.

The situation the McCaugheys encountered of seven fetuses was not something they or their doctor anticipated. Mrs. McCaughey's first pregnancy was a result of fertility treatment and it entailed birth of a single child. This is what usually happens but, in view of what may transpire, increased monitoring might be in order. In any event, prospective parents should be thoroughly informed of the possibility that fertility treatments can result in "higher order" pregnancies and should be encouraged to consider the ramifications of such an outcome *before* they embark on a course of treatment. Health care practitioners should clarify their own beliefs and principles so as not to put themselves in situations in which they might be at risk of compromising their own ethical standards.

CLONING

Approximately 30 years ago the question of cloning humans was included in books of health care ethics. Following a growing consensus that such a thing was impossible, the subject of human cloning was dropped and it remained out of ethical literature until February, 1997, when news of Dolly, a cloned sheep, made headlines throughout the world. Since the arrival of Dolly there has been considerable discussion about the possibility of cloning humans. To date, no human has been cloned and opinion is divided as to whether or not such a thing could be accomplished. However, there is no question of the need for careful consideration of this matter.

Dolly was born on July 5, 1996, and announcement of her birth was made the following February. Dolly was created by Dr. Ian Wilmut at his laboratory, the Roslin Institute in Edinburgh, Scotland. Dolly was identified as the clone of a 6-year-old ewe; she was made from a differentiated adult mammalian sheep cell. Cloning from a differentiated adult cell was considered an astounding feat because, before Dolly, scientists thought that only fetal cells could be cloned. Wilmut said that Dolly came to be through the capacitation of an adult mammalian cell. By "capacitation" is meant that cellular activity was slowed down, the cell was rested and forced into a sort of hibernating state by being starved of nutrients. The capacitated cell was later inserted into an egg cell whose DNA had been removed; an electrical charge tricked the egg into thinking it had been fertilized, prompting it to divide.[24] Thus was Dolly conceived, making yet another unthinkable event a reality of the modern world.

Stunned amazement at Ian Wilmut's accomplishment did not last long. Skepticism from the scientific community began to surface for three reasons. Dolly was Wilmut's sole success in 277 tries, leading to the opinion that the sheep was "an anecdote, not a result." Neither Wilmut nor anyone else was able to replicate the result he claimed to have achieved in Dolly, thus lessening credibility about the effectiveness of the process he described for cloning Dolly. Finally, the adult sheep from which Dolly was said to have been cloned died before Dolly was born, making impossible a comparison which would have proved that Dolly replicated her ancestor.[25]

Skepticism about Dolly's authenticity has set discussion of human cloning back, but the possibility resurfaced in conjunction with a report on cloning mice. Dr. Ryuzo Yanagimachi, a biologist at the University of Hawaii, reported in July, 1998, of cloning 22 mice, seven of which are clones of clones. Dr. Yanagimachi and his colleagues inserted an adult cumulus cell into a mouse egg that had been emptied of its DNA and made the egg develop as though it had been fertilized. They did this by waiting six hours to give the egg a change to reprogram the cumulus cell's DNA and then they chemically prodded the egg to start dividing.[26] Although not yet subjected to the scrutiny of the scientific community, this reported accomplishment has prompted the public to entertain the possibility of human cloning.

It goes without saying that if human cloning is not technically possible, there is no reason to consider whether or not it is ethical. However, since many scientists claim that cloning animals can be achieved and that it is only a matter of time until we can clone humans, it is important to consider the ethical implications of this possibility.[27] Regardless of what science can achieve, there is no question that it is appropriate to ponder the ethical question: Should human cloning be attempted?

Given U.S. culture, there are three ways to answer this question.

First. If people want to clone themselves or their children, and science can help, it is a private matter and up to those who are directly involved.

Second. If people want to make a clone for a weighty reason, such as to get a bone marrow match for a sick child or to replace a dying child, then law should not stand in their way and skilled scientists should be allowed to assist them.

Third. A child ought to be a subject respected in herself, not an object created to satisfy someone's needs. It would clearly be immoral to clone a human being, depriving her of two parents and the traditional relationships of the family.

Even though U.S. society is permissive and pragmatic, most commentators think it best that cloning humans not be attempted. Thus, they reject the argument that all decisions about human reproduction are private and ought to be tolerated. In addition, there is little support for endorsing cloning when its aim is to make a child who would bear replacement parts, or be a replacement, for another child. The ethical principle that a human person is to be an end, not a means to an end, seems too deeply rooted to allow its abandonment in this instance.

Objections to cloning humans go beyond reluctance to accept the unorthodox. The first rule of medicine is to do no harm and opponents of cloning see the possibility of real harm to those who might be created through the technique. Because of the radical manipulation as well as the unknowns attendant to human cloning, abnormalities might be introduced which would be endured by the cloned creature for its lifetime. Beyond this, there is a deeply felt reluctance to tamper with human relatedness. Each and every person who has ever existed has been equally related to two biological/genetic parents, one male and one female. In creating a clone, one would distance the creature from his parents by, in most cases, a generation, placing the clone at a psychological disadvantage. (The exceptions would be a clone made from an embryo which would become an identical twin at a later date, or an identical twin made from a child who, again, would be born at a later date.)

If the current taboo against cloning were lifted, we might stand at the brink of a new eugenic era in which only the best humans currently existing would be reproduced. The government, or some other authority, would need to regulate the replication, giving rise to the creation of a Big Brother, bigger than any which has yet been imagined.

On June 8, 1997, a commission appointed by President Bill Clinton recommended a legislative ban on human cloning which would extend to both publicly and privately financed research groups.[28] This ban would be in effect for three to five years, providing much needed time for a thorough debate on all aspects of this contentious issue. It remains to be seen whether compromise can be reached between those who argue for totally unfettered reproductive freedom and those who maintain that human life within the context of the family is sacred. But it seems safe to say that given the radical and unsettling nature of human cloning there will be no rush to embrace this technological possibility.

CONCLUSION

The areas of technological reproduction and cloning may well be the most complex in all of health care ethics. The easiest way of dealing with these subjects is to decide that extracorporeal conception and early gestation are immoral, as is cloning, thus forbidding almost all novel forms of reproduction. However, most people cannot honestly subscribe to this way of thinking and, hence, are forced to open Pandora's box. It would take a very thick volume to consider in thorough detail all the possibilities that have been raised in this chapter. However, there is enough of a beginning herein to enable the reader to start thinking through the possibilities, especially in conjunction with the introductory chapter and the chapter on abortion. Such a consideration will yield a much fuller picture of the ethics of reproduction, though not a complete one. Today's test tube babies will likely be grandparents before that happens.

ENDNOTES

[1] This is the position of the Roman Catholic Church as expressed in a pastoral statement issued by Joseph Cardinal Ratzinger, "Instruction on Respect for Human Life in Its Origin and on the Dignity of Procreation," March 10, 1987.

[2] Charles F. Bennett, *Conservation and Management of Natural Resources in the United States* (New York: John Wiley & Sons, 1983), p. 31.

[3] Paul Lewis, "World Population Will Top 6 Billion," *The New York Times*, May 15, 1990, p. A9.

[4] Shannon Brownlee, "The Baby Chase," *U.S. News & World Report*, December 5, 1994, p. 84.

[5] "An Infertility Glossary," *The New York Times*, January 7, 1996, p. 18.

[6] Ibid.

[7] Ibid.

[8] Ibid.

[9] Ibid.

[10] Ibid.

[11] Ibid.

[12] The number of abortions has been fairly constant for several years at 1.5 million per year. As for births to unmarried women, the ratio has risen every year since 1952 and is currently 31 percent, almost one-third of all births. Cf., Margaret L. Usdansky, "Single Motherhood: Stereotypes vs. Statistics," *The New York Times*, February 11, 1994, p. 4.

[13] Cf., Mary Beth Whitehead, *A Mother's Story* (New York: St. Martin's Press, 1989); and Thomas A. Shannon, *Surrogate Motherhood* (New York: Crossroad, 1988).

[14] Iver Peterson, "Legal Snarl Developing Around Case of a Baby Born to Surrogate Mother," *The New York Times*, February 7, 1983, p. 10.

[15] "Embryo's Future in Question," *The New York Times*, June 18, 1984, p. B10 and "Australians Reject Bid to Destroy 2 Embryos," *The New York Times*, October 24, 1984, p. A18.

[16] Cf., for example, the case of the seven Stowe-Davis' embryos in Tennessee,

"Man Is Given Embryos After a Custody Case," *The New York Times*, June 14, 1993, p. A11.

[17] For a comprehensive scholarly critique of the Roman Catholic position, Cf., Eileen P. Flynn, *Human Fertilization in Vitro: A Catholic Moral Perspective* (Lanham, Md: University Press of America, 1984).

[18] Cf., Eileen P. Flynn, "Fashioning the Wanted Child: The Ethics of Reproductive Technology," *Commonweal*, March 14, 1986, for an analysis of the case of Corinne Parpalaix; and "Newlywed Hopes to Use Sperm of Dead Spouse to Start a Family," *The New York Times*, June 5, 1994 for an account of the case of Pam Maresca.

[19] Youssef M. Ibrahim, "Ethical Furor Erupts in Britain: Should Unclaimed Embryos Die?" *The New York Times*, August 1, 1996, pp. 1, 4.

[20] Marlene Simons, "Uproar Over Twins, and a Dutch Couple's Anguish," *The New York Times*, June 28, 1995, p. A3.

[21] Laura Meckler, "Multiple births soared in 1996," *The Record*, July 1, 1998, p. A18.

[22] Pam Belluck, " 'Just Incredible,' Says Mother, Holding 1st of Her 7 Babies," *The New York Times*, November 22, 1997, p. A7.

[23] Many Specialists Are Left In No Mood for Celebration: Doctors Say Iowa Woman Put Babies at Risk," *The New York Times*, November 21, 1997, p. A32.

[24] Michael Specter and Gina Kolata, "After Decades of Missteps, How Cloning Succeeded," *The New York Times*, March 3, 1997, pp. 1, B6-B8.

[25] Gina Kolata, "Some Scientists Ask: How Do We Know Dolly Is a Clone?" *The New York Times*, July 29, 1997, p. C3 and Nicholas Wade, "With No Other 'Dollys,' Cloning Report Draws Critics," *The New York Times*, January 30, 1998, p. A8.

[26] Gina Kolata, "In Big Advance in Cloning, Biologists Create 50 Mice," *The New York Times*, July 23, 1998, pp. 1, 20.

[27] Ibid.

[28] Gina Kolata, "Ethics Panel Recommends A Ban on Human Cloning," *The New York Times*, June 8, 1997, p. 22.

DISCUSSION QUESTIONS

1. Consider the range of possible evaluations of the use of technology in human reproduction and choose the position which seems most ethically appropriate to you. What is it about the position you have chosen which makes you think it is ethically acceptable?

2. In respect to assisted reproduction, how do you understand a woman's right to exercise autonomy? Should her right be unfettered, or are there limits on this right? What presuppositions lead you to conclude as you do?

3. Do you think that children should be conceived only within the context of the act of intercourse? Why or why not?

4. Is technological reproduction a question for individual moral consideration to be decided by those who are directly involved, or is it a matter of concern for society which might be justified in issuing restrictions based on concern for the common good? What factors lead you to this conclusion?

5. What is the nature of parenthood and what rights does a child have? In view of the obligations of parents and the rights of children, what restrictions, if any, should be placed on technological reproduction?

6. Consider the various ways in which women can function as surrogate mothers. Are some ways more or less acceptable than others? What leads you to this conclusion?

7. Cryopreservation, or freezing, opens up the possibility of children being born generations after they were conceived. Should this possibility give us reason to pause? Why or why not?

8. Make a list of safeguards society should put in place to prevent tragic surrogate arrangements from taking place.

9. Present an ethical evaluation of artificial insemination by donor along with the rationale which causes you to accept or reject this procedure.

10. Since the embryo is the most vulnerable form of human life, what safeguards should be established to protect it from harm?

11. "Higher order" pregnancies result mainly from taking fertility drugs or following in vitro fertilization with multiple embryo transfer. Outline the issues people face who achieve "higher order" pregnancies and suggest how, in your opinion, they should resolve these issues. What ethical insights lead you to formulate these suggestions?

CASE STUDY

Sarah Johnson, a 32-year-old woman, is unmarried and is not dating. She is busy with her career but she believes that in the next few years she will meet her future husband, marry and have children. She has always assumed that someday she would be a mother; it is very important to her that she have children.

Because Ms. Johnson experiences menstrual irregularities she schedules an appointment with a gynecologist. After a thorough examination, diagnostic tests and visits to additional physicians for more opinions, Ms. Johnson reluctantly accepts the fact that she is midway through menopause. It may be impossible for her to conceive, but, if there is any chance, she must attempt to become pregnant right away. Her anomaly is attributed to the medications Ms. Johnson's mother took when she was pregnant with Ms. Johnson.

Ms. Johnson is shocked by her diagnosis. She is very distressed as she grapples with her options. The options are:

to let go of her hope of biological motherhood, remaining childless or adopting,

to get into a relationship with a significant other as soon as possible in the hope of conceiving quickly, before her biological clock stops ticking,

to try to conceive asexually through artificial insemination. If artificial insemination were ineffective, it would probably be because her ova were no longer viable; should such be the case, her use of donor sperm and ova could posssibly result in a pregnancy,

to determine how she would go about selecting from among donors of sperm and/or ova in order to select persons whose genetic material would be acceptable to her.

Sarah Johnson checks into a country inn for a long weekend to mull over her situation and decide what to do.

Evaluation:

1. Identify the ethical issues contained in this case.
2. Propose possible solutions for these issues.
3. Make a decision relevant to action to be taken or not taken and provide rationale supportive of this decision.
4. Are you satisfied with your decision? Why or why not?

GLOSSARY

Biologism is a way of interpreting the so-called natural law according to which the biological structure of the act of intercourse is assigned a special kind of "oughtness." Thus, people influenced by biologism argue that there is a moral law in the way the act of intercourse is structured and this law (of nature) requires human obedience so that humans *ought not* to procreate apart from the act of intercourse.

The magisterium refers to the teaching authority of the Roman Catholic Church. This teaching authority is exercised in a hierarchical manner so that the pope speaks definitively on matters of doctrine and morality. Collectively, bishops also exercise teaching authority provided that what they say does not disagree with pronouncements made by the pope.

A gray area is an area of ethical inquiry which is colored by grayness rather than "black or white"; what is clearly right or wrong is not apparent. Realizing that an issue puts one in a gray area is helpful because it makes one tentative and patient as she goes about analysis of an issue.

Endometriosis is a medical condition which adversely affects a woman's ability to become pregnant. With this condition tissue resembling the uterine mucous membrane (the endometrium) occurs aberrantly in various locations in the pelvic cavity.

Varicocele is a varicose condition of the veins of the pampiniform plexus (vein shaped like a tendril), forming a swelling that feels like a "bag of worms," appearing bluish through the skin of the scrotum, and accompanied by a constant pulling, dragging, or dull pain in the scrotum.

Superovulation is achieved by taking prescribed hormones which cause the ovaries to produce far more viable ova than normal. In a normal menstrual cycle one ovum is produced; after hormone treatment as many as eight to ten or more ova can be produced.

Laparoscopic surgery is performed by a physician, typically in a hospital. A laparoscope is used to allow a doctor to look directly at such organs as the uterus, fallopian tubes, and ovaries.

Pluralism refers to a tendency to equate the various methods of arriving at ethical judgments so that one is considered as good as another. It is true that there are many different methods for ethical reasoning; opponents of pluralism argue, however, that one method is not as good as another. Instead, they contend that an ethical methodology is as convincing as the rationale which supports it.

Relativism is a tendency to emphasize the specific perspective, conditions, and circumstances of an individual decision maker. Thus, how an individual approaches an issue will have a significant impact on its resolution. For example, in respect to assisted reproduction, a married woman who always wanted to be a biological mother, and who assumed that she would have children, would probably seek out technological assistance if needed. According to relativistic thinking there would be no need for her to defend her decision. From her point of view, or *relatively* speaking, this would be the expected decision.

Extracorporeal conception refers to the fact that an embryo is conceived outside the woman's body in the laboratory. Extracorporeal conception is necessarily accompanied by early gestation in the laboratory rather than in the uterus.

Asexual reproduction refers to generating life apart from the act of sexual intercourse. Asexual reproduction can be achieved in a laboratory using in vitro fertilization techniques or through artificial insemination.

die, a sense of ethical distress was experienced accompanied by a need to clarify the infants' rights along with correlative obligations of parents, physicians, hospital administrators, society, and government. This was far from a simple matter because of the tremendous variability of conditions which can afflict newborns as well as unknowns which have to be factored into each particular case. Nevertheless, starting from distress about some fairly typical cases, a nuanced consensus has emerged in regard to morally appropriate and inappropriate treatment of compromised newborns.

In 1971 at Johns Hopkins University Hospital in Baltimore an infant with Down Syndrome was born with duodenal atresia, a blockage between the higher duodenum and the lower stomach which prevents eating and drinking by mouth that can be corrected by a fairly routine surgical procedure that carries an excellent statistical probability of success. People with Down Syndrome have an extra chromosome, 47 in each cell, rather than 46. They experience varying degrees of mental retardation, have distinctive facial characteristics and a tendency to cardiac or intestinal problems. When the parents were advised that theirs was a Down Syndrome baby who needed surgery they refused to authorize the lifesaving surgery. Pediatric surgeons honored the parents' decision; the courts were not consulted and surgery was not performed. After 15 days without food or water, the baby died.

On April 9, 1982, Infant Doe was born in Bloomington, Indiana. Like the Johns Hopkins baby, this infant also had Down Syndrome and could not eat, in this case because of a tracheoesophageal fistula (an abnormal constriction between the trachea and esophagus which, in this case, made eating or drinking by mouth impossible). Since his parents refused to consent to surgery, the baby died on April 15, 1982. Although the tracheoesophageal fistula is a more serious problem than duodenal atresia, the chances of successful surgery are estimated to be 90 percent, making the cases fairly similar.

In the Bloomington, Indiana, case physicians sought court involvement but the infant died after state courts agreed with the parents and before the United States Supreme Court had an opportunity to intervene.

Between the cases of the Baby Doe from Johns Hopkins and the Baby Doe from Bloomington, Indiana, a provocative article was published by two pediatricians from Yale New Haven Medical Center, R. Duff and A. Campbell, about 43 impaired infants in whose care they had been involved.[1] Duff and Campbell said that all of these 43 infants had died early on because they had honored decisions made by their parents to forgo treatment.

As a result of publicity attendant to the Baby Doe cases and the Duff-Campbell article, consciousness about a distressing situation which happens regularly enough—the birth of a compromised newborn whose continued existence depends upon medical intervention, but who is allowed to die—was raised. Along with the raised consciousness went an awareness that these types of cases contain complex ethical issues and that determining in what morally appropriate responses consist would be far from simple. The process of reaching an ethical consensus was not neat but, nevertheless, it did occur in bits and pieces during the decade of the 1980s.

Perhaps the impetus for moving toward examination of the general subject came from a sense of unease about the way the babies were treated. A documentary film entitled *Who Should Survive?*[2] was based on a discussion of the story of the Johns Hopkins' baby. Watching the film was emotionally trying because viewers were forced to confront the fact that the baby cried in the corner of a nursery for several days before it lapsed into unconsciousness and died 15 days after birth. Thinking about how the nurses suffered was draining; they had to follow the orders "nothing by mouth" and limit what they could offer the child to holding and rocking him. Thinking about what the infant was going through was much worse. Like so many other students of health care ethics I watched the film and experienced moral revulsion. My principal questions were why the physicians were compliant and why the parents considered themselves entitled to decide that their child's best interests would be served by allowing him to die. As it turned out, much of the reservation about allowing compromised infants to die by denying them relatively simple life-saving interventions focused on these very questions.

As physicians, hospital administrators, government officials, journalists, ethicists, and citizens reflected on Baby Doe cases and discussed the many ramifications of these cases, an emerging consensus began to evolve related to putting corrective measures into place. Thus, guidelines for responding to compromised newborns were eventually developed.

At a fundamental level an understanding emerged that there are serious deficiencies in the type of thinking that would conclude, "This baby is not what I had in mind, so let it die." It is true that all expectant parents want Gerber babies, beautiful, bright, healthy infants who are normal in every way and who will enjoy fulfillment, success, and happiness. It is also true that not every baby is a Gerber baby. What should society expect of the parents to whom physically and/or mentally challenged children are born? What are the physician's responsibilities in these cases? In resolving these cases subjectivist thinking was pitted directly against principled thinking, and it was principled thinking which relies on objective standards which won out. As a result, parents who tended to argue, "I just don't feel that this baby ought to live," and physicians who concurred, offering the rationalization that "every situation is different and parents should make decisions according to their preferences" were overruled in the arena of public opinion.

The guidelines which developed related to babies like Baby Doe from Johns Hopkins and Baby Doe from Bloomington, Indiana. These guidelines contain practical directions for making concrete decisions and they assume that certain principles ought to be upheld. These guidelines offer an example of casuistry (see Chapter 1); their general thrust is contained in statements such as the following:

An infant is a human being and is a member of the human community. As
such, the infant is entitled to receive appropriate medical treatment and
to have her existence valued by family and society alike.

It is understandable for parents to experience distress about the birth of a
child who is physically and/or mentally challenged. Parents need counseling and support so that they can come to grips with reality and accept
their child with her limitations. The ideal response would be for them to
accept their impaired child and raise her, with society providing necessary supportive services. If, however, parents cannot accept responsibility for raising their child, substitute child care services should be
provided by society. The infant should not be allowed to die because her
parents do not want her.

As the rationale which undergirds these guidelines was becoming explicit
a parallel development was also under way. This development involved a
rather interesting chapter in ethical history, the formulation in 1984 of the so-
called Baby Doe rules. At the direction of then President Ronald Reagan, the
Justice Department and the Department of Health and Human Services
sought to require treatment of impaired newborns under the auspices of the
Baby Doe rules. These rules were devised under Section 504 of the Rehabil-
itation Act of 1973 which forbade discrimination solely on the basis of hand-
icap. Accordingly, by not treating impaired newborns who were, by virtue of
their impairment, handicapped citizens, those who failed to provide treatment were acting illegally and denying babies their civil rights. A Department of Health and Human Services notice was sent to hospitals detailing
Baby Doe rules, and large posters were placed in hospital nurseries advising
that "Discriminatory Failure to Feed and Care for Handicapped Infants in
this Facility Is Prohibited by Federal Law." A toll-free 800 phone number was
established so that anyone who wanted to could report abuses. As it happened, Baby Doe rules had a short life span because a 1983 suit brought
against these rules by the American Academy of Pediatrics was decided in
the Academy's favor, making the rules unenforceable. Another version of the
same rules met a similar fate in the winter of 1984. During the time Baby Doe
rules were in effect approximately 50 cases were investigated by HHS and in
approximately a half dozen cases impaired children were treated at government insistence.[3]

The reasons the American Academy of Pediatrics and others opposed the
philosophy behind the Baby Doe rules, as well as the actual regulations, are
instructive. Introducing an unrelated group of people or "squad" into what
has traditionally been a limited circle within which family members and
physicians negotiate an agreement appeared unnecessarily intrusive. The
purported need for the rules and the squads was seen as insulting to medicine because the measures presupposed that vulnerable infants were routinely denied life-saving treatment. The disruptive nature of the Baby Doe

squads was a major complaint; these groups tended to swoop down on a hospital nursery at any hour of the day or night, interrogate medical personnel and others, demand to see records, etc., and exert problematic effects on the clinical setting. There were also complaints about the poor judgments reached by Baby Doe squads who, out of incomplete knowledge or ill-advised zealotry, mandated very expensive treatment for severely impaired newborns who did not survive the surgeries or derive benefit therefrom.[4]

The Baby Doe rules turned out to be an unwise response to a few instances of bad decisions not to treat Down Syndrome children but, in the processes of putting these rules in place and dismantling them, as well as in dialogue about the Babies Doe, the right of children to care came to be recognized. A different kind of question was posed in regard to Baby Jane Doe, prompting the formulation of other ethical guidelines.

BABY JANE DOE: HOW PARENTAL DISCRETION DIFFERS FROM PARENTAL NEGLECT

Parental neglect, which would allow an infant to die because he has Down Syndrome, is morally unacceptable. While this type of case is not clearly and absolutely open and shut, it is, nevertheless, close to straightforward. However, every problematic case involving an impaired newborn is not clear and unambiguous. This fact was established in the 1980s by media coverage given to Baby Jane Doe. In considering the case of Baby Jane Doe, society was forced to confront the fact that parental neglect is one thing and parental discretion is another. The outcome of this awareness was an acknowledgement that society needs to honor the family and respect the right of parents to make difficult treatment choices about infants with ambiguous conditions and uncertain prognoses.

Baby Jane Doe was born in 1983 on Long Island, New York; because her medical records were never made public, what has been written about her condition cannot be verified.

After the birth of their daughter, Mr. and Mrs. A., Baby Jane Doe's parents, were informed that the baby was seriously impaired and their options were explained to them. According to court testimony, the baby had spina bifida, hydrocephalus, a damaged kidney, and microcephaly (a small head which might signal lack of part of her brain). The baby's spine was open and a meningocele protruded from it. (A meningocele is a protrusion of the meninges through a defect in the skull. The meninges are the three membranes that envelop the brain and spinal cord.) The two physicians who attended the infant at the Newborn Intensive Care Unit at the University Hospital at the SUNY Campus of Stony Brook disagreed about what should be done for the baby and about the prognosis should one course or the other be followed. One surgeon recommended immediate surgery to drain the hydrocephalus. The other surgeon said that the baby would likely die soon without surgery; his prediction for her if she had surgery was that she would probably be paralyzed, retarded, and vulnerable to bladder and bowel infections.

Mr. and Mrs. A. agonized over their options, consulted appropriate authorities, and reached a decision to allow their daughter to die. Food, fluids, and antibiotics would be provided for the baby, she would be kept comfortable, and they would be present to her. Their expectation was that the baby would die within a matter of days; as it happened, she did not die, the opening on her spine closed by itself, and she did as well as could be expected with the conservative medical regimen her parents authorized.

Baby Jane Doe's birth and her parent's decisions about her treatment would never have come to public attention if it were not for Lawrence Washburn. The Baby Doe rules were in the process of being revised when Washburn became aware of the case. He was a lawyer and right-to-life activist who took Mr. and Mrs. A. to court to force surgery. The case went through three courts in four days. William Weber was appointed the baby's guardian, and the decision of New York Supreme Court was that the baby should have surgery. The New York Court of Appeals overturned this decision, ruling that the suit was offensive because the complainant and guardian had no connection to the individuals in the case. At this point the American Life Lobby complained to the federal government and the Reagan administration became involved.

The United States Justice Department subsequently sued University Hospital in order to ascertain whether or not the infant's rights had been violated. In court proceedings following this suit District Judge Wexler ruled that parents of severely handicapped offspring have the right to withhold life-prolonging surgery and the Second Circuit Court of Appeals upheld this ruling in 1984. Because none of the plaintiffs in the case ever succeeded in obtaining the infant's medical records or in establishing the fact that the baby had been treated in a discriminatory manner, the practical consequence of the case of Baby Jane Doe was the demise of the Baby Doe rules. It would not legally be possible for the Justice Department to function as a final arbiter which invades the family circle to pass on the heart-wrenching decisions parents must make on behalf of impaired newborns with complicated diagnoses and ambiguous prognoses.

Five years after the courts finished deliberating about Baby Jane Doe there was an update about her status in *Newsday*: She was reported to be "doing better than anyone expected—talking, attending school for the handicapped, and learning to mix with her peers. She still can't walk and gets around in a wheelchair but her progress defied the dire predictions."[5]

Several insights derived from the case of Baby Jane Doe led to a refined sense of ethical awareness about how similar cases should be handled. Relevant insights include:

Parents are more closely related to their child than anyone else and they have the responsibilities of caring for and raising their children, so they have the right to make decisions about medical care as long as they act from reasonable motives.

It is difficult to define what constitutes neglect of an impaired newborn and, except in cases wherein there clearly is blatant disregard for the infant's rights, her parents' decision should be respected.

The best medical treatment sometimes is comfort care rather than invasive or burdensome procedures; informed choices of one course over the other should ordinarily be honored.

The right to privacy encompasses parents' reasonable decisions about medical care for their children and this right should not be denied or compromised by government.

Infants have a right to life and this right needs to be upheld. However, pain, suffering, and disability can lead to such a poor quality of life that life-sustaining and life-prolonging medical treatments need not be undertaken if they would result in continued existence for a baby with a very poor prognosis.

THE NEONATAL INTENSIVE CARE UNIT: A MARVEL OF TECHNOLOGY

As recently as the 1950s medical science had little to offer compromised premature infants. Efforts were directed at maintaining the baby's body temperature and perhaps providing oxygen. There was little other technology available and, therefore, parents and physicians could only hope and pray.

During the 1960s, with the coming of precursor technologies, medical science began to hold more promise for compromised newborns. Three developments would prove especially significant: The invention of the ventilator or respirator; the perfecting of artificial means of providing nutrition and hydration, especially total parenteral nutrition; and the discovery of the technique for CPR, cardio-pulmonary resuscitation. (A discussion of various methods of artificial feeding is provided in Chapter 7; explanations of ventilators and CPR are contained in Chapter 11.)

During the following decades, improvements in what was already available along with adaptation of machinery and implements so that these could be used on tiny infants have resulted in the extraordinary sophistication of the contemporary Neonatal Intensive Care Unit (NICU). With a recent 1990s development, the use of surfactant, the technology of the NICU has taken an astounding leap forward. Surfactant is a fatty substance that coats the interior cavities of the lungs and prevents them from collapsing. In 1990 researchers discovered a method for removing surfactant from the lungs of newborn calves and administering it to the lungs of premature infants.[6]

Today's NICU is a maze of modern technology. Equipment adapted for use with tiny newborns includes oxygen tents, oxygen masks, chest compressors, rubber bulbs for suctioning, rubber bags for delivering air, respirators, IV tubes, catheters, stethoscopes, and blood pressure readers. Equipment designed especially for compromised newborns includes tiny cribs called isolettes, warming lights and tables to maintain temperature, plastic wrap to prevent fluid loss, and eye patches to prevent damage from lights. An especially significant and very recently developed piece of equipment is called an oscillator which is a type of ventilator which vibrates a baby's chest with up to 900 tiny puffs of air a minute. This $20,000 machine is gentler than a respirator. Another item of note is a transilluminator which is a blue light that physicians can use in order to check on lung development and examine the lungs to detect whether or not they become torn.

The NICU is staffed by specially trained physicians and nurses. Triage teams, made up of these specialists, are on hand for the births of severely compromised newborns. For the most part, an infant qualifies as a compromised newborn based on weight. Babies weighing less than five pounds are considered low birth weight and may need care in an NICU. Babies weighing less than three pounds are termed very low birth weight and are certainly going to be sent to the NICU. Most low birth-weight and very low birth-weight babies profit from the technology of the NICU and survive to be discharged and progress to normal development.

Today's most difficult clinical situations involve severely low birth-weight babies who may be born after only 24 weeks gestation and who may weigh as little as one pound. (At the present time it is considered impossible for an infant born at less than 23 or 24 weeks gestation to survive.) The biggest risks these babies face are from their immature lungs as well as from the possibility of brain hemorrhage. Should they suffer either an irreversible lung disorder or a brain hemorrhage, it is virtually certain that they will die.

Each year 30,000 babies are born three months before term. Half these infants survive. Neither parents nor physicians have crystal balls to aid them in predicting outcomes. Initial decisions about whether or not to treat have to be made in the instant following birth. Subsequent decisions about whether to continue high-tech treatment or to stop it have to be made under extremely stressful circumstances. Often enough babies develop unremediable complications or die, taking decisions out of caretaker's hands. When these sad eventualities do not occur, however, physicians and parents have to be prepared for what may turn out to be a very traumatic experience.

In a best case scenario, a severely compromised newborn develops optimally in the NICU and leaves the hospital as a thriving baby in her parents' care. There are other predictable scenarios. All possible interventions are attempted and still the baby dies. Interventions are employed and the baby survives, but with devastating handicaps such as blindness, chronic lung disease, mental retardation, cerebral palsy, or a combination of the above. It is also possible that an infant might survive in a respirator-dependent state, meaning that he would never be able to be free of the respirator because he could not breathe on his own.

In addition to treating low and very low birth-weight infants, NICU physicians and nurses are also called upon to educate parents on the spot to the realities of the newborn's diagnosis, prognosis, and treatment options. Since these circumstances are likely to be very distressing to the parents, arrangements need to be made to provide emotional and/or spiritual support to them.

ETHICAL ISSUES ARISING IN CONJUNCTION WITH VERY LOW BIRTH-WEIGHT BABIES AND SEVERELY COMPROMISED NEWBORNS

Babies born 24 to 28 weeks after conception and babies weighing approximately one pound face a very remote chance of surviving. If they beat the odds and do survive, then they have only a slim chance of avoiding mental and/or physical developmental deficits. The situation for these infants is complicated by the fact that no one connected with the decision-making process knows how things will turn out should treatments be employed to sustain and/or prolong life. In addition, these scenarios tend to be very emotional, with lay people inclined to be unrealistic in regard to expectations of the capabilities of medical science. While ethics cannot change the nature of these situations or provide answers about what the future holds, ethics can offer some guidelines which will be helpful to physicians, nurses, and others who become caught up in deciding what to do for these babies.

Decisions should be made on the basis of the infant's best interests, rather than based on unworthy motives of physicians or parents. Examples of such unworthy motives might be a doctor's desire to make a name for herself or a parent's reluctance about raising a physically or mentally challenged child.

If a newborn can be "saved" only to be respirator-dependent for his entire life, a merciful decision to allow the baby to die is ethically acceptable. So is a decision to discontinue treatment if the infant's disabilities would result in a painful and extremely diminished condition.

The public-at-large needs to be educated about realistic capabilities of modern medicine. Too often medical science is thought to be capable of accomplishing impossible goals. It would be better if people understood that there are limits to the capabilities of modern medicine, and these limits are no place more painfully obvious than in the neonatal intensive care unit.

Similar to low birth-weight cases are cases of infants who are severely compromised and for whom the prognosis is unalterably bleak. Deciding whether to treat such infants or allow them to die can be difficult. Cases of **anencephalic newborns,** infants with **hypoplastic left ventricles,** babies with **Lesch-Nyham syndrome** and conjoined infants such as the **Lakeberg conjoined twins** fall into this category. So too would babies with multi-organ failure or an overwhelming pathology for which existing conventional and/or experimental treatments would probably be futile. Sadly, children such as these illustrate the limits of modern medicine to cure or ameliorate disease. As a result, parental refusal to authorize interventions, as well as physician reluctance to pursue the possibility of a one-in-a-million chance of a miracle, are easily understood. It is obvious that this is an area requiring great sensitivity and, in some instances, a reasonable degree of suspicion. One instance is that of medical practitioners who seek to exploit highly emotional circumstances so as to gain notoriety. This may have happened in the 1993 case of the conjoined Lakeberg twins when physicians at the University of Pennsylvania offered to operate even though the likelihood of success was minuscule. As was expected, one baby died during the operation and the second child died several months later.[7] It could be that the Lakeberg babies were a "made for television" phenomenon and that they never had a realistic chance to benefit from medical intervention. In hindsight, allowing the babies to die might have shown better medical and moral judgment than was exhibited by the intervention. In light of the Lakeberg case and other similar cases, it would be helpful to ethics and medicine to explore the ramifications of establishing policy guidelines pertaining to use of futile treatments for severely compromised newborns.

The other side of the coin in regard to severely compromised newborns is parental inability to accept the situation coupled with demands on physicians to employ futile treatments based on the parents' wish to believe that the situation is not hopeless. Parents such as these put physicians in a very uncomfortable place and require sensitivity and compassion. This does not mean, however, that physicians should knuckle under and comply with ill-founded requests for futile treatments. Justice and rationality require that physicians not abandon their professional judgment in order to placate people but, rather, that they take time to educate parents and support them through emotionally stressful times.

Some norms in regard to low birth-weight and severely compromised newborns have taken shape in recent years. These norms include the following:

It is not wise to force treatment if the baby would have to rely on technology such as a ventilator or dialysis for his entire life.

If, following successful treatment, the baby's life would be marred by pain and suffering which could not be alleviated, it would be reasonable to forgo the treatment and allow the child to die.

When there is little to go on in the way of prognosis because physicians do not know how things will turn out, it would be best to err on the side of life, i.e., provide treatment.

In ambiguous cases of severely compromised neonates, follow the instructions of the parents because their relationship to their child gives them authority to make decisions.

CONCLUSION

Dilemmas involving compromised newborns are among the most complex facing society today. Unknown factors frequently cloud the picture, making for a lack of certainty in respect to prognosis. Physicians need to accept the sadness of limitations, and parents need to differentiate between realistic hope and wishful thinking. If and when the media becomes involved, sensitive situations tend to take on sensational overtones to the detriment of both medical science and the family involved; this unfortunate fact needs to be corrected.

Neonatal dilemmas are forcing us to move back to basics in ethical reasoning. Hard cases illustrate the need to establish objective standards grounded in sound medicine and clear-headed reasoning. At stake are justice to vulnerable infants, the integrity of both the medical profession and the human community, and the well-being of the baby's parents. Taking time to reason rightly so as to respond with compassion, competence, and objectivity will be well worth the effort.

ENDNOTES

[1] R. Duff and A. Campbell, "Moral and Ethical Dilemmas in the Special-Care Nursery," *New England Journal of Medicine*, October 25, 1973, pp. 890–894.

[2] Joseph P. Kennedy Foundation, Producer, "Who Should Survive?" Available from Film Service, 999 Asylum Ave., Hartford, CT 06105.

[3] Adrian Peracchio, "Government in the Nursery: New Era for Baby Doe Cases," *Newsday*, November 13, 1983.

[4] Ibid.

[5] Kathleen Kerr, "Legal, Medical Legacy of Case," *Newsday*, December 7, 1987.

[6] Darcy Frey, "Does Anyone Here Think This Baby Can Live?" *The New York Times*, July 9, 1995, p. 29.

[7] William A. Silverman, "Siamese Twins Focus Health Care Issues," (Letter), *The New York Times*, September 5, 1993, p. 10.

DISCUSSION QUESTIONS

1. If you were the parent or grandparent of a compromised newborn, how do you think you would react to news of the infant's physical and/or mental disabilities? What kinds of help and support would be of benefit to you? To whom would you look for this assistance, and what would prompt you to think that these persons or agencies would be of help?

2. If you were a neonatologist and were preparing to meet with parents of a very low birth-weight baby, what medical, psychological, and ethical concepts would you try to communicate to them at the meeting? What led you to decide on these particular concepts? What kinds of support from the health care community and society-at-large would be helpful to you and them? Why?

3. In respect to newborns who are born with anomalies or are of very low birth weight, parents can be motivated by selfishness; physicians can seek fame through possible media exposure; and treatments offered could be futile. Suggest reasons why society should not tolerate these shortcomings. Devise strategies to lessen the likelihood that these possible shortcomings will actually materialize.

4. Prepare a list of principles to be used in conjunction with deciding whether or not to treat a severely compromised newborn. Explain what prompted you to decide to include these principles on your list.

5. Under what circumstances could it be appropriate to allow a severely compromised newborn to die? Provide an ethical justification for allowing nature to take its course in such a case.

6. Would it be morally acceptable to end the life of a compromised newborn through overt means? Why or why not?

7. Some of the Baby Doe cases caused ethical revulsion because compromised infants were neglected and died as a result. Write a definition for neglect, explaining what neglect is and why it is ethically wrong for a parent to neglect his child's care or a physician to neglect to provide care for an infant requiring surgery.

CASE STUDY

Adam Ford was born to unmarried, uninsured teen parents. He was born with severe abnormalities including hydrocephaly, spina bifida, and necrotic small bowel syndrome. Treating Adam would require surgical implacement of a shunt to drain excess fluid from the brain so as to alleviate the consequences of hydrocephaly. The spina bifida would necessitate surgery to close the spine. Finally, the necrotic bowel syndrome would also require surgery and, depending upon how much bowel there was, Adam might or might not be able to be nourished utilizing his digestive system. With or without surgical interventions, his overall prognosis is poor. The maximum estimation of lifespan is two years and a conservative estimate of costs for providing possible surgeries and extended in-hospital care is in the range of $2 million.

Adam's mother was released from the hospital two days after his birth. In the two weeks since, neither she nor Adam's father has come to the hospital or called inquiring about him. Calls to them have not been returned. None of Adam's grandparents has shown interest in his condition.

Adam's attending physician requests a meeting of the hospital ethics committee to discuss the case. She wants advice because she never before encountered a situation in which the infant's family was totally nonparticipative. Her bias is generally in favor of providing treatment but, in this case, she feels uncharacteristically ambivalent. In addition, she feels somewhat guilty, perhaps owing to the fact that in Adam's case she suspects that too much money would be spent for too little return.

Evaluation:

1. Identify ethical issues contained in this case.
2. Propose possible solutions for these issues.
3. Make a decision relevant to action to be taken and provide rationale supportive of decisions.
4. Are you satisfied with your decision? Why or why not?

GLOSSARY

Anencephalic newborns are children born with most of their brains missing, or a significant part of their brains missing.

    Infants with hypoplastic left heart syndrome have a defective development of the left ventricle of the heart. This defect is characterized by respiratory distress and extreme cyanosis (bluish discoloration) followed by cardiac failure and death. Most babies with hypoplastic left heart syndrome die within a few weeks of birth.

Lesch-Nyham syndrome, named for two American physicians, Michael Lesch (born in 1939) and William L. Nyham, Jr. (born in 1926), is a rare disorder which incapacitates infants by burdening them with physical and mental retardation, compulsive mutilation of the fingers and lips by biting, spastic cerebral palsy, and impaired renal function.

Lakeberg conjoined twins were born to Kenneth and Reitha Lakeberg on June 29, 1993, in Indiana. On August 20, 1993, physicians at Children's Hospital, Philadelphia, separated the babies. As was known in advance, because of shared organs, Amy died during surgery. At the outset there was cautious optimism regarding Angela's chances for survival. However, Angela died on June 9, 1994.

PART THREE

MORAL RESPONSE TO NEW TECHNOLOGIES

CHAPTER 5

Applications of Genetic Science

INTRODUCTION

Genetics is a science of relatively recent origin which holds open radical possibilities and engenders enormous complexity. It is a basic science underlying all aspects of health and health care. Specialists in genetics and ethicists who study moral issues related to genetics, as well as a minority of the public, understand what is at stake in respect to genetic science. The vast majority of people, 80 percent according to a March of Dimes poll, have little understanding of either the technological or ethical aspects of genetics, a field which is capable of impacting remarkably on their lives.[1] In keeping with the rest of this book, we shall look first at the science of genetics, familiarizing ourselves in a general way with the field, while bearing in mind that the field itself is constantly changing. After this task is accomplished, we will consider ethical questions arising from genetic science. We shall then suggest an ethical framework within which to evaluate what genetics has to offer.

GENETIC SCIENCE: NEW KNOWLEDGE AND CAPABILITIES BRING NEW CHOICES

The foundations of the possibilities of genetic technology were laid 130 years ago when, in 1866, Gregor Mendel published an account of his theory of heredity. Mendel proposed that inherited characteristics are determined by combinations of two hereditary units, now called genes. Walter Flemming's identification, in 1882, of a substance existing in cells, which he called chromosomes, added to this knowledge. However, neither the work of Mendel nor Flemming received much attention until after 1900.

In 1900, working independently in different countries, Hugo de Vries, C. G. Correns, and Erich Tschermak-Seysenegg reached the same conclusions as Mendel in respect to the inherited nature of characteristics. At approximately the same time these individuals also discovered Mendel's pioneering work and added their knowledge to his.[2] Since that time, the scientific community has shown openness to genetic science and interest in the possibilities it contains. It is an understatement to say that the twentieth century has witnessed breakthrough after breakthrough in the field of genetics.

During the 1920s and 1930s T. H. Morgan and his associates studied very simple organisms, Drosophila (fruit flies), in order to learn about the way in which genetic processes are carried out.[3] In 1944 Oswald T. Avery, Colin McLoud, and Maclyn McCarthy demonstrated that DNA is the hereditary substance of which living cells are comprised, with genes being the individual sections on DNA molecules.[4] Their discovery was followed in 1953 by a watershed event: F. H. C. Crick and J. D. Watson constructed a model of the DNA molecule.[5]

In 1962 it was learned that restriction enzymes can cut DNA molecules into fragments.[6] Building upon this knowledge, in 1972 Janet Mertz and Ronald Davis combined molecules, gene splicing for the first time.[7] By 1978 two independent five-person research teams succeeded in making E Coli bacteria produce human-type insulin.[8] In 1991 the Human Genome Project was begun under the auspices of the United States government. This project is an ongoing attempt to map and ultimately sequence the estimated 80,000 to 100,000 or more genes which make up the human gene pool. Scientists working on the genome project think they will complete their work before the target date of 2005.[9] On November 6,1998, the journal *Science* reported on the work of scientists at the University of Wisconsin under Dr James A. Thomson. These scientists removed embryonic stem cells from laboratory fertilized embryos and intend to use the cells to grow new tissues. If they succeed, this may lead to replaceable organs or new forms of gene therapy.[10]

In order to be able to consider the ethical aspects of genetic technology, we need to have an acquaintance with what is known scientifically about this field. Therefore, it will be helpful to review some building blocks of genetics before moving on to the ethical discussions engendered by genetic science. Let us begin by considering the following list of definitions.

Cell. A cell is the basic unit of life. It consists of a nucleus, an enclosing membrane, and a substance called protoplasm.

Germ Cell. A germ cell or sex cell is a fertile cell which contains 23 chromosomes. Germ cells are either male or female and new organisms develop from germ cells.

Somatic cells are cells that become differentiated into all the various parts of the body (except the germ cells, sperm and ova). Each somatic cell is made up of 46 chromosomes.

Stem cells are the progenitors of all the body's red and white blood cells. Stem cells are needed for gene therapy and bone marrow transplants. At any one time human marrow contains about 10 billion cells; only about 100,000 are stem cells. At the current time scientists are exploring ways of isolating stem cells in order to study them and use them for genetic therapy.

Chromosome. A chromosome is a microscopic rod-shaped body which carries the genes that convey hereditary characteristics. Each human somatic cell is made up of 46 chromosomes; germ cells are the exception.

Gene. Hereditary characteristics are determined and transmitted by genes. Theoretically, each mature germ cell carries a gene for every inheritable characteristic possessed by an individual. Persons receive a set of genes from each parent which determine the unique genotype of each individual.

Dominant (genes). According to Mendel, one gene of each pair dominates over the other and appears in the organism.

Recessive (genes). Also from Mendel, the gene or trait which does not appear but, rather, remains latent is the recessive gene.

DNA. Deoxyribonucleic acid, commonly abbreviated DNA, is the substance of which genes consist. DNA is comprised of four chemicals, identified as A, G, C, and T, which can be combined in an incredible variety of ways. The fact that there are an estimated three billion pairs of cells attests to this variety. Crick and Watson discovered that DNA is configured in the form of a double helix.

Heredity is the transmission from parent to offspring of certain characteristics or, put another way, the characteristics transmitted in the process.

Hereditary characteristics refer to the tendency of offspring to resemble parents or ancestors and in some cases (approximately 5 percent of the time) to be bearers of genetic defects.

Identification of genetic defects. This is the process employed by scientists who study patterns among generations and identify those defects which are transmitted in genes; also, refers to locating and naming the actual genes which transmit defects.

Mutation is a sudden variation in some inheritable characteristic, as distinguished from a variation resulting from generations of gradual change.

Gene therapy is an attempt to correct an intrinsic defect in genetic material. No gene therapies are available to cure genetic diseases at this time but research is underway to develop somatic cell gene treatments for some genetic disorders. Whether or not gene therapy can ever be used on the scale of penicillin remains to be seen.

Gene splicing is a technique for producing hybrid plasmids. Through this process, carried out in vitro (in the laboratory), a new chain of genes which can command the production of new traits is spliced onto (combined with) a DNA molecule. The two fragments join because they have so-called "sticky ends." The process of joining the sticky ends is gene splicing.

Plasmids are small self-reproducing cytoplasmic elements that exist outside the chromosome, as in some bacteria. A plasmid can alter a hereditary characteristic when introduced into a foreign bacterium, as by changing its antibiotic resistance.

Hybrid plasmids are crossbred with plasmids, thus developing new chains of genes in vitro.

Recombinant DNA uses bacteria to manipulate cells because bacterial cells are easier to manipulate than cells of higher organisms. Recombinant DNA also refers to the process by which an individual can acquire new genes.

Transformation is the reintroduction of a hybrid plasmid into a bacterium.

Transduction is the proposed method for repairing genetic defects. It is a process for inserting genes into a host organism by using viruses as carriers or vectors. The issue scientists are struggling with is: If a virus can infect an organism, why can't other genes enter organisms to correct defects? The correcting of defects is the goal of gene therapy.

Monogenic defects are defects caused by one gene; there is cautious optimism that it may be possible in the future to correct monogenic defects.

Polygenic defects are defects resulting from several defective genes. Currently the consensus is that it is improbable that genetic therapies could be developed to correct polygenic defects.

In vivo refers to the human body. Some procedures for treating genetic defects in vivo are under consideration.

In vitro refers to very early human embryonic life as it is found in a petri dish in the laboratory. Procedures for identifying genetic defects at this stage are in place.

Biohazards of gene splicing refers to the possibility that harmful new life forms could be created in laboratories. It is theoretically possible that virulent microorganisms which are resistant to antibiotics could inadvertently be created, causing grave dangers to humans as well as to the environment.

GENETIC SCREENING OF LIVING PEOPLE

Genetic screening can be done on living people to provide information to them about whether or not their specific DNA is linked to pathologies or diseases which have been identified through genetic research. The way to have a genetic test done is to provide blood and/or tissue for analysis; specially trained technicians in specially equipped laboratories carry out the analysis. People can arrange for genetic screening on their own, or, more commonly, do so at the suggestion of their physicians. The motivation to seek genetic screening is usually concern over diseases which occur within one's family or ethnic group. In the future people may be motivated by curiosity but, at present, curiosity does not seem to prompt people to undergo genetic screening. Interestingly, we are probably at the threshhold of a new age of genetic awareness so that within another decade or so people's health histories are likely to include DNA profiles which contain the positive and negative aspects of their genetic makeup.

What can people do with genetic knowledge? The answers to this question will change as genetics becomes more sophisticated both in regard to the kinds of information it can provide and the types of treatments it can offer. For now, if a person learns that she has a genetic predisposition to a disease such as colon cancer or alcoholism, she can put prevention strategies in place, thereby enhancing her chances for overall well-being. In other cases, genetic knowledge can bring relief and peace of mind. It goes without saying that if an individual who has several relatives who suffer(ed) from early-onset Alzheimer's learns that he does not have genetic evidence indicating a likelihood of developing that condition, he will be relieved. On the other hand, however, should a person learn that he carries the gene for this disease, while knowing that the disease has neither treatment nor cure at either the genetic level or the symptomatic state, this would be a stressful burden to bear.

Genetic diagnosis is currently far ahead of genetic therapy. It is hoped that in the years ahead viable treatments will be developed. Until then, however, people who undergo genetic screening need to understand the difficulties which may result.

PREIMPLANTATION AND PREBIRTH GENETIC SCREENING

Genetic screening can be carried out in the laboratory before an embryo is transferred to the uterus. DNA analysis is carried out when the embryo is at the eight-cell stage, approximately two to three days after ova are inseminated. The analysis takes about 8 to 12 hours; embryos unaffected by genetic defect are then either transferred or cryopreserved. In all probability, embryos which have genetic defects would be discarded. People use preimplantation screening to avoid conceiving boys if their sons would likely be hemophiliacs. They can also turn to this procedure to screen for practically any disease which has been identified in DNA mapping.

Genetic screening can also be done on the fetus while it is developing in utero. The most common forms of testing are amniocentesis and chorionic villus sampling. Amniocentesis is a procedure which is carried out as early as ten weeks after conception, but usually several weeks later. Performed by a skilled physician, amniocentesis entails a needle puncture of the uterus together with a suctioning of amniotic fluid. The cells in the fluid are studied to determine whether or not the fetus is affected by genetic abnormal-ity(ies). The major risk factor associated with amniocentesis is miscarriage which occurs about once in 300 procedures.

Chorionic villus sampling (CVS) is another prebirth genetic screening technique. CVS is usually carried out earlier than amniocentesis, at 9 to 12 weeks gestation. Chorionic villi are the forerunners of the placenta. Access to this tissue is achieved through the cervix, and tissue is obtained through a suctioning technique. CVS allows screening for the same genetic disorders as amniocentesis. The risk factor associated with CVS is a 0.5 to 1 percent risk of miscarriage.

GENETIC COUNSELING

Genetic counseling is ordinarily performed by academic geneticists who usually have a master's degree or physician geneticists, who are medical doctors with specialized training in genetics. In essence, genetic counseling is one-on-one education about an individual's genetic endowment or the genetic condition of embryos or fetuses to whom one is related. Genetic counseling can be carried out either before or after an individual undergoes genetic screening. Genetic counselors frequently meet with people before a pregnancy takes place to explain the technology currently available to them. Genetic counselors also meet with expectant parents to go over the results of genetic testing performed during pregnancy.

Sessions with a genetic counselor can bring good or bad news, news which bears far-reaching ramifications. In view of the significance of what is at stake, the dynamics of the interaction are exceedingly important. There-fore, genetic counselors need to be informative, supportive, and nondirec-tive because it is the responsibility of their clients to make decisions on their own behalf or that of their children.

GENETIC THERAPY

There is a general social consensus that it is appropriate to pursue somatic-cell gene therapy, and inappropriate to engage in germ-cell gene therapy. The reason germ-cell gene therapy is unacceptable is because of the unknown and unpredictable risks which might be transmitted in the process. Since it is human life itself which is passed on via germ cells, and since it is these cells which form the links among the generations, there exists a widespread caution in regard to altering germ cells.

As far as somatic-cell gene therapy is concerned, there are three general approaches to correction of genetic diseases. The first is called *ex vivo*. It involves removal of cells from a patient, correction of the cells by addition of a normal gene, and subsequent return of the cells to the patient. *Ex vivo* therapy would be successful if the treated cells functioned in a new way and ameliorated the disease.

A second way to go about gene therapy is called *in situ*; this method introduces a new gene directly into the site of a disease such as a cancer mass or the lining of the lung of a patient with cystic fibrosis. The gene can be attached to a virus, in which case it is called a virus vector, or it can be naked DNA.

The third approach, not as well studied as the first two, is called *in vivo*. This approach relies on a vector (carrier) that can carry a gene through the bloodstream to the designated tissue in an efficient manner. If and when an injectable vector is developed, gene therapy will become as simple to administer as insulin therapy for diabetes.

The good news about genetic therapy is that research and experimentation on all three methods are proceeding in the United States and throughout the world. The bad news is that the results of these trials have not as yet been cures of genetic diseases. Therefore, genetic therapy is not a realistic option for people who have genetic diseases, but medical science holds out the promise that it will be in the not too distant future.

GENETIC SCIENCE: COULD IT LEAD TO A EUGENIC MENTALITY?

A **eugenic mentality** can be a negative offshoot of genetic science. By a eugenic mentality is meant a fascination with genetics resulting in a reliance on genetic means to improve the quality of human beings. The kinds of humans considered undesirable might include mentally retarded, physically handicapped, socially maladjusted, and/or psychologically troubled. Depending on who is defining the category, all kinds of bases for exclusion are possible. People who are too tall or too short, too heavy or too thin, those who have problematic characteristics, e.g., a hereditary predisposition to alcoholism or a gene for homosexuality or a likelihood of developing a specific disease, could be excluded on the basis of these deficiencies. The goal of eugenics is to improve the human gene pool by eliminating negative characteristics and breeding in such a way as to maximize the chances for creating superior human beings. Eugenics seeks to build a better society through eliminating defective members.

There are some obvious problems with eugenics. The first is that there is more at stake in creating a superior human than in creating a superior species of vegetable. Vegetables do not have rights but humans do, and these human rights are possessed by all persons because they are human; human rights do not cease to exist if an individual is "imperfect" in one or more ways. At its core, eugenics tends to cancel out the right of the less than perfect individual to existence and this type of presumptive arrogance is inherently immoral. A second harmful outcome of eugenics could be that through screening programs privileged groups might act on their prejudices against, for example, homosexual persons or those with family histories of substance abuse. Since homosexuality is neither a crime nor a defect and since those with a predisposition to substance abuse can, if necessary, avail themselves of treatment programs, it would be a grave injustice for advocates of eugenics to try to eliminate such classes of people from the human gene pool. Another possible harm of eugenics is that those who promote it do so at the expense of the harmony of the human community. This community, as we know it, is made up of people of all kinds, some more gifted than others, some more troubled than others. The solidarity and prosperity of the human community depend on cooperation and respect among all members, not on a screening policy through which some members lose their right to membership based on the values and biases of those in influential positions. The biggest problem with eugenics is probably the fact that, even if the program were embraced and employed, it would not be possible to carry it out. Humans are the most complex of all the species and, even with carefully orchestrated breeding programs, individuals with physical, mental, social, or psychological limitations would still be born.

In many places in the world today, men are preferred over women, so that female embryos are not transferred, female fetuses are aborted, and female newborns do not receive aggressive medical care or, in some cases, are left to die. If an enthusiasm for selective breeding were to become part of the collective psyche of the Western world, one or the other gender could fall out of favor and be eliminated either in vitro or in vivo. If this were to happen it would be detrimental because the balance nature sets for itself would be disrupted.

Before it became possible to alter human genetic composition, nature, in a sense, took care of itself and humans coped with diseases and deficiencies as these appeared. With the advent of genetic technology, however, it may become possible for humans to alter the genetic makeup of all the various species. While the goals of genetic technologies are to improve the various species as well as to learn about them, this technology also makes possible the producing of harmful mutations or substances which are capable of unknown destructive possibilities. Needless to say, such use of genetic technology would be counterproductive and devastating to people throughout the world.

Finally, widespread ignorance about genetic technology coupled with only limited controls on its execution may result in a situation in which control over life is in the hands of a relatively few, thus radically altering the way things have happened from the beginning of time until now or some time in the near future (i.e., evolution and natural selection). The reason this would be harmful is because there is no way yet devised to guard against the potential for exploitation and manipulation.

GENETIC SCIENCE: POSSIBLE BENEFITS TO HUMANS AND OTHER SPECIES

While it is possible that humans might be harmed by genetic technology, it is also conceivable that they could be helped in wonderful ways. The knowledge which geneticists have accumulated in conjunction with research on subhuman species provides invaluable information about the intricate nature of human genetic dynamics. Since the medical enterprise is principally driven to enhance well-being and cure illness, information provided by genetics may be able to assist in this process. In regard to most illnesses this possibility is still in the future but, in some cases, identification of problems and preventative intervention are already at hand. One such case is the test for **PKU** (phenylketonuria), done routinely since the mid 1960s on newborn infants.

Genetic science may play a role in answering one of the most perplexing of the ultimate questions: Why do individuals act the way they do? The debate on this issue has been split between the nature and nurture camps. Advocates of the nature argument say that people are preprogrammed genetically and merely live out that programming throughout their lives. In other words, to understand their behavior, look to the manner in which their genetic inheritance is arranged. Those who argue from the nurture perspective disagree, reasoning that the way people behave is more connected to the manner in which they have been socialized and to the choices they make than to hereditary factors. The point here is not to settle this matter in a definitive way but, rather, to suggest that genetic science is contributing increasingly to the debate by identifying genes for such conditions as alcoholism, obesity, overreactive tendencies, and others.[11] In so doing genetic scientists have enhanced understanding of these behavior patterns and caused us to come to greater awareness of the complex set of factors that influence us to develop into the people we become. This does not mean that we cannot change our behaviors—but it helps us to understand why it is sometimes so difficult.

One of the most promising (and perhaps frightening) aspects of genetics is the possibility of being able to identify and correct genetic defects in vitro or in vivo. If scientists could remove the gene for such conditions as cystic fibrosis or hemophilia and replace it with a healthy gene at either the embryonic stage in the lab or the fetal stage in utero, this would represent a remarkable achievement. In order for genetic interventions of this kind to be beneficial to humankind, strict safeguards would need to be put in place to ensure that only serious diseases are targeted for remediation. A significant reservation which cannot yet be answered concerns whether or not, in the very act of correcting a genetic defect, technicians might create a more harmful condition and thus be responsible for inflicting this condition on a non-consenting subject.

GENETIC SCIENCE: ETHICAL CONCERNS

Guidelines for implementation of genetic technology are necessary. The reason for this necessity is that individuals should not do harm to themselves or others as they carry out procedures made possible by genetic technology. Society in general and, more specifically, those responsible in particularly relevant ways for the well-being of society, need to exercise prudent control over the implementation of genetic technology. Such interested parties as parents whose children might be affected, government and medical oversight boards, and genetic technologists themselves need to evaluate and, perhaps, restrict procedures which might be carried out.

ETHICAL THEORIES REVISITED

As with many other issues of health care ethics, a key foundational concern involves deciding on the appropriate moral methodology for assessing genetic technology. There are several possible avenues to follow.

Pragmatism is in many ways the most popular approach to ethics in the United States. Essential to a pragmatic approach is willingness to adapt and an unwillingness to draw definitive boundaries or formulate hard-and-fast rules. Pragmatism suggests that since genetic technology is a cutting-edge phenomenon, which holds great promise as well as some reasons for reservation, a cautious trial-and-error approach is in order. Thus, those procedures which yield good results should be continued and, if possible, improved upon and adapted for use in appropriate circumstances. Those procedures with detrimental outcomes should be discontinued, and those with mixed results retained or abandoned, depending on risk-benefit calculations.

While pragmatic attempts at analysis depend upon outcomes, subjective approaches to ethical evaluations of genetic technology most likely occur prior to consideration of the results of using the technology. Hence, hunches or feelings prompt decisions. If an individual has a hunch that a new genetic procedure might work for her, then she would be inclined to opt for it. On the other hand, if a person feels that the same procedure would probably not be advantageous for him, he would act accordingly and reject it. Note in both cases the lack of analysis and absence of rationale in support of decisions. As we note repeatedly in this book, the major flaws of subjectivist theories are their inherent arbitrariness and lack of rational foundation.

There are a number of approaches to ethical decision making about genetic technology which proceed from objective bases. These theories are not all equally reliable or intellectually convincing; nevertheless, they are easier to grasp and dialogue about because of the objective nature of the premise from which they are derived.

Authoritarianism is an approach to ethics which maintains that the analysis of an individual or group in authority represents a sound and reliable appraisal of an ethical issue. Hence, if a government authority, or a medical association, or an informed scientific body, or the leadership of a religious group assessed a particular genetic technology as morally acceptable or unacceptable, the judgment of that individual or group would be decisive. The reason it would be decisive is because of the credibility given to the person or agency rather than from an evaluation of the rationale presented. For practical purposes, appeals to authoritarianism to resolve complex issues of medical ethics are usually unsatisfactory for two reasons. The first is that not many people are willing to turn their decision making over to others; this is especially true of people making decisions about using genetic technology for themselves or their children. These individuals want to know what the authorities have to say, but they realize that ultimately the making of decisions falls squarely on their shoulders. A second reason why authoritarianism has a tendency not to work is because authorities are often at variance with one another, thus canceling out the guidance that might be offered to an interested party who maintains dual loyalties.

Utilitarianism is an influential ethical methodology in the United States. Utilitarianism requires that actions which are taken and policies which are proposed bring about the greatest good for the greatest number. Those who espouse utilitarianism do not find themselves constrained by preset rules or requirements, other than that they maximize the good; there is no mandate specifying that no harmful or untoward effects occur; there is no hard-and-fast methodology for calculating present and future ratios of good to evil/harm. Hence, utilitarians whose bias is in favor of genetic technology have a relatively easy time lending their support to the field of genetics, as well as to discrete technological interventions designed to correct anomalies or improve overall well-being.

Since the aforementioned is true, it also follows that utilitarians with a bias *against* genetic technology would argue *against* genetic interventions, and there is no question that such is the case. While no statistical data are available to establish, factually, which group contains more members—utilitarians with a protechnology bias or utilitarians with an antitechnology bias—my estimate is that in this culture there are more protechnology folks than adherents to an antitechnology position. Thus, the field is fertile for the development and implementation of genetic technology.

The final ethical system to be considered is the so-called natural law approach. Inherent in natural law are concepts of the person and of society, and these concepts are tied to explicit goals.

The concept of person at the core of natural law is of an individual who is distinguished by the dual abilities of being able to reason and to choose and whose lifetime project is to perfect herself by becoming a balanced, happy, virtuous person. Choices that would contribute to this development would be ethically acceptable, while choices that would detract from this goal would be unacceptable. Hence, genetic technology is neither automatically ruled in or ruled out; individuals need to evaluate and assess it in relation to their overall well-being and life project. In carrying out decision making they would consider themselves bound by certain established principles. These principles include the well-known Hippocratic injunction to do no harm, so that there would likely be a healthy skepticism in regard to authorizing untested or unproven procedures for oneself or one's child. Another binding principle which would be recognized and acted upon is the intrinsic dignity of each and every member of the human species, regardless of the individual's deficiency. In consequence, any attempt to reject or eliminate an individual at any time after conception based on genetic defect would be repudiated. There are at least two other relevant principles. One, also based on the dignity of human persons, would condemn placing an adult person with genetic abnormalities at risk by performing experiments on him without his fully informed consent. And the other would require the observance of confidentiality on the part of any health care professional who becomes aware of a person's genetic abnormalities; these are never to be revealed without obtaining consent.

Just as natural law operates on an individual level, so it has a societal component. While this societal component is a less well-known aspect of the system, it nevertheless exists and is relevant to the field of genetic technology. Leaders of society, i.e., government officials and directors of medical associations, according to natural law thinking, should have the well-being of both individuals and the broader human community at heart. This would require enactment of strict controls to eliminate or at least minimize, as much as possible, utilization of procedures which might result in harm. To say the least, this kind of oversight necessitates technical competence and dedication to the good of society.

CONCLUSION

Genetic science may be moving faster than an understanding of what genetics is and can do. Learning about genetics should be encouraged because people need to be well informed about this field in order to be able to avail themselves of its benefits as well as speak up in behalf of appropriate cautions. One thing is certain: Progress in the laboratory will continue and will change the human condition in ways still unimagined.

ENDNOTES

[1] Arthur Caplan, "Ignorance About Genetic Testing Raises Perils for Society," in *Moral Matters* (New York: John Wiley & Sons, Inc., 1995), p. 123.

[2] "Genetics," in William H. Harris and Judith S. Levery, eds., *The New Columbia Encyclopedia* (New York: Lippincott, 1975), p. 1058.

[3] Ibid.

[4] Hugh P. Papazian, *Modern Genetics* (New York: W. W. Norton & Co., Inc., 1967), pp. 110–112.

[5] J.D. Watson and F.H.C. Crick, "Molecular structure of nucleic acids: A structure for deoxyribonucleic acid," *Nature*, 1958: V 171, pp. 964–967.

[6] Richard Hutton, *Bio-Revolution: DNA and the Ethics of Man-Made Life* (New York: New American Library), p. 36, as quoted in Andrew Varga, *The Main Issues in Bioethics* (New York: Paulist Press, 1980), p. 84.

[7] Merrill Sheils, "The Key Breakthroughs," *Newsweek*, V. 93, June 4, 1979, p. 64.

[8] UPI, September 16, 1978, as quoted in op. cit., Varga, p. 88.

[9] Philip R. Reilly, "Genetics and the Law," in Warren Reich, ed., *Encyclopedia of Bioethics* (New York: Simon & Schuster Macmillan, 1995), Vol 2, p. 968; and Nicholas Wade, "Rapid Gains Are Reported on Genome," *The New York Times*, September 28, 1995, p. A24.

[10] Nicholas Wade, "Scientists Cultivate Cells at Root of Human Life," *The New York Times*, November 6, 1998, pp. 1, A24.

[11] Gina Kolata, "Is a Gene Making You Read This?" *The New York Times*, January 7, 1996, p. 4E.

DISCUSSION QUESTIONS

1. Describe the extent of your knowledge of genetics. Do you think it is important for you personally and/or for people in general to learn about genetics? Why or why not? What means could be used in making people aware of genetic science and genetic possibilities?

2. Describe the current state of knowledge about the human gene, identifying genetic defects, correcting genetic defects, and treating genetic defects.

3. What kinds of genetic screening are available before birth and after birth? After people learn the results of genetic screening, what options can they exercise?

4. What is eugenics? What ethical issues does eugenics raise? How should these issues be resolved? Why?

5. Describe the emotional and ethical issues people face when they learn that their unborn child has a genetic disease. In your opinion, what constitutes an appropriate response? Why?

6. If an individual learns that she has a genetic predisposition for a particular disease, how should she respond? In answering this question, consider diseases such as Alzheimer's, breast cancer, colon cancer, and alcoholism.

7. List the skills which a genetic counselor should possess, and provide the rationale which prompts you to include each particular skill listed.

8. Which agencies should have access to an individual's genetic composition? If employers, insurance companies, government, the military, or other agencies obtain this information, how should they use it? What factors lead to this conclusion?

9. Make a list of ethical concerns which arise in conjunction with genetic research, and state why each constitutes a concern.

10. Discuss how genetic science would probably be approached using two ethical methodologies.

CASE STUDY

Students at a government-sponsored military academy are told to report to academy doctors to provide blood and tissue specimens for a DNA registry. The reason given for this order is so that even badly mutilated or decomposed remains of U.S. military personnel could be identified.

One student, Thomas Harding, reports to an academy doctor, not to provide mandated specimens but, rather, to obtain further information before deciding whether or not to comply. Mr Harding has several questions:

Are there any foreseeable uses for DNA samples other than identification of the remains of dead servicemen and women?

Under what circumstances, if any, could DNA profiles of military personnel become available to employers, insurers, medical researchers, law enforcement authorities, marketing companies or others?

Could an individual learn the results of his DNA test before making a decision as to whether or not to allow his DNA profile to become part of the registry?

The academy doctor tells Thomas Harding that he is the only student who has questions. In addition, the physician says that she does not know the answers to these questions. She says that procurement of DNA samples has to be completed in 24 hours and that if Mr. Harding does not comply within that time frame she will have no choice but to report him for noncompliance.

Evaluation:

1. Identify ethical issues contained in this case.
2. Propose possible solutions for these issues.
3. Make a decision relevant to action to be taken or not taken and provide rationale supportive of this decision.
4. Are you satisfied with your decision? Why or why not?

GLOSSARY

PKU (Phenylketonuria) is a recessive single-gene disorder which is detected by means of a blood test administered immediately after birth. Babies born with PKU lack a certain enzyme necessary to metabolize one component of proteins. If these children are fed a normal diet, they go on to develop severe retardation. If their protein consumption is severely limited, however, and if their diet is appropriately modified, children born with PKU can go on to normal development. Thus, identification of and diet treatment for PKU are among the first successes of genetics.

CHAPTER 6

Fetal Tissue:
Research and Transplants

INTRODUCTION

Fetal tissue research and transplants hold out promise for providing scientific information as well as for alleviating symptoms of several extremely debilitating diseases. Clinical promise has not been brought to fruition, however, for two reasons. The first is that funds for research have been very short and the second is that, due to the dearth of research information and funding for transplants, there have been relatively few procedures utilizing fetal brain tissue in transplantation and, hence, there is not much information available.

As far as government support for research and transplants is concerned, it has been of an on-again, off-again nature, mostly off-again. In March, 1988, the Department of Health and Human Services placed a moratorium on use of human fetal tissue for transplant and forbade use of federal funds for research using tissue from aborted fetuses. A panel was appointed in September, 1988, to study the issue and the panel recommended lifting the moratorium; however, the Secretary of Health and Human Services rejected the recommendation and the moratorium was left in place. In November, 1989, the National Institutes of Health issued a statement which said that it was tolerable to use tissue from spontaneously aborted fetuses or **ectopic** pregnancies for research and transplant, and, by executive order of President Bush, in 1992, five banks were established to utilize such tissue. In January, 1993 President Clinton rescinded the moratorium which was in effect and directed that guidelines be formulated in regard to how government funding should be carried out. Clinton's change of policy turned out to be short-lived because, in October, 1993, Congress terminated funding for support of research and transplantation using tissue from induced abortions.[1] Since it costs between $30,000 and $50,000 for an operation to transplant fetal tissue,[2] and since such operations are not covered by insurance, the effect of government policy in this area is determinative of the status of both research and application.

Whether or not fetal tissue should be used in order to treat human illnesses is a complex question. The question forces us to think about limits which we should impose in regard to doing what can be done, or forging ahead, without ethical reservation, trying everything that is technically possible. Those who argue against the use of fetal tissue from electively aborted fetuses do so mainly on the grounds that such usage goes beyond humane and decent conduct. The fetal tissue question represents a classic case in which utilitarian thinking is pitted against ethical systems in which principles are nonnegotiable. Adding to the complexity is the fact that even those who argue on the basis of principle can find themselves reaching different conclusions asserting different, even contradictory, principles.

Just as the fetal tissue issue is very complex, so it is also extremely mundane. Whether or not research funding is available to move the scientific research phase along does not depend on the cogency of moral philosophical argument but, rather, on the political party in power. Advocates for the pro-choice position on abortion support government funding for fetal tissue research projects, while abortion opponents can be counted on to oppose such funding.

MEDICAL DATA

Fetal tissue research uses tissue from dead fetuses obtained through spontaneous or induced abortions. Ideally, these fetuses should be late first trimester or early second trimester and should have suffered as little trauma as possible during the abortion process. Fetal tissue research is undertaken in order to develop vaccines, make advances in prenatal diagnosis, make pharmacological assessments, and develop in utero surgical therapies. Therefore, fetal tissue research benefits vaccine development, helps evaluate risk factors and toxicity levels of drugs, allows development of cell lines, and provides a source of fetal cells for transplantation as an alternative to whole organ transplantation.[3]

According to Fred Rosner, MD, and the co-authors of an article about possible transplant uses of fetal tissue,

> Fetal tissue transplantation has been attempted for a number of disorders including **Parkinson's disease, Alzheimer's disease, Huntington's chorea, diabetes mellitus**; immunodeficiency disorders, such as **Di George syndrome, aplastic anemia** and leukemia; and severe meta-

bolic disorders such as **Hurler's syndrome**. Fetal cells are unlike other tissue in that they engraft easily without producing **graft-versus-host disease**. Fetal cells are able to grow, proliferate and differentiate, and they produce growth factors.[4]

At the present time fetal tissue transplants are at a very early stage of development. Some see these transplants as holding therapeutic promise; others, based on the limited amount of information currently available, are unwilling to endorse them. In a 1992 article the progress of a 64-year-old woman who suffered from Parkinson's disease was discussed. Before her operation in which, using a slender tube, pieces of fetal brains suspended in a liquid solution were implanted in the damaged areas of her brain, she could not take more than a few small steps without falling. Following the operation she could walk "almost normally."[5] Researchers who are involved in fetal transplants for therapeutic purposes caution that, to date, patients who have benefitted from transplants are by no means cured but, rather, the course of their degenerative diseases is not so steadily downhill.[6] Fetal brain tissue transplants, if successful, attach themselves to a recipient's brain, grow and flourish, while resulting in a significant alleviation of symptoms.

The short history of fetal tissue transplantation has been afflicted with false claims and false hopes. Nevertheless, in recent years documented reports of successful procedures have reinforced the belief that these transplants can work. Among these reports are accounts from Sweden,[7] Mexico,[8] Canada,[9] and the United States.[10] While the total number of those throughout the world who have received fetal tissue transplants is approximately one hundred[11] and the status of the transplants themselves remains in the category of therapeutic experimentation, only the future will tell whether or not the procedures which evolve will be essentially therapeutic.

As we shall see, one of the thorniest ethical issues associated with fetal tissue transplants concerns the use of tissue from aborted fetuses. A way around procuring tissue from aborted fetuses would entail using tissue from spontaneously aborted (or miscarried) fetuses or from ectopic pregnancies. There is virtually no ethical reservation in regard to such usage.

Unfortunately, researchers who studied the suitability of fetal tissue from spontaneous abortions and from ectopic pregnancies for transplantation found that this tissue was unsuitable. Their study involved 22,235 obstetric admissions in 1993, 1,250 spontaneously aborted embryos, and 247 products of ectopic pregnancies. Of these, only seven (0.5%) were potentially useful for human transplantation therapy. The reasons the tissue was unsuitable were because of degeneration, bacterial contamination, chromosomal abnormalities, and/or infection with viruses. As a result, researchers concluded that fetal tissues from spontaneous abortions and from ectopic pregnancies are quite limited as feasible sources for human transplantation therapy.[12] They think that tissue resulting from induced abortions would be more likely to provide the material needed for transplant therapy because it would be less likely to be contaminated.

OPINION SUPPORTIVE OF USE OF FETAL TISSUE ON MEDICAL GROUNDS

Before we consider ethical thinking about using fetal tissue, it should be understood that within medical science there is division of opinion in regard to whether or not contemplated procedures would actually work. The scientific case which is made to justify use of fetal tissue consists in two primary arguments. The first is that sufficient success has been achieved in nonhuman species and in limited trials involving human subjects to warrant more widespread use in humans.

The second argument focuses on rationale supportive of recourse to experimental therapies and goes like this: In view of an adult patient's ability to give informed consent along with the severe deterioration associated with such brain disorders as Parkinson's disease, experimental surgical procedures are justified because their goal is to obtain a cure or amelioration of symptoms for an incurable progressive illness. Since continued deterioration and death are the prognosis for conditions such as Parkinson's, there is no question that there is a proportionate reason to attempt a cure through a therapeutic experimental procedure which carries a risk.

OPINION OPPOSED TO USE OF FETAL TISSUE ON MEDICAL GROUNDS

Since the amount of data related to fetal tissue research and clinical usage is relatively small, and since there is more than one possible way to understand what the medical data convey, arguments against the use of fetal tissue are also made based on medical considerations. The essence of these arguments is contained in the five statements which follow.

1. There have not yet been sufficient studies of fetal tissue implants in animals to begin human fetal implants at this time.
2. More needs to be known about the possible harm which might attend unchecked and continued growth of fetal tissue in an adult brain, causing tumors or hydrocephalus, and an estimate of the risks should be formulated.
3. Data available from fetal transplants to humans performed in Mexico, Sweden, Canada and the United States are insufficient to justify carrying out the procedure at this time.

4. Pharmacological treatment of degenerative brain disease holds at least as much promise as surgery with fetal tissue transplant; this approach ought to be preferred.

5. A carefully restricted diet along with medication holds at least as much promise for patients with degenerative brain diseases as do fetal tissue implants.[13]

In view of the fact that two different sets of arguments, one set supportive of fetal tissue use and one set opposed to it, are made by medically informed sources and rest on medical grounds, it becomes apparent that lay people will have to deal with uncertainty at the medical level before they progress to the ethical phase of analysis. In a sense lay people will be forced to determine which professional opinion to accept, a difficult decision to make. Their alternative would be to become sufficiently expert themselves so as to be able to formulate their own educated opinion, or to trust a prerational force, such as their bias for or against experimental medicine.

ETHICAL ARGUMENTS CONCERNING THE USE OF FETAL TISSUE FROM ABORTED FETUSES IN RESEARCH AND IN HUMAN THERAPEUTIC EXPERIMENTATION

At the outset it is important to be aware that those favoring use of fetal tissue in research and transplants think that there is no objection, on ethical grounds, for the use of tissue from spontaneously aborted, or miscarried, fetuses. This is because the parents of the fetus, or its mother, are understood to have similar jurisdiction over it as over a deceased child, in terms of being entitled to authorize the harvesting of the child's organs for transplant. Ethical objections are raised only in relation to fetal tissue procured from abortuses which result from elective procedures. The reasons for this will become clear as the various arguments are examined.

MAKING A CASE IN FAVOR OF USING FETAL TISSUE FROM ABORTED FETUSES

There are ethical commentators who argue that no restrictions should be placed on research or clinical uses of fetal tissue and that there are no reasons to hold ethical reservations in this regard. As long as certain safeguards are in place, this rationale contends, research into fetal tissue use and clinical applications of research findings can bring only benefit. This conclusion stems from several interconnected arguments.

A fundamental contention is that since abortion is morally and legally acceptable, use of tissue from abortuses is also acceptable, provided the mother does not object. This argument presupposes that the woman terminating her pregnancy has jurisdiction over the fetus and the correlative right to determine whether or not to donate its tissue, comparable to the right of parents in regard to deceased children.

The first and most basic moral responsibility acknowledged by health care practitioners is to do no harm. Defenders of fetal tissue use refer to this stipulation to justify what they recommend. They reason that since the abortus is dead, it cannot be harmed by removal of organs or tissues. Since the fetus is beyond harm, there is no reason not to use it to serve worthy ends.

Medical science has advanced through research and experimentation and one significant twentieth-century achievement was largely due to research using fetal tissue. The polio vaccine was developed by scientists in laboratories who worked with fetal tissue. Scientific advancement in curing degenerative brain disease and other breakthroughs may well be accomplished through fetal tissue transplants. Therefore, research and experimentation in this area should move forward.

What happens to the remains of the almost 1.5 million fetuses which are aborted each year in the United States? Cremation and other methods of disposal are used, wasting an incalculably precious resource. Instead of allowing this waste, it would give more dignity and respect to these fetuses to serve science and sick people rather than merely to undergo destruction.

Some people worry that women will more readily have abortions because they will soothe their consciences with the idea that some good can come from the procedure. There is no sound reason for thinking that women would undergo abortions in order to donate tissue or that this option would propel them in that direction. The reasons women procure abortions have to do with the burdens of pregnancy, not considerations about how their fetuses could benefit humanity. Nevertheless, this concern can be addressed by asking for a woman's consent to allow for research or transplant use of her fetus only after she has completed informed consent forms for the termination of pregnancy. As long as the decision to abort and the decision to donate fetal tissue are made separately, there is no reason to think that the possible good to be gained from use of fetal tissue will result in an increased incidence of abortion. Most people agree that under no circumstances should a woman who releases her fetus for tissue harvesting be allowed to designate the recipient of the tissue.

Distressing aspects of organ retrieval revolve around payments being made to donors or medical personnel to obtain organs, as well as transplant personnel using coercive tactics to get physicians who are caring for dying people to speed up the process so as to free up organs sooner. Aware of these abuses, those who argue for procurement of fetal tissue contend that similar forms of misconduct can be avoided by instituting rudimentary safeguards.

Accordingly, as long as there are no financial incentives and no overlapping of abortion and transplant personnel, this argument goes, the procurement of fetal tissue will proceed without conflict of interest.

MAKING A CASE AGAINST USING TISSUE FROM ABORTED FETUSES

There are ethical commentators who argue *against* procurement and use of fetal tissue from elective abortions based on several reasons. The people who adhere to this position advocate an absolute prohibition against procurement and usage, and their opposition does not decrease when guarantees of safeguards or other factors are proposed.

The principal reason for opposing the use of tissue from elective abortions is that abortion constitutes an attack against the dignity of human life. To use the abortus for research would only compound the insult. Just as a human person is an end and should not be used as a means to some end, by extension, the fetus, because a member of the human family, should not be used to achieve a goal. Instead, it should be disposed of in as dignified a manner as possible.

A second reason to oppose the use of fetal tissue is because women are frequently ambivalent about obtaining abortions. Thinking that some good might come from the abortion because of the donation of fetal tissue might provide the incentive to elect that option. Since abortion is an undesirable option, society should unambiguously disassociate itself from enabling rationalizations which could result in more abortions.

When parents consent to donate tissue from their deceased children, their authority to do so comes from their relationship to the child and the legal jurisdiction they have in the deceased child's regard. The decision to donate organs is bittersweet in that their grief is tempered by knowing that their child gives the gift of life to an individual in critical need. Abortion entails a different scenario because there is no one who is in a position to consent to tissue donation. By deciding to end the fetus's life its mother relinquishes her role as parent. If she had wanted to exercise that right, she would have allowed her child to continue to grow in her body until the child was ready to be born.

Abortion does not occur in a vacuum. In the United States the acceptability of abortion is conveyed by a culture which promotes it as a reasonable response to an unwanted pregnancy. Society would add to the immoral climate by endorsing use of tax money for fetal tissue research or experimental procedures involving humans. Society should not become more complicit in the evil of abortion by adding an incentive to undergo the procedure.

A final argument is that since the availability of fetal tissue resulted from an evil deed its being used for a good purpose cannot be justified. Human decency requires that the response to the feticide of abortion be contrition and sorrow, not a crass indifference which seeks to profit from the deed.

REACHING A DECISION ABOUT THE USE OF FETAL TISSUE

The use of fetal tissue is a perplexing question in its own right, but within the field of health care ethics it is also of significant methodological interest. This is because the decision-making process is so complicated and demanding. Individuals need to reach a decision about medical procedures which are recent in origin and which offer limited data. In addition, they have to make these decisions within a context of contradictory medical opinions as well as contradictory ethical opinions. Decisions need to be made by people in very different positions: Physicians or medical researchers considering whether or not to become involved; pregnant women; people suffering from diseases who conceivably could benefit; and relatives or friends who advise any of those who might be directly involved. In addition, burdened with the same limitations is each and every adult who exercises the role of citizen. Citizens must confront the global issue: To support research and experimental use of fetal tissue or to oppose these undertakings.

Regardless of how one approaches this issue, in order to make a serious, informed decision a person needs to evaluate the knowledge, competence and possible biases of the various authorities who present medical data and determine which ones are correct. This will be a daunting challenge for a lay person, and it is altogether possible that her or his judgment will be flawed. Nevertheless, it is the first step in the process.

The second phase of decision making entails consideration of the ethical argumentation put forward by those who favor as well as those who oppose use of fetal tissue. In this regard, the first thing to be determined is whether the fact that fetal tissue would come from elective abortions requires that a person's moral analysis of fetal tissue use be the same as her moral analysis of abortion. In other words, are we looking at one question, the morality of abortion, with two parts or two distinct questions, the morality of abortion and the morality of using fetal tissue, which may be answered as interconnected or as separate and distinct.

The second issue to be decided demands that one take a long, hard look at the fetus. What is the fetus? What is it entitled to in terms of respect? These are not facetious questions; they are difficult and troubling. They are also new. A generation ago people were not challenged to ponder them because the technology for fetal tissue transfer was unavailable. The technology of which we can avail ourselves today is not value-free; evaluating it requires that we ask ourselves demanding questions and exercise our integrity by acting in an ethically responsible fashion.

Finally, a person deciding about the morality of fetal-tissue use would need to name and flesh out her methodological approach to ethics. If she is a utilitarian then, in all probability, she will be in favor of research, use, and tax funding. Utilitarians seek to bring about the greatest good for the greatest number and generally are not troubled by limits on conduct derived from binding moral standards. On the other hand, if a natural law proponent were considering this issue, she would probably oppose fetal-tissue use based on the principles that it offends against the dignity of human life, and its acceptability could lead to a further erosion of society's ethical standards. Should a person be deciding from an intuitionist perspective, she would be inclined to follow her instincts about this procedure. A hedonist would reflect on what kind of pleasure was being sought and how endorsing or restricting fetal tissue use would likely contribute to or inhibit the pursuit of pleasure. Subjectivists would go with their feelings and authoritarians would be inclined to follow the directives of political, judicial, or religious leaders.

CONCLUSION

Research and experimental therapeutic use of fetal tissue presents us with a complex series of interrelated medical and ethical issues. Even though complexity is baffling, attempts to work our way through the maze can cause us to grow in knowledge, insight, and humanity. Let us hope that for individuals as well as for society these are the results of grappling with the fetal tissue question. They are much to be preferred to the divisiveness and ill will which have resulted from confronting some other issues.

ENDNOTES

[1] D. Ware Branch, MD, et al., "Suitability of Fetal Tissues From Spontaneous Abortions and From Ectopic Pregnancies for Transplantation," *Journal of the American Medical Association*, January 4, 1995, 273:1, p. 66.

[2] Gina Kolata, "Evidence Is Found that Fetal Tissue Transplants Can Ease a Brain Disease," *The New York Times*, May 7, 1992, p. B11.

[3] Fred Rosner, MD, et al., "Fetal tissue research and transplantation," *New York State Journal of Medicine*, 93:3, March, 1993, p. 174.

[4] Ibid.

[5] Op. cit., Kolata.

[6] Ibid.

[7] Backlund, E.O., Granberg, P.O., Hamberger, B., et al., "Transplantation of adrenal medullary tissue to striatum in Parkinsonism: First clinical trials," *J. Neurosurg*, 1985: V. 62, pp. 169–173.

[8] Ignacio Madrazo, et al., "Transplantation of Fetal Substantia Nigra and Adrenal Medulla to the Caudate Nucleus in Two Patients with Parkinson's Disease," *New England Journal of Medicine*, January 7, 1988, V. 318, p. 51.

[9] Deborah Jones, "Halifax hospital first in Canada to proceed with controversial fetal tissue transplant," *Journal of the Canadian Medical Association*, February 1, 1992, pp. 389–391.

[10] Gina Kolata, "Fetal Tissue Seems to Aid Parkinson Patient," *The New York Times*, February 2, 1990, p. A31; and op. cit., Kolata, "Evidence."

[11] Aimee B. Schimmel, "A Controversial Catalyst," *Paraplegic News*, Nov., 1994, V. 48, p. 41.

[12] Op. cit., Branch, p. 66.

[13] Cf, Proceedings of the 58th Meeting of the Advisory Committee to the Director, NIH on Human Fetal Tissue Transplantation Research, December 14-15, 1988, NIH, Bethesda, Maryland, and Concurring Statements and Statement of Dissent, John R. Sladek, Jr., and Ira Shoulson, "Neural Transplantation: A Call for Patience Rather Than Patients," *Science*, 240:1386–1388, and Alan Fine, "Transplantation in the Central Nervous System," *Scientific American*, 52–58, August, 1986.

DISCUSSION QUESTIONS

1. Is an elective abortion of ethical relevance to the decision to use human fetal tissue for research and experimentation? Why or why not?

2. In your opinion, should research and experimentation using fetal tissue be allowed? Why or why not?

3. Would the use of the fetal tissue in research encourage women to have abortions that they might otherwise not undergo? If so, are there ways to minimize such encouragement?

4. Does the very process of obtaining informed consent from the pregnant woman constitute a prohibited "inducement" to terminate the pregnancy for the purpose of the research, thus precluding research of this sort? If so, is there any way to get around this problem?

5. If transplantation using fetal tissue from induced abortions becomes common, what impact is it likely to have on activities and procedures employed by abortion clinics? In particular, is the optimal or safest way to perform an abortion likely to be in conflict with preservation of the fetal tissue? Is there any way to ensure that induced abortions are not intentionally delayed in order to have a late first or an early second trimester fetus for research or transplantation?

6. How would utilitarians answer the fetal tissue question? How would proponents of principled thinking or natural law respond? Which of these two methodologies appeals to you as providing the better guidance for making a decision about use of fetal tissue? Why?

CASE STUDY

Bill Townsend is president of a privately funded medical facility established as a regional center to carry out fetal tissue transplants. Mr. Townsend's business is in its start-up phase, and one of the first things he needs to take care of is procuring an adequate supply of fetal tissue. To this end he schedules an appointment to meet with the staff of the largest abortion clinic in the area.

During his presentation Mr. Townsend explains that his program requires fetal brain tissue from fetuses which are 10- to 14-weeks old. A minimum of 200 fetuses would be needed each week with a Tuesday-Thursday pickup schedule being optimal. Should the clinic be able to accommodate Mr. Townsend's project, he promises several inducements. These include free tickets to cultural and sporting events, gifts at holiday time, and several getaway weekends each year. Mr. Townsend explains that it could be ethically and legally problematic for his company to give cash awards, but that there would be no trouble about other kinds of gifts.

After Mr. Townsend completes his presentation, he leaves, and the clinic staff remains at the table to discuss how to respond to his offer.

Evaluation:

1. Identify ethical issues contained in this case.
2. Propose possible solutions for these issues.
3. Make a decision relevant to action to be taken or not taken and provide rationale supportive of this decision.
4. Are you satisfied with your decision? Why or why not?

GLOSSARY

Ectopic pregnancies are established in a fallopian tube instead of in the uterus. Since the fallopian tube does not expand as a fetus grows, it will eventually rupture causing severe trauma. Consequently, ectopic pregnancies are dealt with by one of two surgical procedures: The fetus is removed and the fallopian tube is left, or the tube and the fetus are removed.

Parkinson's disease is a slowly progressive, degenerative, neurologic disorder characterized by tremors, rolling of the fingers, shuffling gait, forward flexing of the trunk, loss of postural reflexes, muscle rigidity, and weakness. Parkinson's disease is incurable. Treatment with dopamine replacement may result in amelioration of symptoms.

Alzheimer's disease is a form of dementia characterized by confusion, memory failure, disorientation, restlessness, speech disturbances, and inability to carry out purposeful movements. This disease usually occurs after age 60; it is progressive and irreversible.

Huntington's chorea is a rare, abnormal hereditary condition characterized by chronic, progressive chorea and mental deterioration that terminates in dementia. Huntington's chorea generally appears when people are in their forties, and they usually die within 15 years. (Chorea is a muscle disorder characterized by involuntary twitching.)

Diabetes mellitus is a complex disorder of carbohydrate, fat, and protein metabolism that is primarily a result of a lack of insulin secretion by the pancreas.

Di George syndrome is a congenital disorder characterized by severe immunodeficiency and structural abnormalities, including hypertelorism, notched, low-set ears, small mouth, downward slanting eyes, cardiovascular defects, and the absence of the thymus and parathyroid glands. Children born with Di George's syndrome rarely live beyond two years.

Aplastic anemia is a deficiency of all the formed elements of the blood, representing a failure of the cell-generating capacity of bone marrow.

Hurler's syndrome is a type of mucopolysaccharidosis, transmitted in an autosomal-recessive trait, that results in severe mental retardation. Characteristic signs are enlargement of the liver and spleen, often with accompanying cardiovascular involvement. Children born with this syndrome usually die during childhood from cardiac complications or pulmonary disorders.

Graft-versus-host disease is a term used to refer to a negative reaction to a tissue transplant, which results in a rejection of the cells or bone marrow which have been transplanted.

CHAPTER 7

Artificially Provided Nutrition and Hydration

INTRODUCTION

Technology has enhanced the practice of medicine while also complicating it. Sophisticated X-rays have made possible an incredible number of diagnoses, thus proving to be a positive improvement in the state of the art. Feeding tubes, on the other hand, have turned out to be a mixed blessing; at times clearly beneficial, but, at other times, the reason for conflicts and conundrums.

Artificial feeding became a routine part of health care during a short interval of time. In the 1960s the possibility of being sustained for a long time by tube feeding was virtually unknown. By the mid 1970s this possibility had become a reality which was available to patients in hospitals all over the United States. As it happened, tube feeding was implemented on a widespread basis without preliminary discussion of extremely relevant questions. Such questions as "Under what circumstances is artificial feeding appropriate?" and "Are there classes of patients for whom artificial treatment should not be implemented?" were neither posed nor resolved before the routinization of tube feeding. As a result, a lot of discussion had to occur after the fact, making for an untidy situation and, not surprisingly, leading to considerable controversy.

DEVELOPMENT AND TYPES OF ARTIFICIAL FEEDING

Feeding tubes provide sustenance to people who are unable or unwilling to eat or drink. Medical techniques for artificial feeding are of two kinds, enteral and parenteral. Enteral feedings bring nutrition to the **gastrointesti-**

nal tract. Tubes which enter the body at the nose are called nasogastric or NG tubes. Two kinds of enteral tubes are surgically emplaced: Gastrostomy or G tubes bring nutrition to the stomach, and jejunostomy or J tubes bring nutrition directly into the jejunum, the second loop of the small intestine.

It is also possible to bypass the gastrointestinal system and deliver nutrition into the bloodstream. This method of feeding is called parenteral nutrition and it can happen in two ways. With peripheral parenteral nutrition, more commonly known as intravenous feeding, liquid nutrition enters the body via small veins in a person's limbs. Total parenteral nutrition (TPN; also known as hyperalimentation or central hyperalimentation) delivers nutrition directly into the superior vena cava, a one-inch vein that returns blood to the heart from the upper part of the body.

Three technological advances led to the widespread availability of enteral feedings in the health care setting: The development of powdered formulas which could be reconstituted by adding water; improvements in the manufacture of plastics so that lightweight, soft, flexible materials could be crafted into feeding tubes; and the perfecting of pumps so that these instruments could be adjusted for proper rates of infusion.

Total parenteral nutrition dates from 1968. An American physician, Dr. Stanley Dudrick, adapted a technique developed by the French surgeon Aubaniac and accomplished the feat of providing nourishment to patients who had nonfunctioning gastrointestinal tracts. In the early 1950s Aubaniac introduced subclavian venipuncture (a surgical incision into a large vein located under the collarbone) as a means of rapidly administering blood to soldiers wounded on the field of battle. Dr. Dudrick benefitted from the engineering model implemented by Aubaniac. At first he worked in a laboratory to design and synchronize the components for TPN; then he tested total parenteral nutrition on animals. By 1968 Dudrick's system was ready for human use. Its parts—a needle for inserting a catheter, the catheter, a filter, IV tubing, a plastic sac-like bag containing the feeding, a pump to regulate the rate of infusion, powdered formulas, and a method for their sterile preparation—had been designed and perfected. Although the individual components have undergone changes through the years, the basic TPN system designed by Dudrick remains essentially the same.[1]

People are tube fed for a variety of reasons. Sometimes tube feeding is employed on a temporary basis because an illness or the need to recover from surgery preclude the possibility of eating and drinking by mouth. At other times very frail people who are not able to consume sufficient nutrients in the ordinary manner receive tube feeding as a temporary or permanent supplement to their diets. At still other times people who suffer from brain injuries such as stroke or coma and who lose their abilities to masticate and/or swallow require tube feeding to stay alive.

After adequate training, insertion of nasogastric tubes can be carried out by a patient herself or by a lay person who assists the patient. Intravenous tubes can be set up by either nurses or physicians. All other forms of feeding tubes require a surgical procedure for their emplacement; thus, only trained physicians can initiate such types of feeding as gastrostomy, jejunostomy, and TPN.

In the late 1960s and early 1970s, the early days of feeding tubes, tube feeding was seen principally in the hospital setting. Since feeding tubes have become commonplace, however, people are tube fed at home and in nursing and convalescent homes as well as in hospitals.

ISSUES RAISED BY ARTIFICIAL FEEDING

The most fundamental issue raised by feeding tubes is to decide what they are: A medical treatment or a form of **comfort care**, similar to being fed by someone else. In the stating of these two possible answers one of the conundrums of artificial feeding reveals itself. Feeding tubes are not a medical treatment because they are not capable of curing any illness. By the same token, feeding tubes are not equivalent to eating or drinking by mouth, even with assistance, because the mouth and throat do not participate in the process; the person being fed is entirely passive and often unaware of what is happening, no eating or drinking utensils are used; and the color, taste, aroma, texture, and social interaction which we identify with eating food at a meal are absent. So, if feeding tubes are equivalent to neither a medical treatment nor the ordinary activity of eating, how can we decide what medical, moral, and social criteria to use in evaluating them? This is a crucial question because we apply different criteria to use and nonuse of medical treatments than we do in respect to eating or refusal to eat. Generally speaking, we approve decisions to reject medical treatments if these treatments are deemed too burdensome or futile in nature. On the other hand, we expect people to nourish themselves by eating and we consider ourselves required to intervene before a hunger striker or anorexic dies from the effects of noneating.

Since feeding tubes are neither a medical treatment nor equivalent to eating and drinking by mouth, and since we need to put them into a category before we can undertake their moral evaluation, it seems reasonable that we decide whether feeding tubes are closer to a medical technology or to the activity of eating. In my opinion, feeding tubes, even though they cure no pathology, are so closely connected to medicine that they belong under the umbrella of medical technology and ought to be evaluated using the same type of criteria as such clearly medical treatments as respirators and dialysis machines. I have four reasons for situating feeding tubes under the umbrella of medical technology:

First, inserting feeding tubes requires skilled medical training or a surgeon's medical license;

Second, designing a feeding formula requires the collaboration of trained professionals: Dieticians, pharmacists, and physicians;

Third, the experience of being tube fed is completely passive and may even be involuntary, without enjoyment of the nourishment or the sensations accompanying feeding oneself a meal;

Fourth, serious medical problems can ensue if feeding tubes are improperly emplaced or if they become displaced, and irritation or abscesses can appear at the sites where tubes enter the body, adding to patient discomfort and necessitating additional treatment.

If feeding tubes are understood as a medical treatment, then a moral, social, or psychological obligation to almost always employ them will not be experienced, allowing for instances of noninitiation or withdrawal under some circumstances. If, on the other hand, feeding tubes were considered equivalent to eating, people would find themselves urging, coaxing, and forcing their use, just as they do with family members, be they infants, the frail elderly, or the ill, who seem not to want to eat.

As mentioned above, feeding tubes came into frequent usage in hospitals over a relatively short period of time and without much discussion as to when they might or might not be appropriate. In recent years, a consensus has begun to emerge in regard to the situations under which feeding tubes should not or should be used. In respect to patients who are actually in the process of dying, or those for whom death is imminent (within a matter of weeks or days), or those who cannot absorb the liquid nutrients delivered by artificial feeding, there is widespread agreement that feeding tubes should not be used.[2] In addition, the wishes of competent patients who state that they do not want to be tube fed as well as clear instructions not to tube feed written in an advance directive or stated by a duly appointed health care proxy are routinely honored.

In regard to when to start tube feeding, there is general agreement that feeding tubes are medically appropriate when their use is envisioned as a temporary measure to provide nourishment for patients who are recuperating from surgery or from an illness which prevents them from eating. Once they heal from surgery or recover from their sickness, they will be able to take nourishment again in the normal fashion.

Many medical conditions are somewhat ambiguous, however, in that the outcome cannot confidently be predicted in advance. The situation of a frail patient who develops stomach ulcers and who cannot eat until her ulcers heal comes to mind. The best medical advice to the patient is that she agree to be fed by means of a J tube (into her intestine) in order to buy time to give medication and her own healing powers an opportunity to clear up the ulcers. This case is a simple one if the treatment works—the ulcers heal and the feeding tube is removed. It becomes much more complex if the ulcers do not improve, if the patient develops other maladies, becomes semicomatose, declines, becoming much more frail, and her prognosis becomes bleak. Under these circumstances, should tube feeding be continued? Now the questioner must face a well-established fact in connection with tube feeding: Physicians, nurses, and family members tend to have significant psychological problems with stopping tube feeding when they know that the death of the patient will inevitably result. Since those responsible for the patient's care cannot in good conscience directly cause her death, it is crucial that they come to terms with an accurate account of how discontinuance of tube feeding would impact on her death. The rationale suggested in defense of stopping artificial feeding proposes that the sick, frail, failing patient dies as a result of the combination of her maladies, that nature has been allowed to take its course.

Yes, **malnutrition** and **dehydration** resulting from the nonreception of nutrition and hydration contribute to the patient's death, but do not *cause* it. Death results from the myriad of factors which caused the ulcers and the subsequent further deterioration. If it is difficult to accept the fact that malnutrition and dehydration contributed to this death, it would be well to remember that up until the availability of feeding tubes, malnutrition and dehydration contributed to each and every death which came at the conclusion of an extended period of dying, culminating in a comatose or semi-comatose condition. By establishing the distinction that those who authorized the removal of artificial feeding and those who carried out the order did not *cause* the patient's death, but rather, her underlying pathologies did, we make it possible to free ourselves to use feeding tubes on a trial basis. If we cannot justify using artificial feeding on a trial basis, we will be forced to accept an untenable position requiring that feeding tubes not be discontinued once their use is begun. Under this mandate, a practice would likely arise of not beginning what might be a successful trial for fear of being required to stick with the therapy even after its futility becomes apparent.

A second distinction also serves to bolster the thinking that tube feeding which does not accomplish its objective need not be continued. This distinction focuses on the fact that there is no medical or moral obligation to initiate a useless or burdensome treatment and, therefore, neither is there an obligation to continue a treatment which has become useless or burdensome. This distinction assumes that noninitiation of artificial feeding and discontinuance of artificial feeding are closely related, so that the same medical and ethical justifications which can be used for one can be used for the other. While the psychological stress attendant to discontinuance of artificial feeding may be much more difficult for the caregivers to deal with than a decision not to start tube feeding, understanding the rationale just presented should enable health care practitioners and surrogates to reach termination of treatment decisions in good conscience.

There is a great deal of concern in contemporary health care ethics about physician-assisted suicide. In connection with tube feeding, therefore, the question naturally arises as to whether a physician who fails to provide artificial feeding is assisting in the suicide of her patient. The answer is *no*, provided that the patient has conditions or ailments which are capable of causing his death. In such a situation, the deprivation of artificial feeding would contribute to the patient's death, not cause it. If a physician refuses to provide temporary tube feeding to a patient for whom it is medically indicated (such as a person with injuries to the mouth and jaw which would, in all probability, heal in time), and the patient dies from malnutrition and dehydration, with no other significant contributory cause, then the physician would be guilty of gross negligence. This negligence would be based on two factors: The physician's not informing the patient of the necessity of artificial feeding and the physician's failure to follow through to see to the emplacement of the feeding tube.

In the situation, however, in which a patient would clearly benefit from tube feeding and in which the physician advocates this treatment but the patient knowingly refuses to submit to it, the physician would bear no fault. Rather, the patient would bear the responsibility for unreasonable conduct, which could be considered suicide, but the responsibility would clearly be the patient's, not the physician's. (Actually, in a case like this, the physician would likely request the assistance of the hospital ethics committee and hospital administration. The end result might be a court order requiring emplacement of a feeding tube based on the rationale that a psychological factor is preventing the patient from making a competent, informed decision.)

One universal fact which every person needs to acknowledge is that each of us will surely die. If we live a long time, our internal organs will inevitably undergo the wear and tear that come from the stresses of a lifetime, and we will die of the accumulated effects of this stress or some other more obvious cause. If we do not enjoy the good fortune of a long life, and we die of natural causes, it will be because of the breakdown of an organ or organs or because of the ravages of a disease. In either context, that of terminal illness or frailty, the issue of artificial feeding is raised and we may be called upon to decide those circumstances under which it is advisable or inadvisable.

In regard to terminally ill patients, those who are at the end stage of a disease such as cancer, AIDS, **ALS (Amyotrophic Lateral Sclerosis** or Lou Gehrig's disease), **emphysema, Multiple Sclerosis** or some other affliction, it is ethically appropriate to respect their wishes if they say that they do not want to be tube fed or if they request discontinuance. It is likewise appropriate to provide artificial feeding if they express a desire for it. If terminally ill patients lose the ability to communicate and physicians are negotiating with surrogates in regard to their treatment, requests to provide tube feeding should be honored if there is reason to believe the feeding will add to the patient's comfort.

For many terminally ill patients feeding tubes present medical and ethical problems. The situation already alluded to, in which the tendency is to continue tube feeding on the grounds that it is already in place, occurs frequently. Another situation which can be encountered entails very weak, terminally ill patients who stop eating. Still other situations involve terminally ill patients who seem to be candidates for tube feeding on the ground that it is so routine and so ubiquitous that it must be called for here. A backlash is beginning to develop against what many people are coming to see as artificial feeding which merely prolongs dying or adds to a patient's discomfort. The evolving thinking tends to argue against tube feeding that does not bring benefit to a patient and, instead, adds to the burdens of the dying process.

In society in the United States a great deal of attention is focused on complying with a patient's wishes or deciding which medical treatments to provide, based solely on the patient's condition. There is no question that the patient's needs are the most important aspect of concern in the patient-family-physician nexus. However, by introducing family members and health care providers into the picture, we are establishing the fact that the way the patient is treated has implications for others. A terrible toll can be endured by loved ones of a patient whose dying is prolonged because of artificial feeding. Doctors and nurses can suffer, too, because the provision of futile treatments can be so at variance with the philosophy they have embraced, to bring healing to the ill and comfort to those who are beyond cure. Members of society also have a stake in the artificial feeding of terminally ill people, because the provision of nourishment by tube and the other medical services which the terminally ill continue to procure add to the overall cost of health care in this country. It is not clear how to resolve the situation so that the interests of family members, health care practitioners and society-at-large are taken into account in decisions related to the artificial feeding of terminally ill patients, but it is obviously an issue with which we need to come to grips.

Perhaps the most perplexing questions about tube feeding have been raised in regard to non-terminally-ill patients for whom noninitiation or discontinuance of tube feeding would result in death. These patients could be comatose persons, either permanently vegetative or with an unknown prognosis; or they could be people with **Alzheimer's disease** or some other form of **degenerative dementia**. If patients in any of these situations have clearly written advance directives which contain stipulations about tube feeding, or if they have properly appointed surrogates, then there is no question about what to do. The directions given in the instruction directive or by the proxy are to be followed.

The situation may become very complicated if there are no written directions and no one has been appointed to serve as surrogate. Such were the circumstances surrounding several highly publicized court cases in the 1980s.

Paul E. Brophy, a Massachusetts firefighter who suffered a **subarachnoid hemorrhage** as a result of a **ruptured aneurysm** wound up in a **persistent vegetative state (PVS)** with his wife, Patricia Brophy, arguing for the cessation of his gastrostomy feeding, and Mr. Brophy's physicians opposing her.[3]

Claire C. Conroy, an elderly, frail, senile nursing home patient was fed by a nasogastric tube which her nephew, Thomas Whittemore, wanted removed so that she could die in peace, but her physician refused to comply with Mr. Whittemore's directions.[4]

Mary O'Connor, an elderly nursing home patient who was disabled as a result of several strokes, was kept alive by a nasogastric tube which her daughters wanted removed, but her physicians refused to comply.[5]

Nancy Cruzan, a woman in her early twenties was in a persistent vegetative state as a result of a protracted lack of oxygen following an automobile accident. Nancy's parents asked her physicians to remove her gastrostomy tube so that she could die, but the physicians refused to comply with this request.[6]

In each of these cases arguments were heard by more than one state court and, in the Cruzan case, the United States Supreme Court[7] itself rendered a decision. Deliberations held in connection with these cases yielded the very complex sticking point around which the controversy revolves. This sticking point was the so-called "nonterminal" condition of the patient who, if frail and elderly, could conceivably be sustained by tube feeding for a matter of months to a few years, or if young and otherwise healthy, as was the case with Nancy Cruzan, could probably continue to live for 30 or 40 years, or more. Conservative judges made the point that the State has no authority to authorize termination of life-sustaining treatment on the grounds that an individual's quality of life is unacceptably low. On the contrary, these judges argued that senile or comatose persons whose lives were sustained by means of artificial feeding were entitled to be protected by the State because of their vulnerability. Among people who think along these lines some hold that tube feeding is equivalent or close to equivalent to eating and drinking by mouth, and thus must be provided as long as it can be absorbed.

The rejoinder to this type of judicial thinking came from those who argued that when a sufficient part of the brain is destroyed or rendered useless to perform its customary functions, a major organ of the human body has been severely impaired, and persons so afflicted should be considered

terminally ill. Since tube feeding cannot bring about a cure or an amelioration of symptoms, in medical parlance, it is a useless or futile treatment and
need not be continued.

Given the movement for advance directives and an increased awareness
about the limitations of tube feeding, it may happen that situations like those
experienced by Paul Brophy's wife, Claire Conroy's nephew, Mary O'Connor's daughters, and Nancy Cruzan's parents will not be replicated. However, if similar situations do occur, in the absence of clear advance directives,
conflicts may occur because of the lack of unanimity of opinion about the
nature of artificial feeding, as well as how to describe the condition of a person suffering from PVS or an irreversible brain disease.

If a patient's preferences are not known and the patient has not given a
relative or friend Durable Power of Attorney for Health Care, there are circumstances under which physicians, after conferring with family members, will be likely to agree not to initiate or to discontinue artificial
feeding. One circumstance is if it can be demonstrated that tube feeding
would not be in the best interests of the patient. The best interests standard
requires that it be shown that any proposed medical treatment or intervention be rejected on the grounds that it would most probably be excessively burdensome to the patient because futile in nature, cause suffering,
or contribute nothing to the relief of suffering. Thus, the patient's best
interests would be ill-served by the treatment. The second circumstance
under which physicians might agree about not starting or stopping tube
feeding entails their having respect for the substitute judgment of a close
relative or friend. Substitute judgment refers to what the patient would
likely choose if he could speak for himself. It should be noted that, in the
four court cases mentioned above, relatives contended that what they
requested was what the patients would have requested had they been able
to speak for themselves but, in each case, serious reservations were voiced
by some judicial authorities in regard to carrying out the substance of the
specific substitute judgment. It should also be noted that if all the members
of a patient's family do not concur in what would represent the patient's
best interests or what would stand as the patient's substitute judgment,
then, in the overwhelming majority of cases, treatment is going to be initiated or continued.

With the case of Helga Wanglie (Minnesota 1993), we were introduced
to an 85-year-old patient with multi-organ failure for whom physicians
wanted to discontinue all treatments except comfort care (exclusive of tube
feeding), on the grounds that these treatments were futile. Mrs. Wanglie's
husband, an attorney by profession, did not agree with the physicians' rec-
ommendations and convinced the court that treatment should be continued, on the grounds that this would be consistent with his wife's beliefs.
The court agreed with Mr. Wanglie because of the status accorded the principle of autonomy: If patients have the right to refuse medical treatments

based on their rights to privacy and self-determination, the reasoning goes, so they have a right to receive any and all treatments, based on the same rights.[8]

The Wanglie decision gives us reason to pause—it opens the door to futile treatments simply because the patient wants them. We can anticipate that discussion of futile treatments will occupy considerable attention in the years ahead.

RELEVANT ETHICAL PRINCIPLES AND MAXIMS

It is important to realize that decisions about artificial feeding are being made in a society which *denies death*. Death is a taboo subject, which individuals and families tend to avoid; it is also a subject which many physicians are reluctant to raise. As a result, when people face questions about the use of feeding tubes, the issue may take them by surprise. They may find themselves trying to grapple with a technology about which they know very little. Add to this state of affairs the fact that today approximately 80 percent of people die in hospitals or nursing homes, and we become aware that artificial feeding has the potential to be at the center of many controversies.

Even if people are realistic about mortality and informed about the technology of artificial feeding, there is no doubt that many questions about using, not using, or ceasing to use feeding tubes will arise under confusing circumstances. This is due in large measure to uncertainties about probable prognoses with or without tube feeding. Knowing that medical science frequently relies on trial and error, it would be helpful if a consensus is established allowing for the discontinuance of artificial feeding when this treatment does not bring the benefits hoped for when it was initiated.

From the point of view of the patient, being guided by the following maxims would promote ethically sound choices:

People should take reasonable care of their health, and medical treatments should be employed to enable the ill to recover from their infirmities.

Since life is a *good*, we should not end a life by overt means.

Illness should be managed with a view to a person's overall good, not just by responding to what seems to be medically indicated. This is because life is not an absolute good to be preserved at all costs. Life should be preserved when its quality is subjectively satisfying. Very sick, frail, or dying life need not be preserved by treatments offering little hope of benefit or by means of very expensive or unduly painful or burdensome treatments.

When individuals are truly in charge of their own decision making, they tend to base their decisions on different standards from physicians. Physicians are inclined to encounter an ailment and prescribe a remedy, i.e., to do what is medically indicated. The patient, on the other hand, is more likely to confront her overall condition, along with the particular ailment which is of concern to her physician, and to reason that the time has come to stop responding aggressively to each new symptom and, instead, let nature take its course. If such a decision is based on the judgment that more treatment, perhaps artificial feeding, would be too burdensome, this reasonable decision should be honored.

From the point of view of medicine, health care practitioners would do well to keep the following maxims in mind:

Artificial feeding is a relatively recent technological innovation; its use, nonuse, or discontinuance does not require the formulation of a whole new body of medical-ethical principles. Instead, dilemmas about tube feeding require an adaptation of traditional standards to contemporary cases:

Do no avoidable harm to any patient.

Provide appropriate remedies to patients who are sick and **palliative care** for patients for whom no remedies are possible.

There is no reason to provide futile treatment or to support false hope.

In regard to surrogate decision makers, awareness of the following guidelines would be helpful:

The expressed wishes of an incompetent should be honored to the extent possible.

If the expressed wishes of an incompetent patient were to require a surrogate to perform an overt act of euthanasia or assistance in suicide, these wishes should not be honored.

In the event that an incompetent patient has not expressed his preferences, a surrogate should decide in such a way as to protect the patient's best interests or to carry out what she feels confident the patient would want under the circumstances.

A surrogate should not make decisions for an incompetent patient based on expedience, self-interest, or with an intent to harm the incompetent.

CONCLUSION

Among the most complex medical decisions to be made today are those relating to artificial feeding. These decisions are especially crucial because patients who are not nourished by mouth or by tube will certainly die within a week or two. Ethical people want to do the right thing: If they are patients, in terms of their health and if they are health care practitioners and surrogates, in regard to those entrusted to their care. Sadly, in many different kinds of circumstances, the right thing, the ethical choice, might be not to start or to discontinue artificial feeding. In order to act in an ethically upright manner, it must be demonstrated that a patient's wishes are being honored and/or that the treatment of tube feeding brings more burdens than benefits to the patient.

ENDNOTES

[1] David Major, MD, "The Medical Procedures for Providing Food and Water; Indications and Effects," in Joanne Lynn, MD, *By No Extraordinary Means* (Bloomington, IN: Indiana University Press, 1986), p. 24.

[2] Eileen P. Flynn, *Hard Decisions: Forgoing and Withdrawing Artificial Nutrition and Hydration* (Kansas City: Sheed & Ward, 1990), pp. 74–75.

[3] Ibid., pp. 24–27.

[4] Ibid., pp. 27–31.

[5] Ibid., pp. 31–35.

[6] Ibid., pp. 40–42.

[7] *Cruzan v. Director, Missouri Dept. of Health,* 110 S. Ct. 2841, 1990.

[8] Lisa Belkin, "As Family Protests, Hospital Seeks End to Woman's Life Support," *The New York Times,* January 10, 1991, p. A1.

DISCUSSION QUESTIONS

1. What are feeding tubes? How is enteral nutrition administered? How is parenteral nutrition administered?
2. How long have feeding tubes been part of customary medical technology? In what kinds of situations are feeding tubes used?
3. When and how did various courts in the United States become involved in cases of discontinuance of artificial feeding? What kinds of decisions did these courts reach?
4. What is meant by the best interests standard and the concept of substitute judgment?
5. What is futile treatment? Under what circumstances can artificial feeding

be considered a futile treatment? Are physicians obligated to provide futile treatments? Why or why not?

6. Describe the cultural factors which prevent people from considering the issues attendant to artificial feeding, even in advance of their actual involvement in a concrete case.

7. State the general maxims individuals should be following in reaching decisions about artificial feeding; discuss your evaluation of these maxims.

8. State the general maxims which physicians should be following in reaching decisions about feeding tubes and comment on whether or not you think they are realistic.

9. State the general maxims which surrogates should be following in reaching decisions about initiation, noninitiation, or withdrawal of feeding tubes; discuss your reaction to these maxims.

CASE STUDY

Susan Stafford was 18-years old when she was in a horrible auto accident. At the accident scene it was apparent that she had sustained profound injuries and might be beyond help. As is standard procedure, she was resuscitated and transported to a hospital where she was treated aggressively. Part of her treatment entailed emplacement of an NG tube.

Ms. Stafford never experienced improvement in her condition. Twenty years after the accident, her parents and siblings concurred that the best thing for Susan and for them would be to let her go. Their reasons were that she was not going to get better. She was trapped by the technology of artificial feeding and prevented by it from dying and entering eternal life, and Susan would never have wanted to be kept alive like this. Unfortunately, her family had no proof of Susan's wishes. She did not have advance directives and had not spoken about the eventuality in which she found herself.

Susan's ailment was severe brain damage. She did not recognize anyone, communicate in any way, or carry out purposive movements. She did grimace occasionally in response to such painful stimuli as pin pricks, overly hot water, and high-pitched sounds. Thus, it was assumed that Susan occasionally experienced pain.

Susan's family asked the director of the nursing home to assist them in formulating the request to have her tube feeding terminated so that she could die. They requested that pain medication be given to her during her last days if there were any indication that she was uncomfortable. The director told them that he was never involved in a case like this before and that there were many factors he would need to consider.

Evaluation:

1. Identify ethical issues contained in this case.
2. Propose possible solutions for these issues.
3. Make a decision relevant to action to be taken, or not taken, and provide rationale supportive of this decision.
4. Are you satisfied with your decision? Why or why not?

GLOSSARY

Gastrointestinal tract is the path of digestion through the stomach and the intestines.

Comfort care is rendered to all patients in health care facilities. It consists of feeding, bathing, turning, attending to discomfort, particularly through administration of medication for pain control, and providing any other services required for the patient's comfort. When people are beyond cure, only comfort care is rendered.

Malnutrition is lack of necessary or proper food substances in the body or improper absorption and distribution of them.

Dehydration is a condition resulting from excessive loss of body fluid. Dehydration occurs when output of fluid exceeds fluid intake. It may result from fluid deprivation, excessive loss of fluid, or reduction in total quantity of electrolytes.

ALS, Amyotrophic Lateral Sclerosis is a syndrome marked by muscular weakness and atrophy with spasticity and hyperreflexia due to degeneration of motor neurons of spinal cord, medulla, and cortex. Prognosis is very poor.

Emphysema is a chronic lung disease characterized by increase beyond the normal in the sizes of air spaces and breakdown in the lung wall. People suffering from emphysema experience chronic breathlessness; oxygen therapy is frequently prescribed.

Multiple Sclerosis is a chronic, slowly progressive disease of the central nervous system of unknown origin.

Alzheimer's disease is a form of dementia which involves irreversible loss of memory, deterioration of intellectual functions, apathy, speech impairment, and gait impairment.

Degenerative dementia is a deteriorative mental state with absence or reduction of intellectual faculties, due to organic brain disease which continues in an unrelenting fashion.

Subarachnoid hemorrhage is an abnormal discharge of blood from the space containing cerebro-spinal fluid.

Ruptured aneurysm is the breaking or tearing of a blood vessel, usually an artery. The probable cause of an aneurysm is a congenital defect or weakness in the wall of the vessel.

Persistent vegetative state (PVS) is a form of eyes-open, permanent unconsciousness in which the patient has periods of wakefulness and physiologic sleep/wake cycles, but at no time is the patient aware of himself or his environment. Neurologically, being awake but unaware is the result of a functioning brainstem and the total loss of cerebral-cortical functioning. Persistent vegetative state patients do not have the capacity to experience pain or suffering. Pain and suffering are attributes of consciousness, requiring cerebral-cortical functioning, and patients who are permanently and completely unconscious cannot experience these symptoms. (Statement of American Academy of Neurology, 1989.)

Palliative care. Same as **comfort care**. See above.

PART FOUR

ETHICAL RESPONSES TO SICKNESS

CHAPTER 8

HIV/AIDS

INTRODUCTION

The subject of HIV/AIDS belongs in a health care ethics textbook, but for different reasons than other issues. Unlike such topics as abortion and euthanasia, HIV/AIDS does not constitute an issue about which individuals and society need to decide one way or another. HIV/AIDS, in a sense, is something relatively new, but it is very different from fascinating recent technologies like respirators and in vitro fertilization, the use of which leads to perplexing dilemmas which must be resolved. Neither can we analyze HIV/AIDS in a manner similar to the subject of patient autonomy, which arose out of a social awakening to the limits of paternalistic medicine. No, HIV/AIDS is different because it represents a *setback* for humanity in the form of a new and deadly virus. In 1981 the HIV virus, which causes AIDS, came into our midst uninvited, out of nowhere, confounding, diminishing, testing, and trying us. AIDS poses some of the most complex dilemmas we will ever try to resolve, but, far more strikingly, AIDS forces health care professionals and all members of society to get in touch with their values, attitudes, beliefs, and habits, a cluster of ethically relevant concerns. Do we value compassion more than judgmentalism? Do we act with bias based on deeply ingrained prejudice? Do we believe physicians and nurses are obligated to care for sick people, regardless of whether or not the sick are socially acceptable? Do we comprehend that virtuous people, those who habitually think nonjudgmentally and act unselfishly, are the people who will respond to HIV/AIDS in a laudable fashion? HIV/AIDS forces us to introspection and calls us to wise, generous, courageous action. In responding to AIDS we are forced to disclose how we analyze issues and, far more profoundly, we are required to reveal who we are.

FACTS OF HIV/AIDS

HIV/AIDS constitutes a worldwide **pandemic** which is ongoing; hence, there is constant need for updating regarding numbers of people living with the virus, experimental and new treatments, research into the **etiology** of HIV and findings from various research programs. What is presented here is intended to convey a rudimentary understanding of the basic facts about HIV/AIDS in order to provide the reader with sufficient information about AIDS preliminary to undertaking analysis of the moral aspects of the subject.

HIV stands for human immunodeficiency virus, the virus which causes AIDS. HIV was identified as the cause of AIDS in 1984.[1] Where did HIV come from, and how long has humankind been at risk from HIV? There are no definitive answers to these questions. Speculation has it that HIV may have been in an animal species such as monkeys and may have crossed over into the human species more than 50 years ago. Working with frozen blood and tissue samples, medical researchers have determined that the inexplicable deaths of some people who died 40 years ago were caused by HIV.[2] We do not know whether or not there were some cases of undetected HIV infection prior to the 1950s, but it is certainly possible that there were. What is known about HIV infection is that medical authorities first became aware of it as a public health threat in 1981 as a result of outbreaks in cities such as Montreal, New York, Miami, and San Francisco. At that time, clusters of patients suffering from the same kinds of symptoms who died after relatively brief hospitalizations suggested that humanity had a new health crisis with which to deal. Within four years the culprit that caused the crisis, the human immunodeficiency virus, was identified; dealing with this virus has been a daunting task for this generation and may well continue to be for as far into the future as anyone dares to look.

AIDS is the acronym, coined in 1984, to express the illness caused by HIV. *A* stands for "Acquired," meaning that no one is genetically infected with the virus but, rather, becomes infected sometime after conception. *ID*, "Immune Deficiency," refers to the fact that HIV impacts on the body's immune system, weakening it and eventually destroying it. A functioning immune system allows people to avoid being sickened by viruses and bacteria, or to get well after being afflicted by an infection; thus HIV contravenes the biological abilities to stay well and to recover. The fourth letter of the acronym AIDS is *S* which stands for "Syndrome." The reason the condition caused by HIV is called a syndrome rather than a disease is because the syndrome or condition of having a weakened immune system opens people suffering from AIDS to a large number of **opportunistic infections** or diseases such as **Kaposi's sarcoma** (KS), **pneumocystis carinii pneumonia** (PCP), and tuberculosis, one of which eventually causes death.

In the early days of AIDS there was a tendency toward hysteria because the public did not know how the virus was transmitted. After HIV was identified and exhaustive research was conducted regarding modes of transmission, the hysteria largely subsided. HIV, as it turns out, is a fragile virus which is difficult to transmit. HIV is transmitted in blood, semen, cervical secretions, and breast milk. It can be transmitted from an infected person during homosexual or heterosexual genital contact. Since HIV is blood-borne it can also be transmitted by people who share intravenous hypodermic needles, through blood transfusions, or, much more rarely, in medical or dental settings in which the infected blood of a patient, medical, or dental practitioner gets into the blood stream of an uninfected person. In conjunction with Magic Johnson's return to the National Basketball Association in January, 1996, discussion occurred as to the possibility of the HIV-positive athlete's transmitting the virus to other players following an accident during a game, and the opinion of experts was that the statistical possibility was so infinitesimally small as to be incalculable.

Fetuses can be infected at birth, by the virus in the birth canal, and breast-fed newborns can be infected by contaminated breast milk. There have also been documented cases of transmission of HIV through artificial insemination and organ donation.

After infection with HIV people ordinarily go through a period of as little as a few years to as many as ten years or more during which they are **asymptomatic**. This means that HIV is latent and that the disruption of their immune systems has not yet begun. The asymptomatic phase is especially dangerous because during this time people who are carrying HIV may not know that they are HIV-positive and may unknowingly transmit the virus.[3]

The asymptomatic phase of infection ends with the emergence of symptoms of AIDS. At this time it becomes apparent that the immune system is compromised. Typically, people suffering from AIDS lose a considerable amount of weight and suffer from a variety of increasingly debilitating illnesses. How long do people live with AIDS, and what is the quality of their lives? There are many variables here; some people live only a few months after diagnosis, while others live five, six, even ten years. People living with AIDS can contribute a great deal to the quality of their own lives. By seeking competent medical care, avoiding reinfection,[4] following a nutritious diet, and keeping an upbeat, positive attitude many people have succeeded in living well with AIDS.

At the time of this writing, no vaccine is available to prevent infection with HIV and there is no cure for those who are infected. There are a large number of established and experimental treatments, however, and the list is constantly growing. Research in the areas of developing a vaccine, a cure, and effective treatments for HIV/AIDS is a rapidly growing field which may some day soon yield hoped-for breakthroughs.

In regard to treatments, up until recently none of the medications pre-scribed to counter the effects of HIV were of significant benefit over extended periods of time. By the summer of 1996, however, scientists learned that by combining several AIDS medicines HIV can become a more treatable condition. In all, 11 AIDS drugs, five of them introduced in the first six months of 1996, are on the U.S. market and more are on the way. The most important new drugs are protease inhibitors which block HIV's repro-ductive cycle. When protease inhibitors are combined with older AIDS drugs the virus appears to stop reproducing. Since experiments with combi-nations of medicines is of relatively recent origin, however, long term results are unknown.[5] In addition, there are two problems with combination drug treatments. One is that doctors frequently do not know how to use the drug combinations effectively. There are 1028 possibilities, using four drugs. The other is that the demands on patients who must follow complicated drug treatment regimens are so heavy that noncompliance is a frequent phenom-enon. In the presence of noncompliance, HIV can mutate, changing into drug-resistant strains that defy treatment, and thus leave patients in a more disadvantageous position.[6]

In view of the fact that AIDS is a deadly affliction, the issue of prevention of infection with HIV takes on the character of an extremely urgent public health concern. Since HIV is transmitted in situations of intimate contact and through infected blood and breast milk, it is in prevention of transmission of contaminated body fluids that a solution can be found. The fact that since 1985 each and every one of the more than 20 million units of blood used annually in the United States has been screened goes a long way to lessen-ing chances of being infected during a transfusion. It will be far more diffi-cult to motivate people to change their behavior so as to lessen or eliminate the possibility of sexual transmission, transmission during drug use, or transmission during breast-feeding.

As of June 30, 1997, there were 612,078 reported cases of AIDS in the United States, and 379,258 people had died.[7] It is estimated that between 600,000 and 1 million people in the United States are HIV positive. The first 100,000 cases of AIDS in the U.S. were diagnosed in the first nine years of the epidemic and the next 100,000 were diagnosed during the following 18 months. For every case of HIV infection the U.S. economy suffers a loss of $600,000 in medical costs and lost wages. And, by the year 2000, if current trends continue, the number of AIDS orphans in the United States will exceed 125,000.[8]

RESPONSIBILITIES OF HEALTH CARE PROVIDERS

The Hippocratic Oath instructs physicians to do no harm. The oath goes on to speak of the self-sacrificing physician whose competence and steadfast-ness are expended in the care of patients. Fortunately, from the onset of

AIDS, many courageous physicians, nurses, and other health care providers have answered the challenging call to render care to those who are stricken. With the spread of HIV/AIDS, however, society has become aware of the phenomenon of some physicians, nurses, and other health care providers who seem motivated by a goal of avoiding harm to themselves.[9] As a result, there have been accounts of health care providers who refuse to render care to persons infected with HIV. Such refusals have generated a backlash of protests the essence of which call on people in the health care professions to live up to their responsibilities to take care of the sick. As a result of this backlash, outright denials of service to people with HIV/AIDS have become rare, but the phenomenon of avoiding AIDS patients still exists. Accordingly, some health care providers go out of their way to keep from coming in contact with people infected by HIV. They do this by avoiding work in metropolitan areas, avoiding certain medical or nursing specialties, or making excuses for not being able to render care when they unavoidably encounter an AIDS patient.

The fact that some physicians, nurses, and other health care providers do not want to assist people infected with HIV/AIDS reveals an alarming reality. Their reluctance points to something amiss in what motivates them to do their work. The health care professions, in particular medicine, are well paid and their practitioners enjoy a privileged status. In the generation or so prior to the appearance of HIV it seemed as if medical science had either wiped out infectious diseases or, with the advent of antibiotics, discovered an effective tool to use in dealing with them. As a consequence, when it became safer to be a physician, men and women may have entered the profession out of a desire for "the good life." However, in light of AIDS, goals which are materialistically based or risk-avoidance oriented reveal themselves as inherently deficient. It is becoming evident that medical professionals ought to be motivated by the traditional goals of medicine: To render service to those in need in accordance with their competence, to render this service from a scientifically based perspective, prescribing treatments as indicated, and contributing the knowledge they gain in the service of the sick to improve humankind's lot by playing a role in the progress of medicine. By so doing, ethical health care providers will increase and develop the inclination towards virtuous service, which should have motivated them at the outset when they entered their professions.

After health care providers pass the first hurdle and admit their responsibility to care for persons living with HIV/AIDS, it will become necessary for them to use their knowledge and skill in two ways: First, to provide education about prevention; and second, to provide treatment and support to people with HIV/AIDS through the various phases of their illness.

For the most part, physicians do not get paid for talking to people; they get paid for carrying out examinations and procedures, or for prescribing medications. Whether it is financially beneficial to physicians or not, the fact remains that by reason of their relationship to their patients they are in a singular position to educate people about prevention of HIV/AIDS. And, since there is no completely effective treatment for this infection, the most sensible strategy for dealing with it is preventing infection from occurring in the first place. Pediatricians could talk to preteens and teenagers about AIDS; children of 11 or 12 are not too young to hear from their doctor that they should not put themselves at risk through drug use or sexual activity. One-fourth of all new reported cases of AIDS are among people between the ages of 13 and 21. Two young people are infected by HIV every hour of every day.[10] Pediatricians and practitioners of adolescent medicine who say that the work of AIDS education should be done in the home or school, not in the doctor's office, should think twice about passing the buck. Yes, the home and school need to do their parts, but there is no reason to underestimate the impact physicians can make by seeking to augment these efforts on a one-to-one basis within the doctor-patient relationship.

Women are most at risk of contracting HIV from heterosexual intercourse and drug use, and the percentage of women with HIV infection is increasing. In the U.S., AIDS is the leading cause of death for black women and the fifth leading cause of death for white women.[11] There are 85,000 cases of women with AIDS in the United States. Women of childbearing age account for the vast majority of these cases. In 1996, women accounted for 20 percent of newly reported AIDS cases.[12] Family doctors and obstetrician-gynecologists are in a unique position to bring up the subject of HIV infection with their patients, to answer questions about the syndrome, and to offer advice about strategies for prevention.

Physicians from other specialties may also become aware of opportunities to be AIDS educators. But, do they have an **ethical obligation** to function in this capacity? The answer to this question depends on a person's approach to ethics. If there is an ethical responsibility for a person to do good according to their competence, then, indeed, physicians should take the lead in providing education for prevention. Such an obligation would be categorized as a so-called "affirmative obligation." An affirmative obligation is a general requirement concerning which a physician is free to exercise discretion as to how and when and under what circumstances to carry it out. If, however, a physician has no ethical sense of being required to act consistently, competently, and proactively in the interest of disease prevention, then we cannot expect that physician to take the lead in discussing HIV/AIDS. Would this be a moral fault? Yes, it certainly would be within a system which requires virtuous conduct of those who have as a goal to complete and perfect themselves as they carry out their professional responsibilities.

Just as physicians have obligations to provide AIDS education during the course of physician-patient interactions, so, too, do health care institutions bear such a responsibility. Accordingly, it would be appropriate for health care administrators to arrange educational forums to explain how AIDS is transmitted, treated, prevented, and managed as well as provide speakers for schools or community groups.

Another responsibility of health care providers is to treat the sick and support them by whatever effective means are available through all the phases of their illness. In order to do the work they alone are trained and licensed to do, such health care workers as physicians and nurses need to overcome any latent fears they might have about coming into contact with people infected with HIV. Before doctors and nurses can educate or treat others, they must be educated themselves. Learning that HIV cannot be transmitted in situations of **casual contact** as well as learning how to practice **universal precautions** in all situations in which there is possibility of exposure to blood or body fluids will do a lot to lessen apprehension. However, some fears are irrational so that no amount of factual education can dispel them. With this in mind, some health care practitioners may need the assistance of support groups or psychological counselors in order to work through their fears and be able to interact maturely and professionally with infected persons.

Still another issue which may require resolution is innate prejudice toward some people who are infected with HIV. One of the most regrettable aspects of the epidemic is that so many people have fallen into the habit of dividing the people who suffer from HIV into categories of innocent or guilty. Within this framework, the innocent have a claim on our care and compassion while we owe nothing to the guilty. This type of thinking leads to a harsh, judgmental attitude and a tendency to disregard the rights and needs of sick individuals. It is an attitude unworthy of a health care provider and, should it characterize a physician or nurse, she should consider herself morally required to correct it.

Treating persons who are suffering from AIDS is a physically and emotionally draining undertaking. The reason for this is because persons with AIDS tend to be young, at the so-called prime of their lives, tend to become very sick with each opportunistic infection, and tend to be extremely emaciated, frail, and sick at the end. It is very hard to watch such scenarios play out over and over again, and it is very frustrating to have to deal with the fact that as a physician one cannot cure what makes the patient ill. Within this context, burnout becomes a distinct possibility, one which doctors, nurses, and other personnel need to guard against. Time off, support groups, stress-reduction techniques, outside interests and other strategies can be employed to counteract burnout. Given the ever-increasing number of AIDS cases (it was estimated in 1995 that in the United States one person is infected with HIV every 13 minutes[13]), burnout is an indulgence doctors cannot allow themselves, and they need to take decisive steps to overcome it.

Besides accepting and supporting HIV/AIDS patients for whom they care, health care personnel need to provide them with whatever medical procedures, treatments, or medications are indicated to improve or sustain their physical well-being. Beyond diagnostic tests, **AZT, aerosol pentamidine, protease inhibitors** and other medications, however, medical professionals need to provide encouragement for patients to become full partners in the project of their care and treatment. Autonomous patients who are urged to exercise their right to self-determination will bring a more informed and determined attitude to their treatment and, thus, will have a better chance to fare well. Another very important thing for doctors to do is to promote positive thinking in their patients. There is a link between the mind and the body; through positive thinking, people suffering from AIDS can maximize their opportunities for well-being.

No amount of positive thinking, however, can alter the fact that AIDS is inevitably fatal. With this in mind, the need for healers to project human warmth, acceptance, and compassion at the end becomes urgently apparent. Young people who die of AIDS, as well as loved ones who gather round their bedsides, face a traumatic event which can be eased by the faithfulness and sensitivity of physicians and nurses who do all in their power to ease the pain and fear of dying.

While physicians have an unquestioned responsibility to provide education and treatment, it is unfortunate that a good bit of attention about care of persons with HIV/AIDS seems to focus on disputes about what constitutes futile treatment and whether or not such disputed treatments should be made available. For example, people in the final stages of suffering from AIDS are often reluctant to authorize **DNR orders**, mostly because they are young and cannot accept the inevitability of their own mortality. Questions about how to broach this subject can occupy health care workers, draining energy which clearly could be spent more fruitfully on education for prevention or treatment of patients who could benefit.

An interesting case involving an experimental treatment for a patient with AIDS raised medical and ethical questions as to whether or not limits should be placed on possible treatments. Jeff Getty, a 38-year-old man with AIDS, received bone marrow from a baboon on December 13, 1995. The hoped-for outcome of the radical cross-species transplant was that the baboon's cells, which are thought to be resistant to HIV, will proliferate in Getty's system, allowing him to develop a parallel immune capacity capable of overcoming the disadvantages of his own damaged immune system. Both Mr. Getty and his physicians consider this outcome a long shot. However, they justify the procedure on the basis that scientific knowledge will be gained from it and that this knowledge may lead to an eventual treatment or cure. Opponents of the interspecies experiment object on the grounds that such procedures may open the door for lethal nonhuman viruses to gain entry into the human community.[14]

In years to come, with increasing numbers of persons suffering from HIV/AIDS and an ever-dwindling amount of public and private money available to spend on health care, dilemmas surrounding futile treatments are certain to capture media attention. As this occurs, dramatic clashes between patients or surrogates who claim that "There is always hope" and health care providers who clamor for realism and medical common sense will force the public at large to engage the issue. Hopefully an ethically reasonable consensus will emerge against the backdrop of heartbreaking suffering which gives rise to the discussion.

SITUATION OF AND RESPONSIBILITIES OF PERSONS LIVING WITH HIV/AIDS

People who are infected with HIV and who are asymptomatic may or may not know their HIV status. If they do not know their status, they will be just like everyone who is not infected, i.e., they will likely think that HIV is not their problem. In the United States in 1993, one out of every 92 men aged 27 to 39 was infected with HIV.[15] In the U.S. in 1993 women were four times less likely to be infected. One of every 1,667 white women had HIV infection, as did one in 98 black women and one in 222 Hispanic women.[16] Those who know that they are infected are not just like everyone else; they must deal with the fact of their antibody status, as well as with the physical, emotional, spiritual, and ethical ramifications of the situation. For some people who become aware of being HIV-positive, life and every day of living can become much more meaningful. For others, the news can be perceived as extremely negative and can lead to a wide variety of emotional problems.

People whose HIV status progresses to the symptomatic phase of AIDS face the task of coping with what turns out to be a difficult life. At the personal level they need to make decisions about whom to tell about their diagnosis and prognosis. In view of the fact that AIDS is a fatal illness, they need to confront end-of-life issues such as their will, advance directives, funeral, etc. Dealing with such matters is emotionally taxing, but refusing to deal with them by employing denial or avoidance strategies may be much more so. Another personal issue inevitably faced by persons with AIDS is that of managing their general psychological state in terms of employing strategies to deal with the traumas they experience or allowing those traumas to cause unmeasurable havoc.

Employment is another issue for people with AIDS. For those who were employed prior to the onset of opportunistic infections, the fact of having a job, as well as the nature of the work performed, contributed significantly to their identity. There comes a time in the progress of AIDS when people become too sick to work, and this represents a major loss. Before this time, when they frequently are absent from work because of illness, they may experience hostility from coworkers who fear working with them and harassment from employers who wish they were no longer part of the workforce. Needless to say, neither of these possibilities is pleasant.

Being unemployed or underemployed results in economic concerns with which the vast majority of people with AIDS must cope. Added to the lack of well-being which their illness causes they confront a loss of income often accompanied by concomitant reliance on family, friends, or public assistance. Connected to general economic need is the specific matter of health insurance coverage. Those without such coverage often rely on indigent care, which frequently leaves much to be desired.

As the breakdown of the immune system continues, the suffering of people with AIDS increases and their ability to care for themselves decreases. At this point, nursing care provided in a hospital, long-term care facility, or at home is needed because the sick are too weak to care for themselves. What people almost universally want, independence and the ability to care for themselves, is lost to people dying with AIDS, adding to their burdens as they live out their final days.

It is obvious that the situation of suffering people with AIDS is a very difficult one which should elicit compassion from others. It is also true that people infected with HIV or suffering from AIDS are members of society who have responsibilities to the society. In this regard, the most sensitive responsibility is connected with the exercise of conduct capable of spreading the virus. Should HIV-positive people engage in sexual relations? Should HIV-positive people donate blood? Should HIV-positive people who use intravenous drugs share needles? Should HIV-positive women get pregnant? Should HIV-positive new mothers breast feed their offspring?

Two of these questions are easy to answer. HIV-positive people definitely should not donate blood. It would be unethical to do so and it definitely is immoral. As a matter of fact, anyone who *could* be infected is instructed not to donate blood. People who have engaged in any risk-related behavior such as homosexual sex, heterosexual sex with a partner whose HIV status is unknown, sex (homosexual or heterosexual) with a prostitute, or sharing needles during intravenous drug use should not volunteer to donate blood. Neither should health care workers who suffer a needle stick with what could be a contaminated needle. While it is true that each of the 20 million units of blood donated yearly in the United States is screened and contaminated blood is discarded, it is also true that HIV-positive blood can go undetected in the first months after infection. In other words, there is a period of time, perhaps as long as 12 months after infection, during which HIV-positive blood can continue to appear uninfected even though it is infected. The reason for this is that the way to screen blood for HIV is to examine the blood to detect whether or not there are antibodies present—and it takes time for antibodies to appear. Nevertheless, after infection with HIV, a person is contagious regardless of whether or not antibodies to HIV appear in her blood. The only way, then, to prevent blood from this source from entering the donor pool is by voluntary self-exclusion of prospective donors. The consensus of ethical thinkers is that it is morally mandatory to require self-exclusion of this group, as well as of all HIV-positive individuals.

It is also clear that HIV-positive new mothers should not breast-feed their babies. Under ordinary circumstances breast-feeding is a good thing because it promotes bonding between mother and child and because it enables women to share their immunity to infection with their children via the milk they produce. If a mother is HIV-positive, however, neither she nor her baby can benefit from nursing because, instead of being a life-enhancing experience, it may become a risk-laden exercise resulting in the baby's contracting a deadly infection. By no process of ethical reflection could any rational person justify placing an infant at such a risk. Therefore, it makes sense to conclude that morally it would be wrong for an HIV-positive mother to breast-feed her child.

In regard to whether or not HIV-positive people should engage in sexual relations, there are two schools of thought. One is an absolutist school which holds that it would be immoral to spread the virus by means of sexual activity and, hence, there can be no justification for such activity. The second school of thought holds that while abstinence from sex is 100 percent effective in preventing the spread of HIV through sex, it is also an unrealistic solution because people cannot be counted on to abstain. Therefore, this way of thinking goes, everyone (except married people who decide to do otherwise) should be educated to use protection (condoms) during sex to prevent unwanted pregnancies as well as the spread of sexually transmitted diseases. Those with HIV infection should be *urged* to follow this precaution, as should homosexuals, promiscuous heterosexuals, and anyone who has had sex with prostitutes. So-called "safe sex" or "safer sex," the thinking goes, is the best possible compromise to lessen the spread of HIV. While condoms are not 100 percent effective, condom use will cut down significantly on the spread of HIV, especially in combination with the application of a spermicide.[17]

A similar problem is met when the issue of intravenous drug users is addressed. If people stop using (or do not start using) drugs, they will not become infected from contaminated needles and, if IV drug users do not share needles, they will not become infected. Therefore, abstaining from IV drugs or not sharing needles will prevent the spread of HIV through contact with contaminated needles. Is it realistic, however, to expect that people who use intravenous drugs will stop or will stop sharing? Those who argue that it is not realistic advocate making clean needles available as an infection-control strategy. Many other people oppose making clean needles available on the grounds that such a gesture would constitute societal approval of illegal drug use. They, therefore, seek to block needle-distribution and needle-exchange programs. While the debate goes on, the epidemic rages.

Should HIV-positive women get pregnant? If they do, and if they receive AZT during pregnancy, they run a less than 8 percent chance of bearing an HIV-positive child.[18] If a woman learns during her pregnancy of an HIV-positive status, should she continue the pregnancy or should she terminate it? This is a very distressing question because by asking it we understand once again the terrible new reality which HIV has introduced into our midst. Women who are HIV-positive will go on to develop AIDS and die; they will not be there for their growing children. Uninfected children born to HIV-positive women will sooner or later lose their mothers and may well wind up as orphans. Infected children face the prospect of suffering from AIDS before the end of their shortened lives. Laying down ethical rules is easy: Do no harm, avoid evil, follow the safer course. According to these sound and reasonable norms, HIV-positive women probably should not get pregnant because of the disadvantages to their offspring. Human behavior is not readily regulated by rules, however, so that women do foolish things and sometimes suffer drastic consequences. Ethicists can only hope to raise the level of awareness of human responsibility, not to change the nature of reality. In view of this, education about what is at stake coupled with compassion toward those who are infected and become pregnant would constitute the most ethically responsible position for health care professionals and society.

PUBLIC HEALTH RESPONSE TO HIV/AIDS

As was noted above, AIDS came seemingly from out of nowhere to threaten the well-being of millions of people. In the United States public-health authorities are responsible for formulating practical, coherent responses to public-health dangers. In this regard, those responsible for safeguarding public health have taken initiatives in four areas.

First, in order to protect the nation's blood supply, public-health authorities have arranged for examination of donated blood to eliminate contaminated blood from the nation's supply. In addition, in order to safeguard the well-being of health care workers and patients alike, universal precautions have been defined and instituted. By the term "universal precautions" is meant that *all* health care workers are to follow strict infection control guidelines in situations entailing contact with blood or body fluids from *any* patient. Depending on the specific type of situation, gloves, gowns, and/or goggles are to be worn, and used needles are always to be discarded in a safe, risk-free fashion.

Second, public-health officials must make budgetary decisions. The first decision entails how much of the public-health budget should go to HIV-related needs and how much to all other health care needs. The second decision requires deciding what percentages to allot for prevention, care, and research. As it happens, there is keen competition for public-health dollars with lobbying from many interest groups. In view of this, public-health authorities face the ethical challenge of being fair and impartial as they reach allocation decisions.

Third, with the discovery of HIV in 1984 and development of a method to test for it, public-health authorities needed to design a program of testing for HIV. Making testing available at locations all across the country presented a huge logistical challenge, which has been met. Greater challenges lay in the necessity of devising a method to insure the confidentiality of people who want to be tested, as well as providing counseling for both the infected and the uninfected. These problems seem to have been ironed out but ethical issues attendant to whether or not to mandate testing for people who fall into certain categories[19] remain unresolved.

Fourth, public-health authorities are key figures in formulating programs of education. Because of this they have been caught up in controversies surrounding safe sex and needle exchanges. While these controversial areas still remain unresolved, an enormous feat has been accomplished in that the overwhelming majority of people are now aware of how HIV is transmitted and what people experience who suffer from AIDS. Whether or not public-health officials will ever compile data related to the content of sexual behavior by U.S. citizens, so as to tailor education to the actual behavior of people, remains to be seen.[20]

ETHICAL DILEMMAS ASSOCIATED WITH HIV/AIDS

It would be impossible to consider all the possible ethical dilemmas stemming from HIV/AIDS, but it will be helpful to consider what is at stake in several paradigmatic cases.

First, responding to unwilling health care providers. As we have already seen, some health care practitioners resist providing or refuse to provide care to HIV-positive individuals or AIDS patients. Their motivation can stem from prejudice, from fear, or from a type of harsh righteousness. No matter what their motivation, it is unethical for them not to care for HIV/AIDS patients, and health care administrators should not tolerate their refusals. Instead, education and psychological counseling should be provided to help them get beyond their reluctance and, if they cannot, they should pursue other careers.

Second, protecting the privacy of HIV-positive health care providers as well as patients. The traditional right of each and every person to have her medical diagnosis and prognosis held in confidence by physicians and nurses extends to people infected with HIV or AIDS. In response to the case of an HIV-positive physician whose practice was destroyed when his privacy was breached and word of his antibody status was spread, hospital administrators have found it necessary to institute safeguards to insure that such abuses do not occur again.[21]

HIV-positive patients as well as patients with AIDS have experienced shunning and ill-treatment from people who have no right to know their diagnosis. Consequently, hospital authorities have had to shore up precautions so as to make certain that all possible safeguards are in place to insure the privacy of patients. Such an undertaking is especially difficult given use of and access to computers. Nevertheless, it presents an ethical requirement which should be honored to the utmost degree possible.

Third, implementing justice and compassion in trials of experimental medicines. People with AIDS have consistently conveyed two ideas to officials at the U.S. Food and Drug Administration: First, they will try anything to keep HIV from killing them and, second, they have little to no patience in respect to long waits for promising treatments which are stalled by evaluative processes. In response to these developments public officials have had to reexamine their dual responsibilities to protect the public health and to respond with decisiveness and swiftness to individuals who look to experimental treatments as their last hope. As a result, expedited review processes have been instituted and, when specific treatments have been thought to offer positive results, people on placebos have been switched from recipients of placebos to recipients of trial medications. In addition, the government has been urged to provide incentives to pharmaceutical companies so that these companies will undertake accelerated efforts to develop new treatments for AIDS.[22] With the advent of protease inhibitors used in combination with earlier medications, the treatment of AIDS is becoming very expensive, generally in excess of $15,000 per year. Therefore, in years to come, the cost of pharmaceuticals and the amount to be spent on uninsured persons suffering from AIDS will need to be resolved.

Fourth. Mandatory or voluntary testing. Mandatory testing denies an individual's right to exercise autonomy by freely choosing to submit to or refuse to submit to an HIV antibody test. Voluntary testing, on the other hand, honors autonomy by protecting the individual's right to choose for himself. In respect to testing the issue to be resolved is whether the individual's right to refuse to undergo testing ought to be protected even when the community or specific members of the community can demonstrate a right to know. Such situations as those involving people who are raped, and physicians who perform surgical procedures in which there is potential for contact with a patient's blood, come quickly to mind. Since the misfortune of Kimberly Bergalis and other patients of Dr. David Acer, so do the rights of dental patients.[23] In spite of sympathy for the right of uninfected people to know, however, most attempts at requiring mandatory testing have been unsuccessful, with the testing issue remaining only one among many of the contentious issues spawned by HIV.

CONCLUSION

HIV/AIDS is presenting society with the most perplexing medical and ethical issues of the twentieth century. Understanding what morality is will not eliminate heartbreak or controversy but will enable people to respond in a rational and compassionate manner to an affliction which has generated abundant strife and confusion.

ENDNOTES

[1] In 1984 research teams in the United States and France, under the direction of Dr. Robert Gallo and Dr. Luc Montagnier, respectively, each working independently of the other, identified a unique retrovirus as the agent which causes AIDS. The U.S. team named the virus HTLV-3; the French called it LAV. In 1988, at the suggestion of the World Health Organization, a uniform name, Human Immunodeficiency Virus (HIV), was adopted.

[2] A 1959 sample from a Bantu man who lived in the Belgian Congo was studied by Dr. Toufo Zhu's research team in New York and identified as infected with HIV1. This discovery led researchers to conclude that "the major group of viruses that 'dominate the global AIDS pandemic at present shared a common ancestor in the late 1940's or 1950's.'" Cf., Lawrence K. Altman, "Study of H.I.V. Family Tree Pushes Back Origins," *The New York Times*, February 4, 1998, p. A16.

[3] It is also possible to transmit HIV intentionally, most likely by deceiving an unsuspecting sexual partner. It goes without saying that such conduct would be unethical.

[4] Although most people are generally not aware of the possibility of reinfection, this possibility does exist. By reinfection is meant that individual X who becomes HIV-positive as a result of contact with individual Y can become reinfected through contact with individuals A, B and C. Since individuals Y, A, B and C each have different strains of the HIV virus, individual X would be placing himself in a significantly more precarious condition healthwise by allowing himself to be infected by these various additional strains of HIV.

[5] Daniel Q. Haney, "AIDS cure no longer seen as unthinkable," *The Record*, July 7, 1996, p. A 7.

[6] Lawrence K. Altman, "AIDS Meeting Ends With Little Hope of Breakthrough: Emphasis On Prevention," *The New York Times*, July 5, 1998, pp. 1, 11.

[7] *GMHC Facts* as of July 1, 1998. (*GMHC Facts* is a monthly summary of facts from the GMHC about the AIDS pandemic. To obtain copies, contact the Gay Men's Health Crisis, 119 West 24 St., N.Y., N.Y. 10011; 212-807-6664.)

[8] *GMHC Fact Sheets* 1994 and 1995.

[9] The fear of health care workers is usually based on the unlikely possibility of being infected during procedures in which they could be exposed to an HIV-positive patient's blood. From 1981 until 1995, 46 of the more than ½ million documented cases of AIDS resulted from exposure to the virus in the clinical setting. In recent years scientists have learned that the risk of infection from HIV can be lessened by 79 percent if a health care worker who has been endangered, generally from a needle stick, is treated with AZT. Lawrence K. Altman, "Drug Seems to Cut Infection for Workers Stuck with Needles," *The New York Times*, December 22, 1995, p. A32.

[10] Bob Groves, "More HIV testing urged for teenagers," *The Record*, June 25, 1998, pp. 1, A 17.

[11] Morbidity & Mortality Weekly Report, February, 1996, as quoted in *GMHC Fact Sheet*, 1998.

[12] Centers for Disease Control Report, December, 1996, as quoted in *GMHC Fact Sheet*, 1998.

[13] Centers for Disease Control Report, June, 1995, as quoted in *GMHC Fact Sheet*, 1998.

[14] Lawrence K. Altman, "Man Gets Baboon Marrow in Risky AIDS Treatment," *The New York Times*, December 15, 1995, p. 1; and Murry J. Cohen, MD, "AIDS Baboon Experiment Is Bad Science," (letter), *The New York Times*, December 25, 1995, p. 38. Mr. Getty continued to be well, with only an occasional setback, in October, 1998. Cf., Claudia Dreifus, "A Conversation with Jeff Getty," *The New York Times*, October 13, 1998, p. 3.

[15] "Study Puts the Risk of HIV in Young U.S. Men at 1 in 92," *The New York Times*, November 24, 1995, p. B19.

[16] Ibid.

[17] The spermicide generally suggested for use with condoms is nonoxynol-9, readily available in pharmacies. Nonoxynol-9 kills the HIV virus; however, individuals who use nonoxynol-9 very frequently (as often as a few times a day) develop an intolerance for it.

[18] Kevin Sack, "House Panel to Draft Bill on AIDS Tests of Newborns," *The New York Times*, July 14, 1995, p. A15.

[19] These categories include either patients or health care providers who experience blood-to-blood contact in a clinical setting, people who sexually assault others, pregnant women, and/or newborns. As it is now, certain states require blind testing of all newborns in order to establish accurate counts of infants born with HIV. Since an HIV-positive infant is definitively indicative of an HIV-positive mother, if the testing were not blind

then the mother's HIV status would de facto be established without her consent. As it is, however, an HIV-positive infant receives no treatment and his mother neither treatment nor counseling in order to preserve a system which protects her confidentiality. Debate about the wisdom of keeping this system intact continues, and the pendulum seems to be moving in the direction of mandatory testing of pregnant women because of the benefits of treatment with AZT for newborns.

[20] Over the years of the AIDS pandemic, various proposals have been made concerning designing research studies to establish accurate data about what the actual sexual conduct of U.S. citizens of varying ages, races, and sexual preferences consists in. These proposals, however, have not met with acceptance from government funders, so that the state of our knowledge of sexual behavior remains limited and sketchy.

[21] Cf, Russell L. McIntyre, Th.D., "Physician With AIDS Properly Restricted In Hospital Privileges," *Info Trends: Medicine, Law and Ethics,* Summer, 1991, pp. 1–11.

[22] "AIDS Group Urges a Plan on Medicines," *The New York Times,* July 3, 1995, p. 6.

[23] For an overview of this tragic story, cf., B. Johnson, "Kim's brave journey," *People Weekly,* October 14, 1991, pp. 44–45 and Tim Golden, "Dental Patient Torn by AIDS Calls for Laws," *The New York Times,* June 22, 1991, p. A7.

DISCUSSION QUESTIONS

1. How have you been affected by HIV/AIDS? In view of what you have read in this chapter, evaluate your response to HIV/AIDS, discussing why you are satisfied or not satisfied with it.

2. Discuss at least two ethical reasons which might motivate health care providers to care for people infected by HIV/AIDS.

3. Discuss at least three reasons why health care workers might want to avoid caring for people infected by HIV/AIDS, and suggest how health care administrators can counter such reluctance.

4. How would you respond to people who argue that most of those who suffer from AIDS got what they deserve? Why do you think as you do?

5. In your opinion, what kinds of sexual and drug-use behaviors are morally acceptable for people infected with HIV? Why do you hold this position?

6. Evaluate the U.S. public-health response to the HIV/AIDS epidemic and discuss how this response could be improved.

7. Relate a specific ethical dilemma associated with HIV/AIDS, either from

this chapter or from your experience. Discuss how you think the dilemma should be resolved and explain the rationale which undergirds your conclusion.

CASE STUDY

Bruce Harlow is a registered nurse who started working at a large metropolitan hospital three years ago. Prior to that Mr. Harlow had been employed by a small rural hospital. In both hospitals he had worked in the area of utilization review and had consistently been commended for excellent performance. Because of a restructuring initiative designed to reduce costs, Mr. Harlow is told that he is being reassigned to a medical floor; several beds on that floor are occupied by AIDS patients.

Nurse Harlow schedules an appointment with his supervisor. He tells her that he is afraid of contracting HIV through accidental puncture and, hence, would be very uncomfortable caring for AIDS patients. He asks for a different assignment.

The nursing supervisor is troubled by Nurse Harlow's request. She knows that other nurses feel as Nurse Harlow does and she fears that if she changes his assignment she will have difficulty getting staff to care for AIDS patients. On the other hand, she worries that should she force Nurse Harlow to accept an assignment about which he has strong reservations his ability to render appropriate patient care will be jeopardized.

She schedules a conference with the director of nursing to discuss the options available to her as well as their ethical ramifications.

Evaluation:

1. Identify ethical issues contained in this case.
2. Propose possible solutions for these issues.
3. Make a decision relevant to action to be taken or not taken and provide rationale supportive of this decision.
4. Are you satisfied with your decision? Why or why not?

GLOSSARY

A **pandemic** is an epidemic which is worldwide in scope. A communicable disease is considered to be an epidemic when its incidence reaches numbers in excess of normal expectancy.

Etiology is the study of causes or origins of diseases.

Opportunistic infections (OIs) are any infections triggered by microorganisms commonly found in the environment which only cause disease in persons with compromised immune systems. It is of one or another opportunistic infection, or a combination of OIs that persons with AIDS eventually die.

Kaposi's sarcoma (KS) is a cancer of the blood vessels that usually appears first on the skin. It is common in equatorial Africa, where it often has an aggressive course and even affects children. In the United States it is mostly found among elderly men of Mediterranean descent, in whom it progresses slowly, rarely kills, and can be treated. As one of the manifestations of AIDS, Kaposi's sarcoma strikes young men and is intermediate in virulence between the African and classical American diseases.

Pneumocystis carinii pneumonia (PCP) is an opportunistic infection from which people with AIDS frequently suffer. This pneumonia, caused by a protozoan parasite which rarely affects people with functioning immune systems, severely weakens persons with AIDS.

Asymptomatic refers to the state of being healthy or of not manifesting symptoms of illness. People who are infected with HIV appear healthy, or asymptomatic, for periods of time of varying length before becoming sick with opportunistic infections.

Ethical obligations of physicians originate in the requirements of professionalism. If one understands a physician to be required by reason of her profession to act in such a way as to enable both her patients and society to benefit from her scientific knowledge and expertise, then physicians, as professionals, have an ethical obligation to provide education about HIV/AIDS.

Casual contact in the context of AIDS refers to all types of human contact which are nongenital in nature and which do not entail exposure to another's blood. Thus, embracing, shaking hands, using the same telephone or bathroom, and all other instances of everyday human interaction constitute casual contact and do not carry risk of HIV transmission.

Universal precautions means that in the clinical setting any procedures in which HIV could be transmitted are enacted with the use of protective measures. Thus, whenever blood is drawn, rubber gloves are worn, and, whenever blood might splatter, goggles are worn. Since health care providers do not know which patients are HIV-positive and which are not, universal precautions are used with each and every patient.

AZT stands for azidothymidine, a drug developed in 1986 by a British pharmaceutical company, Burroughs Wellcome Company, now known as Glaxo Wellcome. AZT functions by causing an immediate drop in the amount of virus in the bloodstream and boosting the number of infection-fighting CD4 cells, the type of blood cells destroyed by HIV. However, the virus eventually overcomes the drug by mutating and becoming resistant to AZT. Side effects commonly associated with AZT include liver damage.

Aerosol pentamidine is a medication prescribed for persons who are HIV positive; it decreases the likelihood of becoming infected with pneumocystis carinii pneumonia.

Protease inhibitors are a category of drugs which prevent the HIV virus from replicating in an infected person, thus stopping the inevitable decline associated with infection.

DNR orders refer to directions given to a physician by a patient or his surrogate and entered on the patient's hospital chart. Those directions stipulate that the patient not be resuscitated if he stops breathing; hence, the acronym DNR which stands for Do Not Resuscitate. In the absence of a DNR order, all hospitalized patients are routinely resuscitated regardless of their diagnosis or prognosis.

CHAPTER 9

Experimentation in Medicine

INTRODUCTION

Medical **science** would not be medical science without an experimental component. The reason for this is because some of the principal purposes of medicine are to cure disease, prevent diseases from occurring through vaccination, and find better ways of correcting physiological anomalies such as broken bones, weakened joints, and failing vision. Physicians are scientists and, as scientists, have a moral obligation to carry out experiments that may have beneficial results. Medical researchers and practitioners begin by identifying a problem that needs correction, then brainstorm and research possible ways of addressing the problem, proceed to test these possibilities, and then assess their progress or lack of same. In regard to developing a cure, vaccine, and effective treatments for HIV infection, the medical research community has completed this cycle tens of thousands of times without achieving its goals, and this community is resolved to continue its quest for as long as it takes. It goes without saying that it is in the nature of medical experimentation for researchers to be positive and hopeful in their attitudes without ever being certain that they will be able to achieve what they set out to do.

Experimentation is a trial-and-error process which occasionally yields success instead of error. And even when medical experimentation concludes without success, which is most of the time, information learned in conjunction with the experiment may eventually prove valuable in another context.

The first phase of medical experimentation occurs in the laboratory. In the laboratory various proposed medications are constituted. Once constituted and analyzed, these medications are tested in culture media, then on animals, and finally, perhaps, on humans. At each of the various phases of testing, rigorous documentation is compiled to record everything which is observed and learned in the trial. If preliminary findings are promising, researchers record their successes in descriptive articles which are submitted to **reputable journals**. After **peer review** and evaluation, if research findings stand up to scrutiny, articles are published in **widely circulated periodicals**, making the broader medical community and the public-at-large aware of what transpired.

As it happens, it is in the area of testing on humans that most of the ethical issues accompanying experimentation in medicine occur and, therefore, in this chapter we shall concentrate on this area.

BRIEF HISTORICAL BACKGROUND

During the 1930s and 1940s medicine was largely paternalistic and patient's rights and participation were not major concerns. In addition, during those decades there were horrible incidents of racism and genocide and, in Nazi concentration camps, human beings were dehumanized and treated in savage and brutal ways. From both these phenomena, patient nonparticipation in medical decision making and mistreatment of human subjects in medical experimentation, society learned valuable lessons which have been incorporated into the ethical regulations governing contemporary medical experimentation.

The most horrible and unethical medical experiments ever performed were done under the direction of Josef Mengele, a Nazi and a physician. Mengele's research interest was in determining the secrets of genetics and his goal was discovering the process or formula for breeding superior human beings. In order to achieve these objectives Mengele subjected people to horrible abuse including torturous, barbarous treatments, and mutilations; afterwards the subjects were killed. At the end of World War II, when war criminals were put on trial at **Nuremberg**, Nazi doctors offered as defense for their misconduct the excuse that they were following orders. This defense was judged unacceptable on the grounds that people are bound by a fundamental obligation to act reasonably and with respect for other humans. Out of Nuremberg came the Nuremberg Code, ten principles which spell out in clear language the limits which must be observed by those who conduct experimental research. What should have been obvious became codified.

A second distressing experiment involving human subjects which led to contemporary regulations in regard to the way experiments are carried out was the infamous Tuskegee Study. Begun about 1930 and ended in 1972, this study is a classic example of poor science and dismal ethics. The reason the scientific component was poor is because the conceptualization of the study, its methodology, and its record-keeping were shoddy. In addition, the possibility that the study would progress to the desired end, observing what happens as untreated syphilis runs its course, could not have been achieved because there was no way to prevent the research subjects from receiving treatment from nonparticipating providers. And, experiments involving humans, which are poorly or improperly designed in that they could not possibly yield significant scientific facts relevant to the matter being studied, are, by definition, immoral.

Many criticisms have been leveled against the Tuskegee study but three specific complaints stand out because in today's climate these practices would never be tolerated. First, the few hundred participants not only did not give informed consent regarding what they were getting into, they were deceived about various aspects of what transpired. Second, they were subjected to spinal taps in order to determine the presence or absence of syphilis; receiving a spinal tap can be uncomfortable and carries some risks and the subjects did not know why they underwent the procedure or anything about possible discomfort or side effects. Finally, in 1934 neosalvarsan was discovered to be effective in treating syphilis, and by 1946 the availability of penicillin, an effective treatment, was widely recognized. In spite of the fact that physicians were aware of the benefits of these medications, none of the doctors conducting the Tuskegee study advised or prescribed these remedies for the subjects, a grave abuse.[1]

Two other experiments which took place in the United States should be remembered in terms of lessons to be learned.

Once secret reports of experiments carried out under United States government auspices from 1944 until 1974 recently came to light. These experiments involved 16,000 U.S. citizens and were designed to study the effects of radiation on humans. According to an article in *U.S. News & World Report*, some of the experiments have resulted in huge lawsuits. At Vanderbilt University in Tennessee, one lawsuit claims 829 pregnant women in anemia studies were fed radioactive iron without their knowledge. Their doctors had little understanding of the chance that it would cause fetal cancers. Another lawsuit claims that doctors in Rochester, N.Y., secretly injected patients with plutonium. And yet another says that physicians in Cincinnati gave cancer patients heavy doses of gamma rays. The doctors said they were trying to cure the cancers but they were also gathering data on the effects of radiation on soldiers. Some patients allegedly died painful deaths.[2]

The presidential advisory board appointed to determine the factual picture regarding the radiation experiments and formulate an ethical evaluation was uncompromising in its condemnation of what transpired. "There was no justification for using dying patients as mere means to the ends of investigators," the panel's report says. Ruth Faden, the committee's chairperson, noted that many people undergo treatment only because they trust their doctors and, in terms of the radiation experiments, physicians violated this trust.[3]

A celebrated case of possible unethical conduct in psychiatric research involved an experiment at the University of California at Los Angeles in which schizophrenic patients were taken off medication to permit researchers to study the condition of schizophrenia. Patients were allowed, in an unmedicated state, to relapse, in some cases with dire consequences. Among these, one patient who was in the study killed himself and another attempted suicide and broke his back. Complaints about the study led to a U.S. government investigation, and this investigation concluded that the study was unethical and violated government regulations primarily because the subjects had not been adequately informed of the risks.[4]

ETHICAL ISSUES ASSOCIATED WITH EXPERIMENTATION IN MEDICINE

Use of Animals. During the past generation the animal rights movement has intensified and strengthened. The main contention of proponents of animal rights is that animals should be treated with respect and should not be exploited or treated harshly or capriciously. Some animal rights advocates oppose killing animals for any reason including to provide food, skins, or for medical research. Other advocates are less absolutist and would draw the line at opposition to cruel treatment of animals or unnecessary or frivolous use.

Medical science maintains that it is necessary to use animals in testing experimental medicines and treatments. Medical researchers, however, have become sensitive to the arguments of animal rights activists and, as a result, tend to make several concessions. In contemporary practice, attempts are made to do as much research as possible at the initial laboratory phases, which do not involve animals so as to use animals more sparingly and only when unavoidable. Researchers have become aware of the capacity of animals to experience pain and, as a consequence, research studies using animals are now designed to keep animals' experience of pain to an absolute minimum or to eliminate it altogether. As a result of raised consciousness laboratory animals are now kept under humane conditions. And, finally, medical and research personnel involved in experimentation with animals have learned not to be dismissive in regard to the contributions animals make to medical progress but, rather, to testify to the contributions made by animals. While opponents of any and all experimentation involving animals would not be inclined to compromise with medical researchers who have changed their attitude and procedures so as to show more respect for animals, most people would probably consider these changes to be evidence of an improved ethical climate.

Use of Fetal Tissue or Embryos. Medical science needs to work from a foundation of knowledge. Some of the most profound secrets of life are hidden in rapidly developing human embryos. In the space of nine short months an organism grows from just two cells into a completely differentiated person. Given the easy availability of human fetal tissue from elective abortions, it is understandable that scientists want access so as to study human development, experiment on embryos to try to correct anomalies, and use fetal material for experimental purposes in order to try to bring about cures for human diseases. In regard to the status of fetal tissue transplants, please refer to Chapter 6, "Fetal Tissue: Research and Transplants."

As far as experimentation on aborted human embryos is concerned, there is widespread reservation about the ethical appropriateness of so doing because it is thought that such experimentation would be extremely disrespectful. As a result, on December 2, 1994, President Bill Clinton issued a terse executive order which forbade such experimentation in any facility which receives federal funds. The main argument supportive of experimentation on human embryos holds that medical science should learn what it can from available embryos. The counter argument is that just as human persons are entitled to respect and are not to be used as a means to an end, neither are human embryos to be used in such a manner. Those who argue thus assert that medical science is morally obligated to respect this boundary and should not consider itself entitled to eliminate the limit for the sake of convenience.

EXPERIMENTATION ON HUMAN SUBJECTS

There are two possible types of experimentation on human subjects: Therapeutic and nontherapeutic. By therapeutic experimentation is meant medications administered or procedures carried out for the benefit of the subject, either to diagnose the subject's illness or to treat the illness. There is no ethical reservation in regard to therapeutic experimentation provided that the subject gives informed consent.

Nontherapeutic experimentation and research refer to prescribing pharmaceuticals or performing procedures not designed to benefit the research subject but to gain knowledge that may be useful to medical science in the future. As with therapeutic experimentation, nontherapeutic experimentation is ethically permissible, with several reservations, provided that subjects give informed consent.

Informed Voluntary Consent. In order to participate in experimental research people need to know exactly what it is that they are getting into and need to agree to do so freely and wholeheartedly. From the outset they need to know that they are free to withdraw if they decide to. What else do they need to know? Certainly they should be told the purpose of the experiment, the exact nature of the procedure with all its constituent parts, the pain and risks which can be predicted as possible side effects of the treatment, and any financial costs involved. This information needs to be communicated in non-technical language and ample time should be set aside to provide thorough answers to questions. The atmosphere should be noncoercive and individuals should be treated with respect regardless of whether or not they decide to consent to participate.

It is ethically right to facilitate and support the process of reaching informed voluntary consent. Just as surely it would be morally wrong to deceive a research subject about any aspect of an experiment. In addition to these white and black conclusions, however, there are several gray areas under the heading "Informed Voluntary Consent" which merit attention.

Because there is so much concern in medical practice about **liability** and **disclosure**, the consent forms given to research subjects have wound up resembling rental car agreements, with pages of hard to read and hard to understand fine print. These forms have become so off-putting that people tend to just sign and hope for the best. No one thinks that short, clear, easy to read forms will soon become part of standard practice; but it is obvious that until such forms come into routine use, there is an inherent weakness in the way informed consent is rendered.

There are two possible moral issues in the relationship between a research subject and the conductor of the research. One issue is that those who design and implement experimental research protocols are experts in what they do and have a wealth of technical knowledge in the area. This is in contrast to the prospective subject who may feel embarrassed at how little he comprehends. Out of this intimidating climate may come a sense of confused obligation on the subject's part to become involved in a procedure which he does not adequately understand. Such a situation would be in indisputable conflict with what is ethically acceptable. Therefore, safeguards should be put in place to correct this unbalance. One possible safeguard might be to require researchers to practice communicating with lay people and not allow them to interact with research subjects until they are competent at communicating in nontechnical language. Another safeguard would be to have patient advocates available to assist prospective research subjects in order to make certain that these lay people understood all that is at stake before consent forms are signed.

A second issue about the informed consent process entails the possibility of the existence of a **conflict of interest** which might prevent the research director and her assistants from being objective when interviewing subjects. It can be assumed that those who design and plan to carry out a research study have a great deal invested in their project and want to see it go forward. Since it cannot go forward without the agreement of individuals to participate, it may happen that those in charge omit negatives, suggest unrealistic positives, or act in an overbearing or coercive fashion so as to enlist subjects. Since all these tactics are within the realm of possibility, and since all are clearly unethical, it follows that the institutions in which experimental research is carried out must put strategies in place to prevent tactics like these from occurring.

OVERSIGHT BY INSTITUTIONAL REVIEW BOARDS

In 1972, the federal government mandated that hospitals and other institutions which conduct medical experimentation on humans and receive federal funds establish Institutional Review Boards, commonly referred to as IRBs. These boards originally functioned by reviewing proposals for medical research before these proposals were submitted for funding. Subsequently, IRBs were also charged with overseeing research on human subjects from social science perspectives. At the present time, Institutional Review Boards exercise oversight during all phases of experimental studies; proposed protocols are evaluated; on-going experiments are scrutinized; and data generated as a result of experiments are reviewed. At each phase of oversight, experimenters must comply with suggestions or revisions proposed by the IRB. Today in the United States there are approximately 4,000 Institutional Review Boards, and these boards are the first line of defense against abuses in medical research and experimentation.

An IRB is as good as its members. By this is meant that the cross section of IRB members who come to the board with the requisite expertise and who act from the dual motivations of advancing medicine and protecting experimental subjects from unnecessary harm can see to it that research and experimentation are carried out in an ethical manner. They can do this by examining each and every aspect of a research protocol in advance of its implementation. A critical element in safeguarding the integrity of an IRB as a whole, as well as of each of its individual members, is for the administration of a hospital or other facility to encourage independence and critical objectivity. The reason for this is because physicians and researchers who come to an IRB to request approval for an experimental program may have a great deal of study, hope, and ego invested in the project. Sometimes cash incentives also come into play when pharmaceutical companies or medical equipment manufacturers contract to reimburse physicians for their agreeing to participate in a research study. In a sense one can expect prospective researchers to be highly motivated salespersons for their projects. There is danger that IRB members will take the easy way out, acting as rubber stamps by routinely passing on whatever comes before them. This possibility will not become a likelihood if the members of the IRB are independent and if their independence and impartiality are expected and affirmed by the administration of the health care facility. Only in such a climate will the balance between hopes for the research and the interests of the patient be adjusted so that the patient is not at a disadvantage.

ISSUES ATTENDANT TO RANDOMIZED CLINICAL TRIALS

Most experimental research studies concerned with evaluating medications or treatments are organized as randomized clinical trials (RCTs). In an RCT patients are randomly assigned to either one of two groups: The group to receive the experimental medication/treatment or the group to receive the **placebo**. The patient who agrees to participate in the trial does not know into which group she is enrolled and, in double-blind studies, neither does her physician.

The biggest ethical issues attendant to randomized clinical trials concern the physician-patient relationship and the patient's possible experience of deleterious consequences. In regard to the first concern, in the Western medical tradition it is understood that a physician will act to benefit her patients, but, in an RCT in which a patient might receive a placebo or undergo a treatment with harmful side effects, the physician is acting with more concern for scientific advancement than for the patient. Those who argue against physician involvement in RCTs do so out of concern for the patient. Those who support physician involvement reason that the patient, as a member of society, may want to promote scientific advancement and agrees to alteration of the terms of his relationship with his physician by giving informed voluntary consent.

The second reservation about participation in RCTs is that patients may be harmed by what they experience in the course of the experiment, and medical practitioners are under an obligation to do no harm. The response to this objection is that patients may also benefit from what transpires and, in any event, they are free to act altruistically to advance medical science if this is what they want to do. Furthermore, there is no explicit intention on the part of the physician to harm the patient, and her expectation is that no untoward results will occur because of the experiment.

THERAPEUTIC EXPERIMENTATION ON CHILDREN

Since children are legally unable to give informed voluntary consent, a question arises as to the ethical propriety of allowing them to undergo experimental treatments. An ethical consensus has emerged that it is morally permissible to allow children access to *therapeutic* experiments, provided that consent is obtained from a parent or guardian. The assumption underlying this consensus is that the child is affected by an anomaly or pathology for which no established medication or treatment exists. Without an experimental procedure, it is further assumed, the child will remain in an unacceptable condition or will deteriorate. An experimental treatment, therefore, offers the child the only hope of benefit available, and the risk to the child of availing herself of this treatment with its unknown side effects may be less than the risks associated with the anomaly or pathology. In other words, the experimental therapeutic treatment presents the best and only hope available, and the child's parent or guardian, clearly aware of this fact, consents to the treatment in order to benefit the child.

NONTHERAPEUTIC EXPERIMENTATION ON CHILDREN

A nontherapeutic experiment is designed to benefit medical science because of the information which it generates. With any experiment there is a scarcity of information about what could happen as a result of doing untried procedures or taking new medicines. In other words, side effects which are unforeseen at the outset may occur, posing a danger to people. These would be quite undesirable but would be unknown beforehand and would only become apparent at some future time, perhaps years after the nontherapeutic experiment is conducted.

Ethicists are divided in respect to allowing children to participate in *nontherapeutic* experiments.[5] Some ethicists argue that since they cannot give informed consent and since nontherapeutic experiments are not designed to benefit the children who could be subject to them, there should be an absolute ban on nontherapeutic experimentation involving children. There are four reasons for this. First, there is no valid reason to assume that the children, were they of adult age, would consent to the experimentation. Second, it is immoral to use children to learn scientific data without anticipating direct benefit to these specific children. Third, no matter how convinced medical researchers might be that a particular nontherapeutic experiment carries no risk and entails no suffering, they cannot offer certitude in regard to these matters and, hence, the existence of doubt precludes the enrolling of children. Fourth, there are three communities involved in the hypothetical possibility of involving children in nontherapeutic experiments: The community of children, the community of medical researchers, and the broader all-encompassing community of society-at-large. Since society-at-large is responsible for protecting children, a vulnerable population, and since medical science could only benefit through exploiting children by putting them at risk, society would abrogate its responsibility to children and weaken the protection due them by allowing participation of children in nontherapeutic experimentation. Therefore, such participation cannot be allowed.

Some ethicists think that refusing to permit children to participate in nontherapeutic experimentation is extremist, and they present arguments to permit participation provided that safeguards are in place. This line of thinking holds that nontherapeutic experiments may be acceptable if the experiment is well designed, if there are no discernible risks, and if there is no discomfort experienced by the subject. Experimental use of **fluoride in water** before this usage became routine is cited as an example of the benign, risk-free, nontroublesome type of experiment in which children should be allowed to participate. Rationale supportive of this position maintains that because children are members of the human community it is reasonable to assume that they would want to undergo benign experiments in order to benefit this community, especially their peers and children in the future.

The lack of ethical unanimity on the morality of using children in nontherapeutic experiments introduces a beneficial tension into this area. Those who argue against any use of children force those who design nontherapeutic experiments involving children to extreme caution in the design and implementation of experimental programs. The tighter the design, the more careful the monitoring, the more intolerance of possible risks and discomfort, the better it will be for children who are involved in experiments.

Of interest in regard to children and medication is the fact that, for the most part, medications are tested on adults, not children. This places physicians at a disadvantage when they need to prescribe medications for minors because doctors are unsure about which drugs are appropriate and at what dosage. On August 13, 1997, President Bill Clinton proposed that drug companies be required to test their products on children before placing new medications on the market. While pharmaceutical company spokespersons agreed that the president's goal, to have accurate information, was a laudable one, they were reluctant to comply. Serious questions concerning risks to minor subjects, not legally qualified to give informed consent, could not be dismissed so as to procure valuable information.[6] It is unclear how this conflict can be resolved. Nevertheless, it seems certain that the reason for the conflict, adherence to the principle of not doing harm by keeping minors from nontherapeutic experiments, needs to be taken with the utmost seriousness.

OBTAINING CONSENT FROM CHILDREN

Strictly speaking, a person cannot authorize any medical procedure, either verbally or in writing, until he reaches the age of 18. Therefore, a parent or guardian must give informed consent for experimental treatments for children up until the age of 18.

Common sense and experience tell us that children are different at 2-years old, 6-years old, 14-years old, and 17-½-years old. As they grow, children mature and we expect them to take more of an interest in their medical care, as well as more of a part in determining in what that medical care should consist. As a result, it makes sense to involve adolescents in medical choices.

There is no formula to follow here. Obviously, 2-year-olds and 6-year-olds lack the maturity to contribute input. Some young teenagers may be level-headed and intelligent enough to merit a respectful hearing of their views, while others may be incapable of mature participation. From an ethical standpoint it is important that parents and physicians be aware of the inherent rights and dignity of minors so as to be open to involving them in decision making to the extent such involvement seems appropriate.[7]

USE OF MENTALLY RETARDED SUBJECTS

Because mentally retarded subjects lack capacity to give informed consent, adult and minor retarded persons should never be enlisted in nontherapeutic experiments. The same rationale as is in place for therapeutic experimentation on children would justify therapeutic experimentation on retarded individuals, provided a parent or guardian gives informed voluntary consent.

USE OF PRISONERS AS EXPERIMENTAL SUBJECTS

There are a lot of benefits for medical science in using prisoners as experimental subjects. Prisoners live in a controlled environment. The components of their diet are determined for them; they spend their days in uniform ways, in terms of number of hours of sleep and the regimens governing their waking hours. A large percentage of early-stage testing of medicine in the United States is done on prisoners. While the use of prisoners as experimental subjects is technically desirable and can be ethically acceptable, several safeguards should be in place to insure that prisoners freely consent to inclusion in experiments.

The most basic requirement of using an adult in an experiment is that the adult freely gives informed consent to participate. Adult prisoners retain this right so that they should never participate in therapeutic or nontherapeutic procedures against their will. Unfortunately, it is difficult to implement this free and full consent requirement in a prison atmosphere. The reason for this is that participation in experimental trials usually entails some benefits for prisoners which might constitute excessive inducements, thus becoming coercive factors. One benefit which often accompanies participating in an experiment is a break from prison monotony, and it is difficult to calculate how appealing this might be to a prisoner. A second benefit could be a specific reward or rewards for participating such as money, increased recreation time, cigarettes or some other commodity, or the possibility of credit on one's prison record possibly leading to early release. Educational programs and strategies need to be devised and introduced so as to minimize the possibility that prisoners will enlist in experimental programs for the wrong reasons.

In addition, other safeguards should be in place when prisoners are used in experiments. Only experiments which fulfill important social and scientific needs should be carried out; if these needs cannot be established, IRB approval should be denied. Prisoners are human beings who are entitled to respect. Accordingly, prisoners should be treated fairly and respectfully, both those who volunteer to participate in an experiment and those who refuse to volunteer. Finally, scrupulous attention should be paid to all aspects of the voluntary consent procedure: The discussion between researcher and prisoner, the comprehensiveness and intelligibility of the consent form, the opportunities provided to ask questions and change one's mind, and the demeanor of the prisoner who is entering the program. Should the prisoner give any indication of not having reached a mature, well-thought-out decision, such as by appearing naively eager, confused, or depressed, further inquiry into her comprehension and motives is essential.

EGO OF RESEARCHERS

The reasons for medical research and experimentation are to advance scientific knowledge, discover vaccines and cures for diseases, bring new or better treatments into everyday medical practice, improve the lives of sick people, and bring about a better standard of living for the human community. Research ought to be patient-centered or scientifically focused. This is not meant to diminish in any way the status or the importance of researchers, but only to point out that the goals of medical research are not tied up with the personalities and ambitions of individuals who carry out research. Medical research is not done so that scientists will become rich, famous, or important; therefore, members of the research community should put scientific and humanitarian concerns ahead of self-seeking and self-aggrandizement. If they do so, research and experimentation will be undertaken in a constructive-collaborative context by scientists who are more interested in doing good for others than in achieving personal rewards.

DISSEMINATION OF RESEARCH FINDINGS

Ordinarily the dissemination of research findings takes some time because editors of medical journals require independent peer evaluations before they agree to publish results of experimental studies and because specialized medical journals may be published only a few times a year. In recent years, with the advent of HIV infection and numerous breakthroughs in cancer research, more and more voices are being raised in favor of more expeditious means of publicizing promising findings. This lobbying is leading to quicker handling and publishing of data, but the position of editors that the peer review process is indispensable remains a sound one.

It sometimes happens that discoverers of medical breakthroughs attempt to bypass established channels and go directly to the media with their news. Such was the case when Drs. Patrick Steptoe and Robert Edwards announced word of the birth of Louise Joy Brown, the world's first in vitro baby on July 25, 1978. While this means of communication should not be condemned out of hand, caution should be stressed because misinformation, hysteria, or false hope can easily emerge in response to scientific-medical news transmitted in a sensational fashion.

CONCLUSION

The topic "experimentation in medicine" is a complex and fascinating one with many ethical aspects. Anyone involved in research or experimentation, as a researcher, research subject, member of an IRB, prospective beneficiary, or skeptical critic should be aware of the many facets of the subject. As with much of medical ethics, with research and experimentation we encounter the black, the white, and the gray and we need understanding and clear thinking to determine which category is applicable, and why.

ENDNOTES

[1] For a scholarly study of the Tuskegee research project, cf., James Jones, *Bad Blood* (New York: Free Press, 1981).

[2] Douglas Pasternak and Peter Carey, "Tales from the crypt," *U.S. News & World Report*, September 18, 1995, p. 78.

[3] Ibid., p. 82.

[4] Philip J. Hilts, "Consensus on Ethics in Research Is Elusive," *The New York Times*, January 15, 1995, p. 24.

[5] For a complete review of thought on this subject, cf., Michael A. Grodin and Leonard H. Glantz (editors), *Children as Research Subjects* (New York: Oxford University Press, 1994).

[6] Robert Pear, "Proposal to Test Drugs in Children Meets Resistance: Ethical Concerns Raised," *The New York Times*, November 30, 1997, pp. 1, 30.

[7] An excellent resource in reference to participation of minors in medical

decision making is "Minors' Rights in Health Care Decision Making," *Bioethics Forum*, Winter, 1995, Volume II, Number 4.

DISCUSSION QUESTIONS

1. Identify ethical principles which have been violated in the course of immoral medical experiments. Discuss the strategies which have been put in place to make certain that unethical practices are not repeated.
2. If you were a parent or guardian of a 15-year-old child, would you authorize your child's participation in a nontherapeutic experiment? Why or why not? If yes, under what circumstances? Do you think the child should participate in the decision and to what extent?
3. If you were a member of an administrative team in a hospital and were charged with setting up an Institutional Review Board, what kinds of people, in terms of character and background, would you nominate? What motivations would lead to your selections?
4. Make a list of the questions you would ask before agreeing to participate in a therapeutic experiment, a nontherapeutic experiment, or a randomized clinical trial. In each case, do you think you would or would not be predisposed to participate? Why?
5. If you were a researcher, what strategies would you employ to assure that your motivation was altruistic rather than self-serving? Why do you think it is important to scrutinize motivation?

CASE STUDY

Fred Nadler is an unemployed medical researcher. He lost his job when his HIV status became known to his employer; the grounds for his dismissal were that he might suffer injuries from laboratory viruses and that such injuries could place his employer at risk of legal action. Mr. Nadler's job loss represented a major setback for him and left him embittered and depressed.

In order to deal with his emotional struggles, Mr. Nadler joined an HIV-positive support group. As it turned out, members of the group were connected to a large network of HIV-positive persons and obtained experimental medications through this network. Within two months of his joining the group, Mr. Nadler became aware of significant improvement in himself and a dozen other group members. They all experienced substantial weight gain, the absence of opportunistic infections, and improved CD4 blood counts. How did this happen? Mr. Nadler and the 12 co-members had all been taking an identical combination of vitamins and antibiotics for seven weeks.

Mr. Nadler was happy for himself and the others. However, he was also somewhat troubled because, as a medical researcher, he was struggling with his conscience. His turmoil centered around several conflicting choices which he was in a position to make.

He could do nothing, allowing word of the efficacy of the vitamins and antibiotics to continue to spread unofficially.

He could go to the "establishment" and share the news with them.

He could get back at the "establishment" for what they did to him by keeping the information from them.

He could set a price for what he knew and sell the information to whomever was willing to pay.

Mr. Nadler decided to ask the members of his support group to brainstorm with him about what to do. Their first task is to determine if there are any objective standards of which they need to be aware and their second task is to determine why they should or should not honor these standards.

Evaluation:

1. Identify ethical issues contained in this case.
2. Propose possible solutions for these issues.
3. Make a decision relevant to action to be taken or not taken and provide rationale supportive of this decision.
4. Are you satisfied with your decision? Why or why not?

GLOSSARY

Science is a field of study concerned with establishing facts and methods through experiments based on theoretically plausible hypotheses. Medicine is a field of theory and practice which aims at understanding the human body so as to maintain physical health or return sick or injured people to health.

Reputable journals are highly specialized publications which appear between 4 and 12 times a year. These medical publications are administered by medical specialists in particular fields, such as cardiology, gynecology, oncology, etc. Specialized journal writing tends to be technical and, thus, inaccessible to lay readers. Reputable medical journals apply very stringent criteria to material submitted for publication because of the fact that by the very fact of publication the material gains credibility.

Peer review is a process by which individuals with the same or similar competence to the writer's (writers') examine the thesis and application in order to render a verdict as to the soundness of both thesis and application. Peer review is carried out prior to publication of articles in specialized medical journals and only articles receiving a positive peer review are published.

Widely circulated periodicals are *Science*, the *Journal of the American Medical Association* (JAMA), and the *New England Journal of Medicine* in the United States and *Lancet* and *Nature* in Great Britain. These magazines appear much more frequently than specialized journals, are more accessible to lay readers, and usually provide material subsequently reported by the media, i.e., news-magazines, newspapers, television, and radio.

Nuremberg is a city in Germany known for the fact that it was the site for the trial of Nazi war criminals following World War II. A tribunal made up of delegates from the United States, Great Britain, France, and the Soviet Union carried out the proceedings against high ranking Nazis charged with war crimes and crimes against humanity. Immoral experimentation was prosecuted under the heading "crimes against humanity."

Liability refers to legal responsibility to make good for harm suffered as a result of a procedure. Since untoward effects cannot be known in advance of an experimental treatment, it is important that experimental subjects grasp this fact in addition to the extent to which the agency conducting the experiment is willing to be accountable or liable for damages. The willingness to provide equitable compensation in case of injury should be regarded as one of the necessary conditions for an ethically acceptable human experiment.

Disclosure refers to the act of revealing in nontechnical language all that is known about the possible benefits and risks of a particular experimental medical treatment.

A **conflict of interest** is an experience of dual loyalties which makes it difficult for a person to honor both. The physician's responsibility is to act in behalf of his patient but, as a scientist seeking to acquire clinical knowledge, he is also motivated to learn from research experiments. It is important to recognize possible conflicts of interest so as to resolve them without jeopardizing either patient care or scientific standards.

Placebo is a medication, usually in the form of a pill, which contains no pharmacological ingredients. In vernacular usage, placebos are described as "sugar pills." Occasionally physicians prescribe placebos in order to placate patients who are hypochondriacs; sometimes placebos are prescribed because they might trigger psychological benefits. In randomized clinical trials, a percentage of those registered receive placebos so as to establish a control group, i.e., a cohort which does not receive medication and which can be clinically observed.

Fluoride in water at the level of one part per million is sufficient to prevent tooth decay and its benefits are greatest for children during the first eight years of life. Most communities which do not have naturally occurring fluoride in their water supplies add fluoride for this purpose. The first tests in which fluorides were added to public drinking water supplies began in three cities, Newburgh, N.Y., Grand Rapids, Mich., and Brantford, Ontario. In the United States today, approximately 50 million people drink artificially fluoridated water.

CHAPTER 10

Organ Retrieval and Transplantation

INTRODUCTION

Medical science does not need a reason to justify its existence but, if it did, it could do so by pointing to achievements connected with organ donation. In this regard, there is no question as to the value of technology which can provide, for example, replacement kidneys, allowing recipients to live normal lives. The state of the art of organ donation is not static but, rather, is ever changing, due to advances in technology, medical knowledge, and pharmacology. While the area of organ donation is generally one to which ethicists and all citizens look with respect, and occasionally awe, nevertheless, it is also an area for which some ethical cautions are in order. These cautions range from subtle to obvious and are the principal focus of this chapter.

ORGAN TRANSPLANTATION: THE STATE OF THE ART

Since World War I, with the development of the technology for blood transfusions, skills surrounding transplantation as well as anticipation of success for transplants have seen continual improvement. As a result, the field of organ transplantation is a vast one and the state of the art is impressive indeed. The organs which can be transplanted include kidneys, cornea, skin, heart, lungs, liver, bone marrow, **blood from umbilical cords**, ovaries, and testicles.

Up until 1984, with the approval and availability of cyclosporin, a medicine which allows a recipient to adjust to a donated organ by repressing the body's tendency to reject the new organ, the possibilities of successful organ transplants were very limited. Since the introduction of cyclosporin, however, the situation has changed considerably so that today people who receive new organs to replace diseased ones can expect full recovery along with the promise of normal lives.

There are several ways in which transplantation can occur. An *autograft* is transplantation of skin or bone within an individual. For example, people who suffer burns on one part of their body can receive a skin graft using skin from another area of their body. A *homograft* is the transplantation of an organ from one individual to another of the same species. Most contemporary organ transplants are homografts. An *isograft* is a transplant between two genetically identical persons, i.e., between identical twins. A *heterograft* or *xenograft*, is an interspecies organ transplant. In 1984 an infant known as Baby Fae was the recipient of a heterograft in the form of a baboon heart. (In respect to terminology, one could also use the words *autotransplant, homotransplant, isotransplant,* and *xenotransplant,* with comparable meanings.)

On April 11, 1996, the first "domino" liver transplant in the United States was carried out. In the procedure a 17-year-old Pennsylvania girl received a liver and a large and small intestine from a donor and her own healthy liver was donated to a third patient. The recipient of the liver and intestines required this combination of organs because of the rare pseudo-obstruction disease from which she suffered. Since her liver had the potential to function normally in a patient who was not troubled by an intestinal anomaly, physicians were pleased that the liver could be transplanted instead of discarded.[1]

It is important to match tissue and blood types between donor and recipient and to monitor recipients carefully, especially in the days and weeks following transplant, for rejection. In regard to matching donors to recipients, sophisticated national and international computer networks have been established. In addition, a system for quick transfer of organs from place to place via courier networks has been instituted; time factors are critical because organs can survive outside the human body only for limited periods of time.

ORGAN RETRIEVAL

Most organs are retrieved from the bodies of the newly dead. The common exceptions to this are retrieval of one kidney from a relative who is a close match, or donation of part of an organ, such as a liver which is expected to regenerate, from a parent to an infant or young child.

In order for hospital officials to procure an organ or organs from a cadaver, one of two things must occur. Either the person who is deceased authorized the donation of organs through prior completion of a written document, or the next of kin of the deceased gives permission for donation of the person's organs. In the absence of authorization, organs may not be removed.

Ideal donors of major organs are accident victims or individuals who die following brain trauma. These people die on respirators in hospitals and a diagnosis of brain death precedes their being removed from the respirator. Should there be permission for organ donation the respirator would continue to run after the declaration of brain death; by continuing respiration the usable organs would be maintained in a viable state. It is estimated that there are at least 10,000 potential donors each year in the United States. Unfortunately, only 40 percent of these potential donors actually become donors. Since there are more than 40-thousand people in the United States on waiting lists for donated organs, the lack of donors represents a serious concern.[2]

ETHICAL ASPECTS OF ORGAN DONATION

Meeting the Need for Organs. The Uniform Anatomical Gift Act is legislation that allows people to will their organs to others so that, if usable, these organs can be taken after death. The UAGA was proposed in 1968 by the U.S. National Conference of Commissioners and subsequently adopted by all states by 1973. Unless a person makes himself an organ donor or the individual's next of kin authorizes donation of his organs, the person's organs cannot be taken. Thus, the system of making organs available for transplant rests on the free consent of the donor or the party responsible for the disposition of the donor's body. The consent requirement is consistent with the culture within which medicine is practiced in the United States. However, as we just saw, there is one significant drawback to this system and it is that an insufficient number of people offer to be donors and too few next of kin agree to donate organs, making for a shortage of donated organs. As a result, a suggestion is frequently made that the United States change the system for procurement, moving to a practice of routine salvaging of organs from the newly dead to obtain whatever organs are available or needed. According to a routine salvaging system, the bodies of all recently deceased would be made available as repositories of organs and no permission would be needed before retrieving organs from these bodies. In respect to people who do not want their organs removed after death, they could go through a procedure for opting out of the system and their wishes would be respected. A term used to refer to this system is *Presumed Consent.*

The argument against routine salvaging or presumed consent is that neither medical science nor the government should require this type of personal altruistic act of people. Instead, what is needed is increased education about the possibilities of organ donation. One body can yield as many as nine organs plus bone, tissue, and skin, providing life-saving assistance for several different people. To the extent that individuals become aware of the possibilities for organ donation, this argument goes, they will become willing to register as donors. By facilitating the registration process through widespread availability of donor cards both government and private sources could promote self-selection into the donor network. These positive initiatives would encourage and expand the voluntary system currently in effect, and this would be preferable to a mandatory government-controlled-and-administered system.

Another way proposed to resolve the shortage of organs is institution of the so-called *Mandated Choice* approach. According to this people would be required to make a choice as to whether or not they want to be organ donors. The occasion on which this choice would be required might be that of obtaining or renewing a driver's license. Unfortunately, when a mandated choice system tied to drivers licenses was tried in Texas, 80 percent of the people did not register to be donors.[3] Their reluctance underscores the necessity of educating the general public about the good to be achieved from organ donation. Such educational efforts might accomplish the purposes of making people more willing to allow for donation of their organs as well as organs from deceased loved ones.

Harm to Living Donors. The first norm regulating medical ethics is "Do no harm." When this norm is added to the general principle that individuals should safeguard their well-being and not mutilate themselves, one becomes aware that allowing for organ donation from living donors requires establishing a rationale which permits exceptions to general rules. This rationale is constructed in three phases. The first phase entails recognition of the implications of autonomy so that respect is given to the free choice of an adult patient, to be a donor or not to be a donor. Accordingly, under no circumstances are children or retarded people allowed to be donors. The second phase of constructing the rationale is to establish a two-fold polemic: The potential donor is a member of society and, as such, is entitled to engage in an altruistic deed so as to benefit someone else. At the same time, the good deed of donating the organ, while weakening the donor, would not so compromise him as to endanger his ability to continue living as a healthy person. Finally, in regard to the role of medical personnel in the transplant scenario, their motivation with respect to the donor would mirror the donor's, so that they would be aiming at restoring health to a person in a very compromised condition through weakening a strong person whose overall strength would, in all probability, be able to absorb the loss.

While it is possible to find ethical justification for weakening a donor in order to benefit a recipient, it is not possible to justify donation of an organ which would result in the donor's death. Thus, the donation of a non-paired or non-regenerative organ such as a heart from one living person to another would be morally unacceptable; this donation would certainly result in the death of the donor and this would be an unacceptable price to pay for the benefit of a recipient.

A provocative case which generated a great deal of interest and violated the principle that children not be used as donors was brought to light in 1990. This case revolved around the decision of Mary and Abe Ayala to conceive a child in the hope that she would be a suitable bone marrow donor for her sister Anissa who had leukemia. As it happened, Marissa Ayala was indeed a suitable donor and Anissa did recover as a result of the transplant. When the parents became aware of the negative response of ethicists to their decision, they were taken aback. They reacted by saying that they were prepared to love and accept the new baby whether or not she proved to be an acceptable donor and they did not seem to understand the principle which the ethicists thought was violated. While, in theory, it may be clear that a person should always be an end in herself and never a means to an end, in practice, in the lives of well-meaning people, translating this theory into action may not be so clear-cut. (The happy fact is that Anissa Ayala-Espinosa has so far beaten cancer because she celebrated five years cancer-free, as reported by news services on June 6, 1996.)

Insuring the Truly Free Consent of Living Donors. While a person has a right to perform the altruistic deed of donating an organ such as a kidney to a sibling, this right does not translate into an ethical obligation to donate an organ in order to save another person's life. The reason for this is because the donation of organs from one living person to another should be a totally free act. To force a person to donate a kidney to her brother would violate the sanctity of the coerced donor and diminish her autonomy and right to choose what good deeds she wants to perform. In view of this fact, during the process of counseling which occurs with donors prior to donation, counselors need to ascertain whether or not the potential donor is experiencing coercive pressure, and, if there is reason to think that she is, she needs to be eliminated from consideration. This holds true even if she is the last possible potential donor and without her organ the needy recipient would surely die.

Determination of Death Prior to Organ Retrieval. The overwhelming majority of human organs are retrieved from the corpses of recently deceased persons. As we have noted, authorization is established if the individual, prior to his death, has executed a donor card, or authorization is procured through negotiations with the next of kin. An assessment is made of the dying patient and a tentative decision is made in reference to the specific organs to be retrieved from the patient.

Word is then conveyed to an organ network as to the status of the patient and the probable organs which are expected to become available. After this the only thing to do is to wait. And the ethical mandate is that all involved wait respectfully for the patient to die before steps are taken to retrieve organs. It would be unethical to retrieve organs from a person who is not dead and it would likewise be unethical to do anything to hasten death so as to make organs available sooner. Respect for the rights and dignity of the prospective donor require that organs not be taken until death occurs.

In view of this fact, determination of death becomes a crucial component of the organ donation process. Since, in the vast majority of cases, the recently deceased will be kept on a respirator to continue heart and lung function, thus insuring organ viability until retrieval, the determination of death will ordinarily be made based on the criteria for **brain death**. By this is meant that once a patient shows no brain activity, neither of the brain stem nor of the cerebral-cortical functioning, and once this is established with certitude, then the patient can be declared dead. Whether or not the deceased continues respiration due to the work of a ventilator is immaterial; the individual is dead because of the determination that all brain functioning has definitively stopped.[4] Without the action of the mechanical ventilator, there would be no respiratory activity either and, in this case, the respiratory activity is not a sign of life but, rather, simply an indicator that the corpse is being maintained until the organs are taken, at which time the respirator will be turned off.

(It should be noted that people who are comatose in a persistent vegetative state do *not* meet the criteria for brain death. Although some people refer to pvs patients as "brain dead" because they lack cerebral-cortical functioning, they are not yet dead because their brain stems function, allowing for the continuance of noncognitive biological existence. Since they are not dead, people in a persistent vegetative state, mistakenly referred to as "brain dead" people, could not be considered as possible organ donors.)

In December 1997, Dr. John Potts reported on a study presented by the Institute of Medicine, part of the National Academy of Sciences, to the U.S. Health and Human Services Department, which had requested the research. The study discussed a potential pool of at least 1,000 organ donors per year whose deaths would be determined from nonbeating hearts rather than from brain-death observations. People whose hearts have stopped, likely because of traumatic injury from a car accident, homicide, or suicide, may evince brain activity because of the effects of life-support equipment. Nevertheless, these people are dead and their organs are viable for only a short time. The Institute recommended allowing organ retrieval from corpses in this category and urged that national standards be set to accomodate retrieval. The most medically significant guideline stipulates that "A five-minute wait should be required after life support is withdrawn and before organ recovery begins to insure that a heart would not resume beating on its own."[5]

Preventing Conflicts of Interest. Two medical teams could conceivably have conflicting interests in regard to a potential cadaver donor. The interest of the physicians charged with caring for the patient is the patient's well-being and comfort, and it is their duty to do everything required to meet these ends. The members of the organ retrieval team, on the other hand, are accustomed to look beyond the donor patient to potential recipients, and their primary interest is in the retrieval of viable organs. It would be unethical if the retrieval team were to put pressure on attending physicians to make compromises or take shortcuts in patient care so as to make organs available faster. It would also be unethical for physicians attending the patient to render less than the customary level of care in order to procure benefits from the retrieval team. In view of the fact that conflicting interests could motivate unethical treatment of a dying patient, patient-care providers and transplant personnel should not overlap so that the same person is on the two teams. In addition, to the extent possible, the two teams should function independently and should not work in proximity with each other or negotiate directly with one another. Thus, having the retrieval team arrive after the patient's death and arranging for negotiations to be handled through hospital administrators or another third party would safeguard against the occurrence of conflicts of interest.

Use of Anencephalics. An anencephalic newborn is an infant born without most of its brain; this anomaly means that the child will not go on to grow and develop and will die within a short period of time. This period of time may be as brief as a few hours or, with technological assistance, as long as a few weeks. About 1,000 anencephalic babies are born each year in the United States. Very rarely do anencephalic newborns live longer than a few months, and never do they grow beyond infancy.

To say the least, having an anencephalic newborn is a heartbreaking experience for the parents. In recent years, however, some parents of anencephalics have sought to blunt their pain by bringing some good out of their personal tragedy through offering their babies as organ donors. The peculiar circumstances surrounding this possibility have given rise to a considerable amount of discussion regarding its ethics.

In order to use an anencephalic's organs such as its heart, lungs, kidneys, and/or liver for transplant, one of two strategies would need to be followed. The first, for which there is virtually no support, would entail mercifully euthanizing the infant and removing its usable organs immediately. Fortunately, physical and moral revulsion is sufficiently strong in regard to contemplating this possibility that it does not seem likely to become an accepted practice.

The second approach to an anencephalic would be to put him immediately on a respirator in order to keep his organs viable. The respirator would then be turned off periodically to determine whether or not the infant could breathe on his own. When it was established that the anencephalic could not breathe on his own, the baby would be declared dead and his organs would be taken.

Contained in the above scenario are the problems inherent in organ donation from an anencephalic. The first problem is that there is no reliable way to measure brain death in this type of infant, so that the trial-and-error method of turning the respirator on and off needs to happen. The baby's caretakers are thus not so much interested in his needs and well-being as in using him to serve a purpose. And using any member of the human race as a means, rather than respecting the person in himself, is considered unethical.

A second problem with using anencephalics as organ donors who give the gift of life to other infants is that the terminology is hollow and meaningless since these infants cannot be understood as in any way consenting to altruistic conduct. They may be sources of organs, but they are not givers of life. Another ethical reservation about using anencephalics revolves around the fact that the most compassionate response to their existence would be to keep them comfortable until they pass away—in other words, to respond to their needs in the most humane manner possible. Putting these babies on respirators in order to keep their organs in a satisfactory condition prevents them from being given the most appropriate care. And, finally, the condition and diagnosis of anencephaly are not black and white. Some infants have barely a brain stem, some have part of a brain plus a brain stem, others have a deformed brain. Acting quickly to declare death and retrieve organs might result in deaths of handicapped children who could have lived and enjoyed some quality of life had physicians been more cautious in reaching a diagnosis of anencephaly and more aggressive in providing therapeutic care.

In theory the issue of the anencephalic newborn is especially interesting because it forces a confrontation between principled thinking, such as is contained in the forgoing, and a utilitarian approach. For the utilitarian, a greater good can be accomplished by using the anencephalic's organs than by rendering compassionate, respectful care to the infant. The good of the lives saved through the salvaging of organs would probably be seen as more straightforward than merely trying to honor principles through serving persons. While this line of thinking can appear rational, clear-headed, and measurable, however, people need to pause and think long and hard before relinquishing principles for a "greater good."[6]

Use of Animal Organs. Whether or not animal organs should be used as replacements for human organs is a disputed question with most of the expert opinion holding that using these organs is not feasible.[7] Currently, experimental work is underway on pigs and baboons to breed animals with human regulatory genes whose organs might be suitable for human recipients.[8] The biggest technical obstacle to overcome in developing such suitable organs is surmounting the physiological rejection factor. To date close to three dozen xenografts have been carried out but none has been successful.

The situation in which animal organs are likely to be used is that of a "bridge" during which a human receives an animal organ as a temporary measure until a compatible human organ can be found. Because of the significant risk of rejection, however, even this temporary strategy is rarely employed.

There are ethical concerns about using animal organs. One of these concerns is voiced by animal rights proponents who argue against killing animals in order to use their organs. These spokespersons for animals contend that humans are not entitled to breed, genetically alter, or kill animals so as to acquire organs. They maintain either that animals have a right not to be killed or that breeding and killing animals constitute an indefensible form of abuse.

Those who hold an opposite position tend to respond by saying that they oppose cruel treatment of animals, breeding more animals than are absolutely necessary for scientific purposes, or using animals in a manner which could be considered capricious. However, they maintain that humans are superior to animals and that humans have a right to use animals for worthwhile purposes. Since saving human lives through replacement of diseased organs is a worthy human goal, people who espouse this mindset find themselves unwilling to compromise so as to satisfy their opponents. In contemporary society proponents of animal rights are a minority and so, for the time being at least, it seems likely that research about the possibility of using animal organs, as well as occasional bridge uses, will continue.

Ethical concern about xenografts was crystallized in the famous case of Baby Fae. Born on October 14, 1984, Baby Fae suffered from **hypoplastic left heart syndrome**, a condition which is almost always fatal within two weeks. On October 26, 1984, a baboon heart was transplanted into the baby, and on November 15, 1984 Baby Fae died. The transplant was performed by Dr. Leonard Bailey, the chief of pediatric surgery at Loma Linda Hospital in California. There was an enormous amount of media coverage of this case and many ethical questions surfaced in connection with it. Was enough effort made to locate a human heart? Was the procedure **experimental therapeutic** or simply **experimental**? In view of the lack of previous success with xenografts, could it possibly have been thought of as experimental therapeutic? If it was, as these questions suggest, a straightforward experimental procedure, how could it have been justified since its consequences were far from benign? Could the suffering and discomfort experienced by Baby Fae be justified? Why were those involved in the technical aspects of organ selection so haphazard? Why did they not take the proper steps to insure that the baboon's blood and tissue matched the baby's? Did Baby Fae's mother give truly informed consent or was she so intimidated by the scenario of meeting with physicians for lengthy consultations that she signed forms without actually realizing all the repercussions of what she was submitting her daughter to? Was the Loma Linda institutional review procedure sufficiently vigorous so as to safeguard the rights of the patient and her family? Was the transplant surgeon motivated to act in his patient's best interests or was he seeking to advance his reputation?

These questions suggest the extent of the ethical unease surrounding animal-to-human transplants involving babies or children. When the story of Baby Fae's transplant first broke, the American public thought it was about to witness a medical miracle. With Baby Fae's death, however, it became apparent that there were good reasons to argue that what had transpired should never have been allowed to happen. It is not surprising that since 1984 there have been no reported cases of xenografts involving minors.[9]

Incentives for Donors. What should motivate a person to donate his organs? Should there be any form of payment to those willing to donate blood, bone marrow, or a kidney? Should there be prepayment to those willing to donate some or all of their organs after death? When one considers the possibility of compensation for organs one begins to understand why bartering organs for cash would not be a good idea. Those most likely to respond to financial incentives would probably be people who need money and who, because of this need, would be unlikely to think about whether or not they really want to experience inconvenience or discomfort or are willing to jeopardize their own health in order to participate in such an undertaking. In addition, the people most likely to opt in based on financial motives would probably be members of the underclass, so that establishing financial incentives would be socially disruptive because it would constitute one more way that minorities and the poor are exploited.

There is an ethical consensus that organs should not be bought or sold and that the only defensible incentive is the assurance of knowing that through organ donation one is offering the gift of life to another person. Thus, the only incentive to be sought in conjunction with organ donation is a subjectively experienced sense of satisfaction because one knows that one may be benefitting others.

Incentives for Medical Personnel. As we inferred in conjunction with the case of Baby Fae, there would be something unseemly about a physician orchestrating an organ transplant if her motivation were to achieve renown as a result. Medical science and organ transplantation exist to benefit people, and since donors should act from this motivation, so should medical personnel who are involved.

It would be unethical for members of a transplant team to offer incentives to attending physicians or nurses in order to get them to pressure patients or family members to agree to organ donation. According to the way the system for organ donation is structured, donors or next to kin should freely opt in and should not experience pressure to donate.

The way the system plays out in the modern hospital, specific nurses and physicians are regularly called upon to broach the issue of organ donation with family members of accident victims. To be sure, these conferences are highly stressful and emotionally charged, and it takes training, skill, and sensitivity for medical personnel to initiate and direct them. No matter how many times a medical professional initiates such a dialogue, it is never easy. Given the circumstances, any thought of offering anxious relatives incentives would be inconceivable. What happens most frequently is that next of kin are made aware of the facts that there is no hope for their loved one and that the person's organs would constitute a gift of life for other people. Then the family members are encouraged to search their souls in order to determine whether or not they would be willing to authorize donation.

Incentives could figure as a part of the process if transplant personnel were to use them to put pressure on the physicians and nurses who interact with families of dying people, usually gun-shot wound, head trauma, or accident victims. The kinds of incentives might be gifts or prepaid vouchers to attend conferences or similar items. The message which these gifts would convey is "Thank you for the organ donations you have arranged and keep up the good work." In order to prevent incentives from getting in the way of the good judgment of doctors and nurses and to insure that the promise of incentives does not prompt medical personnel to exceed the bounds of good taste when they request organs, hospital administrators need to exercise judicious surveillance over this area.

Selecting Organ Recipients. On June 8, 1995, Mickey Mantle, a 64-year-old retired baseball superstar and a recovering alcoholic received a liver transplant; initially this transplant seemed to save his life because his own liver was so badly diseased that he was at the point of death. Within a matter of weeks, however, Mantle was back in the news because his doctors had found evidence of lung cancer. Mantle died on August 13, 1995.

The coverage accorded to Mickey Mantle led to discussion of several interconnected issues. As a matter of fact, many of the issues related to organ recipients are encountered in an examination of the Mantle liver transplant. These issues include:

Social worth Since the early days of organ transplantation there has been an ethical consensus that one human is not worth more than another so that one person should not be considered more worthy of an organ than another. If there are not enough organs to go around, then available organs should be awarded by lottery or based on such a medical criterion as probability of success. Those who allocate organs should not concern themselves with whether a woman is a prostitute or a widowed mother; if they were to do so, organ allocation would quickly become unfair and discriminatory.

Fair allocation system With a general agreement that social worth should not figure in decisions to allot organs, a system has been established to match donors with recipients according to the recipient's place on a waiting list.[10] The waiting list is not as cut and dry as holding a position in a line because specific medical factors could cause a person to move ahead or move backwards. Thus, rapidly progressive total organ failure would be cause for moving ahead, while developing a **secondary condition** which would be a **contraindication** for a transplant would be a reason for reassignment further down the list.

In the case of Mickey Mantle, many questions were raised relevant to these points. As far as social worth was concerned, some people argued that Mantle had made great contributions to sports culture in the United States and was entitled to a liver transplant for that reason. Others objected saying that Mickey Mantle ruined his liver by years of heavy drinking and that he should not have received a replacement organ; their rationale was based on social worth and medical-indications criteria. Still others said that Mickey Mantle catapulted over others on the list because he was famous; they contended that an unknown elderly alcoholic male would not even have been considered for a transplant. The objectivity and competence of Mantle's physicians also came under question because the issue was raised as to whether or not they could have been ignorant of the lung cancer at the time they transplanted the donor liver. Knowledge of the presence of lung cancer would have radically changed the situation, negating the possibility of a liver transplant. But the suggestion was made that perhaps the physicians coveted the limelight into which they stepped because of their relationship to the superstar, and perhaps attaining the limelight was their goal, not rendering appropriate care to their patient while upholding the standards of medical practice.[11]

It will be some time before the issues surrounding Mickey Mantle's liver transplant are resolved if, indeed, they ever are finally settled. In the meantime, there remain other pertinent concerns attendant to the selection of recipients.

Costs Organ transplantation is expensive. According to data gathered by Battelle-Seattle Research Center in Washington and reported in 1995 in the *Encyclopedia of Bioethics*, the average costs for transplants, including hospital, doctor, and organ retrieval fees were as follows: $40,000 for a kidney; $67,000 for a pancreas; $91,000 for a heart; $135,000 for a heart-lung; and $145,000 for a liver. These figures do not include costs incurred by transplant recipients before transplant and after discharge; neither have they been adjusted for inflation.[12] For the most part, costs associated with transplants are borne by taxpayers or people with medical insurance, in other words, by the majority of citizens in the United States. Determining if organ transplants are worth the cost, or under which circumstances the expense is justified, are complex issues which will not yield easy resolution. Still, the fact that some people receive transplanted organs while poor children go unvaccinated should prompt society to look at the big picture and grapple with inequities in the health care delivery system. (It should be noted that currently Medicare covers certain transplantation procedures such as kidney, heart, liver, and bone marrow. Kidney transplants are an entitlement under Medicare provisions, while other transplants are covered on a very restricted basis according to selection criteria that include the length and extent of the disability, the age of the recipient, and the indication for transplantation.[13])

Retransplants It often happens that an organ transplant does not work, raising the issue of a second transplant, or a retransplant. The question then arises as to whether a person waiting for a retransplant or even a third transplant should have priority over a person on a waiting list who would be receiving an organ for the first time. This is a complex issue, not easily settled. From a medical indications perspective, retransplant patients tend to be sicker than patients waiting for an original transplant because they have experienced a significant rejection episode. In addition, medical teams have become acquainted with transplant patients and tend to want to continue to do battle with them. This leads to an unwillingness to give up on a second or third transplant and, perhaps, to a using of influence in order to act in behalf of the patient who is well known. Unfortunately, it is the unknown patient on the waiting list who suffers as a consequence.

While this is a difficult and distressing issue, raising awareness about it and encouraging discussion of its many ramifications may lead to an ethical consensus in regard to how to achieve the desired equity.

Role of the Media With increasing frequency we have been witnessing media attention given to individuals, usually children, who need bone marrow or organ donations in order to survive. This coverage tends to be emotionally wrenching and frequently leads to identification of donors. Is it ethical or unethical to venture outside the established system and bypass waiting lists in order to procure an organ for oneself or a loved one?

While the intention behind the decision to go public is understandable, it is ethically problematic for two reasons. First, it undermines respect for the impartial system which was designed and put in place to prevent organ procurement by just such measures. And, second, it puts the anonymous people on the waiting list at a distinct disadvantage because they are forced to suffer an additional injury because they are not well connected or photogenic enough to be candidates for media coverage. A much better use of the media would be as an educational instrument to inform as to what medical science can do with donated organs and how one could go about declaring herself an organ donor.

PRIORITY TO BE ASSIGNED TO ORGAN TRANSPLANTS

Organ transplants cost a considerable amount of money, both for the operation and for subsequent lifelong maintenance of the recipient following surgery. Many organ transplants do not work, and many people who need organs do not get them. Some transplant surgeries should never take place. And all of this is true within a social context in which more than 40 million people in the United States lack medical insurance, and, in many places, the health care delivery system is strained to the breaking point as it tries to provide routine medical care. It is generally agreed that in the years ahead the United States will have to come to grips with the fact that some kinds of medical treatment are more basic and mandatory than others and that these basic services should be provided before less predictable procedures are routinely attempted. What will this realization or new policy direction do to organ transplant programs? This remains to be seen. As we await developments it is important that we realize that the answer lies at the junction of medical possibilities, financial realities, ethical conviction, and public opinion. These four factors, interacting with each other, will dictate the future of organ transplantation.

A RELATED QUESTION: PRACTICING MEDICAL TECHNIQUES ON CADAVERS

On December 15, 1994, an article in *The New England Journal of Medicine* raised the issue of the ethical propriety of performing practice techniques on cadavers.[14] (This question is relevant to organ donation because it has been established that organs may not be taken from the newly dead without prior permission of the deceased or permission from the next of kin. In other words, the human corpse deserves respect and this respect requires that organs not be removed without authorization.)

The article stated that resident physicians, beginner doctors, and others frequently practice such skills as inserting breathing tubes on cadavers without requesting permission or advising anyone. Subsequent discussion among physicians confirmed that such use of cadavers happens fairly often. The defense for so doing is that no mutilation occurs, the cadaver is beyond the experiences of suffering or discomfort, the doctors need to master the techniques, and it is better that they develop skills by practicing on the newly dead than by practicing on living patients who might be injured by a beginner's lack of expertise.

While all of these arguments are reasonable and cogent, they do not answer those who object to the fact that certain corpses become sites of medical manipulation just because they are available to a physician who needs practice. Respect for the autonomy of living people has been deeply enshrined in medical practice, and using cadavers without permission seems inconsistent with this ethos. For this reason in the next few years a debate about this subject may occur, resulting in the formulation of guidelines to assure respect for recently deceased.

CONCLUSION

The subject of organ donation and transplantation is a large and complicated one. While there are some obvious black and white areas, many
aspects are various shades of gray. Mastering the complexity of this subject
makes one more respectful of the possibilities of medical science and more
humble about the probabilities of reaching ethical certitudes. As a consequence, new life and better lives are not the only results of transplant technology; an increased ethical sensitivity is a parallel, and equally welcome,
development.

ENDNOTES

[1] "Three People Are Involved In 'Domino' Liver Transplant," *The New York Times*, April 28, 1996, p. 26.

[2] Gina Kolata, "Families Are Barriers to Many Organ Donations, Study Finds," *The New York Times*, July 7, 1995, p. A13.

[3] Ibid.

[4] In Chapter 13, "Treatment of the Terminally Ill: Important Distinctions," the position of Orthodox Jews in regard to pronouncement of death is discussed. Orthodox Jews do not accept criteria of brain death as determina-
tive of death but, rather, wait until there is absolutely no sign of breathing.
There is no question that this religious belief should be honored.

[5] "Guidelines Are Urged in Using Organs of Heart-Dead Patients," *The New York Times*, December 21, 1997, p. 38.

[6] In June 1994, the Council on Ethical and Judicial Affairs of the American
Medical Association allowed for physicians to remove organs from living
anencephalics provided the diagnosis of anencephaly was confirmed by
two experts and the baby's parents initiated the discussion about donation. In my opinion, this decision is both wrongheaded and unethical. Cf.,
Gina Kolata, "Donating Organs of Anencephalic Babies Is Backed," *The New York Times*, May 24, 1995, p. C13.

[7] Lawrence K. Altman, "Cross-Species Transplants Raise Concerns about
Human Safety," *The New York Times*, January 9, 1996, p. 11.

[8] Philip J. Hilts, "Mixed-Species Organ Is Set for Transplant," *The New York Times*, July 28, 1995, p. A10.

[9] For a review of scholarly arguments for and against Baby Fae's xenograft,
cf., Judith Mistichelli, "Scope Note 5; Baby Fae—Ethical Issues Surround
Cross-Species Organ Transplantation," National Reference Center for

Bioethics Literature, Kennedy Institute of Ethics, Georgetown University, Washington, D.C., January, 1985.

[10] There is a dispute about a regulation of the U.S. Department of Health and Human Services which in 1998 established a single national waiting list for all individuals who are awaiting organ transplants. The national list replaces several regional waiting lists; advocates of regional lists object to the single national list. The controversy centers around which approach is fairer and more efficient. It will likely be resolved by Congressional action. Cf., J. Scott Orr, "Wait for organ transplant could get longer in N.J., senators say," *The Star Ledger*, June 19, 1998, p. 4.

[11] An account of Mantle's physician's response to negative assessments of his part in the liver transplant are contained in an article written by Lawrence K. Altman, MD, "Defending Tough Decisions in a Case Open to Hindsight," *The New York Times*, August 15, 1995, p. C3.

[12] Warren Reich (ed.), *Encyclopedia of Bioethics* (New York: Simon & Schuster Macmillan, 1995), p. 1878.

[13] "Economic Issues," a publication of the United Network—Organ Sharing, undated, p. 96.

[14] Cf., Gina Kolata, "Hospitals Use Bodies of Dead for Practice," *The New York Times*, December 15, 1994, p. 22A. In this article Kolata describes a study undertaken by Robert D. Truoz and Frank E. Reardon and published the same day in the *New England Journal of Medicine*.

DISCUSSION QUESTIONS

1. Are you willing to donate your organs after you die? Why or why not? If yes, have you filled out the proper forms? Why or why not?

2. If you were in a position to do so, would you authorize donation of a loved one's organs? Why or why not?

3. Donation of a kidney puts the donor at some risk. Donation of bone marrow causes the donor to experience some discomfort. How do you feel about experiencing discomfort or placing yourself at risk to help someone else?

4. Should the United States move from its present opt-in system of organ donation to a system in which there would be routine harvesting except for those who choose to opt out? What prompts you to hold the position you have adopted?

5. Consider the case of an anencephalic newborn who is kept alive on a respirator in order to serve the purpose of being an organ donor when he

dies after a weaning episode. State your moral evaluation of this case, providing rationale supportive of your position.

6. Why should patient care and transplant teams function independently? What are the principles which should motivate each of these teams?

7. At Mickey Mantle's family's request, an organ donors' day was held at the All Star Game, July 11, 1995, in Arlington, Texas. At that time organ donor cards were passed out to fans attending the game and later collected. Suggest at least three other strategies which could be implemented to promote organ donation.

8. Given the fact that routine health care is not available to many people in the United States, should costly organ transplantation procedures be cut back or eliminated and funds rechanneled to other health care needs? Discuss the rationale which prompts you to argue as you do.

CASE STUDY

Theresa Rodriquez is a 34-year-old single mother of two children, nine and 15-years-old. She is an illegal immigrant who lives in the Southwest; she works as a domestic. Since she is poor and has no health insurance, Ms. Rodriguez ignored many symptoms before going to a hospital emergency room. At the emergency room the initial examination revealed a large lump in her right breast. Further tests confirmed the diagnosis of breast cancer. A mastectomy was performed and biopsies of lymph nodes disclosed the spread of cancer. Ms. Rodriquez was told that the best treatment available for her type of cancer is an isograft bone-marrow transplant. In view of the fact that she has a healthy identical twin, the probability of a good outcome is high.

According to the *Wall Street Journal*, the average first-year costs associated with bone-marrow transplants were $172,900 in 1995 dollars. When her surgeon told Ms. Rodriquez that she would need to raise this amount before the necessary arrangements were made, she replied that this would be impossible. Ms. Rodriquez was released from the hospital five days after surgery. Her bill of $13,629 was paid from an indigent fund. Whatever further treatment she receives will be largely a matter of chance.

Evaluation:

1. Identify ethical issues contained in this case.
2. Propose possible solutions for these issues.

3. Make a decision relevant to action to be taken or not taken and provide rationale supportive of this decision.
4. Are you satisfied with your decision? Why or why not?

GLOSSARY

Blood from the umbilical cord as well as the placentas of newborns is rich in stem cells and can be used to treat leukemia and other diseases which damage the blood or immune system. Up until very recently this blood was discarded in the delivery room. However, when it was realized that placental-umbilical blood is rich in stem cells, its usefulness as a substitute for bone marrow became a possibility. Although treatment with this kind of blood requires only a transfusion, clinicians refer to the procedure as a "transplantation." Stem-cell transplants hold promise because researchers think that they are less likely to be rejected than those from bone marrow, less likely to cause graft-versus-host disease, and much easier to obtain than bone marrow. In addition, it is easier to match donors and recipients, thus making it possible to offer treatment to more potential beneficiaries.

Brain death criteria are a way of establishing that a person has died. The most prominent proposal put forward by the medical profession for determining "When is death?" was offered in the 1968 Report of the Ad Hoc Committee of the Harvard Medical School to Examine the Definition of Brain Death; this is ordinarily referred to as the "Harvard definition for death." To read the Committee's detailed criteria, cf., "A definition of irreversible coma," *Journal of the American Medical Association*, June, 1968, V 203, pp. 337–340.

Hypoplastic left heart syndrome is a rare anomaly which affects newborn infants. Those born with this syndrome rarely live more than a few weeks; they experience respiratory distress and a bluish discoloration.

Experimental therapeutic refers to the fact that an individual agrees to a procedure, the outcome of which is uncertain, on the grounds that the procedure represents at least a probability of improving his condition.

Experimental refers to a treatment or procedure about which very little can be asserted as probable. An individual's motivation for participating in an experimental procedure is likely for the advancement of science.

Secondary condition means the occurrence of a second medical problem which complicates treatment of the original problem. For example, a person with kidney failure (original problem) could develop pneumonia (secondary condition) and the presence of pneumonia could prevent the person from receiving a kidney transplant at that time.

Contraindication is a term used in medicine to designate any condition or disease which makes an ordinarily indicated medication or treatment inadvisable. Thus, the appearance of lung cancer would serve as a contraindication to a liver transplant in a patient suffering from end-stage liver disease.

PART FIVE

ETHICAL ISSUES AT THE END OF LIFE

CHAPTER 11

Advance Directives

INTRODUCTION

Ordinarily people make medical decisions about various treatments after consultation with physicians. Some treatment decisions are fairly straightforward: A ruptured appendix needs to be removed by surgery as soon as possible. Other treatment choices are less clear-cut, such as whether or not to undergo chemotherapy after cancer surgery or which particular chemotherapy regimen to choose. While initially it may not be apparent, any situation in which an individual person faces medical decisions has ethical overtones. The reason for this is because people are obligated only to take *reasonable* care of their health. They need not go to extraordinary lengths to achieve a very improbable result; for example, if terminally ill from cancer, a person acts reasonably if she refuses a highly experimental chemotherapy regimen because it is very harsh and/or of unpredictable benefit. On the other hand, it would be unreasonable and morally wrong to refuse medical attention for a broken ankle because, left untreated, the person might well lose the use of his leg and be impaired in all his activities. Furthermore, treatment for the ankle is unquestionably more beneficial than burdensome.

In making treatment decisions, persons employ those faculties which distinguish them as humans, namely, their reason and their will. They also have to get in touch with their values and their attitudes about life and death. Just as the patient has responsibility for taking reasonable care of his health, so the physician's ethical role in her relationship with the patient becomes apparent in the context of health care decision making. This role is no longer to act benevolently in the patient's behalf but, rather, to act respectfully at the patient's behest. Accordingly, the physician is to make the patient aware of the medical aspects of his condition and the various alternatives available in regard to treatment. It is then up to the patient to make informed choices.

In a sense it may have been easier a few generations ago when choices were fewer, paternalism was in vogue so that "the doctor knew best," and individuals merely did as they were instructed. Since times have changed, however, autonomous adult patients are now expected to make informed decisions about their own medical care. They do this after taking into account their medical condition, possible treatment alternatives, and their lifestyle preferences. Because the obligation to reach sound decisions does not cease with the onset of incompetence, instruments known as advance directives exist by which people can leave directions for their care which go into effect when they are no longer able to speak for themselves.

WHAT IS AN ADVANCE DIRECTIVE?

An advance directive is a vehicle which allows for continuation of negotiations between physician and patient after the patient has been temporarily or permanently rendered incompetent either through unconsciousness or a brain disease such as Alzheimer's. Advance directives come in two forms: An instruction directive, and a proxy designation, or a combined form containing both instructions and the naming of a proxy. Advance directives, popularly known as living wills, first appeared about 30 years ago. Their appearance coincided with the explosion of medical technology which made it possible for people to be kept alive in very fragile conditions for long periods of time. The majority of people who draft advance directives do so in order to limit their care should they become incompetent with a poor prognosis. It remains possible, however, to use advance directives for a completely different reason, i.e., to state one's wishes to have maximum treatment rendered for as long as possible.

WHO SHOULD HAVE AN ADVANCE DIRECTIVE?

All persons 18 years of age and older should have advance directives. The reasons which prompt people to draw up advance directives are an acknowledgment of their responsibility to take reasonable care of their health, a desire to express their preferences so that, in accordance with their values, they will not be overtreated or undertreated, and the hope of sparing loved ones the heartbreaking task of having to make difficult decisions under painful circumstances. In spite of the fact that few people would argue about the wisdom of having advance directives, in the United States less than 20 percent of adults actually have completed these documents, and the vast majority of those who have are senior citizens.

What keeps people from formulating advance directives? There are two stumbling blocks which usually stand in the way. One is the tendency to procrastinate, to put off until tomorrow a task which is perceived as emotionally stressful. The other is the discomfort associated with acknowledging our own mortality and directly questioning our values in order to decide how we want to die.

WHEN SHOULD ADVANCE DIRECTIVES BE FORMULATED?

Since the passage in 1991 of the federal Patient Self-Determination Act, each and every adult patient who is admitted to a health care facility which receives funding from Medicaid or Medicare is asked if he has an advance directive or is interested in learning about these documents. There is a positive and a negative aspect to this line of questioning. The positive aspect is that the person's consciousness is raised so that he now needs to consider whether or not he wants to make his wishes explicit. In a sense, he is put on the spot and is forced into a different mode from his familiar tendency to procrastinate. However, there is a negative aspect to the questioning, too, which needs to be mentioned. The occasion of admission to a hospital or nursing home is frequently an extremely anxious and stressful time and suggesting to a patient that she might want to consider eventualities connected to her dying might add to her concerns a heavy additional burden. This is why advocates of advance directives usually suggest that these documents be drawn up at a nonstressful business-as-usual time in one's life, after one has had time to reflect on her values, consult her physician about medically related questions, and talk things over with family, friends, and clergy.

FORMULATING AN INSTRUCTION DIRECTIVE

In order to formulate an instruction directive or living will, a person needs to anticipate various medical circumstances which could result from illness or accident. As it happens, there are a great many individual decisions which need to be made. However, the overall task need not be overwhelming if a person undertakes it from an organized and motivated perspective.

It is generally agreed that there are four different situations in which people might find themselves unable to exercise their fundamental right to self-determination. A brief synopsis of each of these situations follows.

First Situation. A person sustains a head injury and is conscious but incoherent or in a coma from which she may or may not recover. In either case, her condition, should she recover, cannot be predicted.

Second Situation. A person is in an irreversible coma or **persistent vegetative state** with no possibility of recovery. People in such a condition have suffered the permanent destruction of the **cerebral-cortical functioning** of their brains, lack awareness, and are incapable of self-care or interaction with others.

Third Situation. A person suffers irreversible brain damage but otherwise is healthy. An example would be a person with Alzheimer's Disease whose physiological systems (heart, lungs, kidneys, circulatory system, digestive system, immune system, etc.) work quite well.

Fourth Situation. This person is like the one in the third situation, i.e., he has a degenerative brain disease but he differs significantly because he develops a terminal disease such as cancer or blockage of a coronary artery.

Regardless of which situation a person is in, there are at least ten treatments which could be administered. A listing of these treatments follows, along with an explanation of what the treatment entails.

1. *Cardiopulmonary Resuscitation (CPR).* CPR is used when a person's heart or breathing stops. It consists of applying force to the chest with the hands and breathing into the patient's mouth to fill the lungs with air. If available, electric shock may be used or medications designed specifically to restart the heart or stabilize the heart's beating may be administered.

Medical personnel frequently use the terms *Code* and *No Code* in connection with cardiopulmonary resuscitation. In "calling a code," a signal is given to a team of hospital personnel to try to restore a patient's breathing and heartbeat. If a patient is said to be "No Code," no efforts are made to revive the patient.

CPR was developed during the 1960s and hailed for its benefits to accident as well as heart-attack victims. In time, however, CPR became the standard order in hospitals and nursing homes. Now it is automatically administered to all patients who stop breathing unless these patients or their loved ones instruct the attending physician to enter DNR (Do Not Resuscitate) orders on the patient's chart.

A Do Not Resuscitate order means that if a person stops breathing or the person's heart stops beating, no attempt will be made by any method to revive her. The physician is the only person authorized to enter a DNR order on a patient's chart and will do so only if given explicit directions by patients or their loved ones.

Two reasons prompt patients or their loved ones to request DNR orders: (a) Many chronic illnesses are predictable in their downhill course. A DNR decision represents a willingness to accept death by not trying to reverse it when it occurs. (b) Under the best of circumstances, if the very sick, the very frail, and the elderly begin to breathe again after CPR, they stand only a minuscule chance of surviving long enough to be released from the hospital.

2. *Mechanical Breathing—Being on a Respirator or Ventilator.* A respirator or ventilator is a sophisticated machine which delivers air to the lungs and which periodically purges the lungs of excretions. These machines are designed to breathe—partially or totally—for patients who cannot breathe for themselves. Patients are connected to respirators by a tube which goes through the mouth and throat into a lung or by surgical implantation of a tube.

Respirators are frequently employed under emergency conditions to stabilize a patient. Only after a patient is stabilized can medical personnel reach a reliable diagnosis regarding the patient's condition along with a prognosis. It is at this time that medical personnel will want to know what instructions incompetent patients gave in their advance directives.

Connecting a patient to a respirator is often the final step in CPR. Those who do not want CPR will also probably reject respirators.

3. *Tube feeding.* Artificial nutrition and hydration can be provided through a tube into veins, nose, stomach, or intestines. Intravenous feeding, the delivery of fluids to a vein in an arm or leg, is of short-term duration. In contrast, tube feeding, whether into the nose (through a nasogastric or NG tube), or into the stomach (through a G, or gastrostomy, tube), or into the intestines (through a J, or jejunostomy, tube), can be carried on for years. Another type of tube feeding, called TPN, for total parenteral nutrition, feeds into the largest vein in the human body, the superior vena cava, located under the clavicle, or collar bone. TPN can be performed indefinitely.

In contemporary health care practice the tendency is to tube feed patients who are not capable of absorbing nutrients, even the severely demented and those in persistent vegetative states. In view of this fact, those who do not want this type of treatment would be well advised to leave clear directions to this effect.

4. *Kidney Dialysis or Hemodialysis.* The dialysis machine eliminates impurities from and adds vital substances to a patient's blood, thus performing functions which the kidneys cannot. Kidney dialysis can be performed in a hospital or at home.

Kidney dialysis is a medical treatment, which a person may legally reject for any reason and may morally reject if it presents more burdens than benefits.

5. *Diagnostic tests.* Such tests cover a wide range, from blood tests and standard X-rays to very sophisticated X-rays, such as PET (positron emission tomography) and MRI (magnetic resonance imaging) tests, and invasive measures such as using flexible tubing to examine the stomach. Deciding which tests to authorize or refuse in the event of incompetence necessitates coming to a clear understanding of what one wants.

6. *Surgery.* Minor surgical procedures, such as removing infected tissue

from a finger or toe, and major surgery, such as a hysterectomy or heart bypass, can be medically indicated for incompetent patients.

Here again, underlying values come into play. Does a patient want surgery under some circumstances, no circumstances, or all circumstances? In deciding, it is important to keep in mind that surgery carries risks and that the more extensive the surgery the greater the risks. In addition, surgery is a trauma to the patient and requires a period of recuperation. As with diagnostic tests, overall prognosis, evaluated in conjunction with how surgery will lessen or increase pain, will probably weigh heavily in reaching decisions. The cost and availability of the procedure, as well as associated stresses which might be experienced by loved ones, are also factors to consider.

7. *Chemotherapy.* Chemotherapy is prescribed to cure cancers or to bring them under control. One decision about chemotherapy is whether or not a patient wants to fight cancer after entering a state of incompetence from which he will not recover. Another decision is how he would want cancer treated in the first situation described above, i.e., suffering a head injury and facing an uncertain outcome. Here again, beliefs about the value of death sooner rather than later and about the wisdom of employing medical procedures after one's condition has become severely compromised will contribute to one's decision.

It should be noted that, as with any other treatment option, one can begin chemotherapy on a trial basis. If it proves beneficial it can be continued, but if it is ineffectual or causes troublesome side effects, it can be discontinued.

8. *Transfusions.* Many situations can make a person a candidate for the transfusion of blood or blood products, including severe anemia and hemorrhage. The right to refuse transfusions can be exercised in advance directives. In the absence of such explicit instructions, one can expect physicians to take whatever steps are medically indicated. If one's goal is to die quickly when incompetent, with as few medical interventions as possible, it would make sense to state in advance directives that blood transfusions are not wanted. On the other hand, if one takes a less absolute position, it would be good to spell out the circumstances under which transfusions would be accepted or rejected. Any religiously based objections to blood transfusions should be clearly stated.

9. *Antibiotics,* drugs used to fight infection(s). The ability of an individual to recover from infections through the use of antibiotics varies from person to person, and those in very weakened conditions may not respond to even prolonged administration of very strong medicine.

Pneumonia is a serious infection of the respiratory system which usually responds well to antibiotics. A few generations ago, it was considered the "old person's friend" because it brought the peaceful release of death to frail people in failing health. If one might look upon pneumonia or other infectious diseases as a "friend," it is a good idea to stipulate in advance directives that antibiotics are not to be administered. In the absence of specific instructions, the probability is that antibiotics will be administered. Alternately, one may decide to use antibiotics on a trial basis, continuing them if they bring improvement and stopping them if they do not.

10. *Pain Medication within a Regimen of Palliative Care.* Palliative care relieves pain and discomfort; it is not intended to cure. Medication for pain is one aspect of palliative care. Keeping the patient comfortable and clean are standard requirements. Caretakers also must turn the patient, attend to bedsores, and keep the mouth and lips moist.

It goes without saying that all of us desire to be kept clean and comfortable when we are no longer capable of caring for ourselves. There may be some concern, however, about being medicated to control pain. Sometimes, when fatal injuries or diseases cause considerable pain, this pain can be controlled only by increasing the frequency or strength of pain-relief medication. Increased dosages and stronger medications can possibly impede respiration, thus causing death sooner than if less medication were used.

The choice, then, may be between acting decisively against pain, with the likelihood of an earlier death, or treating pain less aggressively, thus stalling death. By leaving clear instructions for one's physician, she will be able to act according to patient preference.

It is important to note that authorities in the field of medical ethics, as well as professional medical societies, do not object to the administration of pain medication that may shorten a patient's life because the intention is to alleviate pain rather than to cause death. (This matter is treated in Chapter 13, "Treatment of the Terminally Ill: Important Distinctions.")

It must now be apparent that writing a comprehensive advance directive is a big undertaking. Those who are concerned because they cannot foresee all possible future medical options should consider designating a proxy authorized to decide about situations and possibilities which cannot be anticipated.

In order to write a comprehensive advance directive a person needs to take into account how she would want to be treated in each of the four situations. An additional consideration is advisable if applicable: Should a woman be of child-bearing years she might want to delineate instructions regarding how she would want to be cared for if pregnant. Most people who decide to do a living will or instruction directive just want to fill in a simple form. What they need to do is determine whether or not the form takes account of the different situations and the full range of possible medical treatments. If it does not, writers might want to add additional comments or even additional pages.[1] It is important to be as comprehensive as possible because one is trying to anticipate circumstances and deal with realities which have not as yet occurred.

APPOINTING A HEALTH CARE PROXY

A proxy given Durable Power of Attorney for Health Care is legally empowered to make health care decisions which are consistent with the values and preferences of an incompetent patient. An ordinary power of attorney authorizes another person to make legally binding decisions and take actions on our behalf. A Durable Power of Attorney for Health Care differs from an ordinary power of attorney in that it goes into effect after the onset of incompetence and pertains specifically to health care decisions.

A proxy with Durable Power of Attorney for Health Care can approve or reject any and all of the treatments and procedures which medical science has to offer. Furthermore, a proxy can employ or discharge medical personnel, obtain medical records, and allocate funds to pay for treatments. She can also go to court, if necessary, to obtain court authorization regarding medical decisions. This last function of a proxy—to take an incompetent's case to court—is an extremely remote possibility. It is likely to happen only if a physician or facility refuses to carry out a proxy's directions and the proxy is unable to transfer the patient to another physician or facility. The reason it is such a remote possibility is that the proxy has the same legal authority as a competent patient and is able to accept or reject treatments just as the competent patient can.

A proxy should be an individual who is well known and trusted. Ordinarily a family member or a close friend serves as a proxy. It stands to reason that the intended proxy should be consulted and should express a willingness to assume this responsibility. A proxy should be familiar with an individual's values and preferences. It should be assumed that a proxy knows what is wanted by the individual for whom she makes decisions. Sincere and thorough discussions covering a wide variety of circumstances should be held with an intended proxy to familiarize that person with one's expectations.

As a general rule, only one person should be designated as a proxy to exercise Durable Power of Attorney for Health Care. However, it makes sense to name second and third alternate choices to serve as proxies should the first and second choice predecease the person they represent or should they themselves be unavailable or become incompetent previous to or at the same time as the person represented.

Since a proxy is expected to carry out our wishes in regard to health care decisions, should we also write a living will? The answer is clear: Yes. A living will which includes a Durable Power of Attorney for Health Care is regarded as the most effective means for dealing with medical decision making when patients are unable to decide for themselves.

Someone can be designated Durable Power of Attorney for Health Care by issuing a witnessed statement in one's own words or by completing a generic form. Some people want to take a shortcut: Not write a living will and simply authorize a relative or friend to make decisions on their behalf. While giving a trusted individual Durable Power of Attorney for Health Care is preferable to doing nothing, it is not as beneficial as writing a living will or instruction directive and designating a proxy. The reason for this is simple. In a living will we detail our wishes as clearly as possible. In the Durable Power of Attorney for Health Care, we allow our proxy to make any decisions which were not foreseen. A proxy can also be called upon to interpret anything which may be ambiguous in a living will. The living will thus becomes a very important document on which our proxy may someday have to rely, should he be making decisions.

QUESTIONS FREQUENTLY ASKED ABOUT ADVANCE DIRECTIVES

Many questions about advance directives come up again and again. These include:

To whom should advance directives be given? Copies of advance directives should be given to close relatives, a close friend or two, perhaps a neighbor, one's family doctor, and the admissions director of the hospital one would ordinarily use and, if one is a patient in a nursing home, the medical director of the facility. One should keep the original document as well as a list of those to whom copies are given.

Where should advance directives be stored? Since it is important to have advance directives close at hand, these documents should not be kept in inaccessible places like safe deposit boxes. Instead, keeping them with important home office items like one's checkbook would facilitate access to them if they need to be produced.

How can advance directives be amended? If a person changes his mind about any specific aspect of an advance directive, it is not necessary to write an entire new directive. Instead, what needs to be done is to cross off what one no longer wants and to write in one's revisions. These revisions should then be signed and dated, and all persons holding copies should be given the amended page(s).

How can advance directives be revoked? An advance directive can be revoked at any time simply by tearing the document into pieces and instructing those holding copies to do the same. It is advisable to provide those holding copies of advance directives with written instructions to destroy the documents and to request that they hold on to that instruction. In this way, should an advance directive which was not destroyed one day be proffered as proof of an incompetent's wishes, chances are good that someone from the incompetent's circle would surface with a copy of the directive of revocation.

How can one affirm that an advance directive continues to represent his wishes? By taking the original copy of one's advance directive out every few years and initialing and dating it, one affirms that one's wishes are unchanged.

What does the law say about advance directives? The federal Patient Self-Determination Act (PSDA) of 1991 promoted the status of advance directives because, with that piece of legislation, the United States Congress gave official recognition to this manner of making choices prior to the onset of incompetence. Before the PSDA people were inclined to fear that their wishes would not be honored because of some loophole which would provide medical practitioners with rationale for treating them against their will. Since the passage of the PSDA this fear has largely disappeared.

Another question which does arise with some regularity is whether or not an advance directive which is completed in accordance with the regulations of one state will be honored in another. There is no reason to think that this will not be the case but, if there are questions about specific states, the matter can be resolved by consulting that state's attorney general.

One final point about advance directives and the law: Since physicians can be counted on to obey the law, and since no state other than Oregon (1997) has laws supportive of physicians who assist their patients in suicide, people who ask that their lives be terminated should not expect that doctors will comply with this type of instruction.

What have the courts said about advance directives? Different courts have said different things. In the 1990 Cruzan case the United States Supreme Court accepted written advance directives as indicative of patient wishes and asserted that these documents should be honored because to do so is consistent with the right of patient autonomy.

Several courts have hampered efforts by relatives of incompetent patients to forgo life-sustaining treatment. An example is the 1988 refusal by the State of New York Court of Appeals to allow discontinuance of Mrs. Mary O'Connor's tube feeding in accordance with the request of her two daughters. When she was competent Mrs. O'Connor had expressed reluctance to have her life extended by artificial means, but she did not write anything down or explicitly designate anyone to act for her. Mrs. O'Connor's remarks were not enough for the court because

> . . . a person who has troubled to set forth his or her wishes in a writing is more likely than one who has not to make sure that any subse-

quent changes of heart are adequately expressed, either in a new writing or through clear statements to relatives and friends. In contrast, a person whose expressions of intention were limited to oral statements may not as fully appreciate the need to 'rescind' those statements after a change of heart.[2]

In a different vein, in the 1992 Wanglie case, the Minnesota Supreme Court decided against physicians who wanted cessation of treatment for Helga Wanglie, a comatose 85-year-old woman. Their rationale was that any treatment would be futile in bringing improvement to the patient. Mrs. Wanglie's husband succeeded in having himself appointed his wife's conservator and, in this role, he argued in favor of the most aggressive treatment regimen so as to leave open the possibility of a miracle. The judge ruled in favor of Mr. Wanglie and against the physicians because he considered the family/surrogate the proper decision maker.

Given the fact that Mary O'Connor's daughters' request was denied while Helga Wanglie's husband's wishes were honored, we cannot know how the decision of a court will go in the absence of clear advance directives. This is yet another reason not to leave the matter to chance.

DECIDING ON HOW TO DIE: ETHICAL ISSUES

As physicians and other health care providers find themselves trying to follow advance directives, some problems are beginning to surface. There is no question about the ethical correctness of following clear written directives or the unambiguous instruction of a duly authorized health care proxy. However, not every situation is distinguished by clarity. A case in point could be a demented patient with a clear living will who gives an oral instruction which contradicts the written directions in his living will. Doctors and nurses have to decide how demented this patient actually is and what his preferences are at this time. It may also happen that a duly appointed proxy gives different directions from those in an instruction directive. What is to be done in such a circumstance?

Both these possibilities point to the need to set out as clearly and thoroughly as possible one's wishes and perhaps to indicate how one would want health care providers to deal with either of the situations just mentioned. The matters of ambiguous directions and proxy counterdirections are of concern to legal and medical policy makers as they seek through research, reflection, and dialogue to address these problematic aspects of honoring patient autonomy.

Is there an ethically right way to die? Or is this matter best left to personal preference or chance?

One way of approaching death is with the decision to fight it at all costs.

This approach would call for the maximization of medical treatments until the matter is taken out of human hands. It is known as vitalism and has as an advantage the fact that few decisions need to be made after the initial decision to "do everything."

There are some ethical reservations regarding a vitalist attitude. The biggest reservation about vitalism concerns its ideological or philosophical underpinnings. Vitalism seems to play into our contemporary culture's inclination to deny death, to make the event of our personal demise an unreality which can be postponed indefinitely. Ethical people and ethical health care professionals need to be truthful. All men are mortal. John is a man. Therefore, John is mortal. John's life, everyone's life, will have an end. Pathetic games are played by physicians, loved ones, and dying patients themselves who are caught up in vitalism. It would be more beneficial to all concerned to try to face death honestly and use life's final weeks or days to say good-bye and express heartfelt sentiments.

Vitalism also raises two other perplexing issues. The first concerns whether or not scarce medical resources should be available to any person who requests them, regardless of the person's condition. With the technology available to modern medicine the event of death can often be postponed for weeks or months even for the frailest, sickest, most decimated patients. Is it morally right to "do everything at all costs" when the benefit is minimal and when there are many other people who are medically needy yet who do not receive the care they need? Sooner, rather than later, this issue will engender a national debate, one aspect of which will necessitate critiquing the philosophy of vitalism.

Another perplexing issue raised by vitalism relates to the mission of medical science. If medicine's purpose is to heal the sick and serve those beyond healing by keeping them comfortable in their dying, then how does the provision of futile treatments fit into this mission? By futile treatments are meant procedures or medicines which cannot be expected to bring cure or improvement to a patient. Futile treatments differ from experimental treatments or improbable but possibly beneficial treatments in that their end result is predictable from the outset. It may happen that treatments begun in the hope of a beneficial outcome become futile over time. In such an event, they need to be assessed as such. It is important for health care providers to examine how the provision of futile treatments is impacting on the culture of the medical profession. If a consensus is reached that the medical profession should not be a party to justifying futile treatments, a concerted effort needs to be made to communicate this message to society-at-large. The issue of futility is treated at greater length in Chapter 13, "Treatment of the Terminally Ill: Important Distinctions."

The experience of dying, under the best of circumstances, is rife with physiological and psychological suffering. Some people respond to this fact in a manner totally opposite that of vitalists. They decide to short-circuit the process by ending life at their own time and in their own manner by euthanasia. As a result, they seek to avoid the final stage of life altogether. Since euthanasia is the subject of Chapter 12, the philosophy of euthanasia requires mention here only to complete the picture.[3]

The third general way of approaching life's final stage is one about which there are no ethical reservations. It is the *via media*, the middle way between vitalism and euthanasia, according to which people seek to take reasonable care of their health. Admittedly, the *via media* is extremely general so that it contains few specific guidelines. Nevertheless, the combination of insights that life does not last forever, that medical technology cannot always achieve healing, and that it is only required to take *reasonable* care of one's health should coalesce to produce more realistic expectations. When it becomes apparent that their health cannot be restored because they suffer from an incurable pathology the ill effects of which can no longer be ameliorated, adherents to the *via media* seek to face their dying and make the most of the time left to them. This is the philosophy of hospice which advocates keeping people comfortable and pain free while accepting the inevitability of death. It is not an easy attitude to acquire but, in the long run, it is the attitude which allows best for realistic preparation for death along with the possibility of accepting the inevitability of one's own dying.

CONCLUSION

In conjunction with a discussion of advance directives, several interrelated challenges become apparent. Individuals should respond to the need to formulate these documents so as to make their preferences known. Relatives and friends need to accept a two-fold responsibility: To support and encourage loved ones who are drafting advance directives and to honor the wishes of loved ones should the time come to act on their behalf.

Physicians need to meet a unique challenge in that their expertise equips them to both explain the limits of medical science and to answer the nuts-and-bolts questions brought by patients who are working on advance directives. Hospitals and nursing homes, medical and legal associations, and community organizations can facilitate understanding of advance directives by sponsoring programs to explain how to go about writing them. The media can remind the public of the importance of advance directives and, further, can introduce a better climate for considering these documents by rejecting the conspiracy of silence surrounding dying and death. Finally, health care professionals and members of hospital ethics committees can set an example of responsibility and maturity by formulating their own instruction directives and Durable Powers of Attorney for Health Care.

ENDNOTES

[1] Both detailed and short forms for instruction directives, as well as forms for use in designating a health care proxy, are contained in my book, Eileen P. Flynn, *Your Living Will: Why, When and How to Write One* (New York: Carol Publishing, 1992), pp. 59–86.

[2] In the Matter of Mary O'Connor, 2 No. 312, *Westchester County Medical Center v. Helen A. Hall, et al.,* State of New York Court of Appeals, decided October 14, 1988, p. 16.

[3] If euthanasia were to become acceptable because of judicial and legislative initiatives, the practice would most probably not be authorized for implementation on incompetent persons. The reason for this is that virtually all proposals for euthanasia consider it acceptable only for conscious competent patients who request it repeatedly and verify at the time it is done that it is indeed what they want.

DISCUSSION QUESTIONS

1. Do you have advance directives? In what form do these exist? If you have them, what prompted you to formulate them? If you do not have advance directives, why have you not written them? Do you intend to do so? Why or why not?

2. If you were to appoint a proxy and were to give that person your Durable Power of Attorney for Health Care, describe the kinds of attributes you would want the person to have, as well as the features of the discussion you would have about the responsibilities your health care representative would be taking on.

3. Consider the four situations in which a person could be incompetent. Are there any significant differences among them? How would these differences alter your treatment choices for yourself?

4. List and explain the ten possible treatments about which people need to make decisions in their instruction directives or living wills.

5. What ethical problems does a vitalist approach to medicine hold? How can vitalism be rejected without having sick people "give up too soon"?

6. Name three specific strategies which could be put in place to make the general public aware of the importance of advance directives. In terms of each strategy, what agency or agencies would be responsible for implementation?

7. There is no ethical question about the moral propriety of formulating and

honoring advance directives. However, many ethical issues come into play in conjunction with advance directives. Identify and discuss at least three such issues.

CASE STUDY

Roger Allen, a 48-year-old divorced father of two daughters, has a serious auto accident and suffers severe injuries. The accident takes place on a tertiary road; Mr. Allen is resuscitated at the scene by a registered nurse. She is uncertain how much time elapsed between the accident and CPR.

Mr. Allen is transported to a hospital emergency room where he is placed on a ventilator in the ICU. At the ICU a nasogastric tube is inserted.

Diagnostic tests reveal significant brain damage and internal bleeding of unknown origin, requiring exploratory surgery.

Mr. Allen's brother brings Roger's instruction directive to the hospital and gives it to the attending physician. The directive says: "If I am in a mentally deficient condition and have no hope of recovering to a normal life, I do not want to be kept alive by medical technology." There is no proxy directive.

The attending physician informs the two daughters that he wants to forgo surgery and stop treatment so as to honor their father's wishes. The daughters object and ask that everything be done for at least six months. They want to see whether or not their father improves or recovers. They agree that after six months of no progress cessation of treatment would be appropriate.

Evaluation:

1. Identify ethical issues contained in this case.
2. Propose possible solutions for these issues.
3. Make a decision relevant to action to be taken or not taken and provide rationale supportive of this decision.
4. Are you satisfied with your decision? Why or why not?

GLOSSARY

Persistent vegetative state, or PVS, is a neurological diagnosis about an irreversible brain condition. In this condition a person has a functioning brain stem but has suffered irreversible destruction of the brain's cerebral-cortical functioning. Accordingly, the person is incapable of any degree of sensate feeling and any possibility whatsoever of human interaction. The diagnosis of persistent vegetative state is usually made by a neurologist and confirmed by two consultant neurologists after a brain-injured patient has been in a coma for at least six months.

Cerebral-cortical functioning of the brain refers to the higher capacities of the brain which enable a person to feel sensation, to think and speak, to recognize others and interact with them, and to carry out voluntary movements.

CHAPTER 12

Euthanasia

INTRODUCTION

At one time euthanasia referred to having a good death, an easy time of dying, or having the painful, traumatic event of death go as well as possible. In the past generation or so the term euthanasia has taken on a different meaning. When we speak of euthanasia today we generally refer to a direct intervention which causes a sick or dying person's death. This action can be performed by the dying themselves, by family members or friends, or by health care professionals. Such actions as the taking of lethal amounts of medication, the administration of poisonous gases, pills or intravenous solutions, or overt killing acts such as suffocating and shooting are the most frequent ways of effecting euthanasia. A common misconception about euthanasia is that there is not much difference between allowing a person to die and ending the person's life by overt action. This misconception reveals faulty thinking because in the contemporary context, what makes euthanasia *euthanasia* is the fact of a direct positive intervention, not the fact that the person has died. In fact, precise speech would require usage of the term "direct, positive euthanasia," qualified by the adjective "active" or "passive." "Active" would convey the fact that death was brought about by the patient's own action, while "passive" conveys the idea that another person performs the deed which causes the death. (When a person ends his own life by some overt action, he commits suicide. It can happen that a person cannot cause his death because of paralysis or some other factor. In such a case he might ask someone else to end his life for him; he would want to be euthanized but would be unable to effect this result, putting his case in the category direct, positive euthanasia in which the subject passively receives the death-causing deed. The person who causes the death would not want to be identified as a "murderer" but, rather, as a helper. Should the movement to legalize euthanasia succeed, society would accommodate this wish.)

A second common misconception about euthanasia is to think that there is no difference between giving a person a large dose of a painkiller to ease the person's suffering or giving the person a lethal dose of any kind of medication for the purpose of causing the person's death. These two acts are significantly different based on the intentions which motivate them. In the first act, the intention to ease the person's pain by providing sufficient medication to accomplish this purpose is a good one so the action is reasonable even if, as an unintended side effect, the person's respiration is suppressed and she dies. On the other hand, to administer a fatal dose of medication to a person for the purpose of ending that person's life constitutes killing the person, albeit mercifully and by request, and killing a person by administering medicine in order to cause death is very different from providing pain medication that might result in suppression of respiration and, indirectly, death. (The difference between killing and letting die is treated at length in Chapter 13, "Treatment of the Terminally Ill: Important Distinctions.")

During the past generation euthanasia has become a major issue in health care ethics. It was always a peripheral issue with limited appeal to a minority of the U.S. populace, but in recent years euthanasia has become a major subject for debate which, predictably, triggers heated controversy. Why is this the case? Actually, this is a complex matter with several related components. Among these components perhaps the most significant are changing conceptions about what constitutes the role of health care professionals, as well as the way we understand rights to which competent adults are entitled.

In the classical tradition of Western medicine which dates from Hippocrates, the physician's responsibility has consistently been to do whatever is possible to bring about cures for sick people or to tend to the care and comfort of people whose illness puts them beyond cure. The role of nurses has been understood in terms of patient education, assistance, care, and supervision. Part of the movement toward euthanasia asks us to expand our concepts of the roles of physicians and nurses to include allowing them to use their expertise to assist terminally ill people in ending their lives. This thinking holds that no one is better able to calculate the proper amount of medication needed to bring death than is a health care practitioner whose learning and experience uniquely qualify her for such tasks. To redesign our concepts of the proper responsibilities of physicians and nurses so as to include participation in euthanasia would constitute more than an incidental revision; it would, instead, constitute a radical change in the nature of the practices of both medicine and nursing. This is one reason why resolution of the debate over euthanasia will entail a thorough reexamination of the nature of the mission of the health care professions.

Contemporary attitudes regarding patient autonomy also affect the debate about euthanasia. When the physician-patient relationship was characterized by physician benevolence toward the patient in a system in which the physician was in a position of superiority in regard to the patient, the issues of patient preference and patient right to self-determination were not accorded much interest. But the practice and culture of medicine have changed so that patients are now accustomed to deciding what kind of care they want and do not want. Within this climate, it is understandable that some people consider themselves entitled to request that they be assisted in bringing death about when life becomes too burdensome.

A few generations ago most people whose death occurred at the end of an illness died at home. Nowadays, 80 percent of people who die following a chronic or terminal illness die in a hospital or nursing home. Institutionalized dying is inevitably accompanied by the apparatuses of technology. The availability of tubes, machines, monitors, and catheters that can be employed to work wonders but, to very sick and dying people, may be perceived as troublesome nuisances, has also contributed to the euthanasia debate. Although people do not actually face the either-or choice between a technologically burdened dying or "self-deliverance," a popular misconception is developing that such is the case. It is not surprising, then, in view of this misconception, that there is growing support for euthanasia as a means for avoiding futile, bothersome technology.

Another factor that is contributing to the acceptability of euthanasia is the reality of the dreadfully diminished capacities of people who suffer from such afflictions as AIDS, some forms of cancer, and other debilitating diseases. Both AIDS and cancer can be treated with a vast assortment of medications and other therapeutic interventions, bringing many good days to those who suffer from them. At the end, however, people afflicted by these diseases tend to be very sick, frail, and in pain. In such circumstances, the issue of fast-forwarding the dying process arises quite predictably, with an increasing inclination to intervene to accomplish this goal.

The twentieth century has witnessed the disappearance of one taboo after another. In the past there were things which could not be spoken of, forms of personal appearance which were unacceptable, social and personal relationships which could not be entered into. It seems almost cliche to say that all this has been changed and that there is much more personal freedom and openness today than there was in the past. In this culture, then, it is not surprising that the widely held and deeply rooted biblical taboo, "Thou shalt not kill," is losing some of its force for those who believe chronically or terminally ill people should be able to choose to end life's final phase "with dignity."

Modern society is secularized and many aspects of life are carried out without regard for a transcendent dimension. In other words, many people acknowledge no connection with a divine higher power so that no obligations to such a power are accepted. The phenomenon of secularization sets men and women free to act in accordance with their own subjective reason and to choose to live and to die as they choose.

To the factors just enumerated we need to add the impact of vocal spokespersons and interest groups whose messages are delivered by the media and who never tire of promoting their pro-euthanasia views. These include Michigan's Jack Kevorkian, the so-called "Dr. Death" who makes house calls to assist in dying, and Derek Humphrey, President of the Hemlock Society and author of a suicide manual entitled *Final Exit*. Recent efforts to legalize physician-assisted suicide, or physician aid in dying, in California and Washington, have also served to make people aware of euthanasia as a possibly acceptable practice.

Since 1998 there has been one state in the United States in which it is legal for physicians to prescribe medication to terminally ill patients who choose to end their lives. The Oregon Death with Dignity Act was approved by voters in a 1994 referendum. In November 1997 a second referendum gave voters an opportunity to rescind their decision but, instead, they reaffirmed it. Following the 1997 vote, the U.S. Drug Enforcement Agency sought to make implementation of the act impossible by threatening sanctions against physicians who prescribe drugs for the purpose of causing a patient's death. The DEA reasoned that such prescriptions would not constitute legitimate medical use and would violate the federal Controlled Substances Act. On June 6, 1998, Attorney General Janet Reno overruled the DEA, leaving open the option for physician assistance in suicide in Oregon.[1]

As written, the Oregon act allows assistance only for Oregon residents. The act stipulates that terminally ill adults have a right to request a lethal dose of prescription drugs if the patient is of sound mind and two doctors judge that the patient has less than six months to live. The law requires that doctors make a determination that patients are not depressed or afflicted by mental illness. Physicians are to impose a 15-day waiting period before completing the drug prescription. Should there be attempts by other states to legalize physician aid in dying, commentators think that those states will structure their procedures in a manner similar to Oregon's because the Oregon model has withstood exhaustive scrutiny by the federal government and been validated.[2]

Before we continue, it should be noted that those who favor euthanasia endorse what is technically referred to as *voluntary positive euthanasia*. To date, there has been no support for *involuntary* positive euthanasia. This distinction means that those who favor euthanasia assert that competent adults who are aware, alert, and emotionally stable have a right to end their own lives by direct actions undertaken for this purpose and also have a right to instruct another person to carry out the death-dealing action. On the other hand, there is no support for causing the deaths of people who do not request euthanasia, i.e., there is no support for involuntary positive euthanasia, regardless of the extent of a person's pain or deterioration.[3]

ARGUMENTS AGAINST AND ARGUMENTS FOR EUTHANASIA

AGAINST	*FOR*
1. God has dominion over life's end. Humans should not intrude into this area.	1. God's dominion is not relevant to nonbelievers. In addition, some people who believe in God believe in a God who would not want dying prolonged.
2. There is a tradition in Western civilization against taking innocent life by overt means. It would be a mistake to abandon that tradition.	2. Western civilization is just one civilization among many. The test of any culture is its ability to adjust and adapt to the issues of its time.
3. The humane response to the suffering person is to tend to her needs, not to kill her. Suffering can be lessened without killing the patient. Killing someone represents an inhumane experience for both the person who carries out the deed and the person who is killed.	3. Ending suffering is a lesser evil than prolonging suffering. We need to respond to the sick and dying who request deliverance with compassion and assistance.
4. All people have a duty not to commit suicide. There is value and dignity in each human life, even in dying life.	4. The life of a suffering person may become useless, at which time the person may choose to have his life ended.
5. It is hard to impossible to ascertain whether or not the decision for euthanasia is sane, sound, and rational. Most very sick people are also depressed. Additionally, oftentimes such people can be subject to coercion from those who could benefit from their deaths.	5. Let a person implement his own choices. Depressed people can make rational choices and so can people whose relatives would be relieved by their demise.
6. Involving physicians and nurses in direct, active euthanasia erodes the ethical foundations of medicine and nursing.	6. Physicians and nurses are in the best position to aid the terminally ill in dying. Those who hold no ethical scruples about practicing euthanasia should not be prohibited from so doing by professional codes or civil laws.

(continued on next page)

AGAINST	FOR
7. By implementing direct, active euthanasia, we would arrange gruesome, dehumanizing scenarios.	7. To set the time, place, and scenario for death would not be inhumane. It would be stressful, but there is no denying that death is a stressful event. To be sure, it is easier to deal with the end of a loved one's suffering than it is to watch the loved one's suffering continue.
8. Legalized euthanasia would add to the fears of the sick and dying who would be afraid of being victims of involuntary positive euthanasia.	8. Sick people would be better off if they thought they could manage their dying.

In order to determine whether or not the practice of euthanasia is morally appropriate or inappropriate, one should consider the arguments for and against it. As it happens, analyzing argumentation is a complex undertaking because there are several different components to both the positive and negative cases and valid points are made by both sides. Let us consider in turn each of the arguments against and for euthanasia.

(1) *Against. God has dominion over life's end. Humans should not intrude into this area.*

This argument suggests that, as is written in the bible, "There is a time to die," and that only God knows what that time will be. For some, God actually sets the time; for others, only God knows when death will occur. Most people who ask physicians how long they will live with a terminal illness, or how long they can expect their loved one to continue to live after a poor prognosis is pronounced, are told what the averages are, followed by a disclaimer that no one knows exactly how long it will be. People who hold this argument think that this is as it should be, that death should come at its own time and that God's mysterious role in regard to life's final moments needs to be respected.

(1) *For. God's dominion is irrelevant to nonbelievers. In addition, some people believe in a God who would not want dying prolonged.*

This rejoinder makes us aware that we live in a secular, pluralistic society in which civil matters should not be decided on the basis of the religious beliefs of some, or even of most, of the citizens. Therefore, amending medical ethics and civil law so that euthanasia becomes permissible should not be hampered based on religious sentiments.

The second part of this rejoinder challenges people to examine their underlying concept of God and suggests that perhaps God is less interested in seeing life played out until the last breath than in the merciful release of suffering dying people. The point of this argument is to show that it is as likely that God is on the side of those who favor euthanasia as that God is opposed to euthanasia.

(2) *Against. There is a tradition in Western civilization against taking innocent life by overt means. It would be a mistake to abandon that tradition.*

This argument seeks to convey the force of the distinction between innocent and noninnocent lives. Humankind in Western societies has always considered itself bound to respect, honor and safeguard innocent lives, and to go to great lengths to protect the innocent. The noninnocent, on the other hand, such as criminals, unjust aggressors or enemy soldiers may be defended against, even by deadly force. To allow death-dealing actions to be directed against innocent people, this argument maintains, would be to take an unjustifiable step down the slippery slope. This thinking holds that it would not be a major progression to move from euthanizing innocent people who request it to euthanizing innocent people (even infants, children, the retarded and the fragile elderly) who do not request it. For the good of society, the taboo against killing the innocent should remain in place.

(2) *For. Western civilization is just one civilization among many. The test of any culture is its ability to adjust and adapt to the issues of its time.*

It may be true that in Western civilization there has been a tendency to allow for the killing of noninnocents while an absolute prohibition has existed in regard to the direct targeting of innocent people. This tradition represents a salutary effort to safeguard the right of the innocent to bodily life. It prohibits others from assaulting or taking that life. However, this tradition should not be interpreted to mean that individuals do not have the right to freely choose to end their lives when living becomes too burdensome due to painful afflictions, frailty, or advanced disease processes. The biblical injunction, "Thou shalt not kill" has always been qualified by exceptions. For society to endorse yet another exception to allow for voluntary positive euthanasia would not undermine civilization, but would, rather, add to its legitimacy by proving its humaneness and adaptability.

(3) *Against. The humane response to the suffering person is to tend to her needs, not to kill her. Suffering can be lessened without killing the patient. Killing someone represents an inhumane experience for both the person who carries out the deed and the person who is killed.*

Human life is marked by finitude. Humans have limited control but, ultimately, are forced to accept phenomena which they cannot change. Sickness and death fall into this category. The humane response to a dying person is to keep him company and alleviate his discomfort. There is no medical or ethical reason to deprive a person of all the pain medication needed to keep him comfortable and, for most people, a regimen of palliation and comfort care can be established in either a health care facility or at home. To be sure, keeping company with the dying and caring for their physical needs is a demanding task, but it is not a task devoid of benefits. In the face of death real communication often occurs and caretakers frequently relate how their experiences with dying patients, relatives, or friends help them come to terms with their own mortality.

Nature has its own laws and, allowed to take its course, each human life will end in death. Mature, integrated people can accept this sobering fact and seek the completion of their human development through grappling with the inevitability of the dying process. If we decide that our role vis-à-vis death is not to be its witnesses while caring for the dying and, rather, attribute to ourselves the right to kill the dying, then we have taken a regrettable step. If euthanasia becomes acceptable, we would need to ask ourselves what would happen to both dying people and to ourselves. The answer to this question is that the lives of the dying would be ended by assaults which would probably be experienced as frightening and uncaring. Things would likely be even worse for the living who kill the sick and the weak, because they would have to live with their consciences while trying over and over to justify what civilized societies and health care ethics have long condemned. It is difficult to rationalize a killing role and more difficult to live with the psychological fallout resulting from assuming that role.

(3) *For. Ending suffering is a lesser evil than prolonging suffering. We need to respond to the sick and dying who request deliverance with compassion and assistance.*

If a person does not want to suffer through the dying process, it does not make sense to force him to do so to satisfy someone else's ethical scruples. No one who opposes euthanasia needs to carry it out, and there is no danger of being euthanized against one's will. To answer a person who wants to end his life by assuring him that you will administer plenty of pain medication and will keep him company will not necessarily be satisfying. For some people, admittedly a small percentage, no amount of pain medication is sufficient. For others, the request for deliverance is not made because of physical pain but, rather, because of some other reason, such as the lack of dignity which comes from frailty and no longer being able to manage personal hygiene. In addition, many dying people are not comforted by having caretakers and loved ones nearby; they would prefer to finish the final chapter of their life as quickly as possible, by euthanasia. The compassionate response to a free and informed request for deliverance is to assist the dying to bring about a swift and pain-free death. Yes, this death is an evil which diminishes the human community, but it is less of an evil than the continued unwanted suffering experienced by a sick or dying person. We shoot horses, don't we? Why is it so difficult for us to accept the fact that we owe at least this much mercy to each other?

(4) *Against. All people have a duty not to commit suicide. There is value and dignity in each human life, even in dying life.*

The responsibility not to commit suicide is a lifelong obligation; it does not cease when a person becomes very frail or terminally ill. There is an ethical obligation to respect and value one's own life as well as the lives of others. This ethical obligation is reflected in the legal sphere by laws which make it illegal to commit suicide or to assist another person in committing suicide. The result of both ethical tradition and legal sanction is the forging of consistent opposition toward suicide. By maintaining that value and dignity are inherent in each and every life, including dying life, we force ourselves to respect and honor dying persons and to assist them to live their last days to the fullest because their humanity entitles them to such assistance.

(4) *For. The life of a suffering person may become useless, at which time it may be taken.*

Healthy, productive people have a duty to contribute to society and, therefore, they ought not to commit suicide. Terminally ill and very frail people, on the other hand, have nothing left to contribute to society, and so they have no obligation to continue to live. It makes sense for social institutions such as the legal system to make a strong case against suicide and assisting in suicide. Such argumentation probably keeps many adolescents and productive adults from taking their lives. But, for people whose time remaining is very brief and whose quality of life is very poor, rationale which prohibits self-deliverance is ultimately unconvincing. If these people feel that they are useless to others and that their lives are terribly burdensome, it is unconvincing to argue that either suicide or euthanasia is morally objectionable.

(5) *Against. It is hard to impossible to ascertain whether or not the decision for euthanasia is sane, sound, and rational. Most very sick people are also depressed. Additionally, oftentimes such people can be subject to coercion from those who could benefit from their deaths.*

Those who argue in favor of euthanasia almost always cite support for an individual's free and unfettered right to say when enough is enough. On the surface, this is an appealing argument because it pertains to the last weeks or months of life and, in regard to a controversial issue, it stipulates that the decision making belongs solely to the sick or dying person. Unfortunately, however, actual decisions for euthanasia by sick people are seldom as straightforward as proponents of self-deliverance would suggest. Most people who are very frail or very sick are also depressed and feeling despondent. This emotional state may be the reason for their request for euthanasia. The reasonable way to respond to a depressed person is to offer support, medication, and therapy to assist the person to deal with the depressed state. Killing the depressed person is neither a reasonable nor a compassionate response.

Sick, depressed people are also vulnerable to coercion. Members of their families and close friends who grow tired of caring for them or anxious about financial issues can communicate in verbal and nonverbal fashion their wish for the end to come. Since it would be virtually impossible to ascertain whether or not accommodating others was the reason motivating a sick person's request for euthanasia, it follows that the ethical and legal prohibitions against this practice should remain in place.

(5) *For. Let a person implement his own choices. Depressed people can make rational choices and so can people whose relatives would be relieved by their demise.*

Patient autonomy and the principle of self-determination demand that we respect the choices an individual makes. Most people who undergo ordeals feel somewhat depressed, but this does not mean that they do not know what they want or that they have relinquished the right to have their wishes carried out. In order to make sure that people are clear and certain about their choice for euthanasia, one or two psychiatric consultations can be arranged and the expertise of these physicians can be used in support or denial of the patient's request.

As far as a person's feeling coerced to accept euthanasia is concerned, there are safeguards which can be put in place to prevent such a situation from dictating patient choices. Careful monitoring of family interactions with patients as well as thorough, repeated interviews with patients should be carried out and noted prior to agreement to assist in euthanasia. In the event of reservations about the patient's freedom in reaching her decision, euthanasia should not be carried out. It is important to safeguard sick and dying people from coercion but it is also important to remember that current practice forces everyone to accept death on its own terms. Noncoerced patients with decision-making capacity have a right to choose to end their suffering on their terms.

(6) *Against. Involving physicians and nurses in direct, active euthanasia erodes the ethical foundations of medicine and nursing.*

Physicians and nurses belong to the health care professions, professions whose identity and ethos are separate from and greater than their individual notions of what is morally acceptable or unacceptable. Doctors and nurses are part of professions dedicated to health care and healing, and their acceptance into these professions requires of them that they carry out their missions. To tolerate the killing of patients by physicians or nurses who mistakenly think this practice is ethically acceptable would render unacceptable and irreparable damage to the healing professions. Physicians, nurses, patients, legislators, judges, philosophers and citizens alike are required to preserve and protect the dignity and integrity of the professions of medicine and nursing. Accordingly, allowing for the practice of euthanasia by individual doctors or nurses on a case-by-case basis would represent an absurd compromise and the ultimate irrationality.

(6) *For. Physicians and nurses are in the best position to aid the terminally ill in dying. Those who hold no ethical scruples about practicing euthanasia should not be prohibited from so doing by professional codes or civil laws.*

In a worst case euthanasia scenario, the deed is botched and the person does not die but, rather, survives in an absolutely wretched condition. This eventuality is likely to happen if the person does not know how much medication comprises a lethal dose or if he does not succeed in swallowing the requisite number of pills. Frequently a lay person who decides on self-deliverance requests the assistance of a friend or relative, but if that friend or relative is not knowledgeable about medications or is not prepared to perform follow-up procedures when necessary, then the assistance is virtually worthless.

What is needed by a person who is intent on ending his life is the skilled support of a physician or nurse or perhaps a pharmacist whose presence will assure that miscalculations of medicine are not made and who will be able to take further steps expeditiously in the unlikely event that a dose designed to be lethal does not work as quickly or efficiently as intended.

To argue that medical practitioners are forever excluded from engaging in euthanasia by the requirements of a vague professional responsibility is to romanticize both the training and the skill of physicians and nurses while imposing on them an identity which many would reject. There should be no barriers preventing technically qualified doctors and nurses who are philosophically comfortable with euthanasia from assisting patients who freely request their services.

(7) *Against. By implementing direct, active euthanasia, we would arrange gruesome, dehumanizing scenarios.*

The significant times of peoples' lives are important social occasions. Birth, religious events, graduations, marriage, grandparenting, dying and death come immediately to mind. Dying and death contrast with the other events enumerated because these are sad happenings replete with emotional heaviness and tears. Most people feel inadequate and diminished in the face of a loved one's dying; they wish it were not so, not yet at least, and do all they can to lessen the pain and suffering. Their hearts are heavy and the best emotional state they can hope for is resignation tempered by acceptance.

To replace the quest for patience, resignation, and helpfulness in the face of a loved one's death with a plan for the time, place and manner of carrying out the loved one's killing would constitute a gruesome, dehumanizing act. On the basis of making such arrangements physical and emotional consequences can be anticipated. As far as the memories associated with active euthanasia are concerned, we can expect that they might trigger such emotional traumas as guilt, nightmares and an abundance of second guessing.

(7) *For. To set the time, place and scenario for death would not be inhumane. It would be stressful, but there is no denying that death is a stressful event. To be sure, it is easier to deal with the end of a loved one's suffering than it is to watch the loved one's suffering continue.*

Death is the final event in each person's life. For some, death represents the end of everything, for others, a transition as the soul journeys to a better life, and for still others a specific demarcation in a continual process of rein- carnation. Regardless of one's beliefs about death, there is general agreement about the fact that in our culture the subject is generally avoided. Death is fearsome and the easiest way of approaching it is to deny its existence.

People who are mature and realistic enough to progress beyond the ten- dency to deny death and to request or assist in euthanasia exhibit an admirable maturity. This strength enables them to deal with the issue of euthanasia as well as the mechanical details surrounding the actual death. There is no question that euthanasia is a stressful business but, for those who are clear-headed and decisive enough to involve themselves, growth in char- acter and courage are to be anticipated.

(8) *Against. Legalized euthanasia would add to the fears of the sick and dying who would be afraid of being the victims of involuntary positive euthanasia.*

What is to prevent a relative, after assisting in involuntary positive euthanasia, to assert that she was following a loved one's instructions? Could sufficient safeguards ever be put in place to keep unscrupulous med- ical practitioners from euthanizing frail, sick people because, in their opin- ions, these people would be "better off dead," or because of incentives offered by relatives? By raising questions such as these and trying to imag- ine how difficult it would be to regulate voluntary positive euthanasia so that it does not disintegrate into involuntary positive euthanasia, we become aware of how dangerous it would be to offer ethical approval for euthanasia under any circumstances.

Should there be any medical or legal acceptance for euthanasia, the suf- fering of sick, frail, and dying persons would be increased as they are forced to add fear of being killed to the other burdens they carry.

(8) *For. Sick people would be better off if they thought they could manage their dying.*

Dying is life's most traumatic event. It is made more traumatic if death insists on coming on its own terms. Sick, frail people who are forced to wait until their diseases sap every ounce of energy from them must endure an inhumane indignity. It would be far more decent to allow them to manage their dying, to make decisions for themselves, to decide when enough is enough. If humans are distinguished by their abilities to reason and to choose, it follows that at the crucial time of their dying they have an unde- niable right to decide for themselves whether they want to wait for death to happen or to cut their suffering short.

To argue that vulnerable people could be at risk of being euthanized against their will if euthanasia were made legal is to attempt to decide the issue based on a far-fetched possibility. If euthanasia were legalized, safeguards would be put in place to prevent such a possibility. In addition, at the present time, all patients in health care institutions are at risk of being overmedicated and dying as a result. What keeps this from happening? The answer is simple: The integrity of the health care professionals who care for patients and whose ethos prevents carrying out of life-ending procedures without the patient's well reasoned request.

THE U.S. SUPREME COURT
AND PHYSICIAN-ASSISTED SUICIDE

On June 27, 1997 the U.S. Supreme Court ruled that states may continue to ban physician assistance in suicide but left the door open to states to revisit the question. By a vote of 9 to 0, the Justices adopted a measured and sober tone, as befits the issue. Hallmarks of the decisions include the judgments that the U.S. Constitution does not grant a right to physician-assisted suicide and that there is no reason to collapse the logical distinction between "assisting suicide and withdrawing life-sustaining treatment, a distinction widely recognized and endorsed in the medical profession and in our legal traditions. . . . It is certainly rational."[4]

In reaching these decisions the Supreme Court found that bans on assisting suicide enacted by the states of Washington and New York do not violate the 14th Amendment of the Constitution. However, Chief Justice William H. Rehnquist seemed to encourage states to continue to explore ways to respond to the suffering of terminally ill patients in intractable pain. He reasoned that state legislatures were the better place to continue the debate:

> The Court should accordingly stay its hand to allow reasonable legislative consideration. While I do not decide for all time that respondents' claim should not be recognized, I acknowledge the legislative institutional competence as the better one to deal with that claim at that time.[5]

CONCLUSION

In considering the arguments for and against euthanasia one thing is clearly apparent: Euthanasia is a complex subject which can be approached from a variety of perspectives. This fact gives rise to two insights. The first is that the debate over legalizing euthanasia ought to be characterized by respect for opposing opinions which people hold because sound reasons can be proffered in support of either position. In view of this fact it does not make sense to attack the sanity, integrity, or intelligence of those whose assessment of euthanasia differs from your own. To do so might result in a similar polarization of society over this issue as is the case with abortion. Polarization accomplishes little that is beneficial. In conjunction with euthanasia what is needed is the forging of a societal consensus to continue opposition to the practice or to allow for euthanasia according to carefully constructed guidelines. Because some degree of compromise is necessary we can anticipate that neither side is going to obtain all that it is after. Once the euthanasia debate is resolved, both sides are going to have to live with each other as well as with the result. Civility and tolerance dictate that an atmosphere of mutual respect during and after the debate will be more productive than an atmosphere of divisive partisanship and hostile factionalism.

A second insight about euthanasia has to do with fundamental ethical issues. The two most fundamental issues about euthanasia concern what the question is and which methodology to employ in answering the question.

There are several possible ways of formulating the question about euthanasia. These ways include asking: Should physicians abandon traditional ethics which require that they do no harm? Should society admit any exceptions to the absolute ban against euthanasia, thus opening the door to unforeseen possible egregious abuses? Should frail, sick and dying people be forced to endure protracted suffering? Should medical professionals be prevented from acting in accord with their consciences by outdated laws which prohibit euthanasia?

On the basis of these possible ways of framing the euthanasia question, it becomes apparent that any number of positions or "spins" can be incorporated within the formulation, thus swaying the analysis. The methodological task is related to the question-formulating task because, in a sense, the way one frames the question gives away one's basic approach to ethics. A question dealing with physician responsibilities within traditional medical ethics reveals a bias in favor of principles, rules, and objective standards. Questions which suggest that allowing for euthanasia under some circumstances would inevitably result in abuses of the practice disclose a pragmatic mindset and a basic distrust of the assumption that all medical professionals can be trusted to adhere to strict guidelines and that monitoring authorities are capable of preventing abuses. The question as to whether or not frail, sick people should have to endure protracted suffering appeals to emotions and intuition and almost seems to require a compassionate response which would allow for legalization of euthanasia. Finally, by asking why medical professionals who favor euthanasia should be prohibited from accommodating suffering individuals who freely request it, appeal is made to the individualism and subjectivism which flourish in this pluralistic society and which resist the imposition of objective standards by people who maintain the binding force of traditional principles.

Is euthanasia morally right or morally wrong? Should those who oppose it be forced to live with it as long as they need not be complicit in it? Should those who favor euthanasia be prevented from obtaining or practicing it based on principles which they do not hold? These questions will continue to be asked until answers or compromises are found to which a majority can assent.

ENDNOTES

[1] Neil A. Lewis, "Reno Lifts Barrier To Oregon's Law On Aided Suicide: Overrules D.E.A. Chief: She Won't Prosecute Doctors Who Prescribe Lethal Doses to State's Terminally Ill," *The New York Times*, June 6, 1998, p. 1.

[2] Robert L. Jackson and Kim Murphy, "Suicide ruling protects doctors: Reno tells DEA to end threat of prosecutions," *The Record* (Special from the *Los Angeles Times*), June 6, 1998, pp. 1, A6.

[3] Two exceptions to the almost total lack of support for *involuntary* positive euthanasia involve the case of severely disabled infants in Holland and an elderly man with Alzheimer's in the U.S. whose family requested assistance from Dr. Jack Kevorkian, Cf., Reuters, "Dutch Bring a Test Case in Euthanasia," *The New York Times*, December 23, 1994, and Tamar Lewin, "Life and Death Choice Splits a Family," *The New York Times*, January 19, 1996, p. A12.

[4] Linda Greenhouse, "Court 9-0, Upholds State Laws Prohibiting Assisted Suicide; . . . No Help for Dying," *The New York Times*, June 27, 1997, pp. 1, A19.

[5] "Excerpts From Decision That Assisted Suicide Bans Are Constitutional. From the Decision in *Washington v. Glucksberg* by Chief Justice Rehnquist," *The New York Times*, June 27, 1997, p. A18.

DISCUSSION QUESTIONS

1. Discuss how society in the United States has changed during the past generation or so, allowing for the possibility of legalizing euthanasia. Identify three positive and three negative consequences of the changing culture.

2. State the first set of arguments against and for euthanasia. Evaluate the

manner in which these arguments are presented and state which of the two has more appeal to you, and why.

3. State the second set of arguments against and for euthanasia. Evaluate the manner in which these arguments are presented and state which of the two has more appeal to you, and why.

4. State the third set of arguments against and for euthanasia. Evaluate the manner in which these arguments are presented and state which of the two has more appeal to you, and why.

5. State the fourth set of arguments against and for euthanasia. Evaluate the manner in which these arguments are presented and state which of the two has more appeal to you, and why.

6. State the fifth set of arguments against and for euthanasia. Evaluate the manner in which these arguments are presented and state which of the two has more appeal to you, and why.

7. State the sixth set of arguments against and for euthanasia. Evaluate the manner in which these arguments are presented and state which of the two has more appeal to you, and why.

8. State the seventh set of arguments against and for euthanasia. Evaluate the manner in which these arguments are presented and state which of the two has more appeal to you, and why.

9. State the eighth set of arguments against and for euthanasia. Evaluate the manner in which these arguments are presented and state which of the two has more appeal to you, and why.

10. Evaluate the roles played by government, the media, medical and nursing societies, and religious denominations in respect to euthanasia. Suggest ways in which these groups could facilitate serious dialogue on a sober subject. Under what circumstances and for what reason should these parties assume a position for or against euthanasia?

11. Suggest at least two strategies to lessen divisiveness as the euthanasia debate is played out in society.

CASE STUDY

Jim Warner is a 37-year-old man who has been suffering from HIV/AIDS for 11 years—7 asymptomatic and the last 4 increasingly debilitating. Mr. Warner's emotional state started to deteriorate about three years after the first symptoms of AIDS appeared. By then he had lost several friends, become indigent, and endured far more bad days than good ones. During a support group meeting Mr. Warner heard other people with AIDS discuss their right to die; a few of them revealed that they were stockpiling pre-scription medication to have on hand if they ever decided that they wanted to exercise this right. He said nothing but resolved that he would follow the same course; Mr. Warner started putting aside antidepressants and pain medication for this purpose.

One day Jim Warner phoned his brother Todd and asked him to come over. Todd and Jim were close and enjoyed a good relationship. When he arrived Todd found that Jim's door was open and that Jim was propped up in bed. Jim had half a vodka and tonic in his hand. He told Todd that he had just swallowed a lethal dose of pills and that once he became unconscious he wanted Todd to hold a plastic bag over his head. The plastic bag was on the night stand.

Within a few minutes Jim started convulsing violently. Todd was horrified at the thought of holding the bag over his brother's head. Instead, he picked up the phone and dialed 911.

Evaluation:

1. Identify ethical issues contained in this case.
2. Propose possible solutions for these issues.
3. Make a decision relevant to action to be taken or not taken and provide rationale supportive of this decision.
4. Are you satisfied with your decision? Why or why not?

CHAPTER 13

Treatment of the Terminally Ill: Important Distinctions

INTRODUCTION

Some of the specific issues treated in this chapter have been addressed in connection with other subjects. However, each of these issues is so important and urgent that it is necessary to consider it separately and at length. People in the health care professions cannot avoid dealing with such questions as cessation of treatment, futility, pain management and the rights of vulnerable patients; therefore, it is important that they understand what is at stake in respect to each one. In order to decide about an issue we need to be clear about all its aspects and feel secure about the choices we make. Of the four questions to be covered in this chapter, some are perennial issues that have been faced by generation after generation. Others are more recent in origin, stemming primarily from advances in medical technology. We will consider each in turn.

CESSATION OF TREATMENT

Stopping medical treatment after it has been started is problematic for at least three reasons. First, the outcome is likely going to be the death of the patient. Even though each and every life ends in death, we live in a culture which denies death and we cling to the unrealistic myth that medical science can fix or cure any ailment. Thus, confronting an imminent death, a situation most of us avoid if at all possible, is very wrenching. In view of this fact, selecting the means that will bring about an undesirable outcome becomes an onerous chore.

The second reason cessation of treatment is so difficult is because there is a widespread psychological tendency to shrink from making such a choice, especially for health care providers or loved ones. The ethos of medicine and nursing requires of physicians and nurses that they cure or heal, and their integrity prompts them to resist giving up. When treatments are stopped and patients die, those in the healing professions may doubt their own dedication to their duty to heal. While it is good that they hold themselves to such high standards and that they are reluctant to stop treatments, reality requires the use of common sense. In the face of a critical diagnosis and a hopeless prognosis, it often is medically and morally appropriate to stop treatment.

Just as medical personnel experience a reluctance to stop treatments, so, too, do next of kin of very sick patients. This is because loved ones feel that they have to do everything or because they cling to an unwarranted hope that a miracle might happen. It would be easier for surrogates if they had the patient's clear directions to follow (see Chapter 11, "Advance Directives") or if they had a more realistic idea of the possibilities and limitations of modern medicine. Education in regard to this latter area would be beneficial, as would psychological counseling to help next of kin understand and deal with inappropriate feelings of responsibility and guilt.

The third reason it is hard for people to authorize cessation of treatment is because of a commonly articulated misconception. This misconception consists in thinking that by stopping a treatment one is *causing* the patient's death; needless to say, neither conscientious health care practitioners nor loving relatives wants to bear responsibility for causing a patient to die. It is of the utmost importance to bear in mind the validity of the distinction between allowing nature to take its course, so that a very sick person dies of his illness(es), and taking overt measures to cause the patient to die. The consensus of ethical thinkers is that it may be morally appropriate to let nature take its course and allow a patient to die of her ailments when treatment is burdensome and there is no reasonable hope of recovery. According to such reasoning the patient does not die because treatment is stopped; she dies because of her pathologies, which could not be reversed. On the other hand, it would constitute an act of killing or euthanasia to employ an overt act such as poisoning or suffocating a terminally ill patient in order to end the person's life. Such an intervention, accompanied by an intention to kill the patient, has traditionally been considered morally unacceptable and illegal. Although the euthanasia movement continues to make progress, the distinction between killing and allowing to die remains valid, and it is a distinction people need to understand if they confront situations wherein cessation of treatment is indicated. It is crucially important to comprehend this distinction because the inability to understand it, coupled with an unwillingness to employ it in appropriate circumstances, results in much of the overtreatment which many people have come to fear.

The rationale which undergirds allowance of discontinuance of treatment can be explained in two ways. The first way is the older way, deeply entrenched in traditional ethics. This way is expressed in the language of *ordinary* and *extraordinary* means, defined as follows.

> Ordinary means of preserving life are all medicines, treatments, and operations which offer a reasonable hope of benefit for the patient and/or which can be obtained and used without excessive expense, pain, or other inconvenience; extraordinary means are all medicines, treatments, and operations, which cannot be obtained or used without excessive expense, pain, or other inconvenience.[1]

Thus, ordinary means must be employed but extraordinary means, often referred to as heroic means, need not be used. Unfortunately, people today tend to find the ordinary-extraordinary terminology confusing. They tend to equate ordinary with "usual" means in terms of very common hospital treatments and extraordinary with very high tech, invasive, or experimental procedures. These are not accurate meanings of these terms. The term "ordinary means" relates primarily to the patient and conveys the idea that what will clearly benefit the patient without unduly burdening her should morally be accepted, provided that there is an overall hope for a positive outcome. In the absence of hope for a positive outcome, as well as in situations wherein medical treatments are excessively expensive, painful, or burdensome, the treatments can be evaluated as "extraordinary" and, therefore, optional. Evaluations are always made relevant to the patient's condition and preferences. The ordinary-extraordinary distinctions are crucial standards from which judgments are made, not the characteristics of particular types of medical treatments.

Because of the inclination to become confused about the meanings of ordinary and extraordinary means there has been a shift in clinical practice to utilization of a different rationale in explaining why it may be morally acceptable to stop treating a patient. This rationale is called the "burden-benefit" principle. This principle recognizes that medical procedures may be discontinued when the burden or risk incurred exceeds the expected or actual benefit. Factors to be considered when assessing burdens and benefits include the effects of a procedure or treatment on the quality and/or length of life and the effects on the patient's overall well-being. The specter of terminally ill patients who are suffering at least as much from interventions to which medical science subjects them as from their underlying pathologies has generated a backlash against inappropriate treatments and in favor of allowing people to die with as much comfort and dignity as possible. Knowing that this is the right thing to do is reassuring both to health care practitioners and to next of kin.

Treatment decisions can be made by the patient himself or by the patient's family. Needless to say, there is much less second-guessing when the patient makes the decision for himself because he is able to carry on negotiations with physicians, make his own calculations about benefits and burdens, and speak his own mind. While it is harder for the patient's family to authorize cessation of treatment decisions for an unconscious or incompetent patient, family members can feel secure about their choice if it is grounded in accurate medical information and sound moral theory.

The types of treatments which are frequently stopped include use of respirators, feeding tubes, dialysis, antibiotics, and chemotherapy/radiation. In respect to discontinuance of the respirator, since the case of Karen Ann Quinlan in 1975–76, consultation with a hospital Prognosis Committee is standard practice before a respirator is turned off. When the patient is competent and conscious, the committee confers with her to determine if she understands the ramifications of her request to discontinue the respirator and to make sure that her decision is arrived at freely. Should a patient be unconscious and/or incompetent, consultation by the Prognosis Committee aims at ascertaining whether or not cessation is in accord with the patient's advance directive or, in the absence of an advance directive, whether discontinuance is a reasonable option given the patient's condition and prognosis. In this latter case, the decision to discontinue would reflect the judgment of the patient's next of kin.

Use of other treatments such as feeding tubes, dialysis, antibiotics, or chemotherapy/radiation is often initiated in the hope that it will ameliorate a sick person's symptoms or restore the person to health. Frequently it happens that neither of these goals is accomplished or that the intervention itself becomes very burdensome. When these eventualities occur, it is reasonable to stop treatment and let nature take its course. Under some circumstances, medical practice requires attending physicians to bring one or two consulting physicians into the decision-making circle in order to ascertain that everyone involved is clear about what is at stake, as well as to offer independent evaluations of the situation.

If it were not possible to stop treatments once started, medical science would be at a disadvantage. This is because trial and error are an integral aspect of medical practice. In the event that treatments could not be stopped if the hoped-for or anticipated beneficial outcomes did not occur, people might pass up the chance to try treatments that could help them, creating an undesirable state of affairs.

It should be noted that the same rationale used for cessation of treatment may support decisions not to use, or to forgo, any medical treatments.

FUTILITY

Medical science is a field of expertise and clinical practice which can be approached in four different ways. People can turn to medicine to learn how to keep healthy or to obtain vaccines to prevent diseases. Sick people can approach medicine in the hope of obtaining cures for their ailments. If cures are not possible, medicine may offer treatments to ameliorate conditions or keep diseases from progressing. Finally, people with terminal diseases can and often do turn to medical science, imploring doctors to do something, anything, in their behalf. This fourth typical situation necessitates that we confront the category of *medical futility* so as to understand and evaluate the intelligibility or unintelligibility of futile treatments. This area is one of the most perplexing and contentious in contemporary medicine. It is an issue which cries out for dialogue in order to advance understanding.

What is futile is useless or ineffectual, that is, incapable of bringing about a desired outcome. The reason the dispensing of futile treatments is a major concern in contemporary clinical settings is that many people are unrealistic about the ability of medicine to provide beneficial treatments to those who have irreversible diseases. The media contributes to the unrealistic atmosphere by announcements of astounding breakthroughs and miracle cures so that people have almost come to believe that the sad realities of sickness, dying, and death can be circumvented. Needless to say, they cannot. Applying futile treatments to patients who cannot benefit will result in one or more of the following consequences:

Physiologic. The treatment cannot maintain pulse, blood pressure or vital functions so that the patient receiving it does not benefit from it and dies in spite of it. When nurses and physicians know with a fair degree of certitude that a proposed intervention will be futile on physiologic grounds, it is not surprising that they are reluctant to employ it. In a sense, by providing futile treatments health care practitioners are violating a basic ethical norm, that they do no harm. It is harmful to a patient and her next of kin to trigger a false hope which cannot come to fruition. And it is harmful to the physicians and nurses themselves because they are carrying out ineffective interventions instead of employing their skills to cure or care.

Outcome. Treatments that have a low probability of having a good effect or will not alter the underlying disease are categorized as futile. In the course of many disease processes such as cancer, emphysema, congestive heart failure, and AIDS, patients reach a point at which conventional treatments offer little or no further benefit. This judgment is a clinical one, based on probabilities and informed by experience garnered from observation of many patients with similar pathologies. While it is not an absolute fact, this judgment about the futility of a treatment based on the likelihood of its outcome needs to be respected by patients and family members. The reason is that no one has a right to be provided with futile medical treatment and no medical practitioner has a responsibility to render such treatment. To contend otherwise is to argue from a premise of irrationality.

Quality of life. The third type of medical treatments understood as futile are those which the patient might survive, but in a terribly compromised condition. Given the technological possibilities of modern medicine to resuscitate patients and sustain immensely frail and feeble people on respirators or by means of tube feeding, the issue of quality of life is frequently encountered. More and more people are balking at being subject to an enfeebled existence made possible by a resuscitation intervention and/or the employment of artificial life support. In cases where a very poor quality of life would most probably result if such techniques were employed, a growing number of medical practitioners and ethicists are moving in the direction of describing these interventions as futile and discouraging their use.

One of the major roadblocks to dealing with futility is the fact that those who would request or demand futile treatments are able to make their case based on the remote chance that the requested intervention will bring about an exception to the general rule. While this is not an area to be treated in a casual or dismissive way, the arguments against rendering futile treatments certainly seem cogent and more compelling than the case put forward by a devil's advocate. One thing about which there is no question is the need for ongoing discussion of this issue, as well as open, respectful communication between physician and patient so that important decisions will not be made on the basis of unrealistic expectations.

An interesting case which illustrates the complexity of opposing parties at odds over futile treatment is that of Mariah Scoon. On February 19, 1996, a five-month-old infant, Mariah Scoon, was admitted to Long Island Jewish Hospital in New York. When he noticed Mariah gasping for breath her father called an ambulance to take the baby to the hospital. Within 24 hours of admittance physicians at Long Island Jewish Hospital declared Mariah brain dead, and they told her parents that she would be removed from the respirator. Lois and Malcolm Scoon objected to respirator removal and, on February 23, 1996, a hospital attorney informed their lawyer that the hospital "would seek judicial relief if the Scoons persist in their objection."[2] The articulated basis for the parents' objection was their born-again religious faith along with their refusal to accept that their baby was dead.

Before a court became involved, in an unusual move, John Cardinal O'Connor of New York arranged to have Mariah Scoon moved to Saint Vincent's Hospital. Even though she remained on a respirator at Saint Vincent's, Mariah ceased breathing on March 13, 1996 and was pronounced dead.

The case of Mariah Scoon raises two issues. The first entails whether or not it makes sense to provide futile treatment in order to accommodate people like Lois and Malcolm Scoon. It cost a substantial amount of money to provide care in the hospital for a baby who was already dead, and, in the act of providing the care health care practitioners may have been placed in compromised positions. Was provision of care a sensitive, compassionate response or an ill-conceived idea which served no rational purpose? If it was the latter, there can be no ethical justification for it.

A second issue raised by this case is whether or not the baby was injured by violent shaking and whether her parents' motive for keeping her on the respirator emanated from their guilt and their desire that brain bruises heal before an autopsy. (On August 13, 1996 New York District Attorney Richard A. Brown announced an indictment against Malcolm Scoon, Mariah's father. Scoon was arraigned the same day in New York State Supreme Court in Queens on charges of reckless manslaughter and criminally negligent homicide in the baby's death. He pleaded not guilty.[3]) Addressing matters such as this one is beyond the purview of this book. I mention it, however, to illustrate the extraordinary complexity of such cases.

PAIN MANAGEMENT

A Study to Understand Prognoses and Preferences for Outcomes and Risks of Treatments (SUPPORT) was carried out by a team of eight principal investigators, all of them medical doctors, and financed by the Robert Wood Johnson Foundation. The objectives of the project were to improve end-of-life decision making and reduce the frequency of a mechanically supported, painful, and prolonged process of dying. Its design allowed for a two-year observational study of 4,301 patients followed by a two-year controlled clinical trial involving 4,804 patients and their physicians. During the control phase a specially trained nurse had several contacts with the patient, family, physician, and hospital staff to elicit preferences, improve understanding of outcomes, encourage attention to pain control, and facilitate advance-care planning, and patient-physician communication. Results of this well-designed, well-financed, and well-executed study were published in the *Journal of the American Medical Association* in November, 1995.[4] The outcomes reported in terms of pain experienced by dying patients were disappointing in that "Families reported that half of the patients who were able to communicate in their last few days spent most of the time in moderate or severe pain."[5]

Physicians are justifiably reluctant to over-prescribe pain medication for people who are recovering from surgery or injury. The reason for the reluctance is not an indifference to the pain people are experiencing but, rather, a wariness about prescribing medications to which people might become addicted. The same caution, however, does not apply at the end of life because dying people do not live long enough to develop addictions to narcotic-based pain killers which provide respite from their suffering. Furthermore, even if the dying did actually become addicted to pain medication, this addiction would be a lesser evil than the suffering experienced by people who are racked by pain. In addition, euthanasia would be a less attractive option if the public were assured that satisfactory treatment of pain was a priority in the treatment of the dying.

Realistically, what can medical science do in respect to providing satisfactory treatment for pain? The Hippocratic tradition establishes as a fundamental responsibility of the physician the relief of pain. This goal is summarized in the ancient French medical adage, "to cure sometimes, to relieve often, to comfort always." By getting in touch with their own tradition, therefore, physicians will come to acknowledge their responsibility to manage the pain of the dying. In so doing, they will need to consider the following points.

First, patients are people with individual histories, likes, dislikes, and needs. This is as true of dying patients as of people at any other stage in their lives. As medicine has become more and more sophisticated it has also become more and more impersonal. Specialist physicians tend to treat particular symptoms and the patient, along with her values, needs and wants tends to get lost in the shuffle. While it is appropriate to follow a medical-indications approach with a trauma patient in the aftermath of an accident, it is inappropriate to adhere to the same clinical style with people who are dying. During the final phase of life physicians need to see patients as unique individuals who are concerned about their loved ones and who bear the enormous burden of their dying. It is for the attending physician to respond to and care for this patient in a humane manner. One of the hardest things for the doctor to do in these circumstances is to talk to the patient and bring up the subject of pain management. The reason this is difficult is because our society denies death, and conversations about dying are among the most difficult imaginable. Nevertheless, shattering this taboo and entering into a compassionate healer relationship with dying patients is an obligation physicians ought not to shirk.

Second, the final days of dying people's lives are often passed in the most forbidding of sterile hospital settings. Medical apparatuses of all kinds serve the dual functions of isolating the patient from family and caregivers and increasing everyone's unease about dying. In conjunction with establishing a commitment to keep dying people comfortable it would probably make sense to reach a consensus about the kinds of settings which would be less off-putting and more agreeable. In this regard, we could learn a lesson from Mrs. Jacqueline Kennedy Onassis who, aware that her death was close at hand, chose to leave the hospital and go home. During her final hours she was visited by family members and friends and surrounded by the furnishings of her own home. We can only speculate about the comfort Mrs. Onassis enjoyed because she died at home but we do know, based on their testimony, that her children felt peaceful about the way their mother passed away.

Third, when we talk about pain management of terminally ill people, we are dis-cussing a complex subject. Pain can be physical, it can be emotional, it can be both physical and emotional, and it can exist in a wide range of intensities. Further complicating the picture is the fact that individuals vary widely both in their ability to tolerate pain and in the threshold at which pain becomes unbearable to them. Pain, like death, is an unpleasant feature of the human condition, something to contend with since it cannot be eliminated.

One of the most helpful sources of information about pain management is the hospice movement. In 1966 in England a physician and former nurse named Cicely Saunders established a format to care for the terminally ill in a humane and dignified manner. Modeled on the medieval hospice in which hosts (hospes) would receive travelers as guests, Dr. Saunders established a modern hospice to look after dying people. A hospice is not meant to be like a hospital where people go to be cured but, rather, a home-like place where the terminally ill receive comfort and care. Since Dr. Saunders founded the St. Christopher Hospice, both hospices and hospice services have been established all over the world. In actual hospice facilities the same type of services are performed as were performed at St. Christopher's by Dr. Saunders and her staff, services designed to keep patients comfortable and to meet their needs. Hospice services provide nursing care, emotional support, respite relief, and pastoral care to terminally ill patients who are cared for at home by a primary care giver assisted by visiting nurses. One of the major pillars on which the hospice movement rests is the commitment to keep dying persons as pain free as humanly possible. Physicians, nurses, and all interested parties stand to gain a great deal from entering into dialogue with hospice service providers and learning from them the wealth of information they have about pain management.

Fourth, there is a need for more education in medical schools about pain man-agement, as well as discussion among physicians about this subject. Once formal education is completed much of what physicians learn comes from what they read, from in-service programs and from informal conversations with colleagues. There is no question that an appropriate and pressing question to be addressed in all these venues is that of competent, compassionate treat-ment of pain for the terminally ill.

Fifth, we need to consider an ethical concern related to pain management. This concern involves the hypothetical case of the patient who is near death and is experiencing considerable pain and it focuses specifically on dosage. In order to properly treat the pain a physician would need to prescribe a large dose of medication which could (or probably would) suppress respiration, thereby contributing to the patient's death. The issue at stake is whether in prescribing and/or administering the pain medication the physician is, in effect, killing the patient. In responding to this case and allowing for ade-quate treatment of pain, we need to make a crucially important ethical distinction. This distinction requires that we look critically at the intention of the physician who prescribes the medicine and/or the physician or nurse who administers it. (It may also be self-administered by the patient.) If the medication is prescribed and administered for the purpose of providing an adequate response to the patient's pain and this is the intention of the parties involved, then giving a dosage sufficient to achieve this result is ethically acceptable. Should the patient die as a result of suppressed respiration, which is either a possible or probable side effect, neither the physician who prescribed the dosage nor the person who administered it is responsible for killing the patient because the patient's death is an unintended consequence of the procedure. This distinction may strike the reader as quibbling because he may think: What difference does it make why one administers medication, it is what happens as a result of taking it that counts. The answer to this is that making a distinction about intentionality is far from beside the point.

In fact, this distinction takes us to the very heart of ethics because, in order to be morally responsible people, we need to intend to do good and avoid evil or, in medical parlance, to do no harm. Even though death at the end of a long illness can be seen as a blessing, for the most part the act of ending a life is understood as one to be avoided, as evil or harmful in nature. Most well-intentioned care givers are repulsed by the thought of killing sick patients. If they are secure in the knowledge that their administering sufficient pain medication to keep patients comfortable cannot logically be construed as a killing act, they will feel reassured because they will understand that they are following a reasonable approach in caring for the dying.

SAFEGUARDING THE RIGHTS OF INCOMPETENT PERSONS

A final important distinction is that an incompetent person differs in significant ways from a competent person, thus necessitating different strategies in carrying out his care. Incompetent persons are those who are unable to exercise autonomy, i.e., make decisions for themselves. Several types of individuals are properly classified as incompetent: Infants and minor children; retarded individuals; the mentally ill; persons who lack consciousness; and those afflicted by degenerative brain disease. The incompetents do not lack the *right* to make autonomous decisions about their care. Rather, they lack the *ability* to conduct thorough negotiations with physicians which are held before informed consent is given. Some types of incompetent patients, such as infants, severely retarded persons and those with advanced Alzheimer's are clearly incompetent. In other cases, however, with patients who exhibit partial or compromised competence, it is very difficult to make the judgment call as to whether or not a specific patient is competent or incompetent.

Generally speaking, persons who manifest certain capabilities are judged to be competent. These capacities include the ability to be able to articulate one's values or goals, the ability to communicate and understand information, the ability to reason and deliberate, and knowledge as to the time, place, and circumstances in which one finds himself. When it is difficult for an attending physician to determine whether or not a borderline patient possesses these capacities, one or two independent consultations, at least one with a psychiatrist, is indicated. In addition, in cases where a patient makes an irrational choice, such as refusing a low-risk medical procedure which promises a substantial benefit, a question of the patient's competence may be raised and appropriate consultations indicated.

Physicians generally carry out negotiations about incompetent patients with surrogate decision makers. If the incompetent patient has advance directives which include the appointment of a health care proxy, then the proxy acts as surrogate. In regard to infants and children, parents are legally responsible to act in the role of surrogate. As children mature through the adolescent years, their input into treatment decisions is routinely requested. However, until youngsters reach the age of 18, only a parent or guardian can authorize procedures. For other incompetents, such as retarded or mentally ill people, the comatose, and those affected by dementia, close relatives typically act as surrogates. There are some cases in which surrogates are appointed by the courts. These cases include situations in which an incompetent person has no relatives, cases in which there is a question as to whether or not a surrogate is acting in a responsible manner, and circumstances of family disagreement in which the relatives of an incompetent patient cannot arrive at the same conclusion. Since court involvement in the clinical setting is slow, costly, and cumbersome, there is general agreement among health care professionals, ethicists, and the public that such involvement should be kept to a minimum.

What responsibilities do surrogates take on in behalf of incompetent persons? Incompetent persons do not surrender their rights through being/becoming incompetent; instead, they lack the means to exercise their rights and surrogates provide this means. Rights are constituent parts of human nature so that all human persons have rights. Rights are powers and privileges to which persons are entitled simply because they are human. These rights include access to and provision of proper medical care. Surrogates act for incompetents, in a sense enabling the incompetents to exercise their choice, by authorizing various treatments and programs of medical care. This is consistent with the obligations we experience as members of the human community, while following from the entitlement of all persons, including the vulnerable, to medical care.

Given the sophistication of medical technology and the compromised status of many types of incompetent patients, ethical issues have arisen around cessation of treatment and forgoing of treatment for incompetents. In regard to both forgoing and withdrawing, the predictable result is frequently the death of the patient. Since death is a negative event and since incompetent patients are also vulnerable, a cautiousness has often become manifest in regard to doing anything which might not be justifiable. As physicians, surrogates, judges, and the public grappled with cases of this kind, some principles began to take shape to give direction for decision making.

One principle is the quality of life concept which considers the patient's level of satisfaction or comfort with or without medical treatment. The emerging consensus is that treatments which will enhance the quality of an incompetent patient's life are morally mandatory and should be chosen. On the other hand, treatments which would cause the patient pain and suffering, and thus diminish the quality of his life, need not be prescribed.

Another standard which is taking shape is known as the best-interest standard. This requires an analysis of the benefits and burdens of treatment, with treatments which are clearly beneficial being required while those which will likely add to the patient's burdens not being morally mandatory. The difficulty with the best-interests standard is that in many instances it is very hard to predict what an outcome is going to be.

Two other approaches to decision making on behalf of once competent adult patients who are now incompetent require application of either the subjective standard or substitute judgment. Using the subjective standard, the surrogate articulates what she knows the patient would want under the circumstances. The evidence the surrogate would need is either written directions or oral testimony which the incompetent patient addressed to her. Substitute judgment is different from the subjective standard in that it is inferential in nature. Accordingly, the surrogate claims to have known the patient, her likes, dislikes, and the way her mind worked, and, on the basis of this knowledge he is able to conclude, "Thus and so is what she would have wanted."

Several watershed court cases, including Quinlan, Conroy, O'Connor, and Cruzan, have been instrumental in crystallizing what needs to be done by surrogates on behalf of incompetent patients in order to protect these patients in their vulnerability, manifest respect for them, even in their diminished conditions, and guarantee their right to proper medical treatment. It is critically important that health care professionals be aware of various aspects of this issue so that they can carry out prudent negotiations with surrogates. If physicians suspect that surrogates do not have the incompetent's welfare at heart, they should alert hospital administrators and stand ready to become involved in court intervention. Finally, and fundamentally, by studying this matter health care providers should foster and maintain attitudes of sensitivity towards incompetents and respect for them because, like us, they are members of the human community and bearers of inalienable rights.

CONCLUSION

One cannot function in the contemporary clinical setting without encountering ethical issues related to cessation of treatment, futility, providing pain relief for the terminally ill, and making ethically sound decisions on behalf of incompetents. Each of these issues is difficult and complex and it places medical practitioners and next of kin in an awkward position: A position in which they need to provide rationale for their motivation as well as for their decisions. If they cannot justify stopping treatment, refusing to provide futile treatments, or prescribing sufficient medication to deal decisively with pain, or why the manner in which they are acting is respectful of the rights of an incompetent, they will fail to act appropriately and will endure troubled consciences. Such a result is ethically unacceptable. If they can offer an ethical defense for their actions, they can respect themselves as upright individuals.

ENDNOTES

[1] Gerald Kelly, *Medico Moral Problems* (St. Louis, MO: Catholic Health Association, 1958), p. 129.

[2] Frank Bruni, "Bid to Seek Taking Baby Off Device," *The New York Times*, February 26, 1996, p. B 3.

[3] Norimitsu Onishi, "Prosecutor Says Rage-Filled Shaking Killed Baby," *The New York Times*, August 14, 1996, p. B4.

[4] The Support Principal Investigators, "A Controlled Trial to Improve Care for Seriously Ill Hospitalized Patients," *JAMA*, November 22–29, 1995, 274:20, pp. 1591–1598.

[5] Ibid., 1595.

DISCUSSION QUESTIONS

1. Do you think you would have a psychological problem asking physicians to stop treatments if your prognosis were grim? Why or why not? Would it be different if you were deciding for a loved one? Why or why not?

2. Why do you think some people are reluctant to stop treatment? Do you think it makes sense to hold out for a miraculous cure? Under what circumstances?

3. What is meant by futile medical treatments? Since no one can know with absolute certainty that a treatment will turn out to be futile, state at least three guidelines physicians can follow so as to evaluate a treatment as futile.

4. Describe steps society can take to enable the general public to become educated about futile, as distinct from beneficial, treatments.

5. How much pain do you think you can tolerate? How much medication would you want if you were in pain? Would your diagnosis and prognosis affect your answers? Why or why not?

6. Since the SUPPORT study did not achieve its purpose, i.e., to have physicians and patients talk about the patient's dying and his/her wishes in regard to treatments and pain control, what strategies would you suggest to accomplish this goal? Prepare an outline which describes your answer to this question.

7. What rights do you believe incompetent persons possess? Describe how quality of life considerations, the best interest standard, the subjective standard, and substitute judgment come into play as decisions are being reached about incompetent persons.

CASE STUDY

Thelma Morgan is a 68-year-old woman who was diagnosed five months ago with inoperable liver cancer. At that time her prognosis was grim; her remaining lifespan was estimated to be six to seven months. Mrs. Morgan opted to undergo chemotherapy but experienced no discernible benefits. In spite of treatment, she continued to lose weight, became jaundiced, and grew progressively weaker. One morning when she awoke Mrs. Morgan had severe pain in her lower back and was unable to get out of bed because her legs could not sustain her weight. Her daughter Stephanie called an ambulance and asked that her mother be taken to the emergency room.

After examination the emergency room doctor told the patient and her daughter that the cancer had probably spread to the spine and this was why Mrs. Morgan was in pain and could not walk. He said that there were no useful treatments available for a patient in her condition and therefore said it did not make sense to admit Mrs. Morgan. Stephanie Morgan is a practicing attorney. She disagreed strenuously with the physician and wanted her mother admitted. The doctor continued to refuse. Ms. Morgan literally left her mother on a stretcher in a cubicle in the emergency room and went to the county court. There she obtained a court order requiring that her mother be admitted and given appropriate treatment.

Mrs. Morgan received an MRI which revealed a tumor on her lower spine. The tumor was treated with a two week course of low-dose radiation. Her pain lessened after the radiation started, but during the treatment Mrs. Morgan became increasingly disoriented and incoherent. Sixteen days after the court-ordered admission, Mrs. Morgan died. Her hospital bill was $38,726, paid by Medicare.

Evaluation:

1. Identify ethical issues contained in this case.
2. Propose possible solutions for these issues.
3. Make a decision relevant to action to be taken or not taken and provide rationale supportive of this decision.
4. Are you satisfied with your decision? Why or why not?

PART SIX

ETHICAL ISSUES
FOR HEALTH CARE PROFESSIONALS

CHAPTER 14

Paternalism
and Autonomy

INTRODUCTION

In recent years the way medicine is practiced has changed. The primary medical relationship is between physician and patient. Up until a generation or so ago, the physician was the active, knowledgeable, in-charge party in this relationship, while the patient was passive, unsophisticated and submissive. A change in the relationship, so that physician and patient become *collaborative partners,* reflects an ideological shift from paternalism to autonomy. How has this significant, far-reaching alteration come about?

The culture of medicine does not exist in a vacuum; it is influenced by the culture of society-at-large. In society, with the Civil Rights movement and the Feminist movement, people of color and women declared their equality with white males. As relationships of superiority-inferiority began to disappear, special privileges traditionally accorded to particular classes of people began to be taken away. Among those to lose some of their prestige were physicians who lost claim to the **moral right** to act on the patient's behalf, without need of the patient's consent. This so-called right was replaced with a very different approach to the physician-patient relationship, wherein the patient assumed the role of partner who is capable of and interested in participating in all aspects of care.

In addition to social movements which led to specific classes of people claiming equality and respect, awareness of harms done to unsuspecting individuals during the course of medical experiments also contributed to the movement away from paternalism and toward requiring that people exercise their liberty by giving informed consent to medical procedures. When people throughout the world became aware of atrocities committed by Nazi doctors during World War II, the content of prescriptive medical ethics changed for succeeding generations. Nazi doctors performed experiments on prisoners in concentration camps in order to learn about the effects of various medicines and procedures. They *used* human persons as lab animals for scientific knowledge. Individuals were used as a means to an end which would be of no benefit to them. And they were used for this purpose with neither their knowledge nor their consent. A unanimous ethical consensus exists that what the Nazi doctors did was morally wrong. A result of that consensus has been the requirement of the exercise of informed consent by autonomous patients before they are subjected to medical treatments. (These matters are addressed in Chapter 9, "Experimentation in Medicine.")

Physicians are still recognized for the specialized training and expertise which they possess. In the current climate, however, doctors would be among the first to admit the limits of their competence and, hence, their reluctance to have complete control over treatment decisions. The transition in physician attitudes is matched by newly assertive lay people; they are better educated than in the past and the media has made the present generation much better informed about physician shortcomings than previous generations were. Medical mistakes, negligence, and malpractice are featured items in print and broadcast news, making everyone aware of the need to give careful consideration to the medical care recommended to them. In addition, at no time in history has the practice of medicine been so complicated, due to the array of medical options available for use in treatment making patient input as to what they want to achieve through medical means more important than ever.

PATERNALISM

Paternalism is a system of social arrangement in which authority and privilege are vested in the male figure who is in charge. In the paternalistic family, the father plays the role of benevolent ruler who is responsible for regulating the life of his family and is likewise obligated to provide for their material needs. By extension, paternalism in medicine implies unquestioned acceptance by all parties that the physician's responsibility is to act on the patient's behalf, not at the patient's behest. From the time of the Hippocratic Oath until relatively recently, the physician's high status required that his actions on behalf of the patient be characterized by competence as well as beneficence. In respect to competence, physicians knew that they were absolutely bound to do no harm and were not to attempt treatments for which they lacked expertise. As far as beneficence was concerned, paternalistic physicians felt obliged always to act for a patient's good and never to offer a treatment which they did not think would be beneficial.

Beneficence comes from the Latin *bene,* good and *facere,* to make, and its meaning is to bring about or to make a good, which, in the medical context, is recognized as well-being or healing. But, with the movement toward patient autonomy, paternalism, with its claim to a commitment to beneficence on the part of physicians, is being laid to rest. Is it a mistake for physicians and patients to reject the good which doctors in previous generations sought to do through beneficence? This is a subtle question which is equalled by the subtle responses appropriate to it. Thus, the offering of beneficence by the paternalistic physician is deficient because of four reasons. First, a paternalistic physician acts on his own values; by not learning the values of his patient and striving to work out a treatment regimen which would be acceptable both to himself and to the patient the doctor does the patient a disservice. Second, there is a sense in which individuals know their own interests better than anyone else; these interests need to be elicited and to be honored in a treatment plan. Third, dangers of abuse could flow from a legitimized paternalism because, if physicians were to be situated beyond anyone's scrutiny but their own and that of their colleagues, incompetent, wrongheaded, or dangerous actions might not come to be recognized. Finally, a patient's medical needs, as defined by a physician, cannot cancel the patient's **substantive** and **procedural rights** to pursue or reject any course of treatment based on subjective preferences.

The ideal toward which contemporary medicine ought to move is for physicians to retain their commitment to act with beneficence toward their patients while relinquishing paternalistic attitudes according to which beneficence would be *imposed.* Within such a scenario patients would understand the good physicians seek to do, they might come to endorse physician-suggested treatments, and they would probably cooperate to facilitate the success of these treatments.

By relinquishing paternalistic attitudes, physicians surrender part of the power and privilege accorded to them by the traditional **ethos, or culture**, of Western medicine. At the same time, however, physicians grow in personal integrity as well as ethical sensitivity because they come to see the patient not as an object upon whom to act but, rather, as a subject whose values and preferences ought to be taken into account.

PATIENT AUTONOMY OR SELF-DETERMINATION

Patients have an uncontested legal right to exercise autonomy in regard to medical treatment. Accordingly, they can refuse to accept absolutely necessary, low-risk procedures such as blood transfusions or appendectomies, and face the prospect of death as a result of their refusals. The common law right to autonomy was articulated by Judge Benjamin Cardoza who argued that "Every human being of adult years and sound mind has a right to determine what shall be done with his own body. . . ."[1] Thus, if treatment is given to a patient against the patient's will, the treating physician runs the risk of being sued for battery. The patient's right to exercise autonomy is insured through the mechanism of giving informed consent for a course of treatment, as well as specific components within the course of treatment such as X-rays or surgery. The standard exemption to the requirement to obtain informed consent from patients is the situation of medical emergency in which a noncommunicative patient needs immediate medical attention. In such situations physicians are expected to do what is medically indicated and should anticipate no legal or ethical objection because they follow such a course.

Just as an adult has a **legal right** to refuse medical treatments which most reasonable persons would consider prudent and desirable, so, too, the autonomous adult has the right to employ all experimental and heroic measures for as long as humanly possible even in view of a fatal diagnosis accompanied by the medically informed opinion that the treatments are futile. Of course, being able to actually follow such a course requires that the patient have financial resources to pay for treatments not covered by insurance, Medicare, or Medicaid, and the patient is able to find a physician who is willing to oversee treatments.

There is no question that the legal system of the United States safeguards the right of the adult to exercise autonomy in regard to making medical decisions. However, a question arises rather naturally in regard to whether or not this legal right is consistent with sound moral principles. The answer to this question is that some aspects of patient autonomy are consistent with reasonable ethical conduct while others are not. Using his reason to choose an appropriate course of medical treatment would represent an ethical exercise of informed consent by the patient. This is because, through the process of reaching informed consent, the patient assumes responsibility for and actively cooperates in his care.

Common sense dictates that beneficial therapies ought to be employed in order to sustain health and correct anomalies. Refusing medical treatment on the basis of whim, aversion, fear, or contempt would be morally suspect because such choices would reveal an attitude which is disparaging toward life. And, ethically, life is to be valued, not disparaged.

The accomplishment of his duties represents a sufficiently compelling motivation to prompt a patient to opt for difficult medical regimens in order to be able to finish his work. An example might be that of a man who reluctantly authorizes a wearing program of chemotherapy and radiation in spite of a small chance of success in the hope of buying enough time to be with his children through adolescence. The altruism and commitment to responsibility evident in such a choice reflect the person's values but could not be demanded or expected of everyone.

It is apparent that an autonomous patient does not have a moral right to disregard his or her health or to refuse necessary, low-risk procedures. Should he or she do so would be to act in an irrational manner which could not be ethically justified.

INFORMED CONSENT

The way in which a patient exercises autonomy is by choosing whether or not to seek medical treatment for a particular sickness or injury, by deciding on which physician or medical facility to use, and by giving informed consent for the treatment. Just as a physician's assumed entitlement to a position of superiority is at the heart of paternalism, so is the exercise of informed consent at the heart of patient autonomy.

What is informed consent? Informed consent is a decision reached by a competent patient to accept a medical treatment or course of treatment. In order for a person to be capable of giving informed consent the individual needs to be sane and oriented; depressed people are capable of giving informed consent as are very sick, frail people as long as they manifest an understanding of what is being offered to them and convey a consistent sense of decisiveness in respect to their choices. A person need not be able to speak to give informed consent, as the person's decision can be rendered in writing. The person needs to be able to understand the information presented to her in order to give informed consent. When there are questions as to a patient's competence to process information and render an accurate account of her wishes, one or two psychiatric consultations are generally requested before the patient's instructions are accepted as representative of her informed consent.

There are several requirements concerning the information presented to a patient in the process of obtaining informed consent. People need to know the purpose of the procedure(s), its actual components, the possible inconvenience and pain which may be connected to it, and any foreseen risks as well as predictable side-effects. Physicians and other health care providers need to present this information in nontechnical language which can be comprehended by patients and members of their families. An unhurried atmosphere is best, and questions should be encouraged and answered fully. Although it is the patient alone who makes informed choices about his medical treatment, it is important to include family members or close friends in the instruction-discussion process because the patient may be as desirous of obtaining their advice as of questioning his doctors.

Deliberate deception on the part of health care providers is morally wrong. It would be less easy to detect, but also wrong, for a physician to try to exploit the upper hand in the physician-patient relationship by putting subtle pressure on a patient to agree to treatments which most reasonable people would not want. It can also happen that a physician seeks to short-circuit the whole expository phase of obtaining informed consent by coaxing acquiescence through such coercive tactics as saying, "If I were in your position, I would definitely authorize this treatment," or "If he were my father, there is no way that I would put him through this."

The actual process of obtaining informed consent usually consists of a discussion between physician and patient or among physician, patient, and patient's family, followed by a request to the patient to read a detailed written form and sign it. Informed consent is generally obtained at the time a person enters a hospital or embarks on an outpatient course of treatment such as chemotherapy. In nonemergency situations informed consent is always obtained from competent patients prior to surgery. Some medical treatments, such as artificial feeding using nasogastric tubes, may be begun without obtaining informed consent. Whether or not this should be done is currently being debated. Given the fact that the exercise of patient autonomy is widely supported by society in the United States, the trend of the future will likely be to obtain informed consent for far more procedures, even those which today are considered so routine that patients are subjected to them without being asked for permission.

Problematic instances in regard to obtaining informed consent involve once-competent but now-incompetent, adult patients, never-competent patients, and children. In regard to once-competent adult patients who become incompetent, written advance directives go a long way toward conveying their decisions about treatments. An instruction directive or living will conveys the sentiments of the person in regard to treatments which are or are not wanted, as well as how these choices might change depending on circumstances. In a Durable Power of Attorney for Health Care, an incompetent names her surrogate decision maker and charges that person with exercising the right to give or refuse informed consent for her in a manner consistent with her preferences and values.

Should a once-competent adult patient who becomes incompetent not have advance directives, it is not clear how his treatment would be carried out. To be sure, since his wishes would not be clearly expressed and since no one would have been designated to act as his proxy, his right to exercise informed consent would be abrogated. Under these circumstances there is a good chance that physicians would follow reasonable instructions given by the patient's family. If, however, in the physicians' opinion, the instructions for the patient's care appeared unreasonable, or if members of the family could not concur as to what to do, decisions about what should be done for the patient or who should speak for him would likely wind up in court.

Never-competent adult patients and children represent special cases in respect to the exercise of informed consent. In regard to children, their parents or legal guardians are legally responsible for giving informed consent on their behalf. As children get older, they become more capable of giving input into decisions regarding their medical treatment and should be allowed to do so. Final decisions, however, rest with parents or guardians. The decision of parents or guardians is almost always honored; the exception is in a case wherein physicians do not think the parents or guardians are acting reasonably or in the best interests of the child. Then, court intervention is a last resort, following hospital-based efforts at mediation.

As far as never-competent adult patients are concerned, family members generally serve as decision makers and physicians ordinarily follow their instructions unless they suspect that a particular decision is not being made with the patient's best interests in mind. In such a case appeal would likely be made to the court to appoint a guardian to negotiate with physicians in order to make treatment decisions for the incompetent patient. In instances in which incompetent adult patients have no close relatives, court-appointed surrogates are entrusted with rendering informed consent for medical treatments.

LIMITED TOLERANCE OF LINGERING PATERNALISM

Paternalism no longer enjoys a special status within the practice of medicine and informed consent forms, which presuppose patient autonomy, are everywhere. In spite of these facts, paternalism has not yet been laid to rest. This is because, for several reasons, it is difficult for patients to exercise autonomy. The status accorded to physicians by society tends to set them above and apart, eroding the possibility that the patient will approach the physician in a spirit of partnership. Whether they admit it or not, some physicians are paternalistic in their thinking and they do little or nothing to encourage patient autonomy. There is also evidence of an inclination by patients to trust physician beneficence; after all, it is easier to trust the doctor than to become sufficiently educated to make truly informed decisions. Finally, in view of the technological sophistication of modern medicine, many people wonder whether nonspecialists could ever acquire the expertise to make intelligent choices.

There are some situations in which paternalistic medicine is considered acceptable. In cases when a patient's decision is clearly unreasonable or when there is sound reason to think that the patient's choices result from coercion, physicians are justified in not following patient instructions and, instead, seeking, through proper **administrative and legal channels**, to do other than what the patient requests. An example of an unreasonable patient decision might be that of a person with a predictably correctable condition which requires surgery. With surgery there is a better than 98 percent chance of a total recovery. Without surgery, death is imminent. The patient refuses to consent to surgery because of irrational, uncontrollable fear. It would be appropriate in a situation like this for a physician to obtain a court order appointing a temporary guardian for the patient. The physician would then carry out negotiations about treatment with the guardian and would more than likely obtain consent for the procedure. In this case, in all probability, a psychiatric consultation would be sought in order for the psychiatrist, through a combination of counseling and medication, to help the patient deal with his fears.

A second case of physician noncompliance with patient wishes which is likely to arise concerns that of a patient who is being coerced by a family member, for a capricious or self-serving reason, to reject medically indicated treatment. An elderly husband, for example, might want his wife to refuse to accept artificial feeding because the artificial feeding would extend her life and her hospital bills. The husband's concern would be his financial security, not his wife's well-being. In such a case, after observing interactions between husband and wife along with feeling suspicious about the sincerity of the wife's instructions not to start artificial feeding, the physician should work through **proper channels** to inaugurate treatment in the patient's best interests, as well as protecting her from harmful coercion.

Because the climate has changed from endorsement of paternalism to endorsement of patient autonomy, in contemporary medicine the burden of proof is on the physician to justify instances wherein patient wishes are not honored. This is due to the fact that the harms to be prevented or the benefits to be provided must unquestionably outweigh the loss of independence and any other benefits the patient seeks by putting himself at risk through not wanting to accept medically indicated treatment.

Cases about which there is little controversy concern patient's turning over their decision making to physicians. If the patient tells the doctor to do what she thinks best because the stresses of analyzing and deciding are just too much for him, then the doctor is justified in treating the patient by employing those treatments which she deems most appropriate.

PHYSICIAN RESPONSIBILITY IN REGARD TO PROVIDING FUTILE TREATMENTS

A perplexing question to consider in respect to the categories of paternalism and autonomy is whether or not physicians have a responsibility to provide treatments which, in their opinion, are unbeneficial or futile. If physicians were to provide unbeneficial or futile treatments as part of standard care, without a specific request to do so, they would be violating professional standards because they would be disregarding the scientific criterion of medical indication and would, therefore, be acting irrationally. What should happen when the patient asks the doctor to provide treatments which the doctor knows to be ineffective or of highly improbable effectiveness to either cure a pathology or sustain/restore the patient to an acceptable quality of life? Such a situation would entail a collision between a patient's prerogative to determine which treatments she wants and a physician's responsibility to act with the patient's well-being in mind.

The way out of this perplexing situation is to confront what is going on. Patients or surrogates who request futile treatments are operating outside of rational standards and, thus, have no claim on medical professionals or for-mulators of public policy for support. Physicians are placed in stressful sit-uations by those who request futile treatments. However, they would violate their own scientific and rational standards if they were to acquiesce to these requests. There is a limit on patient autonomy; the limit is to make reason-able choices within the context of what is medically appropriate.

EXERCISING AUTONOMY BY "DIVORCING" MEDICINE

An especially interesting situation involving patient autonomy has occurred in conjunction with infection with HIV/AIDS. This situation involves per-sons living with HIV/AIDS who assume control of their medical care by self-procuring drugs (either abroad or through the black market) and self-prescribing them (based on consultation with peers or on trial and error).[2] Why does this occur? Should it occur? Is such an exercise of autonomy to be applauded or regretted?

The reasons for this phenomenon are threefold. First, the Food and Drug Administration bureaucracy grinds slowly, keeping new and experimental drugs from the market for months or even years. Second, the criteria estab-lished for admission to experimental programs are very difficult to satisfy and those who are admitted have a 50-50 chance of being given a placebo. And, third, the unusual level of sophistication and extensive networking achieved by some persons living with AIDS make it feasible for them to pro-cure drugs and devise regimens for self-medication.

In regard to whether or not the self-prescribing of medication is to be seen as an ethically acceptable practice by society, society raises a justifiable objec-tion when it expresses reservations about situations requiring medical supervision which occur in the absence of supervision. The involvement of a physician in monitoring a patient on medication is not optional; it is impor-tant and necessary for the well-being of the patient.

Because of this significant reservation there is reason not to applaud the exercise of patient autonomy in this case. The divorce of patient from physi-cian is to be regretted because patients living with HIV/AIDS ought to be partners with their physicians and ought not to become alienated from the medical establishment.

CONCLUSION

Medical decisions are complicated issues which involve many parties. In the past, when people believed that the doctor knew best, things were simpler and more predictable. Today there is an astounding amount of complexity, both in regard to available medical treatments and possible decisions related to employing these treatments. The movement to affirm patient autonomy is a commendable one because it seeks to safeguard a patient's dignity and independence and ensure that he will not be treated against his will. Physicians will undoubtedly benefit, too, as the myth that they are miracle workers is laid to rest, and they are more readily accepted as skilled professionals whose competence is limited to achieving that which is possible.

ENDNOTES

[1] *The Guide to American Law* (St. Paul: West Publishing Company, 1984), Vol. 8, p. 147.

[2] Gina Kolata, "Group Will Import Unapproved Drugs for Treating AIDS," *The New York Times*, March 6, 1989, p. 1.

DISCUSSION QUESTIONS

1. Where do you stand in regard to patient autonomy? If you were ill, would you exercise your right to be let alone? Or would you consider yourself required to seek medical treatment in order to restore your health? What beliefs, values, and/or logic would motivate your choices?

2. In your experience with physicians and other health care professionals, has your ability to exercise autonomy been helped or hindered by them? Explain.

3. Define paternalism and give two examples of how paternalism is still operative in medicine and two examples of how paternalism has been overcome.

4. Can physicians exercise beneficence without being paternalistic? Explain.

5. What is meant by patient autonomy? Do autonomous individuals have a legal right to refuse reasonable medical care? Do they have a moral right to do so? Explain the difference between legal and moral rights.

6. What is informed consent? How can a physician or hospital administrator be certain that a patient has given truly informed consent for a medical procedure? What provisions could be put in place to safeguard patient exercise of informed consent?

7. Describe two circumstances under which paternalistic interventions by a physician can be tolerated and explain what justifies each intervention.

CASE STUDY

Robert Stevens is a 74-year-old man who was hospitalized three days ago because of severe pain in his lower back. Since admission Mr. Stevens has received numerous diagnostic tests, been examined by several specialists, and been taking medication for pain relief. This is the first time Mr. Stevens has ever been in the hospital. His mood is characterized by unease and anxiety; the pain medication may be responsible for his occasional manifestations of disorientation and excessive drowsiness. His wife is a frequent visitor but she could not drive to the hospital today because of inclement weather.

Dr. Julia Phillips, a neurosurgeon, visits Mr. Stevens to explain to him that, in her opinion, elective surgery to repair a ruptured disc represents the best strategy to correct his problem. Her visit is hurried because she is scheduled to perform another operation in 20 minutes. Nevertheless, Dr. Phillips presents a thorough, if technical, account of the patient's condition and the likely outcome of surgery. Once during her presentation Dr. Phillips is summoned to the telephone. When she returns she is surprised to find Mr. Stevens dozing. She rouses him by clearing her throat. After she finishes talking, Dr. Phillips asks Mr. Stevens if he has any questions. He says, "No, Doctor. Thanks very much." When Dr. Phillips leaves a nurse brings Mr. Stevens a four-page consent form. "Where do I sign?" he asks. Mr. Stevens signs the form without reading it. An hour later his preparation for surgery begins; a cancellation in Dr. Phillips's schedule makes it possible for her to operate a day earlier than originally planned.

Evaluation:

1. Identify ethical issues contained in this case.

2. Propose possible solutions for these issues.

3. Make a decision relevant to action to be taken or not taken and provide rationale supportive of this decision.

4. Are you satisfied with your decision? Why or why not?

GLOSSARY

A moral right is rooted in human nature and human community. Individuals claim as moral rights those things to which they are entitled because they are human. Such basic needs as nurture, education, food, clothing, shelter, medical care, and employment are moral rights routinely claimed by human persons. These claims are made to the human community, or society, as goods to which individuals have a moral right. A presumption held by an individual claiming a moral right is that there will be no argument as to its validity because it is self-evident that it should be granted.

Substantive and procedural rights are clearly delineated privileges which belong to a person as a consequence of communal reflection on what it is that humans are entitled to along with establishing uniform strategies through which these privileges or entitlements are to be obtained. Therefore, the patient's substantive and procedural right to exercise autonomy or self-determination has been defined and agreed upon and, thus, would not be contested.

Ethos or culture can be understood as the predictable composite of characteristic and distinguishing attitudes, habits, and manner of being of a group or place. Paris has a different ethos from Tokyo; physicians have a different ethos from fashion models. In connection with the study of health care ethics it is important to be aware of the changing culture of the field of medicine.

A legal right is a claim routinely made by human persons which is protected by law so that, if the person is denied the opportunity to exercise the right, the party guilty of the denial could be tried and punished by the legal system.

Administrative and legal channels vary from one health care facility to another but usually the roles are filled by senior hospital administrative personnel, hospital counsel, patient advocate, bioethics committee, and judges from the local court.

Proper channels vary from institution to institution but usually include senior hospital administrative personnel, hospital counsel, patient advocate, social services, pastoral care, the bioethics committee and, as a last resort, the courts.

CHAPTER 15

Professionalism in Health Care Occupations

INTRODUCTION

This chapter is concerned with several interrelated and important matters relating to how individual health care professionals understand and carry out their work as well as how the professions conduct and regulate themselves. Accordingly, we shall consider the following subjects: What it means to be a professional; upholding professional standards in the context of managed-care arrangements; the value of confidentiality and its perennial importance; the necessity that health care professionals be sensitive to the religious beliefs of their patients, and, finally, how awareness of culturally embedded assumptions can lead to an improved health care climate. Each of these topics contains a significant ethical component.

WHAT IT MEANS TO BE A PROFESSIONAL

To be a physician, nurse or other health care professional is inherently meaningful. This is because being a health care professional provides a person with an identification so that she *is* a physician or he *is* a nurse. The person is, in a sense, identified by her work and the work, or profession, is much more than a job. Frequently, although not always, health care professionals make a lifetime commitment to their work; they intend to perform the work of medicine or nursing or some other health care specialty for virtually all of their working years.

Besides being a source of identification, the work of health care professionals is usually also a source of pride to them. They regard themselves and are regarded by others as learned, and it is known that they would not have been licensed to practice unless they were competent. Furthermore, it is assumed that this competence is an on-going attribute because of the member's continuing good standing within the profession.

The work that health care professionals are involved in is a lofty one: Healing and helping patients. The fact that this work is also the source of one's livelihood and, in the case especially of physicians, a monetarily advantageous livelihood, should be secondary to the commitment to be a good physician or nurse. The health care professions are of their nature powerful professions because the practiced competence of professional healers is so needed by and important to sick people. In addition to all these aspects of the health care professions which impact directly on individual health care professionals, there is another factor which affects them. This factor is their membership in a group and their shared experience of being influenced by the group. This group, of course, is the profession of medicine or the profession of nursing, a distinct and admired association with a specific tradition and ethos which cannot help but form and inform its members.

The identity of the physician, nurse, or other health care professional is ordinarily expressed in relationship to patients so that the very concept of nurse suggests assisting and caring for patients. In order to be a good health care professional, an individual needs to be competent in what she does. This is the absolutely basic requirement. Being a good doctor, an ethical doctor, however, requires much more. It requires that the physician be a person of virtue, i.e., habitually inclined to go about his work while manifesting the full range of positive characteristics which comprise his virtuosity. Truthfulness, empathy, tact, skillfulness, gentleness, sobriety, dependability, and, especially, fidelity. The reason for singling out fidelity is that patients who are terminally or chronically ill have little chance of being cured of their afflictions. What physicians can do for such patients is assure them of their commitment to *nonabandonment*. Accordingly, the patient could anticipate his caretaker's being there for him for as long as needed, and this would be comforting to him.

In regard to the relationship between health care professionals and patients it is becoming more and more apparent that professionals should understand their obligations in regard to educating patients one-on-one as well as in group settings. The reason for this is because preventing disease is much more efficient than treating illnesses. As a matter of fact, symptoms of most chronic and terminal diseases can be ameliorated only while underlying pathologies progress unchecked. Therefore, the manner of response which is most effective is to try to prevent what cannot be cured.

Being a medical professional has several lofty aspects but this does not mean that there is universal agreement about the respectability of the medical profession. In fact, in today's climate it is difficult to assume that medical professionals will be held in high regard for several reasons.

In recent years the practice of medicine has become increasingly special-ized so that frequently patients go to specialists who serve as consultants and who interact with them on a superficial level. In view of this situation people have begun to think of physicians as technical specialists who are employed to provide particular skills. The cumulative effect of this way of thinking is the depersonalization of the medical profession. Once deperson-alized, medicine is in danger of losing its traditional ethos and essential meaning. Another factor contributing to the erosion of the physician-patient relationship is the organization of provision of services into health-mainte-nance organizations. According to these arrangements, patients change doc-tors when their employers change HMOs, thereby contributing to the disappearance of the doctor-patient relationship.

The media exerts profound influence on the way people think about the medical profession. During the past generation media stories about cases of medical malpractice, physicians' earnings, and physicians' shortcomings have contributed to diminished respect for the medical profession. People are therefore likely to think of physicians as overpaid technicians who are better off than they deserve to be. While this cynicism is unfair it also tends to be pervasive. It goes without saying that cynicism needs to be reversed so that the practice of medicine can reestablish the prestige in which it has tra-ditionally been held.

Since the formulation of the Hippocratic Oath over 2500 years ago, physi-cians have defined themselves not only in relationship to patients but also in relationship to other physicians, i.e., as members of a profession or select group. Indebtedness to their forebears who trained and certified them in the practice of medicine is explicitly stated in the oath, so that new physicians make a statement of indebtedness to their teachers and accept responsibility for their financial welfare and the initiation of their children into the profes-sion. Physicians assembled as a group form a community, and it is the com-munity which arranges for training and licensing new doctors. Beyond this, the community of physicians accepts the responsibility for supervising and regulating the practice of medicine in order to insure that only competent practitioners will be permitted to carry out the work that impacts directly on well-being, life, and death.

In carrying out self-regulation, the health care professions can experience problems. A major problem concerns overcoming reluctance to act decisively to prevent technically incompetent or impaired practitioners from harming unsuspecting patients. Because the medical profession is a close-knit com-munity whose members have a presumed ethos of supportiveness for one another and strong bondedness as peers, it is understandable why individ-ual physicians are reluctant to take action against unworthy doctors. Never-theless, inclinations to close ranks and keep silent about incompetent performance or substance abuse by colleagues should not be countenanced. To do so would erode the integrity of the entire profession of medicine and

would impact negatively on each and every reputable physician. Not dealing with abuses would unquestionably be unethical.

The profession of medicine does not exist in a vacuum but, rather, exists
within the broader context which is society. A recent case illustrates how
considerable influence on the way physicians are trained and supervised
emanated from outside the medical profession. The case is that of Libby
Zion, a young woman who was admitted to New York Hospital on March 4,
1984, and who died the following day. Ms. Zion, an 18-year-old college student arrived at the hospital's emergency room suffering from a moderate
fever, aches and pains suggestive of influenza, along with a strange pattern
of on-again, off-again agitated behavior. Ms. Zion neglected to disclose to
doctors her drug use but she did entrust herself to their care. The fact that
under this care she was dead within eight hours astounded her parents,
well-connected journalists, who undertook the task of investigating the competence of the physicians and nurses who cared for their daughter, as well as
the arduous schedule under which interns and residents work in teaching
hospitals.[1] The results of the Zion's tireless crusade, media coverage, and
court proceedings, were a tightening up of standards of accountability and
supervision at teaching hospitals as well as the requirement that interns and
residents have mandatory rest periods and days off instead of the daunting
schedules of pre-Libby Zion days. Thus, from one tragic story the medical
profession has been forced to better regulate itself so as to be able to provide
a better level of care for patients.

PROFESSIONALISM AND MANAGED CARE[2]

Perhaps there never were idyllic simple times in which physicians functioned as trusted confidants and healers. If there were, most people realize
that current times are different, not idyllic, and certainly not simple. Gone,
too, are the days when family members nursed dying loved ones at home
with physicians "protecting" the dying from the hard truth. While people
tend to regret the passing of those days they are also apt to hope that the
unchecked growth of medical expense and ever-increasing escalation of
costs for services has leveled off. Providing and paying for health care is the
subject of Chapter 17, but a relatively new system in which health care will
be provided, i.e., managed care and its effects on medical professionals, is
appropriately situated within the purview of this chapter.

Before beginning this discussion, it is important to familiarize oneself
with the vocabulary which has developed in conjunction with managed
care.

Fee-for-service was, until relatively recently, the way in which medical services were paid for. This means that a patient sought out a doctor for a

medical service and paid the physician what she charged. Sometimes the patient paid the doctor's bill with her own money; more often, part or all of the fee was covered by health insurance.

Customary and usual fees were established by doctors practicing the same specialty in the same area. Thus, charges for similar physician services tended to be rather uniform.

Diagnostic related groups, so-called *DRGs*, appeared during the 1980s, signaling an exercise of bargaining power by those outside the physician-patient relationship with attendant effects on the actual delivery of medical services. Such agencies as Medicare, Medicaid, and insurance companies began to decide how much they would pay for "bundles" of services such as hospital costs, surgery, and supplies. With the appearance of DRGs the phasing out of fee-for-service medical practice and payment was begun.

Managed care is a system for providing health care. Managed care, in varying degrees, integrates the financing and delivery of medical care through contracts with selected physicians and hospitals that provide comprehensive health care services to enrolled members for a set fee.

Health maintenance organizations (HMOs) are subsets of managed-care organizations; they provide comprehensive health care services to enrolled memberships for fixed per-capita fees. HMOs are designed to deliver health care services at lower costs than traditional fee-for-service arrangements.

Capitation is the system of providing physicians with fixed amounts of money to deliver comprehensive health care services. In other words, the amount of money a physician can allow to be spent for patient care is budgeted by managed-care officers and the physician is required to make judicious use of diagnostic tests, specialist referrals, hospitalizations, pharmaceuticals, etc., so as to provide equitably for all his patients and to keep from exceeding his budget. In some capitation agreements, physicians are rewarded financially if they do not allocate the total amount which they are budgeted. Similarly, some capitation plans penalize physicians financially if they exceed their budget.

Gatekeepers are physician-managers in managed-care systems. These doctors are primary-care physicians to whom patients initially report. Gatekeepers take the patient's medical history and supervise their routine care. Referral to specialists and decisions about further medical services are at the discretion of gatekeeper-physicians.

The rationale behind managed-care and health-maintenance organizations is to bring economic forces of the marketplace to the practice of medicine in order to make the provision of services less costly and more efficient. Managed care proposes to accomplish this by introducing competition into health care, encouraging partnerships among physicians and between hospitals, centralizing costly services and eliminating expensive duplication, employing and acting on the basis of cost-benefit and utilization analysis, and, finally, emphasizing and paying for preventive strategies so as to keep people from developing diseases which are expensive to treat. Managed-care proponents claim that health care can be more affordable without compromising quality. They do admit that they try to save money by cutting back on visits to specialists, expensive diagnostic tests, unnecessary surgical procedures, excessive sessions with mental-health therapists and futile end-of-life treatment in intensive-care units. Health-care providers, too, may be realigned or downsized by managed-care organizations so that fewer registered nurses may be assigned to care for more patients and, under some circumstances, registered nurses might be replaced by licensed practical nurses or medical assistants.

In order for managed care to achieve its financial goals physician-gatekeepers have to be committed to making hard-headed decisions; HMO members have to accept the fact that every patient cannot receive every conceivable medical service because it is too expensive and this fact applies to *them*. Finally, people have to live with cheaper treatments or medications which are almost as beneficial as their costlier counterparts because, if everyone were to get, for example, the most expensive pharmaceuticals, health care could bankrupt us all.

ETHICAL EVALUATION OF MANAGED CARE

The ethical evaluation of managed care depends on which perspective one assumes, that of a managed-care advocate or critic. Let us first consider a negative ethical evaluation of managed-care systems.

The most significant reservation about managed care emanates from the situation in which the primary-care or gatekeeper-physician is placed. Within the Hippocratic tradition a physician is joined to a patient in a relationship which requires competence, nonmaleficence, beneficence, justice and nonabandonment. In other words, the patient has every reason to trust the doctor because the doctor is supposed to be committed to the patient's well-being. Critics argue that managed care fundamentally and irrevocably changes the dynamics of the physician-patient relationship to the detriment of the physician's integrity and the patient's well-being. This charge is made because capitation requirements along with accompanying financial incentives and penalties place gatekeeper-physicians in an inescapable conflict of interest. The conflict is between acting in the patient's best interests and making sure not to jeopardize the fiscal soundness of the bottom line. Furthermore, critics contend that the situation is even more insidious than it at first appears because the majority of HMO members lack the sophistication to question the system and the financial resources to purchase services outside the system.

Other criticisms of managed care come from physicians who complain about how tedious and time consuming it is to obtain authorization for services. They argue that their time should be spent in patient care and not in negotiating with managers who know little or nothing of the practice of medicine. This line of argument goes further, suggesting that the bureaucracy is designed to wear physicians down so that they are tempted not to request what they know their patients need because they grow weary of the attendant hassles. Should this temptation become reality, critics contend that gatekeeper-physicians would come to work on behalf of for-profit companies rather than for their patients.

A final criticism about the system of managed care concerns the untenable positions in which physicians are placed. This thinking contends that it is society's responsibility to ration or allocate medical service, not the responsibility of individual physicians who are treating individual patients. Physicians have never before been asked to exercise their professional judgment simultaneously on behalf of both an individual and a collectivity (the entire membership of the HMO). Imposing this responsibility on physicians does not make sense because they are incapable of carrying it out. Rationing, if it comes to that, is a societal responsibility which should be put in place based on a broad-based social consensus.

Proponents of managed-care systems of health-care delivery offer arguments in defense of these systems. They contend that physicians remain in charge of medical judgments and are not hampered by administrators as they plan patient treatment in conjunction with medically sound criteria. The physician-patient relationship remains intact and the quality of patient care is not compromised. Moreover, the system for delivering that care is more efficient causing a wide array of benefits.

With managed care, its advocates claim, both the amount of the U.S. Gross National Product spent on health care and the amount spent by individual patients will stabilize and eventually decrease. This is a necessary economic goal which cannot help but benefit the entire economy. If escalating medical costs are not checked, this line of reasoning maintains, medical expenses have the potential to bankrupt us.

Managed-care advocates also think that the ethos of this system will lead to fundamental and beneficial changes in the way people think about health, sickness, and medical treatment. They think that emphasis on and rewards for preventive strategies are eminently reasonable, and they will result in more well-being, less sickness and disease. And, on the other hand, becoming aware that insurers are unwilling to pay for futile treatments may prompt people to acknowledge the foolishness of seeking futile treatments. In this vein people may also be inclined to execute advance directives which instruct that medical treatments be limited during their final months or weeks of life. Should this happen, those who support managed care envision fewer people dying in the expensive, sterile, and off-putting atmosphere of the intensive-care unit. They say that death would come more peacefully, humanely, and inexpensively at home or in a home-like hospice setting.

How managed care will impact the practice of medicine is an evolving issue and both its opponents and proponents make valid points. For those who have no vested interest either way and who seek to evaluate managed care from medical and ethical perspectives, it is important to assess the degree to which an argument is colored by ingrained bias or self-interest. Both factors tend to lessen the force of the assertions presented.

There is no question that we need change in the economics of health care so that those without access gain access and so that skyrocketing costs are checked. It is also of utmost importance that we seek to safeguard what is essential to the physician-patient relationship, especially the physician's commitment to the patient's best interests and the patient's basis for trust. If we cannot shore up this relationship, the social-ethical ramifications will be disastrous. Lay people will be characterized by sentiments of cynicism and suspicion when they approach physicians, and doctors will be disheartened and demoralized. This grim scenario is one we should not countenance. Therefore, in respect to implementing managed-care arrangements, interested parties need to discuss more than costs and services. They need to return to a consideration of the fundamental ethos of the practice of medicine and decide those steps that need to be taken in order to safeguard the profession.

SAFEGUARDING THE RIGHTS OF PATIENTS IN HMOS

In less than a decade the delivery of health care through health-maintenance organizations has grown to encompass more than 80 percent of the insured in the United States. This major change has occasioned significant problems. The principal problem is dissatisfaction by consumers with changes in their health care. As a result, citizen-consumers are demanding redress of grievances through the political process.

Responding to consumer complaints by instituting legislation to correct problems with the system has turned out to be complicated. Consumers have one agenda, the health-insurance industry another—and these differ from those of the political parties. As the debate unfolds, it turns out that there is general agreement in Congress that health-maintenance organizations should cover emergency-room care if a prudent person were to judge it necessary, as well as access by women to obstetricians or gynecologists without prior authorization. It is also agreed that there should not be rules restricting what physicians can tell patients about treatment options. Legislators recognize, too, that HMOs should be required to disclose information about costs, benefits, and performance, and that service providers are ated to keep medical records confidential. Finally, the need to establis appeals process to be implemented in conjunction with denial of benefits is acknowledged.

While there is convergence on these issues, there is also considerable divergence. Matters to be resolved include whether to limit malpractice awards, how much access to specialists people should have, and expansion of medical savings accounts.

Health-care consumers can anticipate that they will one day be protected by a Patient Bill of Rights, but it is too early to say when that day will come or exactly which rights will be protected.[3]

CONFIDENTIALITY

The word *confidentiality* is derived from confidence which comes from the Latin, *cumfides*, with faith. In respect to the patient-physician relationship, it is assumed that the patient comes to the relationship with faith in the physician, presuming that the physician is a person of discretion who will be a keeper of trust. The Hippocratic Oath spelled out the physician's duty to confidentiality when it declared,

> And whatsoever I shall see or hear in the course of my profession, as well as outside my profession in my intercourse with men, if it be what should not be published abroad, I will never divulge, holding such things to be holy secrets.

The Declaration of Geneva added to the Hippocratic tradition that the physician's obligations to confidentiality extended even to the time beyond the patient's death: "I will respect the secrets which are confided in me even after the patient has died."[4]

Upon reflection, it makes eminent sense that the medical profession require confidentiality of health care providers. This is because in the clinical setting patients are expected to fully disclose their habits, their ailments, their strengths, and their weaknesses. Beyond this, they are frequently required to undress and allow physicians access to their bodies for examination, treatments, and surgery. Thus the patient is vulnerable, needy, and prone to feelings of shame. Patients endure these experiences because they want to be treated for what ails them and because they trust their physicians to keep their secrets. If this trust were eroded it might follow that patients would become unable to seek medical attention.

Confidentiality, therefore, is not an archaic idea. It is directly related to the physician's duties to beneficence and justice and the patient's right to autonomy. Beneficence demands of the physician that she act in the patient's best interests, and justice requires that the physician render to the patient his due. An obligation to hold in confidence or secret all that one learns in the course of a professional encounter, therefore, is derived from both beneficence and justice. Furthermore, patient autonomy implies that patients choose to reveal more or less of themselves to others based on many relevant factors. The two most relevant factors in the physician-patient relationship are that the physician needs to know so that he can competently direct the patient's care and the patient needs the security of the promise of confidentiality so that she can feel assured that personal or embarrassing private matters will not go beyond the doctor's office.

In principle, virtually no health care providers would argue about the ethical appropriateness of confidentiality for the physician-patient relationship. In practice, however, upholding the highest standards of confidentiality is threatened by two realties, the laxness of health care providers and the way medical records are handled.

In respect to the laxness of health care providers, in the hospital setting a casual attitude towards maintaining confidentiality may arise. By a casual attitude is meant that people come to think that confidentiality is not very important and that violations of confidentiality are of trifling significance. Once the status of confidentiality changes from a serious matter to a petty matter, breaches of trust are bound to occur and to be regarded as insignificant. This is because people in general, including health care workers, tend to gossip and to be curious. They may want to enliven conversations with spicy bits of information, and celebrity patients whose HIV-positive status has just been discovered provide such gossip, for example. Add to this the tendency to be curious about why the hospital president's teenage daughter was admitted to the psychiatric ward and a willingness to look at the patient's chart to find out the reason, and we discover a climate in which the confidentiality of patients is in jeopardy.

A second reason why it is difficult to insure patient confidentiality is the way medical records are handled. Third parties such as insurance companies, employers, the government through Medicare and Medicaid or through a surveillance agency, and, perhaps in the future, a DNA registry, may gain access to individual's private medical information. In many instances the person is asked to authorize release of information but this may not be all that voluntary because reimbursement may depend on the authorization. Within the clinical context, too, record handling can jeopardize confidentiality. The sheer number of health care practitioners with a legitimate "need to know" a patient's diagnosis and treatment regimen can number as many as 75 or more.[5] The patient's position, vulnerable to begin with, is rendered more vulnerable by this reality, but this is even more reason to establish the requirement of confidentiality in the strictest possible terms.

Over the past generation, patient records which used to be locked in the family doctor's desk have been entered onto computers, presenting another challenge to confidentiality. At the present time hospital administrators, legislators, providers of managed care, ethicists, and patient advocacy groups are considering how to safeguard computer files which contain the most private and personal information possible, individual's medical data.[6] While the method by which to safeguard this information is not clear, the necessity to do so is unquestionable.

The obligation on a Catholic priest not to disclose what is revealed to him in confession is absolute so that there are no extenuating circumstances under which he is allowed to reveal, hint at, or in any way compromise a penitent's confession. The physician's duty to confidentiality differs from the priest's in that it is not absolute. By this is meant that there can be circumstances in which a physician is excused from the ordinary requirement to respect a patient's confidence. To date, the only situation in which this exception has been recognized is that of protecting the public safety from a probable aggressor. In the 1976 case of *Tarasoff v. Regents of the University of California,* the Supreme Court of California explained the rationale for this exception.

Prosenjit Poddar was a patient of Dr. Lawrence Moore, a psychologist. Poddar was infatuated with Tatiana Tarasoff, but she did not want a romantic relationship with him. During a psychotherapy session, Poddar told Moore that he intended to kill Tarasoff, and Moore, on the basis of his responsibility to patient confidentiality, did not notify either the police or the possible victim. Poddar subsequently killed Tarasoff and was found guilty of voluntary manslaughter. The Supreme Court of California agreed with Tatiana Tarasoff's parents that Poddar's therapist was at fault for not warning the victim of the danger she faced:

> When a therapist determines, or pursuant to the standards of his profession should determine, that his patient presents a serious danger of violence to another, he incurs an obligation to use reasonable care to protect the intended victim against such danger. The discharge of this duty may require the therapist to take one or more various steps, depending on the nature of the case. Thus it may call for him to warn the intended victim of the danger, to notify the police, or to take whatever steps are reasonably necessary under the circumstances.[7]

Thus, confidentiality is a complex matter requiring decency and discretion in all cases, and, in some hard cases, difficult judgment calls. Furthermore, confidentiality now requires supervision of computer entry, storage, and retrieval, as well as sales of computer files. The fact that confidentiality has become such a complex subject ought not to lead to a lessening of respect for this deeply rooted tradition. Rather, it should generate commitment to continue to safeguard confidentiality, especially in view of the obstacles encountered in the contemporary clinical setting.

RESPECTING RELIGIOUS BELIEFS

Some beliefs which are religious in nature bear directly on the practice of medicine, in one case rejecting all that medicine has to offer, in two instances rejecting particular medical interventions and, in the final instance, requiring certain religious prayers and rituals at the time of death. The specific beliefs we will discuss are Christian Science, Jehovah's Witness, Roman Catholicism and Orthodox Judaism. People in the health care field need to be aware of these religious beliefs to pay proper respect as well as to recall, in this context, the extent of the appropriate exercise of patient autonomy.

In regard to Christian Scientists, their belief is that illness is an illusion to be overcome by the mind. Thus, Christian Scientists refuse medical help in fighting sickness. In view of this fact, people holding this belief are unlikely to visit a physician or go to a hospital seeking help. If they do, however, find themselves in a hospital as a result of admittance through an emergency room following an accident, Christian Scientists will likely decline medical services and sign themselves out. Since this decision is freely made and based on religious belief, it should be respected. It would be wrong for medical practitioners to force treatments on adult patients against their will. If the patients who hold Christian Science beliefs are minors, however, and are in need of medical assistance, hospital administrators will likely seek a court order to require treatment. This is because it is generally held that an adult may choose martyrdom if he is so inclined, but he may not require his child to accept the same fate.

As far as Jehovah's Witnesses are concerned, their beliefs allow them to utilize all medical procedures except blood transfusions. They base their refusal of blood transfusions on passages found in the bible, such as, "Only flesh with its soul—its blood—you must not eat" (Gen 9:3–4); and, in 1 Samuel 14:32–34 there is an account of troops in battle slaughtering sheep, cattle, and calves and eating "the meat with the blood in it" along with Saul's condemnation of "eating meat with blood in it."

How does it happen that the Jehovah's Witnesses, a religious group which dates from the 1870s, condemns the medical procedure of blood transfusions based on a small number of biblical texts? After all, the bible was written in ancient times, before anything was known about the medical technology of blood transfusions. Jehovah's Witnesses conclude that blood transfusions were covered in principle in the injunctions against ingesting blood. Their religion teaches them that God forbids them from allowing blood transfusions, and they believe that it would be preferable to die rather than to receive a blood transfusion. Indeed, they think that their eternal salvation depends on their fidelity to God's law, and one part of the law requires rejection of blood transfusions.

Medical professionals who do not share the beliefs of Witnesses may find themselves clashing with Witnesses and may even want to override Witnesses' beliefs under life-and-death circumstances. The physician's conscience and medical ethos, after all, require that she do all that is medically indicated to bring her patient through surgery, and blood transfusions are frequently required in the operating room. While the physician's conscience is unquestionably meaningful and important, if the patient being treated is a Jehovah's Witness, his rights of conscience take precedence. Since Witnesses believe that they must abstain from blood, a physician would act unethically if, from a latent reliance on paternalism, she violated such deeply held religious convictions. In many ways forcing a person to violate his conscience is worse than watching the person die; it certainly constitutes an assault on human dignity.

The consensus of medical and legal opinion supports the right of the autonomous adult Jehovah's Witness to refuse blood transfusions. Many physicians are willing to accommodate this belief and to use techniques acceptable to Witnesses. In respect to specific products which are unacceptable, acceptable, and subject to individual discretion, please consider the following:

> Whole blood and its components are clearly prohibited, whereas the acceptance of albumin, immune globulin, hemophilia preparations, vaccines, sera, and organ transplants is an individual decision. Auto-transfusion of banked blood or blood products is prohibited because they believe that blood that has left the body is best discarded. Blood remaining in circulation within the body, such as during cardiopulmonary bypass, plasmapheresis, or dialysis is acceptable to many Witnesses. Nonblood plasma expanders, erythropoietin, and the new fluorinated blood substitutes are also generally acceptable. Because so much of their philosophy is left to personal discretion, the importance of open and continuous communication between physician and patient cannot be overstated.[8]

There are three situations involving refusals of blood transfusions by Jehovah's Witnesses in which physicians need not necessarily heed the instructions they are given. The first case involves an adult patient who seems ambivalent about refusing blood transfusions. Typically, he tells the doctor that he is a Witness and that receiving blood is against his religion but he also conveys a sense of anxiety over possibly dying during surgery and hints that he might be better off if the doctor did what was medically indicated. Such conversations, to say the least, are most difficult for physicians to deal with because the patient, in a manner of speaking, transfers his ambivalence to the physician with a vague instruction to resolve the matter. Should a physician be convinced that this is what is happening it would be appropriate for him to consult with hospital administration and counsel and perhaps seek a court order mandating a transfusion.

The second problematic case involving Jehovah's Witnesses is one in which a parent instructs a physician not to give a child a transfusion. Under such circumstances, sensitive physicians ordinarily attempt to carry out procedures without recourse to blood transfusions but this is not always possible. When indicated, there is a consistent legal tendency to order blood transfusions to be given over the objections of the parent(s). The reasoning is clear: "Parents may be free to be martyrs themselves. But it does not follow that they are free in identical circumstances to make martyrs of their children."[9]

The most difficult case involving Jehovah's Witnesses and blood transfusions remains unresolved. This is the case of a pregnant woman who wants to refuse a blood transfusion, resulting in the likelihood of her death and that of the fetus. For physicians who reason that they are obligated to only one patient, the woman, a response which honors her refusal seems ethical. To physicians who see themselves serving two patients, the woman and an unborn child, an opposite response seems ethical, i.e., to obtain a court order mandating a transfusion in order to protect the child's rights. Needless to say, in this case we encroach upon many of the thorny issues related to abortion. In view of this fact, it is unlikely that a consensus response will be reached any time soon.

Judaism is an ancient religion whose adherents are divided among Reform, Conservative, and Orthodox branches. In respect to common clinical practice in contemporary Western medicine, there is one belief to which Orthodox Jews adhere which potentially may require accommodation by hospital personnel.

In clinical practice, patients on respirators are sometimes declared dead based on the lack of brain function. Following determination of brain death, life support equipment is routinely discontinued. Should the newly deceased be an organ donor, life support will be continued in order to keep the body oxygenated until such time as the transplant team completes the process of procuring organs, at which time life support is stopped.

Because the only criteria they accept for determination of death are the complete cessation of heart beat and respiration, Orthodox Jews will not allow death to be declared based on neurological criteria or allow life support to be stopped. Orthodox Jews accept that death has happened after it is abundantly clear that a patient has taken her last breath. A wait of as long as 20 to 30 minutes sometimes is observed to make sure that the patient is not merely "in a swoon" but, rather, is unquestionably dead. In some cases a feather is placed in front of the patient's nose in order to determine if it moves; lack of movement confirms the patient's death. Following determination of death by Orthodox Jews, various prayers are said and rituals performed before next-of-kin are willing to allow the corpse to be removed from the bed.

It goes without saying that the beliefs and customs of Orthodox Jews are different from those of the vast majority of people who utilize modern hospitals. A proper, sensitive, ethical response of health care professionals would be to be guided by the wishes of the patient's family and friends and to ask for clarification as to how health care personnel can be of assistance. Allowing for time, space, and accommodation is a small price to pay in order to respect the customs and beliefs of Orthodox Jews.

A fourth religious belief which may impact on clinical practice relates to Roman Catholic teaching on the natural act by which babies are conceived as well as the status of human life in vitro and in vivo. Those likely to hold atypical beliefs in this regard are Roman Catholic women.

In respect to the generation of human life, the teaching of the Catholic Church is that it should follow solely from the act of intercourse, so that technologically assisted reproduction is forbidden. Since Catholics who adhere to this teaching will likely not involve themselves in these kinds of procedures, there should be no conflicts over this issue in the clinical setting. However, physicians and others who counsel women about fertility issues need to be aware of and sensitive to religiously based objections so as not to place those with ethical reservations in an uncomfortable position.

Since Catholic teaching holds that each and every act of sexual intercourse should be open to the transmission of human life, Catholics who follow this teaching are opposed to the use of artificial contraceptives. Most other people take the use of contraceptives for granted and manifest no ethical reservation about such usage. Counseling initiated in the gynecological setting or within the larger women's health system should make allowance for the Catholic position on artificial birth control, taking care to respect those who hold this view. In addition, information about techniques to be employed in conjunction with natural family planning should be made available for those who are interested.

The Catholic Church teaches that life begins at conception and that life should be respected at every point along the spectrum from conception until natural death. The practical ramification of this is that Catholic women who follow the Church's teaching will not submit to abortion under any circumstances, even rape and incest. Physicians and nurses should be aware of this teaching and belief and should stand ready to offer every possible kind of assistance to women with problem pregnancies who reject abortion on moral grounds.

As far as the status of the embryo, either fresh in a petri dish or cryopreserved in a freezer, is concerned, the Catholic Church objects to laboratory fertilization, stating that these embryos should not exist. Based on the belief that human life starts at conception, however, it follows that the Church would oppose destruction of embryos. Clinicians should be aware of the general approach of observant Catholics to reproductive matters in order to avoid giving offense. Since observant Catholics would not likely have been involved in laboratory reproduction, however, clinicians would probably not be involved in such discussions with them.

CULTURE AND HEALTH CARE

Culture is somewhat elusive. It is all around us; we exist in its midst. Still, it is difficult to explain or to grasp exactly what culture is. This is probably because culture is a notion which includes a vast number of variables which exist as generalities and which defy facile description. Moreover, in the United States, melting pot that it is, multiculturalism is very much in evidence. Accordingly, countless cultural subgroups, united by nationality, race, religion, or some other factor, exist as particular entities within the larger whole. United States culture consists of both dominant mores, as well as the cultural beliefs and practices of innumerable subgroups.

It is important to give an account of the elements which go into making up culture in order to concretize the composite reality. Dictionary definitions of culture stress facets such as the concepts, language, habits, dress, skills, arts, instruments, institutions, etc., of a given people at a particular time. Tradition plays a part in culture because one generation transmits its cultural heritage to the next. Nevertheless, culture is not static; it is constantly evolving and changing in subtle ways.

A major issue in regard to culture is whether we belong to culture or culture belongs to us. Since culture is so complex, it is understandable that we give little thought to how its parts function within the whole or how culture affects us. It is important to realize that culture is a human construct; it is what we have made, not how our civilization *must be*. Since people have fashioned all the elements that comprise culture, people can retain, revise, or discard these components. Altering the way things are would not be easy because established patterns would have to be modified or abandoned. Nevertheless, culture is not, and need not be, thought of as static. It can be changed.

To the degree that people approach their culture in an analytical manner they can assume an evaluative role. It is especially important that health care professionals become sensitive to negative aspects of U.S. culture so that they will not be unconsciously influenced by these as they carry out their responsibilities.

NEGATIVE ASPECTS OF U.S. CULTURE

Widely held, deeply ingrained, pervasive detrimental beliefs manifest themselves as negative aspects of U.S. culture. Such faulty theories as sexism, racism, ageism, elitism, materialism, consumerism, xenophobia, homophobia, and the inclination to deny death are present in U.S. culture, producing negative consequences for health care.

Negative beliefs are ways of thinking which are based on faulty rationale or which rest on deficient premises. When negative beliefs impact groups of people, they are harmful to those groups and deleterious to society as a whole. Negative aspects of culture are destructive; they should be brought to light, unmasked, and laid to rest.

It is not easy, however, to rid a culture of negative theories. This is because those who hold negative beliefs tend to deny that they exist or merit the criticisms leveled against them. It can also happen that an alternative rationale, within which the negative cultural thinking is recast as a good thing, is presented by supporters.

The deeply-rooted nature of negative cultural beliefs notwithstanding, it is imperative that health care professionals not appropriate these ways of thinking so as to avoid correlative ways of acting.

SEXISM

Sexism is the domination and exploitation of one sex by another. In the United States sexism is typically manifest as the domination of women by men with a very small percentage of sexism directed at men by women. During the past generation the feminist movement has had modest success in exposing sexism as a pernicious evil. Nevertheless, vestiges of sexism remain as a negative cultural factor in U.S. society.

Sexism is wrong because it denies recognition of women's dignity, resulting in women not being able to exercise the full complement of civil and human rights. Women's opportunities are restricted because of sexism, forcing them to endure inequities. Because sexism has been a pervasive aspect of U.S. culture, up until recently society has had a paucity of role models of fully actualized women. In addition, women who were forced into disadvantageous positions in respect to men, developed a demeaning folklore of coping strategies. Methods for getting what they wanted or needed ranged from nagging, to being coy and manipulative, to being irresistibly seductive. These strategies were based on inequality in male-female relations; employing them was degrading to women and dishonest to men. Our contemporary cultural ethos proclaims that women and men are equal partners but it is difficult to know how to implement partnership because experience and examples are lacking.

The most egregious wrong rooted in sexism is that of abuse of and violence toward women. Abuse and violence emanate from an understanding of woman as an object, less than a full person, someone or something lacking intrinsic worth, who can be used or hurt by a man.

Most women do not suffer physical abuse, but the majority of women have consciously or unconsciously appropriated a loss of self-esteem. They are inclined to disparage themselves just as they have been disparaged by others. Since, in sexist societies, men are wage earners and protectors of women, and since men are attracted to comely women, in sexist societies women seek to secure social and economic advantage through marrying well. Women's attention to physical beauty may be so consuming as to make them unbalanced and unhealthy. And their lack of self-confidence may preclude any possibility for attaining independent self-reliance.

As far as the health care field is concerned, there are many instances of sexism. Female physicians cannot count on receiving respect from male colleagues. In a 1993–94 nationwide survey, whose results were reported in the February, 1998, issue of the *Archives of Internal Medicine*, 47.7 percent of female physicians said that they had been targets of gender-based harassment and 36.9 percent reported having been sexually harassed. Younger female physicians reported higher rates of sexual harassment than older ones; medical schools were the most common sites. In regard to the survey findings, Janet Bickel, vice president for institutional planning and development at the Association of American Medical Colleges said, "Many of us hoped that the increasing numbers of women—now 42 percent in medical schools—and the fact that virtually all medical schools and hospitals now have sexual harassment policies, which we could not say 10 years ago . . . , would (cause the problem) to be going down faster. (But) this shows it's still an issue."[10]

The nursing profession, because of its subordinate status and its care-taking characteristics, has traditionally been considered women's work; thus, male nurses comprise a small minority. Although the nursing profession has made strides in respect to upgrading its status, nursing has not yet succeeded in laying to rest negative sexist stereotypes.

RACISM

Racism is a way of thinking and acting which assumes that one race is superior, making another race inferior. Members of the superior race then discriminate against members of the race which is considered inferior. In the history of the United States, Caucasians considered themselves superior to people of color, especially blacks of African ancestry, and institutionalized many forms of discrimination, the most blatant being slavery.

Racism is morally wrong because it denies individuals recognition of their human dignity, and it rationalizes prejudice against those who are considered inherently inferior. In U.S. history, civil rights such as those to decent housing, adequate education, and job opportunities, among others, were routinely denied to African Americans because of prejudice against them.

Racism contaminated American culture because its injustice eroded the righteousness of the society. It goes without saying that it is impossible to fathom the experience of millions of people who suffered discrimination.

Racism was unmasked during the Civil Rights movement of the 1960s. Laws banning discrimination and providing for equal access were passed at local, state, and federal levels. Corporate and educational leaders adopted strategies to insure fairness and prevent discriminatory practices. Religious leaders and the media preached that prejudice is wrong and that equality for all is consistent with religious and secular ideals. As a result of these initiatives, progress has been made; however, we have still not eliminated racism from American culture.

Racism exists in health care just as it does in other parts of U.S. society. Researchers studying elderly cancer patients in nursing homes learned that many are severely undertreated for their pain. The study found that white patients were the least likely to be ignored; about 25 percent reporting undertreatment. But of 188 African-Americans, 64, or slightly more than one-third, were untreated for pain. Similar trends were identified among those of Hispanic, Asian, and Native American descents, although the statistical significance of prejudice against members of these latter groups could not be established. One reason for these findings, according to Dr. Kathleen Foley, chief of pain and palliative care service at Memorial Sloan-Kettering Cancer Center in Manhattan, is that outright prejudice is at work.[11] Should this be the case, it is unethical and demands immediate correction.

An indirect consequence of racism is that people of color have less access to education and employment than do whites. As a result, they have less money because they earn less. Hence, their access to both health insurance and health care is jeopardized by economic factors.

It is hard to keep hospitals fiscally sound in urban ghettos, many of which are populated by people of color. Therefore, hospital administrators are less inclined to build or expand facilities in inner cities, thus depriving people living there. Similarly, physicians are more apt to establish private practices in areas with large pools of insured people. Since physicians are unwilling to locate in minority neighborhoods, people who live in those neighborhoods are at a loss when they require a doctor's attention.

Finally, in health care professions the number of people of color who are physicians, nurses, pharmacists, physical therapists, respiratory therapists, etc. is small, while the number of minority workers who handle menial tasks is large. This disparity is the result of hundreds of years of racist practice which denied education, opportunity, and the American dream to members of minorities.

AGEISM

Ageism is discrimination against older people. Human life follows a universal pattern from birth and infancy to old age, sickness and/or frailty, and death. In U.S. culture the season of life which is valued is when people are vibrant and flourishing, from youth to middle age. During this time people are attractive, energetic, and productive. As middle age gradually evolves into old age, people grieve the loss of their youth. The grief may be so profound that panic sets in, prompting employment of surgical, pharmacological, or cosmetic treatments to stall a natural biological process.

In some cultures, deference is shown to elderly persons—but this is frequently not the case in the United States. Senior citizens are treated with dismissiveness; they are not valued as an asset. Because of our innovative technological ethos, we are a forward looking people who tend to focus our attention and regard on the future. This leaves aged members in an alienated situation because their lives and accomplishments are mostly in the past.

The fact that senior citizens get increasingly older, becoming frail means business to the health care establishment. For this reason, the elderly are courted by health-maintenance organizations, assisted living and nursing home facilities, pharmacies and related health care agencies. However, in spite of the fact that health care providers want the business of the elderly, ageism exists as a pervasive form of discrimination with which elderly patients must contend.

An example of a medical disadvantage experienced by elderly people is that too few older cancer patients have been included in clinical trials of cancer drugs, thereby handicapping physicians who remain uncertain as to the most effective treatments for this population. In regard to this issue, Dr. Frank Haluska, a cancer expert at Massachusetts General Hospital in Boston, moderated a news conference during the May 1998 meeting of the American Society of Clinical Oncology at which experts speculated about why the Society had left questions concerning treatment of older cancer patients largely unexamined. Two reasons were suggested: "One is the added complexity of studying the effects of a therapy for cancer among people who have other ailments. Another is that doctors are generally reluctant to recommend patients for cancer trials, which may be perceived as too demanding for older people."[12] Unexpressed, but equally plausible, is the possibility that medicine, like the broader culture, has been subtly affected by ageism. If this is the case, state of the art treatments are defined relevant to young patients, while those who are older are ignored. Needless to say, if such a bias is operative, it requires speedy rectification.

When patients are advanced in years, the physician-patient relationship is frequently not what it ought to be. It can be the case that physicians disesteem elderly patients and do not invest sufficient time to thoroughly listen to them and discuss health concerns. As a consequence, elderly patients endure disrespect which they may internalize, leading to a loss of self-esteem.

Many elderly patients gradually develop dementia which, in advanced stages, results in an inability to care for themselves. At this point it often becomes necessary to hire caretakers or to select institutionalized care. Those who need this care remain persons with rights, individuals with dignity. It happens frequently, however, that demented elderly are treated as objects, not persons, and that their dignity is not upheld. It is ageist discrimination, deeply ingrained in our culture, which is at the core of this kind of disrespect.

There are so many frail, demented elderly in nursing homes that their management has become a serious issue. It is easier to over-medicate, physically restrain, and tube feed these patients than it is to give each of them the time and attention they need. If ours were not a culture contaminated by ageism, we would find the will and wherewithal to care for frail, demented, institutionalized elderly on a one-on-one basis, responding appropriately to the needs of each. Such a change in our way of doing things would require a profound change in our collective psyche.

Ageism is a sad reality which is deeply ingrained in our culture and often manifest in the health care context. It will be difficult to correct this prejudice, but the way to begin is through awareness and resolve.

ELITISM

Elitism exists as a feature of our culture according to which far more attention and regard are paid to elite members of society than to ordinary people. Such categories of people as the wealthy, celebrities, high achievers in business, sports and entertainment, government officials, members of prominent families, and the spouses and children of these people constitute the elite of U.S. society.

Even though our cultural ideals of individualism and egalitarianism support equality and equal respect, elitism is a negative aspect of our culture with which the overwhelming majority of people, the nonelite or ordinary, contend in various contexts, including health care.

The elite benefit in the health care setting because all eyes are on them, and special attention is given to every aspect of their care. When a member of the elite is a patient in a hospital, the media may be in evidence, reporting on the patient's situation. Under these circumstances, health care workers tend to bend over backwards to insure the best possible outcome. No one wants a famous patient to render a negative account of the hospital stay upon release. No one wants a famous individual to die on his shift. To prevent these things from happening, every effort is made to make sure that famous patients are well cared for.

As far as the elite are concerned, there is no problem with elitism. However, if one takes a big-picture view, one is forced to acknowledge that there is a two-tiered system and that the nonelite do not fare nearly as well as the elite.

With respect to physicians' counseling their patients in regard to lifestyle and health, a study reported in *The Journal of the American Medical Association* recounted that doctors are more likely to advise well-to-do patients than poor ones to lose weight and exercise. "The researchers speculated that poor patients might get less advice on diet and exercise because they tend to have more illnesses than the rich and doctors might devote their time to more pressing matters." But subtle discrimination may also be a cause because "doctors may underestimate their ability to persuade patients to change at all income levels."[13]

In addition to the fact that elitism is inherently unfair, the existence of special treatment for a minority in the health care context raises the issue of why excellent treatment is not the standard of care for everyone. It should be. Then the distinction between the celebrity and the ordinary person would disappear, resulting in improvement for the culture.

MATERIALISM/CONSUMERISM

Materialism is the tendency to be more concerned with material things than with spiritual values. Consumerism is a belief that the abundance of goods and services one purchases will bring happiness. In U.S. culture materialism and consumerism go hand in hand, producing deleterious consequences for people who embrace these philosophies.

Materialism and consumerism encourage unreflective, shallow, superficial, and acquisitive habits. Foolhardy, wasteful and, ultimately, trivial pursuits, materialism and consumerism constitute an unworthy philosophy of life. Regrettably, it takes maturity and clear-headedness to recognize and avoid the materialist-consumerist trap into which it is easy to fall.

The carryover of a materialistic-consumeristic mentality into the field of health care can be seen in the person of a health care consumer who approaches medical science to satisfy her wants. This individual may think of the baby she wants from reproductive technology as similar to a beautiful item of jewelry. The problem with this is that a child is a person, not a possession. And children have traditionally come from the loving, devoted union of married people, not from the recent achievements of medical procedures. This is not to say that under no circumstances should children be conceived by means of technologically assisted reproduction. Rather, it suggests a caution that parents-to-be need to understand that human offspring are not possessions before they seek to become parents by assisted reproduction.

The case of assisted reproduction which is furthest removed from traditional procreation involves use of donor gametes. This case holds the greatest potential for deteriorating from a human relational encounter to a shopping trip. It costs approximately $16,000 for an attempt at a pregnancy with specially selected sperm and egg donors. There is something chilling about making embryos on speculation and selecting egg and sperm donors according to their looks, education and ethnicity. Lori B. Andrews, a professor of law at Chicago-Kent College of Law, said "It does seem like a supermarket approach to embryos," adding that these embryos inhabit ambiguous legal territory. Such legal issues as the status of embryos formed in the laboratory and who the guardians of these embryos are remain unresolved. There are also ethical issues, such as the potential, in theory, for siblings to be raised by separate parents without any knowledge that they have brothers or sisters.[14] It is important to consider setting limits in this area so as to lessen the likelihood of harm to children, parents, and society as a whole.

In addition to couples seeking to become parents, materialism comes into play for those who sell gametes for use in assisted reproduction. This is more true for women than men because ova donation is more complicated and demanding than sperm donation, bringing a much higher price. Those who sell ova subject themselves to a stressful and risky course of hormone treatments and surgical harvesting for a payment in the range of $2,500 to $5,000. If the woman who purchases the donor's ova has a successful pregnancy, the donor will have a child or children who, in all likelihood, will never know their genetic mother. Donors need to ask themselves whether materialistic needs are so great that they would be willing to endure physical risks for monetary compensation. Understanding the force of cultural factors which are at work is important for potential donors before they embark on a course which is rife with problems.

There are other examples of consumerism and materialism manifest by persons who turn to medicine for what they want. Some want new organs, and they do not want to wait for them, so they seek to bypass waiting lists by trying to purchase organs. Others want pharmaceutical agents not available in this country because not yet tested, so they go abroad to obtain them. Still others want to stall or reverse the aging process, or to disguise it, so they buy surgery or treatments with this end in view.

The strongest argument against the materialist-consumerist attitude as it manifests itself in the purchaser of health care is that this attitude betrays a lack of wisdom. It is wise to cultivate a graciousness in accepting life's limits because, like it or not, these limits impose themselves on each of us. Rather than denying our limitedness, it would be wiser to accept it, valuing what is instead of pursuing that which we ought not to covet.

XENOPHOBIA

Xenophobia is hatred or contempt directed to foreigners. It is inconsistent with mainstream culture in the United States because the United States is a melting pot, a place where foreigners from every corner of the world have been assimilated.

In spite of this fact, xenophobia has become apparent in the United States during the past decade or so. This negative attitude is directed against illegal immigrants, purportedly because they deprive citizens of jobs and cost taxpayers money through services they require. Xenophobia is also present in the form of long-lived feuds between members of various ethnic groups; there are old grudges which linger in this country generations or centuries after the hatreds came into existence in the old country.

While xenophobia is far from pervasive, it should, nevertheless, be regarded with zero tolerance. This is because contempt for any group is wrong based on the facts that such an attitude denies persons the respect which is due them. Beyond this, xenophobia results in the denial of human rights and callous treatment of vulnerable people, in total variance with the ideals present in our national ethos.

Respecting foreigners requires of health care institutions that they adapt to meet the specific needs of these patients. A case in point reveals a failure in this regard. For many years Montefiore Hospital in the Bronx, New York, employed full-time interpreters who spoke Vietnamese and Khmer to assist patients from Vietnam and Cambodia. But, in April 1998, because of financial pressures, hospital administration cut back on this service. The hospital now relies on employees who hold other jobs in the hospital to assist as necessary. But this realignment has been problematic. Staff have reported that they have been forced to scramble to find bilingual employees who may be busy tending to other tasks. Patients have been forced to wait. This situation represents a subtle example of foreign-speaking people being placed at a disadvantage. The solution is far from subtle. The hospital needs to take steps to insure that efficient communication again becomes standard practice.[15]

Xenophobia is manifest in health care in respect to illegal immigrants who lack access to a rudimentary level of care. Since their point of entry into the system is far along the continuum, i.e., when they are quite ill and appear at a hospital emergency room, they tend to need more elaborate, expensive care than should be the case, and they are burdened by worse diagnoses. Since they are not covered by private or government insurance, illegal immigrants must rely on charity care, which, because of problems in funding, is fast drying up.

Illegal immigrants who require expensive treatments, such as bone marrow transplants, organ transplants, or cardiac surgery, face a high probability of not being able to obtain the care they need. Instead, once their illegal status and health status are established, they are likely to be deported. In the third world countries from which they came seeking a better life, they will have little or no chance of obtaining the type of treatment they need.

The solution to xenophobia is not deportation. Instead it is to find the money and the heart to expand health care coverage so that people who find themselves in this country and in need of costly medical care will receive it.

In the United States the bottom line counts for a great deal. But so does our ethos as melting pot and secure harbor for all those wanting to be part of the American dream. It is in our best interests to overcome xenophobia and be compassionate to the stranger in our midst.

HOMOPHOBIA

Homophobia consists in fear towards those who are different from the majority in terms of sexual orientation along with distaste or repugnance toward the manner of gay sex.

Homophobia is a widespread prejudice which is readily apparent in our culture. Homophobia makes life difficult for gay men and lesbians because it forces them to hide their sexual orientation and to endure the consequent stress which results from this. Gay people who reject the closet, coming out to family, friends, and colleagues risk rejection, derision, discrimination, and, in extreme cases, assault and death.

The reality of life for gay people impacts on straight people, too. To the extent that the culture directs that gays not be accepted, nongay people tend to be fearful and suspicious of gays. These sentiments prevent heterosexuals from manifesting respect for gays and entering into productive engagement with them. This diminishes the human community. Beyond this, avoidance of the fact that individuals are gay and lesbian results in an unhealthy deception. Truth, not deception, is a prerequisite for a healthy culture; so denying or pretending that gay people are not gay weakens the collective unity known as culture.

In regard to health care, an example of the occurrence of homophobia illustrates the complex and far-reaching nature of the phenomenon. This example requires a long hard look at homophobia directed towards a HIV-positive gay man who is a hospital patient. This person is entitled to respect, as is his significant other. However, innumerable times since the advent of AIDS this respect has not been forthcoming.[16] Health care providers who find themselves ill at ease with gay patients, fearful of them, or intolerant need to work through their prejudice and get over it. This is because health care workers are responsible for cultivating respectful, courteous, professional ways of acting with all patients.

In respect to homophobia in the health care setting, there is a need to help health care workers understand and articulate the essence of their own personal attitudes. If providers identify themselves as homophobic, they need help to correct this unfortunate prejudice. The goal for hospitals and other facilities is that gay men and lesbians should be treated with respect and provided with the same standard of care as other patients. Hospital administrators and key personnel from medicine, nursing, and allied areas should collaborate to formulate appropriate guidelines in this regard and then put policies and procedures into effect in order to attain the objectives.

DENIAL OF DEATH

Denial of death is manifest in the universal tendency not to think about our own mortality. While we are not likely to claim, "People do not die. Death does not happen," we are apt to hold fast to the myth of our own immortality.

Unless people hold a strong belief in eternal life or in reincarnation, they tend to understand death as an enemy which robs them of life, relationships, work, enjoyment—everything—and which leaves grieving survivors broken-hearted. Since no one has come back from the dead to tell us what (if anything) lies on the other side of human consciousness, there is a pervasive fear of the unknown.

Because death is seen as so painful, wrenching, and fearsome, most people avoid thinking about it or confronting it. By putting it out of sight and out of mind we can pretend it does not concern us and can manage better to enjoy our workaday lives. Denial of death and avoidance of the subject are widespread phenomena which weaken culture in the United States because of the radical way in which they distort reality.

In terms of health care, it is impacted in negative ways by our unease about death. Individuals, content to avoid the subject, procrastinate until it is too late to execute advance directives. Thus, they leave their care, should they become incompetent, to chance. And caretakers then find themselves at a loss. This is what happened to Christina Walker Campi who wrote of how her dying husband's oncologist went off duty for three days, leaving her alone in a darkened room with a "frantic dying man." She was unprepared for the physical and emotional exhaustion she experienced.

She wrote:

"I do not know what would have helped. When we made the decision to terminate treatment, the doctors should have handed my husband's care over to a palliative care team. A pain management specialist, a social worker, and a chaplain were needed, but such a team didn't exist at the hospital. His dying needed to be managed as much as his treatment did. I needed to feel that I wasn't left alone to make decisions I wasn't emotionally or clinically competent to make."[17]

Ms. Campi recounted her ordeal because she wanted to help others deal better with the dying of a loved one. Her intention will be realized to the extent that the conspiracy of silence surrounding death ends and a necessary conversation commences.

Physicians and nurses, reluctant to broach the most taboo of subjects, tend to be less than forthright with terminally ill patients, thus inflicting painful isolation on the dying and compromising their own professional standards. Dying patients do not face what is happening to them and reject the hospice alternative entirely or until their days are truly numbered. In so doing, they fail to avail themselves of the most compassionate and practical agency which exists to help.

The last days of the dying are not used to human advantage. The dying are not helped to see that they are putting the final frame of their life in place, a life during which many good and loving deeds were done. They do not get to tie up loose ends, make amends, say goodbye. Because death is handled so poorly, family members and health care workers are left with sadness, dissatisfaction, and guilt. They feel that they failed the dying person and, accordingly, are troubled.

It will be very difficult to overcome our inclination to deny our mortality and to stop avoiding death. But that is not to say that the task is impossible. What is needed are education, opportunities for frank discussion, and time spent with the dying. Should we take these steps, death will lose some of its fearsomeness and unreality and all of us, health care professionals, patients, and family members, will be in a better place.

It is morally imperative that courses in medical ethics include consideration of how cultural factors impact on the delivery and practice of health care. As we have seen, our culture contains assumptions and ways of acting which are deeply embedded but seldom examined. To strengthen our culture we need to reject aspects which are detrimental. This is a multifaceted project, one that requires patience, thoughtful analysis, and unfettered good will.

CONCLUSION

To be a health care professional is to assume an important and honored status which continues to be valued and respected. Being a physician or nurse gives a person an identity; being a good nurse or doctor imparts a sense of pride and integrity. Understanding how our feelings of worth and self-esteem are enhanced by acquitting ourselves of our responsibilities in a forthright, professional manner is a precondition for actually doing so. Reflecting on the inherent importance of this task and committing ourselves to it are among the most meaningful steps we need to take in facilitating professional development.

ENDNOTES

[1] Cf., Natalie Robins, *The Girl Who Died Twice: Every Patient's Nightmare: The Libby Zion Case and the Hidden Hazards of Hospitals* (New York: Delacorte Press, 1995).

[2] The system of managed care is relatively recent in origin and, as a consequence, the subject has received limited treatment in ethical literature. There is, however, a useful publication which examines managed care from the points of view of many different interest groups and I recommend it as a valuable resource. Russell L. McIntyre, ed. and publ., *Health Care, Law & Ethics*, "Managed Care" a double issue consisting of 38 articles, Winter/Spring, 1995, 10: 1/2.

[3] Robert Pear, "2 Patients' Rights Bills Take Divergent Roads: Democrats and Republicans Are Far Apart," *The New York Times*, July 4, 1998, p. A9.

[4] *British Journal of Psychiatry*, October, 1976, "News and Notes: Confidentiality," as quoted in Ian E. Thompson, "The Nature of Confidentiality," *Journal of Medical Ethics*, 1979, p. 57.

[5] Leonard M. Fleck, "Confidentiality: Moral Obligation or Outmoded Concept," *Health Progress*, May, 1996, p. 18.

[6] Gina Kolata, "When Patients' Records Are Commodities for Sale," *The New York Times*, November 11, 1995, pp. A1, C14.

[7] *Tarasoff v. Regents of California,* 529 P. 2d 553 (Cal. 1974), vacated, reheard in bank and affirmed 131 *California Reporter* 14, 551 P. 2d 334 (1976). A second landmark case relating to a psychiatrist's duty to confidentiality is scheduled to be tried in Federal District Court in Bridgeport, Connecticut late in 1998. The case involves Joseph De Masi, MD, a resident in training to become a child psychiatrist, who allegedly told Douglas H. Ingram, MD, the psychiatrist conducting his therapy, of his sexual interest in children. Dr. Ingram did not warn or notify anyone; neither did he take steps to have De Masi's residency terminated. De Masi went on to sexually abuse boys. Because of abuse of Denny Almonte when he was a 10-year-old patient at Danbury Hospital, charges have been brought against Ingram and New York Medical College (which De Masi attended) and at which Ingram was a faculty member. Commentators expect that deliberations about this case will result in directions for psychiatrists whose patients give voice to criminal proclivities without naming specific intended victims. Cf., Frank Bruni, "Child Psychiatrist and Pedophile: His Therapist Knew but Didn't Tell; a Victim Is Suing," *The New York Times*, April 19, 1998, pp. 35, 40.

[8] Marianne Culkin Mann, MD; John Votto, DO; Joseph Kambe, MD; and Michael J. McNamee, MD, "Management of the Severely Anemic Patient who Refuses Transfusion: Lessons Learned During the Care of a Jehovah's Witness," *Annals of Internal Medicine*, December 15, 1992, p. 1043.

[9] *Prince v. Commonwealth of Massachusetts*, 321 U.S. 158 (1944).

[10] Brenda C. Coleman, The Associated Press, "Many female doctors sexually harassed," *The Record*, February 23, 1998, p. A8.

[11] Sheryl Gay Stolberg, "Study Finds Pain of Oldest Is Ignored In Nursing Homes," *The New York Times*, June 17, 1998, pp. 1, A26.

[12] Lawrence K. Altman, "Treating Elderly's Cancers Is Frustrating Many Experts," *The New York Times*, May 20, 1998, p. A14.

[13] "Doctors' Counseling Is Linked to Wealth," *The New York Times*, November 6, 1997, p. A36.

[14] Gina Kolata, "Clinics Selling Embryos Made For 'Adoption,' Couples Can Even Pick Ancestry for $2,750," *The New York Times*, November 23, 1997, pp. 1, 34.

[15] Somini Sengupta, "Hospital Cuts Back on Translators: At Montefiore, Southeast Asian Refugees Face a New Obstacle," *The New York Times*, June 1, 1998, p. B4.

[16] For accounts of prejudice directed against gay men with AIDS, cf., Eileen P. Flynn, *AIDS: A Catholic Call for Compassion* (Kansas City: Sheed & Ward, 1985).

[17] Christina Walker Campi, "When Dying Is as Hard as Birth," *The New York Times*, January 5, 1998, p. A19.

DISCUSSION QUESTIONS

1. What does it mean to be a nurse or physician? How does being a doctor or a nurse differ from "having a job"? What kinds of responsibilities and privileges go with having professional status?

2. The medical and nursing professions regulate themselves. List at least four strategies which could be put in place to assure that self-regulation is carried out in an ethically upright manner.

3. Present the reasons why managed care is an ethically good and economically practical system for meeting health care needs. State why you support or reject this rationale.

4. Present the reasons why managed care may not be an ethically good or economically practical system for meeting health care needs. State why you support or reject this rationale.

5. Assume that you are a patient and describe your thinking about the physician's duty to confidentiality.

6. Assume that you are a health care provider and describe your thinking

about maintaining confidentiality as well as the difficulties you experience in conjunction with keeping patient information private.

7. List strategies which could be put in place by hospital administration to enhance the climate of confidentiality as well as safeguard the handling of patient records.

8. Why is it important for health care providers to be sensitive to patients' religious beliefs? Discuss how patient beliefs might collide with a professional's responsibilities. How can these conflicts be resolved?

9. Discuss at least four ways negative cultural assumptions can detract from the ethical provision of health care services.

CASE STUDY

Marilyn Hudson is a 59-year-old woman who recently lost her job due to downsizing. Her HMO coverage remains in effect for six months.

The job loss proved to be an emotionally upsetting experience for Mrs. Hudson. In addition to being troubled by insomnia and loss of appetite, she experiences occasional nausea, dizziness, shortness of breath, and chest pains. Although she is somewhat depressed, Mrs. Hudson is motivated to take care of herself and recover from the stress related to her job loss. Therefore, she makes an appointment to see Dr. Robert White, the primary care physician assigned to her by the HMO.

Her first and only visit to Dr. White was a difficult experience for Mrs. Hudson due to the fact that she waited 90 minutes to see the doctor, and the doctor was interrupted twice while attending to her.

Except for the interruptions, the physician-patient interaction proceeded in a routine fashion. The doctor performed a cursory examination, listened to a brief account of the patient's symptoms, and asked questions about her family history and lifestyle (smoking, alcohol, and caffeine use). The doctor then wrote a prescription for a mild antidepressant and suggested that the patient join a support group for people who lost their jobs.

As she waited to give the receptionist her $12 copayment Mrs. Hudson overheard the doctor dictating his notes to the receptionist: "Patient related symptoms of anxiety probably related to job loss; R_x prescribed; no follow-up."

Evaluation:

1. Identify ethical issues contained in this case.
2. Propose possible solutions for these issues.

3. Make a decision relevant to action to be taken or not taken and provide rationale supportive of this decision.
4. Are you satisfied with your decision? Why or why not?

PART SEVEN

MEDICINE AND THE COMMON GOOD

CHAPTER 16

Roles of the Courts, Government, and Professional Societies in Health Care Ethics

INTRODUCTION

Generally speaking, ethics is concerned with what *ought* and *ought not* to be done. Applying ethics to health care is a complicated undertaking, both because ethics is an intricate and subtle discipline and because the delivery and practice of health care are complex and multifaceted. Health care, after all, is made up of several components, including, but not limited to, the relationship between physician and patient, scientifically based procedures which yield diagnoses, prognoses, and treatment options, treatments provided by many kinds of professionals, possibilities of employing a wide range of technologies and a need to allow for or prohibit such medical procedures as abortion and physician-assisted suicide. The practice of medicine can also involve dealing with vulnerable patients, resolving conflicts between patients and physicians, safeguarding the well-being of communities, and devising strategies to maintain professional standards of health care practitioners along with the freedom, dignity, and autonomy of patients. Add to this reality the need to answer new questions, under the pressure of time constraints, with life and death literally hanging in the balance, and we begin to grasp the difficulties confronted by such social institutions as courts, legislatures and professional societies faced with analyzing or resolving contemporary questions related to health care.

COURT INVOLVEMENT IN BIOMEDICAL CASES

In the past generation we have become aware of a number of perplexing cases which required settlement but for which no apparent solution was readily at hand. In some of these cases what constituted the patient's best interests was disputed, in others, proper conduct of physicians, and, in still others, a more complex combination of issues, for example, cases about whether to treat low-birth-weight newborns or to let the babies die. We have spoken of Karen Quinlan and Nancy Beth Cruzan, two young women in their twenties whose lives were maintained by medical technology for years after each of them sustained severe brain injury which caused them to languish in persistent vegetative states. Then there are two physicians of widely divergent repute, Jack Kevorkian[1] and Timothy Quill[2], who assisted patients in dying, helping to push this issue to the fore. And, you will remember Marybeth Whitehead and William Stern, parents of a baby girl conceived as a result of a surrogate agreement, whose disagreement about who should raise the child triggered a national debate.

In respect to some cases of forgoing medical technology, physician-assisted suicide, surrogate motherhood, and other relatively novel questions, health care practitioners and society as a whole have found themselves needing quick answers for questions which had never before been posed. In regard to some of these questions, court intervention has been most helpful in clarifying what is at stake as well as in resolving the issue. It would probably have been better if resolution of these types of cases had come from legislative processes that yielded guidelines and laws. This is because the legislative process is communal and participatory, with guidelines formulated on the basis of consensus, and opportunities provided for interested parties to articulate their positions. To have courts decide, instead of legislatures, is, in a sense, to put the cart before the horse. While decision making by courts is less than ideal, however, it is the way several matters of medical-ethical importance have been settled. And, given the benefit of hindsight, most commentators would probably agree that the courts have done an adequate job.

When a perplexing case goes before a court, the task of the justices is to weigh arguments, principles, and options in order to decide upon the right course of action. Justices do not possess formulas, insights, or norms unavailable to lay people. Selected to serve society, ideally they should be clear thinkers who have competence in interpreting precedents established in past decisions. Justices need to be balanced and impartial. They learn their values and ethics in the communities from which they come. When moral consensus regarding particular health care issues has not been reached by society (or when a particular question has not even been raised), it may fall to the judiciary to play a key role in articulating what might best represent such a consensus. In regard to questions such as those mentioned above, courts in the United States have been playing just such a role.

When the United States was established, the Constitution was adopted and the Bill of Rights was soon added. In the United States the tradition of respecting and insuring individual rights has a long and honored history. Late twentieth century medical technology presents justices with the challenge of determining how the explicit Constitutional right to privacy along with the common law right to self-determination impact on vulnerable people in a variety of circumstances. Judicial decisions reached in this country attempt to be faithful to the unique context of the tradition of individual rights established by the Constitution as well as the legal heritage based on **English common law**.

In addition to attending to the rights of particular individuals, justices must also pay heed to a second aspect of the decisions they reach. The state has an interest in respecting the biological life of vulnerable persons, safeguarding the integrity of the health care professions, and insuring that institutions such as hospitals and nursing homes are free to act in conformity with their moral standards. Resolving the tensions which sometimes arise as a result of conflicts between concern for individual rights and a need to preserve the common good may result in division among justices as is evidenced by the issuance of majority and minority opinions. Even when a court reaches a unanimous decision, difficulty can be experienced in achieving a balance which respects both the interests of an individual and those of the state.

In addition to having difficulty with balancing individual and state interests, justices can also have a hard time deciding which standards and principles are relevant to the case at hand, and whether those standards and principles which are identified make an **absolute** or a **relative claim** on society. For example, what principles and standards apply in situations wherein a child born as a result of a surrogate contract is claimed by both its biological parents, with the biological birth-mother refusing to honor the contract she signed and demanding that she be allowed to keep her baby after birth?

In regard to novel cases, that is, truly new cases involving the use of new technology or cases that simply did not come up in the past, justices have to reach decisions without reference to precedents from cases characterized by similar facts. This does not mean that no guidance is available from other kinds of cases. On the contrary, precedents set in the past in conjunction with different kinds of cases can be instructive. Even though such instruction is informative, however, justices still have to plow new ground as they confront new questions.

When courts decide new cases, they establish new precedents. A precedent is a decision or a ruling in a particular case which becomes established as a standard which is then applied to similar cases. For example, in the case of *Griswold v. Connecticut,* in 1965, the U.S. Supreme Court established that married people have a right to privacy and, therefore, that state laws banning physicians from giving prescriptions for contraceptives to married persons are unconstitutional. The right to access to artificial contraceptives is a precedent set by Griswold. This precedent was cited in *Roe v. Wade* in support of a woman's right to privacy in coming to the abortion decision. The Griswold precedent did not answer the *Roe v. Wade* question, but it contributed to it. Should a court one day face a question about a right of homosexual men to acquire condoms (a highly unlikely possibility), the Griswold precedent would undoubtedly be cited, not because this precedent bears directly on the right of homosexuals to condoms, but because the precedent would have some relevance in such a case.

The precedents established by courts are in the nature of legal guidelines. By the term "legal guidelines" is meant what the Constitution and laws allow, given the intent of these documents and the best insight of justices, for example, in regard to new biomedical questions. Legal guidelines, however, are not necessarily *ethical* guidelines. They are only ethically sound if they incorporate valid ethical principles in a coherent and consistent manner. An essential aspect of any court decision on a question of health care ethics is the court's engagement with the moral dimensions of the question. This engagement requires that the court discuss why it believes one course of conduct or another would be the morally correct thing to do and to offer as much justification as possible for why this is so. On the other hand, the court would also need to take account of contrary ways of thinking and present the strongest possible refutations for these rejected positions.

One thing that is certain about court decisions and precedents is that no physician (except a maverick) and no health care facility is going to act contrary to the directives contained in court decisions. The reason for this is that physicians fear being disciplined by civil or medical authorities; hospital administrators, while holding the same fear, also tend to be conservative and want to situate themselves on the safest side of the law. These providers of health care tend to welcome instructions or reassurance conveyed by court intervention.

Knowing the significant precedents established by courts in the United States is important for anyone who deals with issues of health care ethics. While the legal and the ethical spheres are not **coextensive**, neither are they **mutually exclusive**. The reason for this is that courts can be wrong, but ethics, since its raison d'etre is to identify the morally right action and explain what it is about a deed which makes it morally right, cannot be wrong. The assumption should be that decisions of courts are ethically sound but, should a court decision be unethical, the ethical task becomes to overturn the decision and establish new and valid precedents.

During the 1970s and 1980s individuals frequently sought court intervention in termination of treatment cases wherein respirators or feeding tubes were involved. Cases such as Quinlan (1976), Bartling (1984), Bouvia (1983 and 1986), Conroy (1985), Brophy (1985 and 1986), O'Connor (1988), and Cruzan (1990) were all complicated and disputed, and each was decided by a court. Some of the most difficult recent health care ethics cases entail deciding whether or not to treat premature babies of very low birth weight, and under what circumstances to discontinue treatment; as we noted in Chapter 3, in *Weber v. Stony Brook Hospital* (1984) the Appellate Division of the New York State Supreme Court scrutinized the decision of Baby Jane Doe's parents not to subject the child to various surgical procedures and supported their decision to follow a conservative course which at the outset did not include surgery. In the past few years courts have been asked to decide if divorced women are entitled to maintain control over frozen embryos conceived before the divorce and what rights and responsibilities, if any, would accrue to the divorced husbands, should they become fathers.

In the process of considering some of the kinds of issues with which the courts have been involved during that past generation we might be tempted to think that it is fortunate that we have courts and that we should routinely turn to the courts for solutions to health care conundrums. For the most part, however, this is not a practical strategy.

Traditionally medical decisions have been reached within a rather intimate circle after negotiations involving physicians, the patient, and the patient's family. Within this small group it has been possible to respect the patient's rights to privacy and confidentiality and to allow physicians to exercise their judgment and the prerogatives of their profession with appropriate discretion. In addition, the preferences, values, and beliefs of family members can be taken into account and, if appropriate, honored within this small circle. This is as it should be. To routinely invite court involvement would be unnecessarily intrusive and could be destructive of the interactive relationship among patient-physician-family.

When courts are involved in clinical cases everything associated with the clinical context gets put on hold until the court decision is handed down—which could be a very long time. Is it morally acceptable to make concerned parties wait for as long as it takes courts to decide and **appeals** to be heard? Perhaps we can justify lengthy delays the first or second time cases arise, but once these cases become fairly common it would make more sense to resolve them without recourse to the courts. The other side of this argument is that just as patients and surrogates are entitled to a quick response to their dilemmas, so the courts need not have their calendars tied up with medical case after medical case. Courts have other issues to adjudicate, making it necessary to free them from excessive concentration on cases of health care practice.

One reason why courts establish precedents is so that health care practice can be carried out under the instruction such precedents convey. In other words, precedents serve as guidelines which provide health care practitioners with the guidance they need to carry out their work.

Finally, the role of the courts is to settle *disputed* matters which fall outside the purview of existing laws or of traditional medical practice. As we have seen, many novel matters neither addressed by law or traditional medical practice have surfaced in recent years, frequently as a result of technological innovations. These issues have been referred to courts, discussed by judges, and resolved with the articulation of decisions and new precedents. At this stage, however, it has generally become appropriate for courts to step aside and let legislatures enact appropriate laws.

THE UNITED STATES CONGRESS AND HEALTH CARE ETHICS

Legislatures are empowered to enact laws. Enacted laws are of two kinds: Compulsory laws which require that some action be performed such as those which mandate that parents or guardians have children vaccinated, and negative laws which forbid specific actions such as removing organs from people who are not dead. Laws are enacted by the United States Congress or by a legislative body at a state, city, or local level.

The United States Congress is made up of the Senate and House of Representatives. Each of the 50 states elects two people to the Senate and these Senators serve six-year terms. Representation in the House of Representatives is proportional, based on population. Representatives serve two-year terms. Laws passed by Congress are federal laws and are binding on citizens in each and every state. Probably the greatest influence of Congress on health care ethics is in the area of establishing and funding administrative bodies which provide health services.

As far as administrative bodies which provide health services are concerned, two stand out as especially significant. Medicare and Medicaid provide health care for people over 65 and for the indigent, respectively. While the provision of health services does not immediately appear to be an ethical issue, once one probes beneath the surface and confronts many related concerns, several ethical aspects become apparent. The amount of money spent on Medicare and Medicaid, per year, is enormous. Since a large percentage of this outlay goes to expenditures for end-of-life treatments which are ineffective in bringing about remission of symptoms or cure of pathologies, the economics of these systems, which some people fear could bankrupt us, becomes an ethical concern. There are also concerns about the way entitlements are administered, with layers of bureaucracy absorbing a large percentage of public funds without delivering health care. And, with the unwieldiness of the systems comes the possibility of exploiting them so that unscrupulous health care providers are able to engage in fraudulent activity. This reality occurs in the context of the contemporary United States in which more than 40 million people are not covered by Medicare or Medicaid or by privately purchased health insurance. This specific situation actually occupied Congress for much of 1993 and 1994 as President and Mrs. Clinton pushed for universal coverage against a background of controversy about problems with existing programs, as well as reservations about the practicality of designing a new system. Congress still lacks a viable plan for providing universal coverage and a program for correcting present and future problems with Medicare and Medicaid.

An issue which Congress may take on someday soon is that of the status of tobacco by considering whether or not this disease-causing substance should be classified as a harmful addictive drug. Should such a decision be made, there would be literally dozens of ramifications in regard to the tobacco industry and adult smokers, and health care ethics would be affected as well.

The 1973 *Roe v. Wade* decision of the United States Supreme Court has not been accepted by a significant number of U.S. citizens and, from time to time, those who object to legalized abortion consider reversing *Roe v. Wade* through an amendment to the United States Constitution. This amendment would either make provision of abortion illegal in most circumstances or would stipulate that allowing and regulating abortion procedures be under state jurisdiction. In order to amend the Constitution, two-thirds of each house of Congress must approve the proposed amendment and three-fourths of the states must ratify the amendment. Whether this process will ever be used successfully to establish a norm of health care ethics remains to be seen. Thus far, in regard to abortion, enacting a constitutional amendment has been unsuccessful.

The issue of "partial birth" abortions which is mentioned later in this chapter in conjunction with the president's veto power was addressed by Congress in recent years. By passing legislation in March 1996 forbidding physicians from performing this specific procedure Congress sought to exercise jurisdiction in limiting the practice of abortion. As the reader shall see, this Congressional initiative did not become law because of the president's veto. (The House of Representatives voted on July 24, 1998 to override Clinton's 1997 veto of partial birth abortion. The vote was 296 to 132. Action by the Senate, scheduled for the fall term, had not taken place as of Spring 1999.)

STATE LEGISLATURES AND LAWS
WITH BIOMEDICAL IMPLICATIONS

All matters not explicitly claimed as part of the jurisdiction of the federal government fall under the jurisdiction of the governments of the 50 individual states. In the United States the individual states vary considerably one from another. Some are largely urban, others almost totally rural. Some are large in population or area, others are small. Some are conservative, with a large percentage of people practicing their religions, others are liberal, still others possess relatively small numbers of church-goers. Some state legislatures are **unicameral**, others are **bicameral**. Some legislators are well informed and conscientious, others are neither. Some legislators give political considerations top priority while others place principles over politics. The face of state legislatures and legislators is a varied and at times disconcerting one. Yet it is to these chambers that some of the most vexing issues in health care ethics now routinely come.

In recent years the 50 states have faced several medical-ethical issues. Whether or not, and in what circumstances, to allow third parties to participate in surrogacy arrangements for the purpose of procreation, deciding about the status and contents of advance directives, putting in place limits on the practice of abortion, and, in a few cases, deciding about physician-assisted suicide[3] have occupied state legislatures. In some cases, bills have been proposed from within legislatures, debate has ensued, votes have been tallied, and laws have or have not been put in place. In other cases, referenda have been formulated by legislators and put before the voters for approval. If approved by a majority vote, a **referendum** becomes law. In still other cases, an **initiative** can be formulated by a special-interest group, and the initiative can then become law through being approved by voters in a referendum or being approved by vote of the legislature.

Issues of health care ethics touch just about everyone at one time or another, and these questions cause doubt and confusion. Deciding them in a legislature where ignorance or political considerations could make a vote go one way or another is far from ideal. Probably the only way to guard against poor laws regarding medical-ethical questions is by encouraging education and debate. Through education about values and ethics people mature in regard to their moral sensitivity, thus enabling them to make better decisions. And through open debate the various facets of issues are articulated and evaluated, thus providing for the likelihood of a nuanced and balanced decision.

THE INFLUENCE OF THE EXECUTIVE BRANCH ON HEALTH CARE ETHICS

Two ways in which the executive branch of the United States federal government impacts health care are through the Department of Health and Human Services and through task forces, generally referred to as Presidential Commissions. As it happens, in carrying out their work both these agencies of the executive branch unavoidably encounter ethical issues.

The Department of Health and Human Services has been known by this name since 1980. From 1953 until 1980, its precursor agency, the Department of Health, Education and Welfare, was in operation. The Department of Health and Human Services is organized in five divisions. In terms of the subject matter of this book, the purview and work of the Public Health Service is of greatest significance. The Public Health Service is presided over by the Surgeon General of the United States. The Surgeon General is nominated by the President and ratified by Congress. The mission of the Public Health Service is to promote the protection and advancement of the nation's physical and mental health.

The most visible agencies within the Public Health Service are the Food and Drug Administration, the Health Resources and Services Administration, the National Institutes of Health and the Centers for Disease Control. Among its responsibilities, the Food and Drug Administration oversees the safety, effectiveness, and labeling of drugs and medical devices. The nature of this oversight requires that the FDA exercise caution so as not to allow distribution of pharmaceuticals which could cause unforeseen harm. In recent years this prudent policy has prompted protests from persons living with AIDS and from AIDS advocacy groups. The rationale behind the protests has been that people with fatal diagnoses do not have time to wait for drugs which might be helpful to them. As a result of these protests and a sober rethinking of its way of operating, some concessions have been made by the FDA to make medicines available on an expedited basis to persons living with HIV/AIDS.

The Health Resources and Services Administration supports states and communities in providing health care to underserved people, especially migrant workers, mothers and children, the homeless, and other groups with special needs. This agency also carries out provisions of the Ryan White Comprehensive AIDS Research Emergency (CARE) Act, which seeks to support a comprehensive medical response to HIV/AIDS. In regard to both these initiatives the Health Resources and Services Administration exercises an ethical mandate. This mandate requires that citizens, through the state, provide for the well-being of vulnerable populations, including their medical needs, because the human dignity of needy people demands provision of medical services.

The Centers for Disease Control and Prevention are based in Atlanta and were established in 1973. The Centers came into prominence in conjunction with the identification of AIDS. Such sensitive judgments as decisions about imposing quarantines to prevent the spread of diseases fall under the jurisdiction of the CDC. Early on in the history of AIDS in the United States a decision was made to respond to the epidemic through education and strategies for reducing the risk of transmission. This seems to be the only reasonable and just course. However, in opting not to impose a quarantine, a controversial decision with ethical ramifications was made. The reasons the CDC did not advocate a quarantine were because it could not justify requiring people infected with HIV to live apart from their communities and because it would be impossible to identify asymptomatic infected individuals and remove them from the population.

The mission of the National Institutes of Health is to employ science in pursuit of knowledge in order to improve human health. Accordingly, the NIH supports medical and behavioral research at home and abroad. An example of an issue with ethical ramifications which the NIH has had to resolve is that of equitable representation of various infected populations in research studies of medications for AIDS. People infected by HIV tend to fall into predictable categories: Homosexual men, intravenous drug users, hemophiliacs and other recipients of infected blood or blood products, sexual partners of IV drug users or hemophiliacs, and children born to HIV-infected women. In order not to favor any population, and especially in an effort not to discriminate against any group(s), the NIH has had to consciously implement strategies to allow just access to AIDS medications to a fair representation of each infected population.

The Health Care Finance Administration has oversight of the Medicare and Medicaid programs. The HCFA serves 68 million Americans who are entitled to coverage because of age, disability, or poverty. Because of the enormous amount of money spent by the federal government on health care and the increasing cost of medications, diagnostic procedures, and treatments, the day may be near when the HCFA will find it necessary to put limits on what government is willing to pay for. Limit-setting is inherently controversial and sensitive; it also requires a strong sense of ethical probity. This is because neither the lobbying of special-interest groups nor the advantages to be gained by creating favorable public opinion should dictate policy decisions. Rather, a clear-headed commitment to fairness by achieving the most salutary medical outcomes for the largest possible number, without compromising justice, is called for. Will it be possible to join utilitarian ideology to principled thinking? Only time will tell.

It is the Surgeon General who presides over the Public Health Service and, in recent years, the Surgeon General's positions on various health-related issues have occasioned considerable controversy. This is primarily because of the ethically sensitive nature of the issues as well as the fact that there are deep divisions of opinion with regard to these issues. One example involved Dr. Jocelyn Elders, an appointee of President Bill Clinton, who advocated access to artificial contraceptives for adolescents and whose suggestion met with sustained resistance from people who object to premarital sex. Another example relates to President Clinton's nomination of Dr. Henry Foster. Once it was learned that Dr. Foster performed approximately two dozen abortions, anti-abortion groups protested his nomination, which was eventually withdrawn. Thus, we can see that the Surgeon General, who should be concerned solely with the health and well-being of U.S. citizens, can be evaluated based on personal decisions she or he has made that have political and ethical overtones. Citizens who disagree with either the Surgeon General's ethics or politics can be counted on to mount opposition and force the Surgeon General to answer their objections. This situation is both good and bad. It is good in that it requires accountability of government officials. It is bad in that it can preoccupy government officials with the task of defending themselves, preventing them from attending to the work of overseeing efficient health care delivery, as well as providing education for disease prevention.

The executive branch of the federal government also functions in the arena of health care ethics through the work of presidential commissions. Such issues as human in vitro fertilization, forgoing and withdrawing artificial feeding, deciding about research and transplant of fetal tissue, developing a comprehensive strategy for responding to HIV/AIDS, and cloning have occasioned the appointment of presidential commissions. These commissions are ad hoc in nature, meaning that they cease to exist once they have accomplished their particular mandate. Broad based in representation and expertise, presidential commissions have contributed significantly to the analysis of complex issues, as well as to formulating policies in relation to these questions.

A final way in which the executive branch of government can affect matters of medical-ethical import is by exercise of presidential veto of legislation with which the president disagrees. Should a president choose to exercise veto power, then the president's ethical position and rationale come under scrutiny. This was the case on April 11, 1996, when President Bill Clinton vetoed a bill outlawing some late-term abortions. HR1833 sought to make it illegal for physicians to perform so-called "partial birth" abortions in which the fetus is extracted feet first and its brain then suctioned out to allow its compressed head to pass through the birth canal. Proposed legislation can become law in spite of a presidential veto upon repassage by a two-thirds majority in both the Senate and House of Representatives. The House achieved such a majority in July 1998; at this writing, Senate action has not taken place, as noted earlier.

PROFESSIONAL SOCIETIES AND ETHICAL
DECISION MAKING

Several independent organizations have considerable interest in the practice of medicine and, hence, are also concerned about ethical issues. In one sense, these organizations grapple with the implications of ethical questions, trying to understand in what an ethical response would consist, and why. In another sense, these organizations may be interest groups, seeking to promote their own agendas. It goes without saying that organizations will contribute more to an ethical climate, ethical awareness, and ethical insight if they are singlemindedly pursuing these goals rather than trying to protect their special interests.

Founded in 1847, the American Medical Association is based in Chicago and is composed of two types of members—individual physicians and medical specialty associations. These associations are represented in the House of Delegates, the AMA's policymaking body. The AMA is involved in issues with medical connotations, including medical-ethical issues. Its policy positions on medical-ethical issues tend to be centrist and pragmatic. Anyone interested in considering specific issues in health care ethics would do well to review the policy position the AMA has taken on that issue.

Supported by private donations, the Hastings Center for the Study of Bioethics was established in 1969 and is located in Garrison, New York. The Hastings Center functions as a think-tank, supporting scholarship in medical ethics and conducting conferences on specific issues. Its publication, *The Hastings Center Report*, is an influential vehicle which addresses cutting-edge issues. The influence of the scholars from the Hastings Center is felt by both governmental and nongovernmental agencies responsible for policy formation.

Two church-sponsored agencies, the Kennedy Institute for the Study of Bioethics and the Park Ridge Center, contribute to the development of health care ethics. Based at Georgetown University and organized with ties to the Roman Catholic community, the Kennedy Center supports scholarship in bioethics and maintains an extensive library with comprehensive holdings in medical ethics. The Park Ridge Center, affiliated with the Lutheran Church, is located in Park Ridge, Illinois, and supports research in medical ethics as well as interfaith understanding.

There are countless special-interest groups which influence bioethics. Organizations such as the Hemlock Society and New York-based Choice in Dying lobby for societal acceptance of euthanasia and physician-assisted suicide. Opposed to such groups is the United Handicapped Federation of St. Paul, Minnesota, which advocates that public policy be formulated with an eye toward protecting handicapped people so that members of this group need not fear being subjected to measures which might shorten their lives and which they do not freely choose. In regard to abortion, two groups are well known: Right to Life, which defends vulnerable life in the womb, and Planned Parenthood, which lobbies for a woman's right to choose abortion.

CONCLUSION

Ethical judgments about health care come from many sources including courts, legislatures and policy-making bodies. The reason for this is because decisions have to be made, and the situations that arise tend to be complex.

It stands to reason that the judgments made by intelligent, well-informed people who work collaboratively to achieve the right answer to a complex problem should be taken seriously. It is also true, however, that given the fact that the issues are complicated and the "reasoners" might be flawed in their thinking, the conclusions which are put forth need not be accepted at face value but, rather, should be probed so as to ascertain whether or not they can stand up to critical scrutiny.

ENDNOTES

[1] Jack Kevorkian is a 69-year-old retired pathologist who has stated that neither the actions of the legislature, the executive, nor the judiciary will sway him from his work. As of October 2, 1996 Kevorkian had assisted 41 people in ending their lives. Cf., Aaron Epstein "Supreme Court enters assisted suicide debate," *The Record*, October 2, 1996, p.8.

[2] Timothy E. Quill, a physician and long-time advocate of physician-assisted suicide, supported the decision of a terminally ill patient to end her suffering and prescribed medicine for this purpose. Quill's decision and his explicit assistance have met with much more approval than Kevorkian's approach because Quill is considered more thoughtful, careful, and nuanced. For an account of Quill's reasoning, cf., Timothy E. Quill, "Death and Dignity: A Case of Individualized Decision Making," *The New England Journal of Medicine*, March 7, 1991, pp. 691–694.

[3] Three instances of state involvement in regard to allowing physicians to aid patients to end their lives by overt means are briefly outlined here. First, an attempt in California in 1988 to gather 372,178 signatures so as to put the Humane and Dignified Death Act on the ballot in the general election fell short by 100,000 signatures. The Dignified Death Act would have made it legal for physicians to give lethal injections to the terminally ill.

Second, in 1991 in the state of Washington Initiative 119 was defeated. This initiative would have allowed physicians to engage in both assisted suicide and active euthanasia. Physicians could do so only in response to patient requests and if the patients had less than six months to live.

Third, in 1994 voters in Oregon approved a measure to allow physicians to prescribe lethal doses of medication which dying patients could self-administer. Upon appeal this law was ruled unconstitutional by a federal judge on August 3, 1995. The law's supporters appealed the federal judge's decision. On March 3, 1996, by a vote of eight to three, the United States Court of Appeals for the Ninth District, located in San Francisco, gave broad support to the 1994 Oregon measure.

A separate decision rendered shortly thereafter, on April 2, 1996, by the Court of Appeals for the Second Circuit in Manhattan, New York, represented a parallel development. This decision struck down a nineteenth century state statute that made it illegal for doctors to help terminally ill patients end their lives. Attorney General Dennis C. Vacco filed an appeal to the decision of the Second Circuit Court on May 15, 1996.

On October 1, 1996 the United States Supreme Court announced that it would decide during its 1996–97 term whether the Constitution gives terminally ill patients a right to a doctor's assistance in hastening death. After this decision by the Supreme Court the status of this issue will be clarified from a legal perspective. Cf., Linda Greenhouse "High Court to Decide if the Dying Have a Right to Assisted Suicide," *The New York Times*, October 2, 1996, p. 1. On June 27, 1997, the Supreme Court overturned the decisions of the federal Appeals Courts in the Ninth District in San Francisco and the Second Circuit in Manhattan, ruling that there is no Constitutional right to physician assistance in dying. In essence what the Supreme Court did was force states to craft different arguments for euthanasia. It remains to be seen whether or not these "different arguments" will withstand judicial scrutiny.

DISCUSSION QUESTIONS

1. Describe the situation in which new, complex, and emotionally charged medical-ethical issues emerge in the contemporary United States. Discuss the manner in which these issues are resolved taking care to comment on the confusion, disruption, and polarization they frequently engender. In your opinion, is there any way to lessen the confusion, disruption, and polarization and, if so, how could this be accomplished?

2. Sometimes courts decide that a particular medical practice is ethically appropriate and a significant percentage of the population disagrees with the decision. The right of a woman to obtain an abortion is a case in point. How would you go about deciding whether the court is morally right or the position held by the dissenting group is morally right? Why do you think the approach you advocate is sound and rational?

3. State two decisions made by courts which have ethical ramifications and two ethically relevant principles defined by courts.

4. What legislative bodies make decisions with medical ramifications? How are these decisions reached? Discuss the positive and negative aspects of involving legislative bodies in ethical matters.

5. What role is played by professional societies and special-interest groups

in the formulation of ethical positions and guidelines? Design a list of criteria by which to evaluate the reliability of these societies and groups.

6. At the present time in the United States the health effects of smoking and being in proximity to cigarette smoke are topics of widespread interest. What specific ethical ideas or norms need to be included in the national dialogue on this subject? How can ethics impact on this issue for the well-being of both the individual and society as a whole?

CASE STUDY

Judge Patricia Smith-Martin handles medical decision cases in Green County. She has served as a judge for seven years and has been called on in a medical decision-making capacity an average of once or twice a year.

A perplexing case is brought to Judge Smith-Martin's court in July, 1996. Tanya Hunter, a 24-year-old woman who sustained severe head injuries as a result of an auto accident, is comatose; early diagnostic tests do not disclose an accurate account of the extent of her injuries. Thus, it is too soon for physicians to establish a secure diagnosis and prognosis. Ms. Hunter is approximately seven weeks pregnant; she has no advance directive and no one who knows her can recall her ever expressing wishes about her treatment should she be in circumstances similar to those which she currently endures.

Three physicians, all neurologists, meet with Ms. Hunter's parents and her boyfriend, Michael Wilson, the acknowledged father of the fetus. Two of the three doctors express the opinion that Ms. Hunter would stand a better chance of recovering if she were not pregnant; the third physician says that she can offer no opinion because there is insufficient data to guide her.

Following their consultation with the neurologists, Ms. Hunter's parents meet with a gynecologist and schedule an abortion for the following day. Michael Wilson strenuously objects to this decision and hires an attorney to assist him in blocking the abortion. Mr. Wilson and the attorney go to Judge Smith-Martin's court to obtain an order blocking the termination of pregnancy procedure. The judge says she will take six hours to consider the case and will then render a decision.

Evaluation:

1. Identify ethical issues contained in this case.
2. Propose possible solutions for these issues.
3. Make a decision relevant to action to be taken or not taken and provide rationale supportive of this decision.
4. Are you satisfied with your decision? Why or why not?

GLOSSARY

English common law is the system of law in the United States, Great Britain, and other English-speaking countries. Common law represents the law of the courts as expressed in judicial decisions. Previous decisions of the highest courts in a jurisdiction are binding on all other courts in the jurisdiction. The common law system is both authoritative and flexible. Its authority comes from the firmly established precedents it honors. Its flexibility comes from its freedom to adapt these precedents to new questions or technologies.

A **relative claim** differs from an **absolute claim** in that it is not always binding in all circumstances. Thus, a relative claim on the part of a patient does not establish an undisputed obligation on the part of a health care provider. The claim of an injured person to medical care is, thus, a relative claim. Under ordinary circumstances it should be honored but, in the aftermath of an accident, it may not be possible to do so because physicians need first to care for those who will best benefit from their care and some individuals may die before doctors or nurses get to them. The name given to the system of dividing accident victims into groups and designating these groups as first, second, and third in order of access to medical care is triage.

Coextensive, in this context, means having the same content. The reason the ethical and legal realms are not coextensive is because their reference points are different. The legal system in the United States seeks to make decisions in accord with established precedents and the Constitution. The purpose of ethics is to conform actions to objectively existing valid moral standards or to some other criterion or criteria.

Mutually exclusive means that two ideas or systems cannot exist in a manner of interrelationship with one another. As an example one cannot assert belief in the values of standard Western medical care and Christian Science at the same time. However, common law courts cannot disallow ethical aspects of questions because morality is pertinent to the formulation of legal decisions. Thus, the realms of law and ethics are not mutually exclusive.

Appeal is a legal term which means that a decision of a lower court is brought to a higher court for a second hearing. Frequently the reason for an appeal is the hope of a different decision. Occasionally, however, an appeal is instituted in order for a higher court to validate the decision of a lower court on a novel or very complex question.

Unicameral means one legislative chamber; one legislative body makes the laws for a state. The only unicameral state legislature in the United States is in Nebraska. Many local governing bodies, such as county boards and township boards, are unicameral.

Bicameral means two legislative chambers, ordinarily a Senate and an

Assembly acting in consort; these bodies make laws for a state. Forty-nine states in the United States have two-house, or bicameral, legislatures.

A **referendum** is the referral of proposed laws or constitutional amendments to the electorate for a vote.

An **initiative** is the act of originating a law or constitutional amendment through popular petition. By formulating an initiative the electorate can formulate legislation independent of the legislature provided that a majority of voters support the initiative.

CHAPTER 17

Providing Health Care in the United States

INTRODUCTION

Providing health care in the United States is a different kind of moral issue from those we have discussed thus far. In this chapter we will be considering the system which is in place for delivering health care. Many people argue that the health care provided in the United States is the best in the world but, whether or not one agrees with this claim, almost all knowledgeable people admit that there are problems with the system of health care delivery. These systemic problems are complex, deeply ingrained and pervasive; whether or not they are intractable remains to be seen. The matter of actually designing an appropriate system for providing health care in the United States is beyond the scope of this book and shall not occupy us here. Rather, we shall set two modest goals: To indicate in a general way the problems inherent in the current system and to suggest which ethical principles need to be implemented in modifying the system.

PROBLEMS OR ISSUES ARISING IN CONJUNCTION WITH PROVISION OF HEALTH CARE IN THE UNITED STATES

Background Issues. During the first 50 or 60 years of this century provision of health care was a relatively simple matter. Doctors carried most of the equipment they used in a black bag and the same doctor was likely to attend a patient for most, or all, of her or his life. During those days the range of medical and surgical interventions was quite modest. Today, sophisticated diagnostic technology complements an extensive array of medical and surgical options making medical care a very complex, highly specialized, and costly commodity. In 1992 more than $800 billion was spent on health care in the United States and the cost of health care is growing at a rate of approximately ten percent per year.[1] The dollar amount spent for health care, as well as the fact that health care expenditures represent an ever-increasing percentage of our gross national product,[2] are beginning to give us cause for concern. The reason for health care is to prevent or cure pathologies or attend to people with chronic or terminal illnesses. It may be possible, however, for health care costs to undermine the soundness of our economy, and such an eventuality would be undesirable. Hence, a pressing background issue entails how to achieve a situation in which expensive medical care can continue to be available while, at the same time, the total cost of health care is scaled back so as to keep this cost in line with the overall rate of inflation.

A second background issue is that many purchasers of health care are unaccustomed to paying for medical care with their own money and so they tend to think of it as without cost. This is because medical consultations, treatments, and prescriptions are covered, in whole or in part, by some form of insurance. However, whether people reach into their own pockets or not, health care costs money and its aggregate costliness eventually impacts on everyone. There would be greater efficiency and economy in the provision of medical care if its recipients exercised a similar kind of vigilance in respect to purchasing medical services as people do when making other kinds of spending decisions. Determining how to motivate the medically insured public to get over the "I don't have to pay for it (or pay much for it) so I don't care how much it costs" attitude will not be easy. It will be necessary, however, if the system is to work economically.

A third background issue is that the lifestyles of many citizens of the United States predispose them to deleterious health consequences which require expensive medical treatment. Cigarette smoking, excessive consumption of alcohol, overeating and poor nutrition, use of illegal narcotics, dependence on prescription medicine, lack of exercise, and high-risk sexual behaviors contribute to a wide array of diseases. Not only does it cost a great deal to treat these diseases, it is also true that those afflicted with them would have fared much better healthwise had they prevented the occurrence of these diseases. In order for U.S. citizens to take prevention strategies seriously it will be necessary for them to understand both their own responsibilities in respect to their well-being and the harm they are causing to the common good by irresponsible conduct.

A final background issue requires that we acknowledge how individualism flourishes in our culture to the detriment of concern for the common good. Personal rights, opinions, desires, satisfactions, and goals are championed in the United States. The individual's circle tends to be a small one: Significant others, perhaps a few friends, neighbors and coworkers, and not many others. Gone with the doctor's black bag are, for the most part, barn raisings and extended families which provide care for frail elderly members. Energy is spent on protecting our own self and possessions, with little attention devoted to the needs of those outside of our circle. As a result of American individualism and materialism, concern for the common good has eroded. This erosion is causing serious difficulties in respect to crafting a program of health care reform because health care reform necessitates real concern for the common good, or the well-being of society, while individualism cares little about the total human community.

Specific Problems. There are many problems or issues which arise in conjunction with providing or delivering health care in the United States. Fourteen of these problems will be described below. Neither the list nor the descriptions presents the full picture; rather, they are meant to suggest a fairly comprehensive overview of the main shortcomings in the contemporary system.

Access. The biggest problem associated with provision of health care in the United States is that everyone does not have access to the system. Those who fall into this category are the more than 40 million people who are uninsured and who, in all probability, cannot afford to pay for health care services.

Health Care Dollars which Do Not Pay for Health Care. The overwhelming amount of health care purchased in the United States is paid for by the government through Medicare and Medicaid or by privately owned health-insurance companies. Both Medicare-Medicaid and health insurance firms employ personnel, process claims, and issue payments. Their procedures and personnel are expensive and add to the cost of health care without actual medical benefit to anyone. A study based on medical consumption during the year 1985 showed that the administrative cost of providing health care in the United States totaled $95 per U.S. citizen; in contrast, the cost per Canadian citizen was $21.[3] Proposals have been made to dismantle the so-called third party infrastructure and change to a single-payer system in which government would provide and pay for health care. Taxes would be adjusted to cover the costs and administrative bureaucracy would be kept to a minimum so as to maximize efficiency. While a single-payer system has obvious merits, a national consensus in favor of such a system has not emerged. Thus the problem of health care dollars paying for administrative infrastructure remains, and there is no clear indication as to how to resolve it.

Access to Health Insurance. One problem arises with predictable regularity in respect to people's ability to get health insurance. It is that health insurers often deny coverage to people who have specific preexisting conditions that are likely to require costly medical care. From the point of view of the insurance company, refusals of coverage may appear to reflect sound economic policy but, from the perspective of the person who is denied coverage, the refusal constitutes an incalculable disadvantage.

Caps. A cap is a maximum allowable benefit. It can be a dollar amount, a set number of weeks or months of hospital care, a set number of hours of home care, or a specific amount of visits to a certain kind of provider, such as a chiropractor or psychologist. One problem with caps is that the needs of many individuals for treatments are greater than the number allowed. Another problem is that individuals with catastrophic illnesses rather quickly use up all their benefits and are left with enormous needs and no coverage. People who face the devastating effects of caps argue persuasively that this broken part of the system needs to be fixed. One of these people is Christopher Reeve, the actor who suffered a broken neck as a result of a fall from a horse. A quadriplegic, Mr. Reeve's lifetime insurance coverage is capped at $1.2 million. With annual costs of close to $400,000, Mr. Reeve's coverage lasts three years.[4]

Cost of Private Health Insurance and Government Programs. All forms of health insurance are rapidly becoming prohibitively expensive. Uninsured individuals and families can buy health insurance but few can afford the very high cost.[5] Most Americans receive health insurance as a benefit provided by employers. Employers have begun to register alarm at the size and predictability of the yearly increases in the cost of covering their workforces. As a consequence, employers have begun to organize and exert pressure to hold the line on health-insurance costs. Switching to managed-care companies is one of the strategies employed to this end. (See Chapter 15.)

Government, too, has been shaken by the ever-increasing costs of its programs, Medicare, for the elderly, and Medicaid, for poor people. No one favors the growing costs of these programs but there is no consensus in respect to how to fix entitlement programs so that they become less expensive.[6]

Negative Consequences of Economizing. In recent years many different kinds of initiatives have been put in place in an effort to reign-in escalating health care costs. Some of these initiatives have had negative consequences, so that attempts at fixing a broken system have resulted in still more ruptures in the system.

Several strategies for economizing have tried to reduce costs by reducing time spent in hospitals. Some procedures which used to be performed in hospitals were moved to physician offices or free-standing clinics. Some procedures which formerly required in-patient hospital stays are now done on a same-day basis. Time allowed in a hospital for childbirth, surgery, and other treatments has been cut back. In most cases physicians and patients, hospitals and other facilities have adapted to the attempts at cutting back expensive in-hospital care without deleterious consequences. In some cases, however, this is not the case. Patients discharged too soon after surgery have developed costly and life-threatening complications; new mothers and infants released too soon have suffered; and some patients undergoing procedures in doctor's offices or clinics who have experienced distress have been at a medical disadvantage because of the unavailability of back-up hospital resources. As awareness of this state of affairs has increased, so has a backlash against cutting costs at what might be the expense of the well-being of patients.

The Plight of the Uninsured. The more than 40-million uninsured people in the United States get sick and need medical care. Since they have no insurance and probably have limited financial resources, they are unlikely to go to a family doctor when they get sick because they do not have the money. Unfortunately, they are unlikely to get better without treatment and so they are apt to get sicker. Uninsured people in very compromised conditions tend to seek help at hospital emergency rooms. Emergency-room care, whether provided to indigents, paying patients or insured patients, is more costly than care rendered in a physician's office. In addition, the indigent patient's condition is probably going to be much worse than it would have been had she sought intervention at the start of symptoms. (Treating a more advanced illness costs more than dealing with the illness during its early phases.) Thus, by virtue of their point of entry into the medical system, as well as their escalating medical problems, the uninsured eventually exert a detrimental effect on the health care system to which they lack access.[7]

Malpractice Litigation. The United States is a litigious country in which people believe it is necessary to be able to receive monetary compensation when they suffer because of a physician's negligence or ineptitude. On the face of it this appears to be a reasonable belief and it could be said to promote competent conduct on the part of physicians. However, there is another side to malpractice litigation that needs to be examined and, perhaps, corrected.

The other side is that medical malpractice judgments against doctors can run into the millions of dollars, resulting in very high premiums for malpractice insurance. Even if physicians are vindicated in court, the cost of defending themselves against charges of malpractice is prohibitive. Of course, the expenditure for malpractice insurance is passed along to those who purchase medical services, and, as with some other costs, money spent for malpractice insurance does not buy medical care.

There is general agreement that capricious suits brought against doctors and/or hospitals should be discouraged. There is also discussion about limiting the size of awards so as to contain costs. Better communication between patient and physician and better oversight of the clinical setting are encouraged, to prevent situations which lead to malpractice cases in the first place. It is apparent that there are no easy answers to the problems attendant to malpractice litigation but the fact remains that this matter requires resolution.

Waste and Fraud. Wasting medical resources is wrong; these resources are supposed to be used to effect beneficial outcomes. Fraud is wrong, too; physicians should not try to collect payment for services they do not perform. Both waste and fraud cost money and this money usually comes from the government or from private health insurance companies. It is money which could be spent on people who lack health care, or it is money which could be saved, thus lowering the overall amount spent on health care.

While there is no support for waste and fraud, there is also a remarkable lack of resolve to expose and punish it. The reasons waste and fraud occur are because of greed, indifference, and lack of administrative oversight. In respect to greed, some health care providers are dishonest and covetous, and they submit false bills in order to receive payments to which they are not entitled. Waste and fraud do not happen in a vacuum; many indifferent people need to look the other way so that scams can be carried out. The fact that waste and fraud occur also points to the deficiencies in the administrative structures which exist to monitor provision and reimbursement of services, indicating obvious inadequacies.

Waste and fraud are demoralizing and frustrating aspects of our health care delivery system which need to be eliminated in order to improve the system.[8]

Competitive Climate. In just a few years the ethos of the marketplace has taken hold in the field of medicine so that physicians compete to establish practices in desirable locales and hospitals compete to attract patients to come for expensive operations, treatments, and procedures. At the same time, health care is downsizing so that fewer registered nurses (RNs) take care of larger numbers of patients and, in some cases, lower priced licensed practical nurses (LPNs) or medical assistants are assigned to responsibilities which used to be filled by RNs. Some of the money saved in staff reductions is being spent on marketing programs to induce would-be patients to procure their care at facilities which strive to maintain an excellent public relations image. There seems little question that the entry of health care facilities into the competitive marketplace has negative aspects which must be addressed if the health care system itself is to provide appropriate services.

Physician Compensation. The primary providers of health care are physicians. Physicians are highly trained, highly skilled professionals who earn a good livelihood. This is as it should be. A question arises, however, as to how much is reasonable compensation for a physician. In 1990 a physician's average annual income after expenses and before taxes was $155,800, more than seven times the average salary.[9] The physician's average annual income rose to $164,300 in 1991.[10] Under recent managed-care arrangements doctors' salaries have begun to decrease slightly. Accordingly, the median income of physicians dropped 3.8 percent in 1994, for an average salary of $150,000.[11] Physicians earn a substantial amount of money because they charge hefty fees to their patients or the insurance companies which employ them. Up until relatively recently, few criticisms were raised about how much doctors charge but, in the last few years, their high earnings have come to be regarded as yet another problem with the health care delivery system. Perhaps future negotiations with doctors will result in lowered income requirements for them. Such a concession would constitute one concrete step toward rectifying the system.

Provision of Unnecessary Medical Services. Futile medical treatments cost money and do not provide patient benefit. Therefore, the provision of futile medical services should be discouraged in the strongest possible fashion. To so argue seems clear-headed and realistic but, nevertheless, the provision of futile treatments is an everyday occurrence. This is because many patients, family members, and physicians have difficulty accepting the fact that specific conditions are beyond help by medical means. If it becomes possible to confront reality more truthfully there will be less recourse to futile treatments, thereby allowing those energies and therapies to be directed to rational goals.

A group of people which routinely seeks medical services without a corresponding need is *hypochondriacs*. These individuals suffer from a delusion which makes them believe that they are sick even though there is no physiological basis for their belief. When medical care cost less and when hypochondriacs were less likely to take up the time of specialists, the tendency was to humor them and get them out of the doctor's office as quickly as possible. These new times require a less gentle, more straightforward approach to hypochondriacs. Just as waste and fraud cannot be tolerated by our overtaxed system of health care delivery, neither can the drain which hypochondriacs put upon it.

Statistics disclose that a significant amount of an average individual's expenditures for health care are incurred during the last year of life. Of the $900 billion spent for health care during 1993, $300 billion was spent on persons aged 65 or older, and one-third of that amount, $100 billion, was spent during the last year of life.[12] Expenditures during the final 30 days of life account for 40 percent of what is spent during the last year, because most deaths occur in the costly hospital setting.[13] If society is to bring health care costs under control and arrange for provision of health care to the uninsured, measures need to be taken to correct what may be disproportionate outlays at the end of life. It goes without saying that this is a sensitive subject; however, unless this significant piece of the big picture is evaluated so that needed corrections can be made, the provision of health care to all in need will continue to go unrealized.

Charity Care. Up until a few years ago charity care was provided by doctors on a pro-bono basis and by hospitals through a surcharge paid by all paying patients, those who had insurance and those who paid from their own funds. Medicare and Medicaid funding also paid for the care of the poor. Recent court decisions made it unacceptable to charge people for care they did not personally receive, thus cutting off one source of funding for charity care in hospitals. In addition, government's scaling back of Medicare and Medicaid funding is compounding the problem. As it is working out, economically sound hospitals with few indigent patients will probably be able to absorb the losses incurred by treating the indigent. Hospitals in disadvantaged areas, with large cohorts of indigent patients, are finding themselves in a very different position. Strained to the limit by lack of coverage for indigent care, these institutions face insolvency if funding is not promptly reinstituted. This is a major systemic problem which demands resolution.[15]

Cost of Pharmaceuticals. Medicines take a long time in research, development and testing phases, and companies which produce pharmaceuticals take big risks and incur huge expenditures in so doing. The pharmaceutical industry is one among many industries in our capitalist society; paramount among its aims is the realization of a profit. Knowing these facts is preliminary to considering what to do about the high cost of medications, yet another systemic issue to be resolved. Few people would argue that pharmaceutical companies have a right to make a profit, but most are beginning to question the amount of the profit, as well as the cost of prescription medicines. Recognizing that an issue exists is the first step on the road to resolving it. As far as making medicines less expensive and so more easily procurable, society is at the early stages but will probably progress quickly, because lowering these costs is emerging as one of the primary goals of health care reform.

PRINCIPLES TO BE HONORED WHILE MODIFYING THE SYSTEM OF HEALTH CARE DELIVERY

The health care delivery system in the United States needs to be changed or modified so that people who live in this country receive an appropriate level of health care and so that the percentage of the gross national product spent on health care does not undermine the economic health of the nation.

Preliminary to understanding how principles impact in this area we need to examine two crucial notions: That of "an appropriate level of care" and that of "the economic health of the nation." As we shall see, neither of these matters is simple.

Appropriate Level of Care. In regard to an appropriate level of health care it seems obvious that some services would fall outside this category. Included in the list we would probably find cosmetic surgery, futile treatments, and very expensive procedures which carry a very low medical probability of success. Home health care assistance during the night hours when the client is sleeping, supplying assisted-reproduction services to poor infertile couples and performing eye exams on uncooperative nursing-home patients with Alzheimer's disease would also likely make the list. We need to remember, however, that in our democratic system dissenting voices have a right to speak and to act to change decisions which they consider unfair. Thus, much energy might be expended in defense, for example, of not providing home health care throughout the night, and, in the end, a consensus might be reached that this care should be provided. According to such a scenario the net result for the system would be more spending rather than less. Furthermore, specifying particular types of treatments for nonprovision is not even the main task in determining an appropriate level of service; deciding how much to spend on which populations is the more important undertaking.

Reprioritizing for Economic Efficiency. All of us are going to die but, in general, death is closer for those with terminal illnesses as well as for those of advanced years. Yes, medical science can be utilized by people in these categories but to limited benefit because medicine cannot prevent death or cure terminal illnesses. Therefore, it would seem to make more sense to invest health care dollars in prenatal care, attending to children and adolescents in their formative years, and providing education in wellness for people of all ages. Reprioritizing in this manner would represent a major change in the philosophy of health care delivery and would be a difficult goal to achieve. Whether or not it is achievable is questionable, for several reasons. This question would have to be addressed in the United States, a society in which people only seem capable of joining forces in opposition to something, not in order to work together on crafting constructive social policies. In addition, the issue would have to be aired anew only a few years after the 1993-1994 government-led effort at health care reform ended without achieving systemic changes. Finally, the debate would need to include health care special-interest groups, and strategies would need to be devised to prevent these lobbies from exercising more influence than they are rightfully entitled to. In view of the daunting nature of the total task of deciding on a comprehensive description of an appropriate level of care, it should not be surprising that many people are unwilling to participate in the exercise. Perhaps the injustice inherent in the fact that more than 40 million Americans lack access to health care will, nonetheless, provide the impetus to embark upon this challenging undertaking.

Economic Issues. In respect to our second preliminary issue, the economic health of the nation, it is important that we understand the need to keep the growth of the health care sector in line with other segments of the economy so as not to jeopardize the nation's overall economic health. Provision of health care is one good among many. Besides providing health care our economy also needs to produce goods and provide a wide array of other services. Significant among these services are care for the environment and improving the educational system. No one economic need should gain ascendancy at the expense of other equally meritorious needs. Thus, there should be a balance so that health care spending does not grow at a rate significantly in excess of the rate of inflation.

In respect to the overall economy of the United States it goes without saying that this is a complex reality. Much like the delivery of health care, the economy has evolved into its present form. When there are problems with the economy adjustments are made in order to correct the problems. A blueprint for healthy economic design does not exist; trial and error is the approach used in order to generate the dynamisms which will result in a strong economy. There is no argument that health care spending should be kept at a reasonable level and should not continue to grow at an astronomical rate. Deciding on precisely how much should be spent on health care and how much growth in overall health care spending should be tolerated are matters about which there is bound to be disagreement. Difficult as the economic issue is, however, if attention is not focused on these matters, we will not move toward the goal of providing health care for all people in the United States.

Ethical Issues in Provision of Health Care. After resolving these two preliminary issues, we need to grapple with the even more difficult *why* question: Why should basic health care be provided to everyone in the United States? In engaging this why question we will unavoidably encounter relevant ethical principles.

The reason why basic health care should be provided is because justice requires that human rights be met and the right to health care is a human right to which each and every human person is entitled. The correlative to rights is obligation so that, if everyone has a right to health care, some collectivity has an obligation to honor or satisfy that right. In this case a general consensus is evolving to the effect that it is society as a whole, through its agent, government, which ought to exercise this obligation.

Since the obligation to provide health care arises in conjunction with the principle of justice, it is important that we consider what justice is. At its most elemental level, justice entails giving each other what is due or providing what we owe each other. In view of the fact that we believe that health care is a basic right, justice requires that we (society-government) insure that it be provided for anyone who needs it.

Two ways of looking at justice are especially relevant to this discussion. One is a consideration of so-called "legal justice." Legal justice suggests the general responsibilities of citizens to act in behalf of the common good. People acknowledge responsibilities to perform military service, pay taxes, serve on juries, and care for the environment. By extension, an obligation that is both individual and collective, i.e., to provide basic health care, also falls under the purview of legal justice, requiring cooperation of all who are able to assist.

Distributive justice is another aspect of the principle of justice. According to distributive justice society as a whole is obligated to provide basic health care for everyone. It requires that government agencies provide for the uninsured because the current situation in which more than 40 million people lack access to health care is an unjust violation of their rights. The facts that so many Americans have health care as a result of having health insurance or being covered by Medicare or Medicaid does not let us off the hook in respect to the uninsured. The system cannot be seen as just, or sound, or working until each and every person has access because each and every person has rights. The requirement under distributive justice entails the honoring of the right to health care.

The requirements of distributive justice will not go away even though there are many issues to work out. One of the biggest issues is determining how to deal effectively with special-interest groups which want to retain all their current status and privileges even though this prevents progress in putting health care reform in place. Civic virtue may require that special-interest groups be willing to compromise and give back some of their entitlements so that everyone will be able to attain access to basic health care.

Another principle which should be affirmed in bringing health care reform to fruition is the principle of subsidiarity. By *subsidiarity* is meant that decision making, control of funds, and plans for distribution of services should come from the local level, not from a remote bureaucracy lacking firsthand knowledge of the identity and needs of a particular community. The principle of subsidiarity is reasonable and, should it be applied, many of the inefficiencies connected with remote government should be eliminated. This is not to say, however, that supervision from state or federal agencies would not be needed to prevent mismanagement as well as discriminatory practices from arising in conjunction with the provision of services.

Many people fear health care reform because they object to rationing. By *rationing* is meant the setting of limits to the provision of services. In the medical context, rationing implies that everyone would not be able to procure everything, so that perhaps the very frail elderly or the very low-birth-weight newborn or the person with very advanced cancer would not be offered every possible technological intervention. It is understandable that people do not want to give up services they assumed would be available for themselves or their loved ones. Reservations regarding rationing are understandable. Understandable or not, however, rationing is already a reality in respect to access to health care in the United States. In the current system the criterion for establishing whether or not an individual has access is the person's insurance status—whether covered by a private health insurance plan or a government program. Those who are covered have access to medical treatments. Those who are not covered have access to little or nothing. Rationing limits the health care access of more than 40 million Americans to little or no care. The current system of rationing is, therefore, immoral. If limits are to be set, then these limits should be on everyone and the limits should be put in place after everyone has access to basic health care. There is a need to promote in the national consciousness (and conscience) the notion that the virtue of concern for others needs to evolve into a commitment to securing access to health care for everyone.

CONCLUSION

Providing health care for everyone in the United States should not be approached from a negative perspective. It is a daunting challenge which will only be met by virtuous people who understand the problems in the current system and are committed to the ideals of fairness and justice. While the recent national debate on health care reform was discouraging in its tone and distressing in its outcome, people of good will should not make excuses for not moving forward in the interest of insuring access for everyone. Common decency and communal integrity demand no less of us.

ENDNOTES

[1] Arnold S. Relman, M.D., "Foreword," in Marc A. Rodwin, *Medicine, Money and Morals* (New York: Oxford University Press, 1993), p. IX.

[2] Ibid. Relman said, "At the present rate of growth more than 16 percent of our gross domestic product would be devoted to the health sector by the end of this decade—a circumstance that would be disastrous for competing public and private needs."

[3] Philip S. Keane, S.S., *Health Care Reform: A Catholic View* (New York: Paulist Press, 1993), p. 52.

[4] Trip Gabriel, "Will the Insurers Feel His Sting?" *The New York Times*, April 11, 1996, p. C8.

[5] Lindy Washburn, "Families fear loss of health coverage," *The Record*, March 10, 1996, p. A1. Washburn recounts recent hikes in rates for family coverage from Blue Cross and Blue Shield of New Jersey. Premiums which cost $9,600 in December 1994 soared to $16,900 on April 1, 1996. As a result of large increases in the cost of insurance the number of customers decreased from 160,000 in 1993 to 30,825 in early 1996.

[6] Robert Pear, "Shortfall Posted by Medicare Fund Two Years Early," *The New York Times*, February 5, 1996, p. A1. Medicare hospital expenses are paid for with income from a trust fund and the balance in the trust fund results from payroll taxes. At the present time a gap is developing in the trust fund because there are not enough dollars deposited to make up for those which are spent, creating a situation of depletion of principal. Consequently, according to Richard S. Foster, chief actuary of the Federal Health Care Financing Administration, "This gap, which barely showed up in 1995, will grow in future years. In the absence of legislation, it will keep getting worse. . . . We have enough assets to cover the shortfall in each of the next few years. But once the assets of the trust fund are

depleted" probably before 2002, there will not be enough assets to cover expenses.

[7] Vicki Cheng, "Access to Health Care Cuts Hospitalization For Chronic Illnesses," *The New York Times*, July 26, 1995, p. C8, and Raymond Hernandez, "Assembly Passes A Bill Regulating Childbirth Stays," *The New York Times*, January 17, 1996, p. A1.

[8] Cf., Pam Bulluck, "In Crackdown on Health Care Fraud, U.S. Focuses on Training Hospitals and Clinics," *The New York Times*, December 22, 1995, p. A32 and "Health Executive Tells Senators Medicare Fraud Is Widespread," *The New York Times*, February 15, 1996, p. B13.

[9] Op. cit., Rodwin, p. 5.

[10] Ibid.

[11] Milt Freudenheim, "Doctors' Incomes Fall as Managed Care Grows," *The New York Times*, November 11, 1995, p. 1.

[12] R. Sean Morrison, M.D., and Diane E. Meier, M.D., "Managed Care At The End Of Life," *Trends in Health Care, Law & Ethics*, Volume 10, Number 1/2 (Winter/Spring, 1995), p. 91.

[13] James D. Lubitz and Gerald F. Riley, "Trends in Medicare Payments in the Last Year of Life," *New England Journal of Medicine*, April 15, 1993, p. 1092.

[14] Cf., Katherine Eban Finkelstein, "Bellevue's Emergency," *The New York Times*, February 11, 1996, p. 45 (Magazine) and "Failure on charity care," (editorial), *The Record*, March 24, 1996, p. RO2.

DISCUSSION QUESTIONS

1. Do you have access to health care? How have you achieved access? Describe what having access to health care means to you. If you do not have health care, how have you adjusted to your situation? Describe any feelings you experience as a result of not having access to health care.

2. The health care delivery system in the United States has several positive attributes. Identify as many as you can and explain why you consider each attribute a positive one.

3. There are systemic problems arising in conjunction with the delivery of health care in the United States. Make a list of these problems and state how each problem impacts on people's ability to gain access to health care.

4. There are more than 40 million Americans who have no health insurance

and, hence, little or no access to health care. Is this situation an insurmountable problem? What factors cause you to answer as you do?

5. In what would basic health care consist? What prompts you to formulate this definition?

6. How could the continued growth of the health care sector undermine the economic viability of the United States?

7. What is meant by "the common good"? Why is it so difficult to provide for the common good by assuring access to health care for uninsured Americans?

8. Define legal justice, distributive justice, subsidiarity, and human rights. Discuss the relevance of each in respect to access to health care.

9. Should there be rationing of health care in the United States? Why or why not?

10. Describe how a system of rationed health care should be designed and administered.

CASE STUDY

Dr. Pierce Franklin, an internist and member of a moderately successful practice, received an unsolicited mailing which contained a sign to be posted in the office. The sign read, "If you want the compassion of the IRS, the efficiency of the post office and the prices of the Pentagon, support efforts to establish National Health Insurance." The sign was sent by a managed-care company. The mailing also contained post cards which doctors could ask patients to send to government officials in order to register opposition to "socialized medicine."

The members of Dr. Franklin's group meet every Monday morning to discuss items of mutual interest. Dr. Franklin decided to put discussion of the mailing (and other similar efforts) on the agenda. His reason for doing so was to try to determine whether medicine and politics should mix. He also wanted to discuss how far it was appropriate for physicians to go in order to attain monetary advantages. Dr. Franklin felt especially uneasy about lobbying patients and he was concerned that the changing economic and political climates could have demoralizing effects on him and his colleagues.

The meeting is about to begin. Each of the four physicians at the table approaches Dr. Franklin's agenda item with a sense of confusion and dismay. The one thing of which the group is certain is the need to clarify the principles and values at stake so as to be able to formulate an intelligent response.

Evaluation:

1. Identify ethical issues contained in this case.
2. Propose possible solutions for these issues.
3. Make a decision relevant to action to be taken or not taken and provide rationale supportive of this decision.
4. Are you satisfied with your decision? Why or why not?

Appendix

CONTINUED READING AND RESEARCH ON ISSUES IN HEALTH CARE ETHICS

Now that you have reached the final pages of this book you are undoubtedly aware of the enormity and complexity of the subject of health care ethics. You also understand the open-endedness of this field and how new cases as well as new technological developments lead to changes in and reappraisals of established ways of thinking. What can you do to keep abreast of this ever-evolving discipline?

Media coverage, electronic and print, is the most likely medium from which to learn news of import. When you hear about a new type of case or a novel technology from a segment on a radio or television program or a wire service article, you can begin the task of learning about the entire story. The way to accomplish this is to scan major U.S. newspapers such as *The New York Times* for feature-length articles on breaking subjects. Such articles generally include references to medical specialists, articles from medical journals, or leads on attorneys for people who are involved. These leads will provide a direction to take to dig more deeply into the story so as to attain a fuller picture of what is going on.

Should you be interested in carrying out research on issues of health care ethics, you would benefit from being aware of some basic resources. These basic reference tools will lead to innumerable further sources from which to learn about the particular subjects which make up the field of health care ethics. Following is a listing of sources with which you should be familiar.

ENCYCLOPEDIA AND SOURCE BOOK

Warren T. Reich, editor-in-chief, *Encyclopedia of Bioethics, Revised Edition* (Simon & Schuster Macmillan, 1995). This five volume encyclopedia is 2,950 pages and accessible to the lay reader. Articles are written by people with expertise in their subjects, and there are extensive bibliographies for each subject. A helpful index is located at the end of Volume Five.

Albert R. Jonsen, Robert M. Veatch, LeRoy Walters, editors, *Source Book in Bioethics: A Documentary History* (Washington, DC: Georgetown University Press, 1998). This volume brings together core legislative documents, court briefs, and reports by professional organizations, public bodies, and governments around the world. Covers period from 1947 to 1995. 510 pages.

MAJOR JOURNALS

American Journal of Law and Medicine
Bioethics (from Australia)
British Medical Journal
Cambridge Quarterly of Healthcare Ethics
Ethics
Hastings Center Report
IRB: A Review of Human Subjects Research
Journal of the American Medical Association
Journal of Clinical Ethics
Journal of Health Politics, Policy and Law
Journal of Law, Medicine and Ethics
Journal of Medical Ethics
Journal of Medicine and Philosophy
Journal of Religious Ethics
Kennedy Institute of Ethics Journal
Lancet
Milbank Quarterly
Nature
New England Journal of Medicine
Philosophy and Public Affairs
Science
Theoretical Medicine

INDEXES

Bibliographic Index. A cumulative bibliography of bibliographies. Published since 1937.

Index Medicus. Lists scholarly articles published in technical medical journals. Published by the U.S. Public Health Service since 1960.

New York Times Index. Lists articles, editorials, op-ed features, and letters under general subject headings. Published since 1851.

Philosopher's Index. Indexing and abstracts from books and journals in philosophy and related disciplines including ethics, law, and religion. Published since 1940.

Reader's Guide to Periodical Literature. Author and subject index of articles from over 175 of the most widely read magazines, plus book review section. Published since 1901.

Capsule Surveys of Major Current Issues with Bibliographies are contained in the *Scope Note Series* from the Kennedy Institute of Ethics, Georgetown University, Washington, DC 20057–1212.

ONLINE INFORMATION RESOURCES

Bioethicsline. Provides references to print and nonprint materials on value questions arising in biomedical and behavioral fields. Includes citations appearing in the *Bibliography of Bioethics.* Prepared by the library staff at the Center for Bioethics, Kennedy Institute of Ethics for the National Library of Medicine. 1974 to present. Over 13,000 records. BIOETHICSLINE is accessible via telnet through the MEDLARS system. Persons with MEDLARS accounts can telnet to 'medlars.nlm.nih.gov' and choose *B - Biomedical Databases* from the initial menu. At the first user prompt enter the command *file bioethics* to access the BIOETHICSLINE database.

Bioethics Thesaurus and Searching Manual. The Bioethics Thesaurus and a manual for searching BIOETHICSLINE are available via anonymous ftp from the National Library of Medicine (ftp to 'nimpubs.nlm.nih.gov'). Bioethics publications are in the /online/medlars/manuals directory. Persons with only e-mail access to the Internet can also obtain documents from the anonymous ftp server. Send a message to mailserv@nlm.nih.gov with ONLY the word HELP in the body of the message to get instructions on using this process.

COMPENDIUM

Bio-Law: A Legal and Ethical Reporter on Medicine, Health Care, and Bioengineering. James F. Childress and Ruth D. Gaare, eds. University Publications of America. Publishes monthly updates on legal aspects of 14 topics in bioethcs. 1983–present.

WORK BY EILEEN P. FLYNN

Finally, my previous work in health care ethics might be useful to you either in respect to methodology or scholarship, or both. In view of this possibility, please be advised of the following:

Eileen P. Flynn,

Books with medical-moral content:

Your Living Will: Why, When and How to Write One, Carol Publishing Group (Citadel Press, 1992).

Hard Decisions: Forgoing and Withdrawing Artificial Nutrition and Hydration, Sheed & Ward, 1990.

Teaching About AIDS, Sheed & Ward, 1988.

AIDS A Catholic Call for Compassion, Sheed & Ward, 1985.

Human Fertilization in Vitro: A Catholic Moral Perspective, University Press of America, 1984.

Pamphlets with medical-moral content:

"Making a Loving Life-Support Decision," Abbey Press, 1990.

"Talking to Your Children about AIDS," Abbey Press, 1988 (reprinted, 1992).

Articles with medical-moral content:

"Explaining AIDS to Your Children," *Marriage & Family*, November, 1988.

"Heterosexual Transmission of AIDS Raises Serious Ethical Issues," *Journal of Theta Alpha Kappa*, Spring, 1987.

"The Seamless Garment and Persons with AIDS," *Service*, Fall, 1986.

"Tragic Circumstances and Direct Abortion," *Journal of Theta Alpha Kappa*, Spring, 1986.

"Fashioning the Wanted Child: The Ethics of Reproductive Technology" *Commonweal*, March 14, 1986.

"Technological Reproduction—Ethical Considerations," *Journal of Theta Alpha Kappa*, Spring, 1985.

"*The Sensus Fidelium* and the Morality of Human Fertilization *in Vitro*," *Journal of Theta Alpha Kappa*, Spring, 1983.

"Procreative Morality in Contemporary Catholicism," *Journal of Theta Alpha Kappa*, Fall, 1983.

Index